Agriculture in Capitalist Europe, 1945–1960

In the years before the Second World War, agriculture in most European states was carried out on peasant or small family farms using technologies that relied mainly on organic inputs, and local knowledge and skills, supplying products into a market that was partly local or national, partly international. The war applied a profound shock to this system. In some countries farms became battlefields, causing the extensive destruction of buildings, crops and livestock. In others, farmers had to respond to calls from the state for increased production to cope with the effects of wartime disruption of international trade. By the end of the war, food was rationed, when it was obtainable at all. Only fifteen years later, the erstwhile enemies were planning ways of bringing about a single agricultural market across much of continental Western Europe, as farmers mechanised, motorised, shed labour, invested capital and adopted new technologies to increase output.

This volume brings together scholars working on this period of dramatic technical, commercial and political change in agriculture, from the end of the Second World War to the emergence of the Common Agricultural Policy in the early 1960s. Their work is structured around four themes: the changes in the international political order within which agriculture operated; the emergence of a range of different market regulation schemes that preceded the CAP; changes in technology and the extent to which they were promoted by state policy; and the impact of these political and technical changes on rural societies in Western Europe.

Carin Martiin is Associate Professor in Agrarian History in the Department of Urban and Rural Development at the Swedish University of Agricultural Sciences in Uppsala, Sweden.

Juan Pan-Montojo is Associate Professor of Modern History at the Universidad Autónoma de Madrid, Spain. He has been the editor of *Historia Agraria* and currently edits *Ayer*, the journal of the Spanish Association of Modern Historians.

Paul Brassley is an Honorary University Fellow in the Land, Environment, Economics and Policy Institute, University of Exeter, UK.

Rural Worlds: Economic, Social and Cultural Histories of Agricultures and Rural Societies

Series Editor:
Richard W. Hoyle, University of Reading, UK

We like to forget that agriculture is one of the core human activities. In historic societies most people lived in the countryside: a high, if falling proportion of the population were engaged in the production and processing of foodstuffs. The possession of land was a key form of wealth: it brought not only income from tenants but prestige, access to a rural lifestyle and often political power. Nor could government ever be uninterested in the countryside, whether to maintain urban food supply, as a source of taxation, or to maintain social peace. Increasingly, it managed every aspect of the countryside. Agriculture itself and the social relations within the countryside were in constant flux as farmers reacted to new or changing opportunities, and landlords sought to maintain or increase their incomes. Moreover, urban attitudes to, and representation of, the landscape and its inhabitants were constantly shifting.

These questions of competition and change, production, power and perception are the primary themes of the series. It looks at change and competition in the countryside: social relations within it and between urban and rural societies. The series offers a forum for the publication of the best work on all of these issues, straddling the economic, social and cultural, concentrating on the rural history of Britain and Ireland, Europe and its colonial empires, and North America over the past millennium.

Series Advisory Board:
Paul Brassley, University of Exeter, UK
R. Douglas Hurt, Purdue University, USA
Leen Van Molle, KU Leuven, Belgium
Mats Morell, Stockholm University, Sweden
Phillipp Schofield, Aberystwyth University, UK
Nicola Verdon, Sheffield Hallam University, UK
Paul Warde, University of East Anglia, UK

Titles in the series include:

The Farmer in England, 1650–1980
Edited by Richard W. Hoyle

Coping with Crisis: The Resilience and Vulnerability of Pre-Industrial Settlements
Daniel R. Curtis

Agriculture in Capitalist Europe, 1945–1960
Edited by Carin Martiin, Juan Pan-Montojo and Paul Brassley

Observing Agriculture in Early Twentieth-Century Italy
Federico D'Onofrio

Agriculture in Capitalist Europe, 1945–1960

From food shortages to food surpluses

Edited by Carin Martiin, Juan Pan-Montojo and Paul Brassley

LONDON AND NEW YORK

First published 2016
by Routledge
2 Park Square, Milton Park, Abingdon, Oxon OX14 4RN

and by Routledge
711 Third Avenue, New York, NY 10017

Routledge is an imprint of the Taylor & Francis Group, an informa business

© 2016 selection and editorial matter, Carin Martiin, Juan Pan-Montojo and Paul Brassley; individual chapters, the contributors

The right of Carin Martiin, Juan Pan-Montojo and Paul Brassley to be identified as the authors of the editorial material, and of the authors for their individual chapters, has been asserted in accordance with sections 77 and 78 of the Copyright, Designs and Patents Act 1988.

All rights reserved. No part of this book may be reprinted or reproduced or utilised in any form or by any electronic, mechanical, or other means, now known or hereafter invented, including photocopying and recording, or in any information storage or retrieval system, without permission in writing from the publishers.

Trademark notice: Product or corporate names may be trademarks or registered trademarks, and are used only for identification and explanation without intent to infringe.

British Library Cataloguing in Publication Data
A catalogue record for this book is available from the British Library

Library of Congress Cataloging in Publication Data
A catalog record for this book has been requested.

ISBN: 978-1-4724-6965-6 (hbk)
ISBN: 978-1-315-46593-7 (ebk)

Typeset in Bembo
by Cenveo Publisher Services

Contents

List of figures   *vii*
List of tables   *viii*
Notes on contributors   *x*
Acknowledgements   *xv*
List of abbreviations   *xvii*

1   European agriculture, 1945–1960: an introduction   1
PAUL BRASSLEY, CARIN MARTIIN AND JUAN PAN-MONTOJO

PART I
International politics   21

2   International institutions and European agriculture: from the IIA to the FAO   23
JUAN PAN-MONTOJO

3   Political stability, modernization and reforms during the first years of the Cold War   44
EMANUELE BERNARDI

4   International agricultural markets after the war, 1945–1960   64
ÁNGEL LUIS GONZÁLEZ ESTEBAN, VICENTE PINILLA AND RAÚL SERRANO

PART II
Market regulation and the motives behind it   85

5   The policy of wheat self-sufficiency and its impact upon rural modernization in Greece, 1928–1960   87
SOCRATES D. PETMEZAS

vi *Contents*

6 British agriculture in transition: food shortages to food surpluses, 1947–1957 107
JOHN MARTIN

7 From food surplus to even more food surplus: agrarian politics and prices in Denmark, 1945–1962 125
THOMAS CHRISTIANSEN

PART III
Technical change 143

8 Mechanisation and motorisation: natural resources, knowledge, politics and technology in 19th- and 20th-century agriculture 145
JURI AUDERSET AND PETER MOSER

9 Technology policies in dictatorial contexts: Spain and Portugal 165
DANIEL LANERO AND LOURENZO FERNÁNDEZ-PRIETO

10 Tractorisation: France, 1946–1955 185
LAURENT HERMENT

PART IV
Rural society and structural policy 207

11 Structural policy and the State: changing agricultural society in Belgium and the Netherlands, 1945–1960 209
ERWIN H. KAREL AND YVES SEGERS

12 From food scarcity to overproduction: saving the German peasant during the miracle years 229
GESINE GERHARD

13 Farm labour in the urban–industrial Swedish welfare state 246
CARIN MARTIIN

Conclusion 265

14 Similar means to secure postwar food supplies across Western Europe 267
PAUL BRASSLEY, CARIN MARTIIN AND JUAN PAN-MONTOJO

Index 275

Figures

P1	Par le Plan Marshall (1950) by Gaston van den Eynde	21
4.1	International trade in agricultural and food products, 1951–1970	66
4.2	Evolution of the Nominal Protection Coefficient, 1951–1970	78
P2	The small-scale pig trade in 1962	85
5.1	Wheat area cultivated, production (left axis) and yields (right axis)	93
5.2	Domestic wheat consumption	95
5.3	Production of cereals and imports of wheat in tons, 1927–1960	99
P3	Demonstration of milking machinery, 1959	143
8.1	A widely used draught-training method for horses and cattle in the 19th century	146
8.2	Educating instead of breaking horses	147
8.3	Horses and tractors in Swiss agriculture, 1866–1956	151
8.4	An industrial technique adapted to the power available on the farm	155
8.5	Only the development of the power take-off and its perfecting in the 1950s made the tractor 'a power centre of the farm', enabling it to multitask	159
10.1	Evolution of tractors and horses (in thousands) 1948–1966	189
10.2	Age of farmers in 1955	190
10.3	Oise, tractors per 1,000 hectares	191
10.4	France, tractors per 1,000 hectares	191
10.5	Horses on farms equipped with a tractor in 1950	194
10.6	Horses and tractors by farm	194
10.7	Wage-labourers and tractors by farm	195
10.8	Diversity at a *départemental* level for the whole of France	196
P4	A typical Swedish farm of the 1950s	207

Tables

1.1	Cereals: changes in output pre-/postwar	3
1.2	Pre-/postwar changes in potato production ('000 tonnes)	4
1.3	Imports of bread and feed grains ('000 tonnes)	7
1.4	Output of selected commodities in 1952 expressed as an index	9
1.5	Land and labour use and productivity, 1950–1962 in European market economies	10
1.6	Percentage changes in the numbers and sizes of farm holdings	11
1.7	Technical and structural variations in the late 1950s	16
3.1	The post-war Communist vote	45
3.2	Utilization of the ERP *lire* fund for agriculture	46
3.3	Foodstuffs as a percentage of the total imports through ERP aid	47
4.1	International trade in agricultural and food products, 1938–1954	65
5.1	Estimation of wheat production and imports	90
5.2	The KYDEP system of the collection of wheat (1953–1957)	98
5.3	The growth of factors of production in agriculture	101
6.1	Production of the major agricultural commodities	118
6.2	Price review determinations, 1949–1957	119
6.3	Government subsidies to agriculture	120
7.1	Cultivated area	127
7.2	Vegetal output	128
7.3	Animal output	128
7.4	Number of animals	128
7.5	Number of farms by size, 1946–1966	133
9.1	Evolution of land consolidation in Spain (1953–1959)	168
9.2	Spain (1950–1964): numbers of tractors	169
9.3	Fertiliser consumption in kilograms per hectare in Spain (1930–1960)	170
9.4	Yields per hectare of the main Spanish agricultural products (1950–1959)	170
9.5	Evolution of the consumption of animal products in the Spanish diet, 1935–1975	171
9.6	Active agricultural population as a proportion of total active population in Spain and Portugal (1930–1970)	179

9.7	Agricultural output (percentage) in Spain (1931–1975)	180
9.8	Agricultural sectoral growth (constant prices, per cent) in Portugal (1930–1973)	180
9.9	Agricultural labour productivity, land productivity and land-labour ratio in Portugal and Spain (1950–1972)	181
10.1	Output of the main food crops (except wine) between 1935 and 1955	187
10.2	Millions of cattle, sheep and pigs	188
10.3	Agricultural inputs	189
11.1a	Production of some agricultural products in the Netherlands, 1935–1950	214
11.1b	Production of some agricultural products in Belgium, 1935–1950	214
11.2	Agricultural exports in the Netherlands, 1935–1950	215
13.1	Number of farms in different farm size categories	248
13.2	Total labour in Swedish farming, 1951–1966	249
13.3	Number of people in working age and at work in Sweden, 1945–1965	253
13.4	Proportions (%) of the labour force in agriculture and other sectors	254
13.5	Types of labour (%) in Swedish farming, 1951–1966	255
13.6	Percentage changes in various types of farm labour, 1951–1966	256
13.7	Average male labour on Swedish farms of different sizes, 1956–1966	256
13.8	Average female labour on Swedish farms of different sizes, 1956–1966	257
13.9	Decline in male and female farm labour on holdings of different farm sizes	258

Notes on contributors

Juri Auderset
Scientific collaborator, Archives of Rural History, Berne; Reader in Contemporary History, Department of History, University of Fribourg, Switzerland.

Recent publications: (with Beat Bächi and Peter Moser), 'Die agrarisch-industrielle Wissensgesellschaft im 19. / 20. Jahrhundert: Akteure, Diskurse, Praktiken', in Brodbeck Beat, Ineichen Martina and Schibli Thomas (eds) *Geschichte im virtuellen Archiv. Das Archiv für Agrargeschichte als Zentrum der Geschichtsschreibung zur ländlichen Gesellschaft* (=Studien und Quellen zur Agrargeschichte, Bd. 3), Baden 2012, 21-38; 'Texte, Kontexte, Politische Kultur. Intellectual History bei Keith Michael Baker und Lloyd S. Kramer', in WerkstattGeschichte 60 (2013), 76–95; (with Peter Moser), *The Agrarian-Industrial Knowledge-Society in the 19th and 20th Centuries* (forthcoming).

Emanuele Bernardi
Researcher in Contemporary History at the Faculty of Letters of 'Sapienza' in Rome since 2016.

Recent publications: Two books on the letters of Manlio Rossi-Doria and Emilio Sereni (Rubbettino, 2011). His book *La riforma agraria in Italia e gli Stati Uniti* (Il Mulino, 2006) and the thesis from which it originated received several awards. He is a member of the Scientific Committee of the historical journal *Studi Storici*.

Paul Brassley
Honorary University Fellow in the Land, Environment, Economics and Policy Institute, University of Exeter, UK

Recent publications: (with David Harvey, Matt Lobley and Michael Winter), 'Accounting for Agriculture: the origins of the Farm Management Survey', *Agricultural History Review* 61 (2013); (with Yves Segers and Leen Van Molle (eds)), *War, Agriculture and Food: Rural Europe from the 1930s to the 1950s.* New York and London: Routledge, 2012.

Thomas Christiansen

Recent publications: *The Reason Why: The Post Civil War Agrarian Crisis in Spain.* Zaragoza University Press (2012); *Crime and Punishment in the Black Market in Spain. 1940–1953: An Analysis of the Fiscalía de Tasas.* Centro de Estudios Sobre la Despoblación y Desarrollo de Areas Rurales/AGER, 2005.

Lourenzo Fernández-Prieto

Professor of History and Director of the HISTAGRA Research Group, University of Santiago de Compostela (Spain). He was Vice-President of the Spanish Society of Agrarian History and a member of the editorial board of *Revista de Historia Agraria*.

Recent publications: *Agriculture in the Age of Fascism: Authoritarian Technocracy and Rural Modernization, 1922–1945*, with Miguel Cabo and Juan Pan-Montojo (eds): Turnhout, Brepols, 2014; 'El Atlantico no es el Mediterráneo: el cambio agrario al otro extremo de la Península Ibérica: el mismo estado, otros paisajes, ¿los mismos campesinos?', with David Soto in Ricardo Robledo (ed.): *Sombras del pasado: las huellas de la historia agraria*, Barcelona, Crítica, 2010, pp. 231–264; *El apagón tecnológico del franquismo: estado e innovación en la agricultura española del siglo XX*, Valencia, Tirant lo Blanch, 2007.

Gesine Gerhard

Associate Professor of European History, and Associate Dean and Director of General Education, University of the Pacific, Stockton, California.

Recent publications: 'The modernization dilemma: Agrarian policies in Nazi Germany' in *Agriculture in the Age of Fascism: Authoritarian Technocracy and Rural Modernization, 1922–1945*, edited by Miguel Cabo, Lourenzo Fernández Prieto and Juan Pan-Montojo. Brepols Publishers, in press; 'Das Bild der Bauern in der modernen Industriegesellschaft – Störenfriede oder Schoßkinder der Industriegesellschaft?' In *Das Bild des Bauern: Selbst- und Fremdwahrnehmungen vom Mittelalter bis ins 21. Jahrhundert*, edited by Daniela Münkel and Frank Uekötter. Göttingen: Vandenhoeck & Ruprecht, 2012, pp. 111–130. She is also under contract to Rowman & Littlefield to write a book on *Food in the Third Reich*.

Ángel Luis González Esteban

Currently enjoying a four-year grant within the research project 'The Livelihood of Man: Natural Resources, Institutions and Technology in Agriculture during the 20th Century' (Department of Economics and Economic History of the University of Salamanca, Spain) and working on his PhD thesis on agrarian policies after the Second World War, with special regard to policies concerning national and international wheat markets. He has recently been awarded the Spanish Agrarian History Society (SEHA) prize for young researchers for his work on the theoretical framework of the food sovereignty approach.

Laurent Herment
Chargé de Recherches (première classe). CNRS-CRH. EHESS, Paris.

Recent publications: *Les fruits du partage: Petits paysans du Bassin Parisien au XIXe siècle*. Presses Universitaires de Rennes, 2012; Hyperinflation et mouvements de la rente dans les campagnes d'Île-de-France. Fortunes et infortunes d'une bourgeoise rurale, in *Annales Historiques de la Révolution Française*, 2013-4, no. 374, pp. 129–155.

Erwin H. Karel
Erwin H. Karel is Lecturer in social and economic history at the University of Groningen, Netherlands, and research fellow at the Dutch Agricultural History Institute (NAHI).

Recent publications: Karel, E. and Segers, Y. (2015), 'The Low Countries 1750–2000' in *Rural Economy and Society in North-western Europe, 500–2000: Struggling with the Environment: Land Use and Productivity* (Vol. 4, pp. 260–306). Turnhout: Brepols Publishers; Karel, E. and Paping, R. (2013), 'In the shadow of the nobility: Local farmer elites in the Northern Netherlands from the 17th to the 19th century' in D. Freist and F. Schmekel (eds), *Hinter dem Horizont: Projection und Distinktion ländlicher Oberschichten im europäischen Vergleich 17. bis 19. Jahrhundert*. (pp. 43–54). Münster: Aschendorff Verlag; Paping, R. F. J. and Karel, E. H. K. (2011), 'The rural succession myth: Occupational careers and household formation of peasants' and farmers' offspring around 1800'. *Tijdschrift voor Sociale en Economische Geschiedenis*, 8(4), 44–75.

Daniel Lanero
Lecturer in History and Scientific Manager of HISTAGRA Research Group, University of Santiago de Compostela (Spain).

Recent publications: 'The Portuguese Estado Novo: Programmes and obstacles to the modernization of agriculture (1933–1950)', in Lourenzo Fernández Prieto, Miguel Cabo and Juan Pan-Montojo (eds): *Agriculture in the Age of Fascism: Authoritarian Technocracy and Rural Modernization, 1922–1945*, pp. 85–111. Turnhout, Brepols, 2014; *Historia dun ermo asociativo. Labregos, sindicatos verticais e políticas agrarias en Galicia baixo o franquismo*, Santa Comba, tresCtres, 2011; 'The Iberian dictatorships and agricultural modernisation after the Second World War' with Dulce Freire in Peter Moser and Tony Varley (eds): *Integration through Subordination: The Politics of Agricultural Modernisation in Industrial Europe*, pp. 183–201. Turnhout, Brepols and COST, 2013.

Carin Martiin
Associate Professor in Agrarian History in the Department of Economics at the Swedish University of Agricultural Sciences in Uppsala, Sweden.

Recent publications: 'Modernized farming but stagnated production: Swedish farming in the 1950s emerging welfare state' in *Agricultural History*, 2015.89.4. *The World of Agricultural Economics: An Introduction* (Routledge, 2013) and 'Farming, favoured in times of fear: Swedish agricultural policy 1935–55', in P. Brassley, Y. Segers, L. Van Molle, *War, Agriculture, and Food* (Routledge, 2012).

John Martin
Reader in Agrarian History, School of Humanities, De Montfort University, Leicester, UK.

Recent publications: 'The transformation of lowland game shooting in England and Wales in the twentieth century: The neglected metamorphosis', *International Journal of Sports History* (2012); 'Rex Paterson: (1903–1978) Pioneer of grassland dairy farming and agricultural innovator', in R. Hoyle, *Farmers and their Records*, (Ashgate, 2013).

Peter Moser
Director, Archives of Rural History, Berne, Switzerland.

Recent publications: (together with Tony Varley (eds)), *Integration through Subordination. The Politics of Agricultural Modernisation in Industrial Europe*, Vol. 8, series Rural History in Europe, Brepols, Turnhout, 2013; 'Zugriff auf die Lithosphäre. Gestaltungspotentiale unterschiedlicher Energiegrundlagen in der agrarisch-industriellen Wissensgesellschaft', in Traverse, Zeitschrift für Geschichte 3/2013, 37–48; (with Juri Auderset), *The Agrarian-Industrial Knowledge-Society in the 19th and 20th Centuries* (forthcoming).

Juan Pan-Montojo
Associate Professor of Modern History at the Universidad Autónoma de Madrid, Spain. He has been the editor of *Historia Agraria* and currently edits *Ayer*, the journal of the Spanish Association of Modern Historians.

Recent publications: *Apostolado, profesión y tecnología : Una historia de los ingenieros agrónomos en España* (Madrid, 2005). He has coordinated or edited the following collective publications: *Más se perdió en Cuba. España, 1898 y la crisis de fin de siglo* (Madrid, 1998), *Bodegas, vinos y mercados. El cambio técnico en la vitivinicultura española, 1850–1936* (Zaragoza, 2001), *La inspección de Hacienda en España: una mirada histórica* (Madrid, 2008), *El sueño republicano de Rico Avello* (Madrid, 2011) and *Agriculture in the Age of Fascism* (Turnhout, 2014).

Socrates D. Petmezas
Professor of Modern Economic and Social History in the Department of History and Archaeology of the University of Crete and a Collaborating

Faculty Member of the Institute for Mediterranean Studies/Foundation of Research and Technology-Greece. He is currently the representative for Southern Europe in the Management Committee of the European Rural History Organization (EURHO).

Recent publications: *The Economic Development of Southeastern Europe (1830–1914)* (co-edited with E. Eldem and H.A.-Alpha Bank: Athens, 2011).

Vicente Pinilla
Professor in Economic History at the University of Zaragoza, Spain. Vice-Rector of Budget and Economic Management of the University of Zaragoza 2000–2004. He has held appointments at the University of Bristol, London School of Economics, University of California at Davis, University of Maastricht and Ecole des Hautes Etudes en Sciences Sociales, Paris.

Recent publications: Co-editor of *Agriculture and Economic Development in Europe since 1870* (Routledge, 2009) and editor of *Markets and Agricultural Change in Europe from the 13th to the 20th century* (Brepols, 2009). His latest book is *Peaceful Surrender: The Depopulation of Rural Spain in the Twentieth Century* (with F. Collantes) (Cambridge Scholars Publishing, 2011).

Yves Segers
Professor doctor of rural history (Faculty of Arts) and Director of the Interfaculty Centre for Agrarian History (ICAG) at the University of Leuven, Belgium. He is co-promoter of the research network CORN: Comparative Rural History of the North Sea Area.

Recent publications: *War, Agriculture and Food: Rural Europe from the 1930s to the 1950s* (edited with P. Brassley and L. Van Molle, Routledge, 2012); *The Agro-Food Market: Production, Distribution and Consumption* (edited with L. Van Molle, Brepols, 2013).

Raúl Serrano
Assistant Professor in Management at the University of Zaragoza, Spain. He has been a visiting researcher at the Idaho State University and the London School of Economics.

Recent publications include papers in *Agribusiness, Applied Economics, Economies et Sociétés, Journal of Iberian and Latin American Economic History, Journal of Wine Economics and Revista de Historia Industrial*.

Acknowledgements

This book is the result of more or less continuous discussions about European agricultural history in the mid-twentieth century. An earlier stage was reached through the book *War, Agriculture, and Food: Rural Europe from the 1930s to the 1950s* (Routledge, 2012) edited by Paul Brassley, Yves Segers and Leen Van Molle. The present volume deals primarily with the years between the end of the Second World War and the establishment of the Common Agricultural Policy about fifteen years later.

The idea of focusing on this time period came up during the preparations for the Rural History Conference in Bern 2013, and the work begun there was followed up at a workshop in Zaragoza, Spain, in 2014. We are most grateful to Peter Moser and colleagues who arranged the RH 2013 conference in Bern, and to Vicente Pinilla and his colleagues at the University of Zaragoza who arranged the workshop.

We are also very grateful to Richard Hoyle, Series Editor of 'Rural Worlds: Economic, Social and Cultural Histories of Agricultures and Rural Societies' who accepted the book for publication in this series. Finally, we want to thank everyone, but especially Michelle Antrobus and Emily Yates, at Ashgate and Routledge who have been involved in publishing this book.

Abbreviations

BAE Bureau of Agricultural Economics
CAP Common Agricultural Policy
CDU *Christliche Demokratische Union Deutschlands*
CEA *Confédération Européenne de l'Agriculture*
CEEA *Centro de Estudos de Economia Agrária*
CEIL Committee of Experts on Indigenous Labour
CFB Combined Food Board
CIA (a) Central Intelligence Office
CIA (b) *Commission Internationale d'Agriculture, Confédération Internationale de l'Agriculture*
CSIC *Centro Superior de Investigaciones Científicas*
CSU *Christliche Soziale Union*
DBK *Deutsche Bauernkorrespondenz* (the German Peasant Correspondence)
DBV *Deutscher Bauernverband* (German Peasant League)
DC Christian Democratic Party, Italy
ECA (a) European Committee for Agriculture (FAO)
ECA (b) Economic Cooperation Administration (ERP)
ECO Economic and Financial Organisation of the League of Nations
ECSC European Coal and Steel Community
EEC European Economic Community
EFTA European Free Trade Association
EPA European Productivity Agency
EPTA Expanded Programme of Technical Assistance
ERP European Recovery Program (Marshall plan)
ESSE National Confederation of Unions of Agricultural Cooperatives, Greece
FAO Food and Agriculture Organisation of the United Nations
FATIS Food and Agricultural Technical Information Services
FDP *Freie Demokratische Partei*
FNSEA *Fédération Nationale des Syndicats des Exploitants Agricoles*
FSA Farm Security Administration
GATT General Agreement on Tariffs and Trade
IBRD International Bank for Reconstruction and Development
IEFC International Emergency Food Council

IFAP International Federation of Agricultural Producers
IIA(a) International Institute of Agriculture
IIA(b) *Instituto de Investigaciones Agrarias* (Agrarian Research Institute)
IKF Institute for Crop Improvement, Greece
ILO International Labour Organisation
ITO International Trade Organization
IMF International Monetary Fund
INIA *Instituto Nacional de Investigaciones Agrarias* (National Agrarian Research Institute)
INRA *Institut National de la Recherche Agronomique*
IRA *Institut des Recherches Agronomiques*
JCI *Junta de Colonização Interna* (Internal Colonisation Board), Portugal
KEPES Central Committee for the Protection of Domestic Wheat, Greece
KESDES Consortium of Unions of Agricultural Cooperatives for the Administration of Domestic Wheat, Greece
KYDES Central Service for the Administration of Domestic Wheat, Greece
LoN League of Nations
MSA Mutual Security Agency
NATO North Atlantic Treaty Organisation
OECD Organisation for Economic Cooperation and Development
OEEC Organisation for European Economic Cooperation
OFAR Office of Foreign Agricultural Relations
OMGUS American Office of Military Government for Germany
PAEGA Privileged Anonymous Society of General Warehouses, Greece
PCI Italian Communist Party
RNS *Reichsnährstand* (Reich Food Estate)
SAF *Société des Agriculteurs de France*
SBV *Schweizerische Bauernverband*
SDGM Centre for Testing Agricultural Machinery, Greece
SEA *Servicio de Extensión Agraria* (Agricultural Extension Service), Spain
SPD *Sozialdemokratische Partei Deutschlands*
UN United Nations
UNECE United Nations Economic Commission for Europe
UNRRA United Nations Relief and Rehabilitation Administration
USDA United States Department of Agriculture
USSR Union of Soviet Socialist Republics
VER Voluntary export restraints
VRA Voluntary restraint agreements
WHO World Health Organisation

1 European agriculture, 1945–1960

An introduction

Paul Brassley, Carin Martiin and Juan Pan-Montojo

This book is about the emergence of modern agriculture in Western Europe. In the years before the Second World War, agriculture in most European states was carried out on peasant or small family farms that still relied substantially on muscle power and other traditional inputs, aided to some extent by technologies that would become established in postwar agriculture. The resultant products were supplied into a market that was partly local and partly international. The Second World War applied a profound shock to this preexisting system. In some countries, farms became battlefields, with the extensive destruction of buildings, crops and livestock. In others, farmers had to respond to calls from the state for increased production to cope with the effects of wartime disruption of international trade. By the end of the war food was rationed when it was obtainable at all. Only fifteen years later, the erstwhile enemies were planning ways of bringing about a single agricultural market across much of continental Western Europe, as farmers mechanised, motorised, shed labour, invested capital and adopted new technologies to increase output.

The curious thing is that this period of dramatic technical, commercial and political change has been overshadowed, in the historical literature, by the dramatic events that preceded and followed it. While much has been written, and written recently, on the Second World War, and political historians in particular have recently become interested in what the emergence of the Common Agricultural Policy in the early 1960s tells us about the process of European integration, virtually nothing has appeared on the period between these two climactic events since the last edition of Michael Tracy's classic *Agriculture in Western Europe*, the bulk of which was written over fifty years ago.[1]

The purpose of this book is to fill this partial vacuum in European rural history. How rapid was the postwar recovery? How was it produced? Why was the Second World War *not* followed by an agricultural depression in the way that the previous global conflict had been? Why did an agricultural population that had been content to survive in their youth or middle age before the war have the confidence to innovate and invest in their middle- or old age after the war? These are the issues that are explored by historians from a dozen different countries, of which some were original members of the Common Agricultural Policy whereas others joined later, with the exception of Switzerland.

Their work is structured around four themes: the changes in the international political order within which agriculture operated; the emergence of a range of different market regulation schemes that preceded the Common Agricultural Policy; changes in technology and the extent to which they were promoted by state policy; and the impact of these political and technical changes on rural societies in Western Europe. First, however, it is desirable to sketch in the major changes in the state of Western European agriculture between the end of the Second World War and the signing of the Treaty of Rome (from which the CAP emerged) in 1957.

Agriculture in Western Europe at the end of the Second World War

There have been several recent accounts of the impact of the Second World War on food and agriculture in Europe.[2] They all tell stories of food shortages, in some cases to the point of starvation (in Greece and the Netherlands, for example), rationing, the emergence of food substitutes, contrasts between social cohesion and the emergence of black and grey markets, state control, the disruption of traditional patterns of agricultural trade, shortages of labour and other inputs, and the different experiences of the various belligerent and neutral states as far as agricultural production was concerned. In the countries of continental Europe, where the land battles occurred, their impact on land, farm buildings and farm animals was greater than in the UK, where, although there was some damage to farms from aerial attack, much good land became airfields, and less good land military training areas, direct damage was generally less.[3] Among the neutral countries, changes in Spanish agriculture were more a result of the Civil War and the autarkic economical programme that was implemented by Franco's regime, than of the world war. In Portugal there was significant growth in agricultural output, admittedly from a very low base.[4] Ireland benefited from the proximity of the UK market, whereas the more industrialised Swiss economy was surrounded by belligerent countries and so found it difficult to obtain both food imports and fertilisers. Swedish farmers had to cope with greater levels of bureaucracy and consumers with food rationing, but calorie consumption was only a little below the levels of the 1930s.[5]

One simple way of illustrating these differences is to examine agricultural production and trade figures for the immediate postwar years. The following discussion is concerned only with the major Western European countries. This would have made no sense for a pre-war context, when Eastern European countries were important suppliers of agricultural products to the German market in particular, but should be acceptable for the postwar years, since by the time production in Eastern Europe had recovered enough for exports to be possible, all of the countries involved, with the partial exception of

Yugoslavia, had been isolated from Western markets as a result of the political tensions between the USSR and the West. The data source used in Table 1.1 is the FAO *Yearbook of Food and Agricultural Statistics*, which has the advantage of carrying on and reporting the data collected before the war by the International Institute of Agriculture. Thus, the level of postwar production can be contextualised by comparison with an average of the pre-war years – normally, an average of 1935–1938. The data, where it can be checked, appears to be reliable for the pre-war period, and even reasonably reliable during the war.[6] Deciding which year to choose to represent the state of Western European agriculture at the end of the war is a little more tricky. The devastation of continental agriculture might perhaps be best captured by using 1945 figures, but these are not available for every country. Alternatively, there might be a case for using an average of the years 1945–1947, but the harsh winter of 1947 seems to have affected production in the subsequent summer over much of Europe, so rendering the figures atypical. Therefore, figures for the single year 1946 have been used in Tables 1.1 and 1.2.

Table 1.1 traces changes in the output of all cereals (i.e. wheat, rye, barley, oats and maize). It is immediately apparent that in eight of the thirteen countries, cereal production was lower than in the pre-war years, by an average of about 25 per cent, with Germany and Austria, not surprisingly, being especially affected. The Swedish figure is explained by high yields in the late 1930s rather than by the surrounding war. Figures for individual crops show that not all were affected equally. Barley production in Belgium and France, for example, was higher in 1946 than before the war. But the overall trend was that cereal production fell in countries that had been fought over or occupied during the war. In contrast, the greatest output increases were in the UK, where increased

Table 1.1 Cereals: changes in output pre-/postwar

	Pre-war 000 tonnes	1946 000 tonnes	% change
Austria	1,851	859	−53.7
Belgium	1,620	1,232	−24.0
Denmark	2,772	3,059	+10.3
France	15,099	12,265	−18.8
Germany	16,558	10,109	−38.9
Greece	1,371	1,270	−7.4
Ireland	886	1,299	+46.6
Italy	11,152	8,821	−20.9
Netherlands	1,404	1,424	+1.4
Portugal	1,006	1,375	+36.7
Spain	8,688	7,159	−17.6
Sweden	2,575	1,936	−24.8
UK	4,555	6,634	+45.6

Source: FAO, *Yearbook of Food and Agricultural Statistics: Part 1, Production*, Rome, 1948.

Table 1.2 Pre-/postwar changes in potato production ('000 tonnes)

	Pre-war	1946	% change
Austria	2845	1533	−46
Belgium	3,169	1,477	−53
France	15,883	9,882	−38
Germany	33,607	23,466	−30
Italy	2,626	2,288	−13
Spain	4,954	2,272	−54
Denmark	1,349	1,810	+34
Greece	139	238	+71
Ireland	2,583	3,279	+27
Netherlands	2,022	3,071	+52
Portugal	555	848	+53
UK	5,011	10,329	+106

Source: FAO, *Yearbook of Food and Agricultural Statistics: Part 1, Production*, Rome, 1948.

cereal cropping was one of the purposes of the plough-up campaign, and Ireland, which presumably also responded to cereal trade difficulties by increasing domestic production. In the Netherlands, decreases in wheat and rye production were roughly balanced by increases in production of the feed grains, especially barley and oats. This probably represented a postwar recovery, since the feed-grain area had been restricted during the war and yields had suffered as a result of fertiliser shortages.[7] Denmark, where cereal output was also a little greater than before the war, had been treated differently from other occupied countries in an attempt to maintain its exports to Germany.[8]

As far as human food was concerned, the overall decline in cereal production was to some extent offset by increases in potato production. As Table 1.2 reveals, countries such as the Netherlands, which had seen a decrease in cereal production, managed to increase potato output, with still greater increases in the UK, Ireland and Denmark.

On the other hand, animal numbers were rarely maintained during the war, and in consequence consumers ate less fat and meat. Only in the UK were cattle numbers in 1946 higher than before the war, although they had been more or less maintained in Italy. Pig numbers fell almost everywhere, although again they were roughly equal to pre-war numbers in Italy. Production of fats in 1945 and 1946 was at best only at about 80 per cent of its pre-war level, and in Belgium and Austria only 40 per cent of that level. Sweden, where consumption of fats was up by 20 per cent, was the only exception to this generalisation, but even there meat production was down, as it was in all other Western European countries. In Germany and Austria it was at only about 40 per cent of its pre-war level in 1945 and 1946. As far as food consumption was concerned, therefore, the general pattern in Western Europe was for consumption of grain products to be greater, by up to 20 per cent, than it had been before the war (only in Germany, Austria, France and Italy was it less), and for consumption of fats, meat and sugar to be less. The calorific value of daily food supplies in north-western countries was about 3,000 calories per head before the war, but averaged only about 2,800 calories in 1946/7, and in Germany and Austria in 1945/6 fell as low as 1,600 calories.[9]

As Judt argues, with memories of the years after the First World War still present in their minds, both Europeans and Americans expected the twenty years after 1945 to be marked by, at best, poverty and toil, and possibly by civil war. In October 1945, General de Gaulle had warned the French people to prepare for twenty-five years of 'furious work' to repair the French economy. Eighteen months later, the French Minister of National Economy was predicting economic and financial catastrophe, a view supported at about the same time by the American diplomat George Kennan, who had been in the Prague embassy at the time of the Nazi takeover, and wrote of the exhaustion of physical plant and spiritual vigour in Europe resulting from the war. In July 1947 the American journalist Hamilton Fish recorded his impressions of a visit to Europe as 'There is too little of everything – ... too little flour to make bread without adulterants, and even so not enough bread to provide energies for hard labour; ... too little seed for planting and too little fertilizer to nourish it; ... too little leather for shoes, wool for sweaters ... sugar for jam, fats for frying, milk for babies ...'.[10] Virginia Potter, an American woman who had spent the war years in England but returned to the USA and Canada for a short visit in the spring of 1946, encapsulated these transatlantic contrasts in recording her feelings of depression as her ship returned to England: 'We are passing the Devonshire coast, it is, needless to say, raining, which makes me think of cold and seagulls, and more rain – and boiled turbot with photographic paste sauce, and then I try to switch my mind back to Canada, to that glorious sunshine, ... martinis at the Ritz, filet mignon at Café Martin, the hot baths!'.[11] It is therefore hardly surprising that the section on the world food situation in the report prepared for discussion in the Economic and Social Council of the United Nations in February and March 1948 began with the sentence 'The world food situation is as critical this year as at any time since the end of the Second World War, but crisis is an inadequate term to describe the current food situation'. Moreover, the officials of the newly formed UN Food and Agriculture Organisation, who had prepared the report, did not see this as a temporary problem: 'Food shortages have become a chronic feature of the postwar world', they wrote, and 'there are long-term elements which will prevent a rapid elimination of major shortages'.[12]

These long-term elements affected both demand and supply, and not only in Europe. World demand had risen as a result of population increase and a greater realisation by governments of the benefits of an adequate diet. At the same time, production was held back by the wartime loss of farming resources and delays in replacing them. In April 1946, the UK Minister of Food presented a report on *The World Food Shortage* to Parliament. It argued that the world transport system had been 'wrenched to the purposes of war' so that fuel, fertilisers and animal feedstuffs became unavailable; that shipping shortages had prevented exports of grain from Australia and Argentina (where grain and linseed were burned as fuel owing to a lack of oil and coal); that unsettled economic conditions, consequent lack of faith in the currency, and a shortage of consumer goods, made producers unwilling to sell for cash; and that trade and transport disruption made farm populations maintain their own feeding standards at the expense of those in towns.[13] Two years later, the UN report noted that rice production in the Far East was lower in 1947 than before the war, and in India and Pakistan had been reduced by both bad weather and 'civil strife'. In the USA a record wheat crop in 1946 was more than offset by much lower outputs of maize and oats.[14] In Europe, as we have seen, cereal and potato production in 1946 was lower than before the war in some countries and higher in others, but the general pattern was that people consumed more cereals and fewer animal products than before the war. Then, the winter of early 1947 was marked by a prolonged spell of unusually cold weather over the whole of Europe, which damaged or destroyed large areas of autumn-sown crops. It was followed by an unusually dry summer. In consequence, crop yields fell and the overall European output of wheat, rye, oats and potatoes in the 1947 harvest was lower than in the previous year, and much lower than the pre-war average. However, it was not simply a problem of domestic production. Since the latter part of the nineteenth century several European countries had been regular importers of bread grains, and many others of animal feedstuffs.[15] However, as an article in the journal *Economic Geography* in 1948 argued, postwar economic conditions, specifically low industrial production and low gold and dollar reserves, affected Europe's ability to buy agricultural commodities.[16] The UN report concurred: 'At the present time, some of the large deficit countries do not possess financial resources for the purchase of their appropriate shares of the very insufficient exportable grain supplies'.[17] In other words, foreign exchange, not nutritional need, would determine the international distribution of food if this pattern persisted.

In these circumstances, it is hardly surprising to find that agricultural commodity imports after the war were generally lower than the pre-war average, as Table 1.3 shows. It takes wheat as a proxy for all bread grains and maize for animal feedstuffs, as these were always the major commodities in these two categories. The italicised figures in the table are for those countries in which the 1947 figure is greater than the pre-war figure, and it is clear that there were usually some special circumstances to account for this, such as the postwar emergency requirements in Germany and Italy, and pre-war policy in Spain and Portugal. What stands out in this table, however, is the significant decrease, especially in feed grains, in some of the major pre-war importers such as the UK, Belgium, Denmark and the Netherlands. If Europeans were to benefit from increased food supplies, it appeared that they would have to produce them for themselves.

In addition to labour shortages, a lack of fertilisers and draught power, in the form of either horses or tractors, held back production on wartime European farms. With the end of the war the labour problem should have

Table 1.3 Imports of bread and feed grains ('000 tonnes)

	Wheat pre-war	Wheat 1947	Maize pre-war	Maize 1947
Austria	205.6	No data	368.8	0.3
Belgium	1,159.8	597.1	799.3	291.6
Denmark	256.6	32.9	332.1	18.3
France	579.3	288.8	688.4	513.7
Germany	673.3	2,021.2	979.3	741.9
Greece	429.2	353.7	44.3	55.3
Ireland	410.7	117.6	299.2	76.6
Italy	700.5	1,045.1	153.0	420.9
Netherlands	541.4	489.6	934.3	297.6
Portugal	30.2	167.2	39.9	128.0
Spain	0.4	298.6	56.8	5.6
Sweden	48.4	81.2	116.7	40.5
UK	5,111.8	4,261.2	3,285.4	485.7

Source: FAO, *Yearbook of Food and Agricultural Statistics: Part 2: Trade*, Rome, 1948.

disappeared, although of course it took time for soldiers to be demobilised and prisoners of war (POWs) to return home. Repatriation of German POWs from the UK did not begin until 1947 and was completed by the middle of 1948, and one estimate calculates that they made their greatest contribution to the UK economy, and especially agriculture, in the two years after the war.[18] Repatriation from the USSR took even longer for those who survived. Horse numbers were higher in 1946/7 than before the war in Austria, Belgium, Denmark and the Netherlands, and only lower by about 7 per cent in Germany and 12 per cent in France, which makes the UN report's statement that 'the reduction in draught power during the war was so great that the provision of 23,000 tractors and 260,000 draught animals to countries assisted by UNRRA is estimated to have replaced less than five per cent of the loss' somewhat surprising.[19] Calculating the number of horses required on European farms in the immediate postwar years is difficult because this was the middle of the period in which tractors began to replace horses to a significant degree, but horses retained a significant role in farming. There were twice as many horses as tractors on British farms in 1946, for example.[20] The Economic Commission for Europe estimated that 213,000 tractors were needed on European farms in 1947/8, when tractor production in the main producing countries, the UK, France, Italy and the western zones of Germany, totalled 158,400. With the end of the war, nitrogen fertilisers became more easily available, since their constituents were no longer needed in explosives, but phosphate and potash fertilisers were still affected by transport problems in some areas.[21] In summary, European agriculture at the end of the Second World War and in the two or three years following had not returned to pre-war levels of output or to pre-war patterns of trade, and was struggling to feed the people of Europe.

The major changes from 1945 to 1960

We have gone to some lengths to emphasise Europe's postwar problems in the previous section because it is too easy in looking at long runs of statistics to overlook them. From a viewpoint in the early twenty-first century, the immediate postwar years seem like a short extension of the Second World War, easily overlooked, despite the pessimism of the time. And, in fact, there is a grain of truth in this impression, because both in the world as a whole and in many European countries, agricultural production expanded – or returned to the pre-war normality – much faster than General de Gaulle and the UN experts had predicted. The volume of world food supplies exceeded its pre-war level in 1948/9, although world population growth meant that supplies per head were still about 8 per cent below the pre-war figure. Compared with weather-affected 1947/8, food production everywhere, except Australia and New Zealand, 'showed great improvement' according to the FAO's annual report on the state of food and agriculture.[22] According to Michael Tracy's calculations, based on data for countries in the Organisation for European Economic Co-operation (OEEC) at the time (essentially Western Europe but without Spain), 'In the crop year 1949/50, agricultural production in the OEEC area exceeded the pre-war level; even in Western Germany production was back to the pre-war level by 1950/51'.[23] The volume of agricultural production in Europe as a whole, excluding the USSR, exceeded pre-war levels for the first time in 1951/2. In the previous year, the calorie content of all European diets was above 90 per cent of pre-war levels, and in many countries it was higher than the pre-war average. Crop production led the way. It was almost up to pre-war levels per head by 1948/9, when output of animal products per head was only 72 per cent of its pre-war level.[24] An estimate by Martin-Retortillo and Pinilla, based on FAO data, suggests that agricultural production in Western, Mediterranean and Nordic Europe, plus Germany, amounted to $US67.8 billion in 1950 (calculated at 1999–2001 prices), compared with a figure of $US66.4 billion for the pre-war years calculated on the same basis.[25] Breaking down the FAO data into individual agricultural commodities and countries, as in Table 1.4, reveals a rather more complex picture, although the overall result remains the same. As Table 1.4 suggests, not all countries shared in the return to normality: Austria and Spain are the obvious exceptions, and both had political reasons for their slow agricultural expansion. Until the end of occupation in 1955, much of the east of Austria lay in the Soviet zone, 'notorious for the brutality of its administration, and its ruthless, destructive, economic policies'.[26] Spanish output was kept low by the after-effects of the civil war and the subsequent drive for autarky. Except in Austria, horse numbers were in general decline after the war as farmers began to turn to tractors, and the acreage of oats fell as a consequence. These factors explain 30 of the 48 cells (of the 104 that contain data) in Table 1.4 in which the figures are in bold, indicating that the production of the commodity in a particular country remained below the pre-war level. And apart from Austria

Table 1.4 Output of selected commodities in 1952 expressed as an index (pre-war = 100)

	Wheat	Rye	Barley	Oats	Maize	Potatoes	Cattle	Pigs	Horses
Austria	**96**	**63**	**88**	**78**	**72**	**90**	**87**	**87**	120
Belgium	129	**52**	300	**71**	n.d.	**67**	136	160	**95**
Denmark	**79**	136	193	**94**	n.d.	172	**92**	113	**71**
France	103	**63**	161	**73**	**90**	**70**	104	101	**88**
Germany	130	100	103	**59**	**31**	119	**96**	115	**92**
Greece	139	**97**	107	147	**94**	326	**87**	148	**80**
Ireland	149	200	192	102	n.d.	105	106	**77**	**77**
Italy	109	**90**	125	**93**	**80**	103	115	129	**95**
Netherlands	**76**	100	194	138	n.d.	216	102	116	**76**
Portugal	118	164	361	141	155	193	n.d.	n.d.	n.d.
Spain	**94**	**82**	**70**	**73**	**91**	**69**	n.d.	n.d.	n.d.
Sweden	112	**69**	n.d.	**65**	n.d.	100	**81**	106	**59**
UK	135	455	288	140	n.d.	159	115	106	**38**

Source: FAO, *Yearbook of Food and Agricultural Statistics: Part 1, Production*, Rome, 1948. Note that the data for animal production are based on livestock numbers, not meat or animal products output. All figures less than 100 are shown in bold.

and Spain, only France had a majority of commodities in which the index of 1952 production was less than 100. Writing in 1955, Elizabeth Wiskemann, who had known pre-war Germany well, described the evolution of food supplies in West Germany as 'unexpectedly satisfactory', and by 1956 production had further increased almost everywhere.[27]

Table 1.4 is a relatively crude measure of the variation in European postwar agricultural recovery, but it supports the overall conclusion, based on total farm output, of rapid expansion in the three or four years after the weather-induced problems of 1947. International trade, too, was returning to pre-war levels by the 1950s. Wheat imports for Europe as a whole were a little greater in 1952 than before the war, with Germany and Italy being major importers. The wheat market was still dominated by the UK as it had been before the war, but UK imports remained at less than pre-war levels for the 1950s as home production increased. European imports of maize, the major imported feed grain, were only at about half of pre-war levels by 1952, and again the UK, which remained the largest single importer, was buying less than half of its pre-war purchases. Imports of barley, oats and rye were always less than those of wheat and maize. Despite its postwar production increases, the UK remained the dominant European – indeed, world – food importer. In the butter trade, UK imports never quite recovered to pre-war levels in the 1950s, but Germany, the other main pre-war importer, was back to pre-war levels by 1957. Denmark and the Netherlands, the major exporters, had not returned to pre-war levels by 1957. Similarly, with cheese: again, the UK and Germany were the major pre-war importers. The UK exceeded its pre-war import levels in the late 1940s but then reduced imports as domestic milk production increased, whereas by 1955 Germany was importing more than it had before the war. The beef market, too, returned to pre-war levels by 1957. The principal live cattle exporters were Ireland, Denmark and Yugoslavia, and the main importers the UK, West Germany and Italy, and in each case the 1957 figures exceeded pre-war levels. The UK also dominated the fresh and frozen meat trade. Denmark, Poland and the Netherlands, the main pre-war exporters of bacon and ham, exceeded their pre-war exports by 1947, by which time the UK was back to its pre-war import levels.[28] One of the notable features of international agricultural trade in this period was the spread of bilateral trade agreements. The UK made such an agreement with Denmark for the supply of butter, and with Poland for bacon. Italy made agreements to purchase various commodities from the USSR. By 1949 the FAO claimed that 80 per cent of world trade in food and agricultural products was covered by such agreements, with the result that there was no single world price. The UK paid $US80 per tonne for Canadian wheat, but $US140 for wheat from Argentina, whereas Canada received twice as much for meat and bacon as Argentinian producers.[29]

Agricultural production in the European market economies rose further in the 1950s: Martin-Retortillo and Pinilla's figures suggest by nearly 40 per cent on average between 1950 and 1962.[30] The Mediterranean countries performed slightly below this average, and France and Germany well above it. These output increases were produced using a little less land, a lot less labour, and more capital and purchased inputs. As Table 1.5 shows, the area devoted to crops decreased slightly in the 1950s, so production per hectare rose, and the agricultural population fell much more, so that output per head nearly doubled, according to this calculation. It is worth noting that Tracy's OECD-derived data for 1949–59 suggests a range of increases in labour productivity from 27 per cent in Ireland to 61 per cent in France, 72 per cent in Germany and the highest, 77 per cent, in Denmark. Interestingly, all these increases are higher than the changes in output per head in other industries, although the output per head in non-farm industries remained higher than it was in agriculture. Again, this varied between countries. In Ireland in 1960 nearly 40 per cent of the civilian labour force was employed in agriculture, but it produced only about 25 per cent of the Gross Domestic Product; similarly in France,

Table 1.5 Land and labour use and productivity, 1950–1962 in European market economies

	1950	*1962*
Net production ($US million at 1999–2001 prices)	69,438	97,433
Cropland 000 hectares	96,202	95,911
Net production per crop hectare $US	721.8	10,15.9
Active agricultural population (000)	34,588	25,918
Net production per head $US	2,007.6	3,759.2

Source: Own calculations from Martin-Retortillo and Pinilla, 'Patterns and causes of the growth of European agricultural production', Tables 1, 2 and 7.

over 20 per cent of the labour force produced only 10 per cent of GDP, whereas the figures were closer to parity in the Netherlands, where 10 per cent of the labour force made the same contribution to GDP, and the UK, where the figures were just under 5 per cent in each category.[31]

The data in Table 1.5 show that nearly 10 million people in the European market economies left agricultural employment in the 1950s. The rate at which they did so was higher in Germany, France, Italy, the Netherlands and Denmark than in the UK, where the level of farm employment was already less than in the rest of Europe. It was also higher than in Spain, where another data source suggested that the rate of outmigration from farming was only about a third of the French or German level in the 1950s, or in Greece, where there is some evidence for an increase in the agricultural population in this period.[32] By 1962 over half of the agricultural population of Western Europe could be found in Portugal, Spain, Italy and Greece.[33] At the same time, as Table 1.6 shows, the number of agricultural holdings decreased, although not as quickly as the total labour force, with a consequent increase in average farm size.

Those who left the land were usually (but not exclusively) young people, and landless labourers and younger children of farmers were more likely to leave than those who either had a farm or had reasonable prospects of succeeding to one.[34] There was much discussion at the time over whether labour was pulled from the land by the prospect of higher earnings in industry or pushed from it by farm mechanisation. As Vinen observes:

> It seems reasonable to assume that pull was stronger than push in France, where the demand for labour was intense and mechanisation was low, and that push was stronger than pull in Germany, a country with a strong tradition of agricultural mechanisation, and where labour was relatively abundant.[35]

Table 1.6 Percentage changes in the numbers and sizes of farm holdings

	% change in number of holdings	% change in average holding size
Austria 1951–60	−7	+10
Belgium 1950–59	−21	+21
Denmark 1946–61	−6	+4
Germany 1949–62	−19	+19
Netherlands 1950–59	−12	+22
Norway 1949–59	−8	+6
Sweden 1951–61	−17	+12
Switzerland 1939–55	−14	+10
UK 1950–60	−11	n.a.

Source: C.E. Bishop, *Geographic and Occupational Mobility of Rural Manpower*, Paris: OECD, 1965, p. 58.

On the other hand, the rate at which agricultural wages increased in comparison with machinery costs was roughly the same in both countries. Over Europe as a whole, farm wages increased faster than the costs of fertilisers, feedstuffs and farm machinery in the 1950s, and in Germany twice as fast.[36]

It is consequently unsurprising that the use of capital in European agriculture increased, although it is not easy to measure the extent to which it did so. There are various kinds of capital employed in agriculture. A common categorisation differentiates between fixed capital, which is mostly farm buildings and machinery, and working capital, meaning breeding livestock, seeds, stored crops, etc. Since the former lasts over several years and may remain in operation long after it has been written off in the farm accounts, it is notoriously difficult to measure, although it is possible to find indicative proxy measures. The most easily available involves farm machinery: the number of tractors on farms in the OEEC countries increased from 500,000 in 1947 to 3 million in 1960. An alternative estimate for Western Europe, which covers many of the same countries, suggests that the number of tractors per worker increased by more than five times between 1950 and 1962, from 0.049 to 0.238. The number of tractors per worker in West Germany and the Nordic countries in 1962 was slightly higher, but in the Mediterranean countries it was considerably less, at 0.032 in 1962.[37] Some idea of changes in working capital may be gained by examining the number of animals on farms, which, according to one estimate, measured in terms of livestock units which account for the differing sizes of the animals, increased by a little over 17 per cent between 1950 and 1962. However, it is important to remember that, as the authors point out, this figure incorporated contradictory trends. Draught animal numbers were decreasing, while breeding animal numbers were increasing, although they were only a part of the total, which also included fattening animals. On the whole, therefore, the percentage change noted above probably underestimates the increase in working capital employed in European agriculture.[38]

The other major input change was in purchased inputs, such as fertilisers, feedstuffs, pesticides, veterinary medicines, tractor fuel, and so on. The most readily available figures are for fertilisers. Consumption of fertiliser nitrogen, phosphate and potash in Europe as a whole exceeded pre-war levels by 1948/9, although the use of potash in Western Germany, cut off from supplies in what was now the eastern zone, remained below the pre-war level. Martin-Retortillo and Pinilla's calculations from FAO data show consumption (of all fertilisers) doubling in the Western European countries, and also doubling in the Mediterranean countries, but from a much lower base.[39] The late 1940s and 1950s were years in which more and more farmers began to use selective herbicides such as MCPA and 2,4-D on cereal crops, insecticides such as DDT, and antibiotics to treat animal diseases, but these changes are more difficult to quantify.

These economic, structural and technical changes in European agriculture did not take place in a political vacuum. There had been agrarian parties in several European countries before the war, and their numbers alone would have made farmers and their families politically significant in many countries. But there was more to it than that. In countries where the working class was predictably left wing, and the bourgeoisie consistently conservative, the agricultural population could be supporters of middle-ground parties that were often part of coalitions, or volatile in their affiliations, supporting whichever political group would give the greater concessions to agriculture. Elsewhere, they had powerful and well-financed pressure groups that were effective in putting the case for farm support. And underlying all of the politics was the cultural significance of agriculture, which was widely seen as a repository of virtuous traditions.[40]

In this political environment, it was not surprising that the world food crisis at the end of the war led many governments to conclude that the expansion of domestic agriculture was desirable, if not essential, and could be assisted by supportive government policies. As the FAO noted in 1949, the volume of food production was no longer so influenced by market price changes as it had been before the war: 'A large number of governments now guarantee prices to farmers through a variety of procedures, all of which give the farmer a greater degree of security, thereby stimulating or stabilizing production'.[41] Agricultural prices were supported by import controls in France and Germany, Belgium supported the price of wheat, and a little later Germany intervened to take any surplus production off the market, while Italy subsidised wheat exports. The common feature of policy in these continental European countries was that a relatively free internal market operated within a ring of protection from the world market. In the UK, with a much longer tradition of food imports and a still remaining involvement as a major importer in many markets, a different support system was used, in which the market was open to world trade but internal prices were supplemented by taxpayer-funded subsidies.[42] As early as 1950, the French Minister of Agriculture, Pierre Pflimlin, and his counterpart in the Netherlands, Sicco Mansholt, began to advance proposals for a common European agricultural market, even though their interests were not identical; France appears to have been primarily interested in regulation and the Netherlands in a free market. Their initiative was in part a recognition of the common interests and problems of European agriculture, and in part a response to the rapid expansion of production in the late 1940s. Pflimlin saw that French agriculture would soon need a larger market than France itself could provide, and that the continent had two major importers, the UK and Germany. There were also comparisons with the European Coal and Steel Community, which was beginning at this point in time. Despite this logic, negotiations to establish a 'Green Pool' failed in 1954, and it appeared that the opportunity had been lost, although, of course, within only a few years the 1957 Treaty of Rome laid the foundations for the establishment of a Common Agricultural Policy in the 1960s.[43]

European agriculture and rural society in 1960

The fifteen years from the end of the Second World War saw a Western Europe that was short of food, in a world that was short of food, change to a better fed continent in a better fed world. Nevertheless, it would be a mistake to think that Europe's agricultural problems were over and that there was no room for change or development. In 1956, The Twentieth Century Fund, a private philanthropic foundation in the USA concerned with questions of public welfare, initiated a survey of the economic needs and resources of Europe. As part of this, Paul Lamartine Yates was asked to write a study of Western (i.e. non-communist) European agriculture. Yates was employed by the Fund at that time, but he had previously worked for the UN Food and Agriculture Organisation, and before the war he had produced a major study of Western European agriculture, so he was well qualified to summarise its condition at the end of the 1950s.[44] His book appeared in 1960, and contained, in addition to various analyses of agricultural economics, food consumption and trade, a short survey of the state of farming in various countries. His findings demonstrated not only the changes that had been seen since the war, but also the remaining problems that had yet to be resolved.[45]

Beginning in the north, Yates described a rural Norway with a high population density and small farms, largely self-sufficient in animal products but unable to grow enough arable products for her own market, whereas Sweden had more arable land, more efficiently sized farms, and an expanding industrial sector that was drawing labour from the land. In Denmark, the technically progressive and well-capitalised farms were large enough to provide sufficient employment for a farming family, although they remained dependent upon access to foreign markets for their pigs and dairy products. The two big islands off the north-western shores of the continent demonstrated considerable differences. Some 40 per cent of the working population in Ireland were still in agriculture and the farms were neither intensive nor efficient, whereas agriculture in the UK was different, not only from Ireland, but from most of continental Europe too. Farms were bigger, the proportion of employed, as opposed to family, labour was greater, they were highly mechanised, and there was little pressure to move labour off the land, although it was happening.[46]

In his accounts of agriculture in the countries of continental Europe, Yates constantly found the same themes emerging: farms that were too small to provide full-time employment but too far from towns for their workforce to take advantage of industrial employment, so leading to under-employment; land that was fragmented into numerous fields, often at a distance from each other; and an expanding population that could with advantage be moved into industry. He admitted that France was too big a country to admit of easy generalisations. It was the biggest country in Europe and most varied in climate, topography and types of farming, from the big arable farms of the Paris Basin to the small farms and market gardens around Avignon in the south. In general, farm output was increasing rapidly and labour was 'streaming off the land', but there was still a long way to go. Many farms were cursed with fragmentation into numerous plots, and there were still areas, such as Brittany and the south-west, that remained isolated and overpopulated. In Belgium, the labour-intensive agriculture on very small farms was also beset by problems of under-employment and fragmentation. There was a variety of high-technology farming types in the Netherlands, where there were still active land reclamation projects, but farms were generally small and there was pressure to find new export markets and to transfer labour to industry. Farms in southern Germany were also small and fragmented, although they were bigger in the north, and in both areas farmers had been helped by recent mechanisation and a buoyant domestic market. But they were still making only slow progress in regrouping fragmented farms. In Austria, too, despite recent rationalisation, some under-employment remained. Farming in northern Italy, in the Lombardy plain, was similar to French and German agriculture, whereas the south was dominated by Mediterranean crops. In the country as a whole 40 per cent of the labour force remained in farming, far more than necessary, and further industrialisation was urgently needed. In Greece, half of the labour force remained on the land, farms were small and yields were low, but there had been remarkable technical progress since the war, and the country would soon be self-sufficient in food. The fertile north-western and southern coasts of Spain were separated by a big, dry, infertile area in between, where yields and the level of mechanisation were low, and under-employment was frequent. Many people in dry and overpopulated Portugal had a poor diet, but their incomes were too low for them to acquire more food. Industrialisation was urgently needed.[47]

This cursory summary of Yates's rapid survey hardly does justice to either the variety of Western European farming or the changes that had occurred to it since the war, but at least it demonstrates that problems remained and that there were differences between countries. The range of intercountry variation is illustrated in Table 1.7, the data for which is derived from a survey carried out at the end of the 1950s by the European Productivity Agency in an attempt to delineate agricultural regions, mainly in member states of the then newly formed European Economic Community.[48] It shows that average wheat yields in the Benelux countries (Belgium, Netherlands and Luxemburg) were twice those in Italy, and average milk yields per cow in France almost half those in the Benelux countries. The variation between individual regions was greater still. Highest yields of both wheat and milk were found in the intensively farmed Dutch coastal area from Friesland down to the Rhine and Meuse deltas. There the wheat yields were four times greater than those found in Sardinia, the region with the lowest yield, and about three times greater than in the rest of Italy south of Rome.[49]

In northern Italy, however, in the Po Valley and its delta, wheat yields approached those of the Dutch coast. The region with the lowest milk yield was the French Massif Central, even though it included the Cantal dairying district. There were even greater disparities in the structure of agriculture. The

16 *Brassley, Martiin and Pan-Montojo*

Table 1.7 Technical and structural variations in the late 1950s

	Germany	Benelux	France	Italy	Highest region	Lowest region
Wheat yields (tonnes/ha)	2.8	3.4	2.3	1.7	3.8 Dutch coast	0.95 Sardinia
Milk yields (kg/cow/year)	2941	3815	1948	n.a	3941 Dutch coast	1390 Massif Central
Area covered by farms of less than 10 ha as % of total farm area	39	35.4	16	n.a	62 Middle Rhine	4 Paris Basin
Area covered by farms of more than 50 ha as % of total farm area	10	8.5	25	n.a.	60 Paris Basin	2 Bavaria
Active agricultural population as % of total active population	23	n.a.	26.8	42.2	53.7 Po Delta	8.5 Paris Basin

Source: K.H. Olsen, *Agricultural Regions in the O.E.E.C. Countries*, Paris: OEEC, 1961.

Paris Basin, with its surrounding districts of Picardy, Champagne and the Beauce, stood out as having the lowest area of small farms, the greatest of large farms, and the lowest proportion of its labour force in agriculture. In contrast, in neighbouring Normandy, 47 per cent of the labour force remained in farming, almost as high a proportion as that in the Po Delta, the region with the highest proportion of agricultural labour. The regions with the highest area in small farms, and the lowest in large farms, were both in Germany, in the middle Rhine Valley and Bavaria respectively, but nearly comparable figures showing the preponderance of small farms were found in several other regions of Germany and much of the Low Countries. Had data on this variable been available for Italy, it would probably have shown a similar pattern.

This survey, and the others discussed above, have, in one way or another, dealt with the technical and structural problems that remained for Western European farming after fifteen years of postwar change. The following chapters provide partly different views and deal also with questions such as: why was agricultural change after the Second World War so different from the post-First World War changes; why did technical and structural change happen; why were pro-agriculture policies so common and how effective were they in producing agricultural change?

A literature survey

As the footnotes to this Introduction suggest, the number of historical works in the English language literature dealing with European agriculture as a whole between 1945 and 1960 is extremely limited. In fact, the only clear candidate for inclusion in this category is Chapter 11 of Tracy's *Agriculture in Western Europe*, originally published in 1964. Its main and more recent competitor is the multi-author volume edited by K.K. Patel, but the main focus of this book is on European political integration and the extent to which the origins and development of the CAP can shed light upon the process. The article by Martin-Retortillo and Pinilla, frequently mentioned above, deals with the whole period between 1950 and 2005, but includes data points at 1950 and 1962 and therefore includes some useful analysis of agricultural change.[50] Most of the volumes in the CORN and COST series contain chapters relating to individual countries rather than analyses of Europe or Western Europe as a whole.[51] One of the conclusions that emerges from an examination of this limited range of historical work is that the relevant archives remain largely unexplored, possibly because there were so many official publications from national governments and international organisations, in addition to the works of contemporary writers such as Lamartine-Yates and Dovring referred to earlier.

A brief introduction to the contents

In Part I of this book, the international political order in food and agriculture is discussed by Juan Pan-Montojo, who explores the initial framing of international institutions in the field, and their functions during the early post-Second World War period of new economic and political realities. Emanuele Bernardi focuses on the Cold War era and discusses the European Recovery Program ('the Marshall Plan'), the role of the US and of the Catholic Church, and the impact of the Korean War. In the third chapter Vicente Pinilla, Ángel Luis González Esteban and Raúl Serrano claim that both national trade policies and the international set of regulations after the Second World War were deeply dependent on the domestic agricultural policies and the so-called farm adjustment problem.

Part II focuses on the range of market regulations that emerged in between the Second World War and the Common Agricultural Policy, which in many countries had roots in earlier decades of the twentieth century. Socrates Petmezas explains the policy of cereal self-sufficiency, public intervention and extension services in Greek agriculture that managed to achieve nutritional self-sufficiency in the late 1950s. In Britain, food shortage in the late 1940s was turned into food surplus in the 1950s, which John Martin discusses with references to the 1947 Agriculture Act and the state support of agriculture. From Denmark, Thomas Christiansen explores the Danish agrarian sector and explains how a surplus of food during the war was developed into even more surplus production.

Part III deals with technical change, public research, extension services and the increased use of commercial agrarian inputs after the Second World War. Peter Moser and Juri Auderset emphasise the interaction of theory and practice in these processes, with special attention to changes in the use of natural resources in agriculture. Technological change in a dictatorial context is highlighted by Daniel Lanero and Lourenzo Fernández-Prieto in their chapter on how the fascist ideological sphere intervened in the agricultural sectors in Spain and Portugal. The Iberian study is followed by Laurent Herment's investigation of French agriculture after the Second World War, where farms in many regions were small, and the process of tractorisation rather a matter of adaptation of farms to tractors than the other way around.

The fourth and final part of this book focuses on rural society, structural policies and structural change in agriculture and their links to political aims concerning welfare and urbanisation. Yves Segers and Erwin H. Karel provide a comparative study of Belgium and the Netherlands, emphasising similarities with regard to increased state intervention, scaling up, modernisation and, in the Dutch context, social engineering. Gesine Gerhard explores the agricultural transformation in West Germany in the 1950s, the so-called 'miracle years', explaining how the dramatic structural change occurred without any major social conflict and the role played by agricultural interest organisations in the process. In Sweden, Carin Martiin argues, the fact that self-sufficiency in food had already been achieved paved the way for policies aimed at producing the same amount of food, but with less labour and fewer, more efficient, family-operated farms. Finally, the concluding chapter highlights some of the main results of these studies.

Notes

1 M. Tracy, *Agriculture in Western Europe: Crisis and Adaptation Since 1880*, London: Cape, 1964; there is a good survey of the work of political historians (and some agricultural economists) in the introductory chapter to K.K. Patel (ed.), *Fertile Ground for Europe? The History of European Integration and the Common Agricultural Policy since 1945*, Baden-Baden: Nomos, 2009. We are grateful to Vicente Pinilla for providing us with a copy of this book.
2 Among those treating Europe as a whole and going beyond the experience of individual nations are F. Trentmann and F. Just (eds), *Food and Conflict in Europe in the Age of the Two World Wars*, Basingstoke: Palgrave Macmillan, 2006; L. Collingham, *The Taste of War: World War Two and the Battle for Food*, London: Allen Lane, 2011; I. Zweiniger-Bargielowska, R. Duffet and A. Drouard (eds), *Food and War in Twentieth-Century Europe*, Farnham: Ashgate, 2011; and P. Brassley, Y. Segers and L. Van Molle, *War, Agriculture and Food: Rural Europe from the 1930s to the 1950s*, New York: Routledge, 2012.
3 B. Short, *The Battle of the Fields: Rural Community and Authority in Britain during the Second World War*, Woodbridge: Boydell, 2014.
4 J. Pan-Montojo, 'Spanish Agriculture, 1931–1955: Crisis, wars, and new policies in the reshaping of rural society', in Brassley *et al.* (eds), *War, Agriculture and Food*, pp. 88–90.
5 C. Martiin, 'Farming, Favoured in Times of Fear: Swedish agricultural politics, 1935–1955', in Brassley *et al.* (eds), *War, Agriculture and Food*, p. 162.
6 Its reliability is discussed in P. Brassley, 'International Trade in Agricultural Products, 1935–1955', in Brassley *et al.* (eds), *War, Agriculture and Food*, pp. 40 and 45.

7 K. Brandt and associates, *Management of Agriculture and Food in the German-Occupied and Other Areas of Fortress Europe: A Study in Military Government*, Stanford, CA: Stanford University Press, 1953, p. 408.
8 M. Nissen, 'Danish Food Production in the German War Economy', in Trentmann and Just (eds), *Food and Conflict*; M. Nissen, 'From War Profits to Post-War Investments: How the German occupation improved investments in Danish agriculture in the post-war years', in Brassley *et al.* (eds), *War, Agriculture and Food*.
9 All these figures are in the UN Department of Economic Affairs, Economic Report, *Salient Features of the World Economic Situation 1945–47*, New York: Lake Success, 1948, pp.147–155. There is an interesting fictional study of the impact of post-war food shortages in Hamburg in Rhidian Brook's novel *The Aftermath*, London:Viking, 2013.
10 T. Judt, *Postwar: A History of Europe since 1945*, London: Pimlico, 2007, p. 89.
11 A. Potter, *Shared Histories: Transatlantic Letters between Virginia Dickinson Reynolds and her Daughter, Virginia Potter, 1929–1966*, Athens, GA: University of Georgia Press, 2006, p. 245.
12 UN, *Salient Features* p.191.
13 Minister of Food, *The World Food Shortage*, Cmd.6785, London: HMSO, 1946, p. 3.
14 UN *Salient Features*, pp. 194–195.
15 Brassley, 'International Trade in Agricultural Products'.
16 R.E. Birchard, 'Europe's Critical Food Situation', *Economic Geography*, 24(4) October 1948, p. 278.
17 UN *Salient Features*, p.198.
18 J. Custodis, 'Employing the Enemy', *Agricultural History Review*, 60(2), 2012, pp. 262–263.
19 FAO, *Yearbook of Food and Agricultural Statistics: Part 1, Production*, Rome: FAO, 1948; UN, *Salient Features*, p. 200.
20 P. Brassley, 'Output and Technical Change in Twentieth-Century British Agriculture', *Agricultural History Review*, 48(1), 2000, p. 74.
21 UN *Salient Features* pp. 144, 200.
22 FAO, *The State of Food and Agriculture: A Survey of World Conditions and Prospects*, Washington, DC, FAO, 1949, pp. 8, 9 (henceforth referred to as SOFA 1949).
23 Tracy, *Agriculture in Western Europe*, p. 232.
24 SOFA, 1949, p. 8; SOFA, 1952, pp. 15, 19.
25 M. Martin-Retortillo and V. Pinilla, 'Patterns and causes of the growth of European agricultural production, 1950 to 2005', *Agricultural History Review*, 63(1), 2015, pp. 132–159.
26 S. Beller, *A Concise History of Austria*, Cambridge: Cambridge University Press, 2006, pp. 252 and 260.
27 E. Wiskemann, *Germany's Eastern Neighbours: Problems Relating to the Oder-Neisse Line and the Czech Frontier Regions*, London: Oxford University Press, 1956, p. 173.
28 FAO, *Yearbook of Food and Agricultural Statistics: Part 2: Trade*, Rome: FAO, 1958.
29 SOFA, 1949, pp. 15–16.
30 Martin-Retortillo and Pinilla, 'Patterns and causes of the growth of European agricultural production', p. 5.
31 Tracy, *Agriculture in Western Europe*, pp. 233, 236; P. Lamartine Yates, *Food, Land and Manpower in Western Europe*, London: Macmillan, 1960, p. 150, compares farm and non-farm productivity per worker, and shows that the former was normally lower than the latter, but to varying degrees. Whereas farm labour productivity was 88 per cent of non-farm in Denmark, the figure was only 30 per cent in Portugal.
32 F. Dovring, *Problems of Manpower in Agriculture*, Paris: OECD, 1964, p. 16; C.E. Bishop, *Geographic and Occupational Mobility of Rural Manpower*, Paris: OECD, 1965, p. 17.

33 Martin-Retortillo and Pinilla, 'Patterns and causes of the growth of European agricultural production', Table 7.
34 Dovring, *Problems of Manpower*, pp. 19–21.
35 R. Vinen, *A History in Fragments: Europe in the Twentieth Century*, London: Abacus, 2002, p. 338.
36 Bishop, *Geographic and Occupational Mobility*, p. 57.
37 Tracy, *Agriculture in Western Europe*, p. 232; Martin-Retortillo and Pinilla, 'Patterns and causes of the growth of European agricultural production', Table 5. There are further figures for tractor and farm machinery numbers in SOFA, 1949, pp. 133–5 and Bishop, *Geographic and Occupational Mobility*, p. 57.
38 Martin-Retortillo and Pinilla, 'Patterns and causes of the growth of European agricultural production', Table 3.
39 SOFA, 1949, pp.129-130; Martin-Retortillo and Pinilla, 'Patterns and causes of the growth of European agricultural production', Table 5.
40 Vinen, *A History in Fragments*, p. 337; Tracy, *Agriculture in Western Europe*, pp. 248–250.
41 SOFA, 1949, p. 9.
42 Tracy, *Agriculture in Western Europe*, pp. 235–42.
43 G. Thiemeyer, 'The Failure of the Green Pool and the Success of the CAP: Long term structures in European agricultural integration in the 1950s and 1960s', in Patel, *Fertile Ground for Europe?*, pp. 47–51.
44 P. Lamartine Yates, *Food Production in Western Europe: An Economic Survey of Agriculture in Six Countries*, London: Longmans Green & Co., 1940.
45 P. Lamartine Yates, *Food, Land and Manpower in Western Europe*, London: Macmillan, 1960.
46 Yates, *Food Land and Manpower*, pp. 103–112.
47 Yates, *Food Land and Manpower*, pp. 112–131.
48 The European Productivity Agency was established in 1953 as a branch of the Organisation for European Economic Co-operation (OEEC, later the OECD) to stimulate productivity in agriculture, industry and government and private services.
49 The Sardinian wheat yield of less than a tonne per hectare was a quantity with which farmers in late sixteenth-century England or late eighteenth-century France would have been dissatisfied. See S. Broadberry et al., *British Economic Growth 1270-1870*, Cambridge: Cambridge University Press, 2015, p.95; A. Moulin, *Peasantry and Society in France since 1789*, Cambridge: Cambridge University Press, 1988, p. 8.
50 Tracy, *Agriculture in Western Europe*; Patel, *Fertile Ground for Europe?*; Martin-Retortillo and Pinilla, 'Patterns and causes of the growth of European agricultural production'.
51 See, for example, P. Moser and T. Varley (eds), *Integration through Subordination: The Politics of Agricultural Modernisation in Industrial Europe*, Turnhout: Brepols, 2013. Details of other volumes in both series may be found on the Brepols website, www.brepols.net.

Part I
International politics

Figure P1 Par le Plan Marshall (1950) by Gaston van den Eynde (courtesy of the George C. Marshall Foundation, Lexington, Virginia)

2 International institutions and European agriculture
From the IIA to the FAO

Juan Pan-Montojo

Introduction

Agriculture and food became after 1945 a major field of regulation for national states and, at the same time, political issues framed by supranational agreements, transnational tendencies and intergovernmental decisions and programmes. The international institutions that were behind those 'external' factors were not, though, an innovation of the postwar period. The organisations that were established during or after the Second World War responded to models, projects and ideas that had been developed in the interwar period, especially in the 1930s under the pressure of the Great Depression. Their foundations were laid even earlier: in 1887, the French government established a Commission Internationale d'Agriculture (CIA) that displayed a public activity beyond the congresses it regularly organised; and in 1905, a first intergovernmental organisation specialising in agriculture, the International Institute of Agriculture (IIA), came into existence. Therefore, despite the numerous new elements of the postwar agricultural settlement, 1945 was not a year zero. A longer look is hence the first task of a chapter which does not want to address either international agricultural and food organisations in isolation or their role as precedents and promoters of European integration. Our aim is summing up certain results of these two disciplinary traditions, the one that has studied concrete institutions and their role in food or development history and the other that deals with the prehistory of the Common Market, in order to concentrate on the impact of international politics and policies on Western European agriculture.[1]

Mixing both approaches in one article has many risks: it can easily slide into a shallow description of too many agents combined with a far-fetched explanation of their evident, and difficult to measure, influence. But without a general picture of all these international and supranational agents and platforms, our approach to agricultural changes between 1945 and the 1960s would be incomplete. Post-Second World War agricultural policies in Western Europe were almost everywhere characterised by a thorough national regulation of production and foreign trade under a protective umbrella; therefore, the relevance attributed to international actors may seem a paradox unless we can discover a close interdependence between protectionism and internationalism. We will argue, following Milward, that such interdependence existed and that most of the international organisations came to the rescue of national policies.[2] This is not, though, the only story. Food and agriculture organisations were set up in an international system torn apart by the Cold War and, as we shall see, both their actual programmes and the limits of their action reflected somehow the pervasive nature of this international rift and the dominant position of the United States in the West. Agriculture and food became additional weapons in the East–West confrontation, apart from relevant political instruments of Western countries in their imperial and foreign policy. Finally, international organisations, whatever the intentions of the nationally minded politicians that designed them, did produce as well new discourses, networks, institutions, and new professional and political profiles – those of international civil servants and negotiators – that contributed to the homogenisation of national agricultural policies.

International institutions before the Second World War and agriculture

In the late nineteenth century, agricultural 'exceptionalism' became a widespread, perhaps we could say hegemonic, discourse. We use this term to refer to the growing consensus that agriculture was an economic sector with peculiar features, which deserved special treatment.[3] Agriculture was special, many voices argued, because of the role it played in the reproduction of rural society, which was seen as a cornerstone of society, because of the strategic function of food and because of the difficulties encountered by small farmers in surviving in global markets. Exceptionalism was voiced by the new agricultural associations that appeared in nearly every European and American country and by the 'agrarian politicians'. One of the first institutions to be born out of exceptionalism was the International Institute of Agriculture (IIA). It was established in 1905, after a long campaign by a US citizen, David Lubin, who obtained the backing of the king of Italy and wide support from a coalition of European agrarian forces. Lubin, a successful American businessman who invested in agriculture in California in the 1880s, dedicated much time and energy in the final decades of the 19th century to studying the causes of the high risks involved in agricultural ventures. He concluded that the main problem was the imbalance of power between agriculturalists and other economic sectors, a situation deeply rooted in the asymmetry of information about crops and prices between farmers on the one hand, and dealers and industrialists on the other.[4] His solution for this imbalance – the establishment of a permanent organisation aimed at uniting agrarian interests and strengthening their position through the collection and publication of data and studies in different fields – did not find any support until he managed to meet and convince the king of Italy, Vittorio Emanuele III, in 1904. The king put Italian diplomacy at the service of the project and a founding conference met in Rome in May 1905.

The International Institute of Agriculture, after a failed attempt by some of its early supporters to build it up as an international parliament of aristocratic and corporatist lobbies, became an intergovernmental international institution that gathered data, published comparative works and supported conferences.[5] Its members tended to be diplomats, rather than technicians, a fact that, along with other structural problems (among them its reduced budget), seriously limited its accomplishments, according to Asher Hobson, the representative of the USA at the IIA in the 1920s.[6]

Despite its shortcomings, the Institute played a significant role during the interwar period in different fields.[7] It promoted several international conventions among specialists and created a set of advisory councils and commissions, which were the bases of transnational professional, scientific and bureaucratic networks. It favoured the development of a common agenda and facilitated the coining of a common vocabulary in the field of agricultural economics. Finally, the Institute published a long list of regular statistical studies on the basis of figures provided by member states and tried to fix standards to homogenise the data. In many of these levels it carried out research or facilitated information to the League of Nations' conferences, as it was doing when, between 1928 and 1930, it led the first international agricultural census and after 1936 undertook the preliminary works for a second one.

Even before the IIA had taken shape as an idea, the Commission Internationale d'Agriculture had been created in the international congress of agriculture celebrated in Paris, in 1889, under the presidency of Jules Méline, the French republican who brought about the protectionist turn of 1892. The CIA's main role was ensuring the continuity of the congresses and therefore to fix the agenda for international discussion.[8] The CIA changed its nature after the Great War. In March 1925, under the leadership of Louis de Vogüé, President of the Société des Agriculteurs de France, and Ernst Laur, President of the Schweizerische Bauernverband, it passed new statutes in order to become 'the truthful and only organisation representing general interests of agriculture in the international field'.[9] After the readmission of German organisations in the CIA, Andreas Hermes, a Catholic politician who had been the first minister of agriculture in the Weimar Republic and would play a very relevant role after the Second World War in the German agrarian organisations, joined in the CIA.[10] In 1927, coinciding with the announcement, by the League of Nations (LoN), of an International Economic Conference, the French associations gave in, renounced their previous rejection of 'uncontrollable' supranational schemes and accepted the transformation of the Commission Internationale into a Confédération Internationale de l'Agriculture, with its headquarters in Paris, and a large and variegated membership, representing agricultural organisations from 18 European countries.[11]

Even though international agricultural markets had been highly volatile in the 1920s, the 1929 depression turned instability into a generalised crisis as González Esteban, Pinilla and Serrano explain in Chapter 4. In this context, international economic forums, including the agricultural ones, acquired a new political relevance. However, the IIA did not fare well. Its inefficiency and its internal political climate produced a growing mistrust among the experts of the Economic and Financial Organisation of the LoN (ECO), which had previously recognised the IIA as an associate organisation.[12] ECO developed its own agricultural projects. In 1935, when the invasion of Ethiopia brought about LoN sanctions on Italy and pushed it towards an explicit autarkic programme with self-sufficiency in food supplies at its core, the fascist regime appointed a relevant politician, Acerbo, as head of the Institute.[13] This step reduced even more the role of the IIA. The CIA did better: its new profile as a European organisation after 1927 enabled its leaders, who had the strong support of their governments, to play an active role in the international economic debates of the 1930s.[14] The leaders of the CIA rejected both free trade and autarky, opposing to them a new concept that tried to combine international trade, stability and protection of the farmers: the organisation of agriculture – that is to say, the regulation of international production via multilateral agreements, combined with national regulation of the domestic markets, agreed upon by organised producers.

Autarky and the organisation of agriculture were not the only discourses that acquired a final shape and had strong impact in public opinions and agrarian policies in the 1930s. Before their development, those whom Trentman has called 'new internationalists' framed a wider approach to food and agricultural: international coordination.[15] In the 1930s, this vision that interacted with autarkic and protectionist views – presenting itself often as an alternative to them – attained an increasing audience among the international organisations of Geneva. In a memorandum written in 1934, 'The agricultural and the health problem', F.L. McDougall, the Australian delegate to the League's economic section, summed up the views of the British nutritionists John Orr and Wallace Aykroyd. These two scientists distinguished between 'energy food' (primarily cereals) and 'protective food' (fresh fruit and vegetables, meat, fish and dairy products), argued that a good diet implied a balanced intake of both types, and emphasised that in order to overcome the widespread malnutrition of the world population it was necessary to lower international prices of 'protective food'.[16] If tariffs on agriculture were lowered, a new world specialisation of production would emerge that would increase the supply of 'protective food' in industrialised countries and multiply exports especially of 'energy food' from food-exporting countries, improving nutrition and hence living standards everywhere. International trade, the memorandum continued, needed to be supplemented by the redistribution of wealth within the countries and a more efficient distribution of primary products. These views, known as the 'nutrition approach', were very successful in the international arena in the late 1930s, first, in the International Labour Organisation (ILO), where a working team was set up in June 1935 and, after its inquiries, published a book, *Workers' Nutrition and Social Policy*; then at the League of Nations itself, which created a mixed committee in September 1935, and published its final report in 1938. As a result of the League's recommendation, at least nineteen countries established national nutrition committees which were to have relevant roles when the war imposed rationing on many of them.

Beyond this immediate consequence, the LoN adopted a policy language that stressed the relationship between agriculture, human welfare, international trade and price stability. The conference on European Rural Life, planned for 1939, was the last act of an evolution that, starting in hygiene concerns in 1931, fashioned a full list of food and agricultural policy recommendations. Out of this new language, and of the personal efforts of a group of committed LoN people, came between 1943 and 1945 the design of the Food and Agriculture Organisation (FAO) of the United Nations.

The League of Nations was not the only organisation that challenged the IIA's monopoly of agriculture in international society. We have already mentioned the ILO, which had started working on rural labour conditions from its foundation in 1920, despite strong legal resistance. In 1922 the Permanent Court of International Justice delivered two positive advisory opinions 'pertaining to the competence of the ILO in regard to International Regulation of the Conditions of the Labour of Persons Employed in Agriculture' and 'the Competence of the ILO to Examine Proposals for the Organization and Development of the Methods of Agricultural Production'. In later years, pressures came from state delegates and employers, who voiced the uneasiness of big farmers and landlords before rural labour conventions.[17] ILO experts largely contributed to the projects of the Health Committee of the League of Nations on rural hygiene, which prepared two relevant meetings: the European Conference on Rural Hygiene in June 1931 and the Intergovernmental Conference of Far-Eastern Countries on Rural Hygiene, held at Bandoeng, Java, in August, 1937. The following year, 1938, the ILO established the Permanent Agricultural Committee, which continued working after the war.

International and transnational organisations after the war

The Second World War interrupted the normal work of the interwar institutions. Most of them, though, either resumed their work or were merged with the new agencies created during the war to confront the food supply problems of the Allies. In the field of agriculture, there were in fact many institutional continuities, despite the major changes in the architecture of international society under the leadership of the USA, especially after the beginning of the Cold War.

The economic commissions of the League of Nations were recreated as agencies of the United Nations. The one established anew, the Food and Agriculture Organisation, accepted the premises and part of the administrative personnel of the IIA in 1945 and moved to Rome in 1951. The FAO found thus a solution to the situation created by the Hartman Report that, in 1945, characterised the IIA as a dysfunctional institution subordinated to fascist aims and recommended its dissolution.[18] The IIA's statistical instruments, its large scientific resources in the field of plant diseases and their prevention, and its academic, technical and political networks were to a certain extent inherited by the FAO. The ILO survived the war and maintained and increased its rural sections: it established the tripartite Committee of Experts on Indigenous Labour (CEIL) (1946), and the tripartite Committee on Work on Plantations (1950). By the 1950s rural employment had become a clear ILO priority, prompting collaboration with the FAO and the Organisation for European Economic Cooperation (OEEC), and strengthening the ILO's international mandate in rural contexts. The ILO highlighted some core areas for involvement, such as vocational training, cooperatives, rural industries and migration. Finally, the Health Committee of the League became the World Health Organisation and took over the staff and experiences of its predecessor. During the 1950s it concluded numerous agreements with the FAO to fight livestock diseases and promote health controls on food processing. The interwar institutionalisation of internationalism was therefore continued and its achievements consolidated into a new set of organisations.

However, despite these continuities in organisations and – as we shall see – in discourses, there were profound changes too. New forms of agricultural multilateral organisations among governments came into existence: some were short-lived, since they were supposed to meet immediate reconstruction needs; others were longer term undertakings. The second relevant novelty was the multiplication of non-governmental institutions that put together national agricultural or specialised associations or agricultural experts. The third new element was the triumph of intervention in agriculture in the USA. American agricultural regulation included, already in the first postwar years, a renovated approach to food security and development aid by Washington. It meant the transformation of food aid into an instrument of American market regulation but it also involved the encouragement of a strong commitment among agribusiness firms and agricultural technicians to export technological options and institutional arrangements which had been developed in the country in the previous years.[19] And, last but not least, all agricultural projects were read after 1947 under the new light of the Cold War: preventing the spread of communism, competing with Soviet development and preparing for a possible war with the USSR were targets openly or implicitly shared by the majority of experts in international organisations.

Among the intergovernmental organisations, those configured to address the war needs on the Allied side and the postwar food and reconstruction problems were the most short-lived, although they did have a longer influence. On 9 June 1942, Roosevelt and Churchill set up a temporary war government agency, the Combined Food Board (CFB), to pursue a common policy in relation to food during the war. The CFB played a relevant role in the organisation of allied food resources and after 1944 it became a tool to ensure food supply in Europe and Asia. In 1946 the CFB was turned into the International Emergency Food Council (IEFC).[20] Two years later, the Council transferred its activities and responsibilities to the Council of the FAO and its Central Committee continued working within the organisation. The Sixth Session of the Council of the FAO finally dissolved the IEFC in June 1949. Between 1946 and 1949 the different emergency bodies had an internal division in commodity committees where government representatives sat and tried to agree on allocation recommendations for each agricultural product that could then be concurred with or not, and finally implemented or not by member countries.[21] The IEFC had no authority of its own: it just suggested how food could be better distributed to match demand and eliminate surpluses and deficits at a world level, but its proposals did not bind governments.

A year after the foundation of the CFB, in 1943, a second organisation had been created: the United Nations Relief and Rehabilitation Administration (UNRRA). The UNRRA became part of the United Nations in 1945. This international agency was in direct charge of coordinating the supply of first-aid products, clothing, food and shelter, to refugees in Asia and Europe and to civilian populations in areas ravaged by the war. It was initially thought of as a means to use the commodities accumulated during the exceptional circumstances of the war and, at the same time, win over the cooperation of liberated countries.[22] The majority of the UNRRA resources were spent on its programmes in central, eastern and southern Europe. In fact, by 1946, most of its work was done in regions beyond the Iron Curtain. This and the growing tensions among the different visions of internationalism within the organisation led to its termination in 1949, although by then most of its functions had been taken over by the FAO.[23]

The FAO was the third organisation designed during the war, in the course of the United Nations Conference on Food and Agriculture celebrated in Hot Springs in 1943. Organised by the American authorities, the meeting in Virginia between 18 May and 3 June assembled nutritionists, economists and agronomists to think about a food international order based on the idea of 'international coordination' – that is to say, supranational planning.[24] The 'Interim Commission', with representatives of the 44 United Nations, was set up the same year and started to work on what would be the FAO. This latter organisation was actually established as a UN agency in October 1945 and, under the direction of John Orr, opened its headquarters in Washington DC, moving to Rome in 1951.

Orr had a very ambitious project: he wanted to create an international authority that was able to lead the construction of a multilateral free-trade order, finance credit lines for food-deficient countries, and stabilise world prices through bulk purchases and sales, so as to combine an expanding international trade, specialisation and fight against famine.[25] He and other people who had been behind the nutrition approach and were also in the new organisation were therefore trying to turn it into the embodiment of their projects in the 1930s. However, as he says in his memoirs, the FAO as it was actually designed between 1943 and 1945 had to 'limit its activities to collecting statistics on food production and distribution, promote research and give technical assistance to food deficit countries'.[26] After Orr's resignation in 1948, Norris E. Dodd took over and proposed a less ambitious International Commodity Clearing House, which was, however, once more rejected. Technical assistance, and technical and economic information, both biased in favour of large companies and big landowners, who had a more direct capability of fully utilising FAO's resources, became the central task of the organisation.[27] Under the third Director-General, Philip Cardon, the FAO reached what seemed to be the maximum regulation of food aid accepted by the USA: the FAO principles of surplus disposal that set certain limits to food aid to avoid it becoming dumping.[28]

In a publication of the FAO in 1955, *So Bold an Aim: Ten years of co-operation toward freedom from want*, P.L. Yates classified the achievements of the organisation in three sections.[29] The first one on 'Scarcities and surpluses' concluded that in the field of international trade the main result had been keeping interest in the question alive. In the second one, 'Information services', Yates listed an impressive amount of publications; however, in relation to statistics, he said that the FAO had taken too long to catch up with the level reached by the IIA and had not quite equalled the IIA's data presentation. The third section, on 'Technical activities', was in fact the only one in which FAO outcomes were highly valued. On the basis of the UNRRA programmes, staff and finance transferred to the FAO in 1947, the organisation created its first technical assistance resources. With the Expanded Programme of Technical Assistance (EPTA), passed as Resolution 222 (IX) in 1949 by the UN and funded after 1950, the FAO was allocated a relatively large sum of money, which enabled it to hire agricultural and nutrition experts, finance grants for national specialists, and put in place training centres in different countries. In spite of the various shortcomings of projects that needed yearly extensions by financing countries and often did not find adequate experts to fulfil its ambitious tasks, Yates stressed the relevance of the programme to create an operating international network of institutions and experts for technical change.

Yates's book was published in a year that was a turning point in the organisation's history. In 1956 Binay Ranjan Sen was appointed Director-General. Thanks to his activity and to a political context characterised by the acceleration of the decolonisation process, he managed to multiply the FAO budget by ten.[30] From this position the Indian technician launched in 1960 an ambitious programme: the Freedom from Hunger Campaign. It was the culmination of a rapid expansion which went beyond technical consultancy and started a systematic promotion of national extension services.[31] By 1959, the FAO had developed a large programme: over 1,700 experts had served field projects, 1,600 fellowships had been awarded and 100 training centres organised.[32]

The FAO opened regional branches. Among them, one of the most active was the European Committee for Agriculture (ECA), which in fact carried on most of the coordination tasks of FAO at a Western European level. The ECA had an executive permanent body and two subcommittees: one for agricultural research and one for diffusion and professional formation. It dedicated most of its efforts to sharing the results of experimental projects launched by agricultural and agro-industrial associations on one hand, and by public institutions of research and agricultural administrative agencies on the other.[33]

It was not only the FAO that established its own regional organisations. The United Nations Economic and Social Council, the heir to the League of Nations' Economic and Financial Organisation, created its own regional agencies too. The United Nations Economic Commission for Europe (UNECE) was established in March 1947. It aimed at becoming the coordinating supranational authority to reconstruct European economic links.[34] It was, however, marginalised once the USA administration that very year decided to set up a new organisation under Western control to intermediate the Marshall Plan. The UNECE explicitly maintained throughout the Cold War an all-European perspective: before 1955, it contributed to keeping links between East and West thanks to its secret diplomacy; after the death of Stalin it increased its open activities, and fostered economic and technical contacts.[35] The Committee of Economic Advisers of NATO underlined in 1958 its utility as a means of obtaining technical and statistical information on the Eastern Bloc.[36]

The UNECE decided in June 1948 to start a Committee on Agricultural Problems and a Committee for Timber. These committees were in charge of laying down the programme of studies for the secretariat and discussing their results in order to make policy recommendations. The UNECE Committee on Agricultural Problems established a general market report system and published as well data and reports on both political blocs. However, the main task of its Committee on Agricultural Problems took place in the field of harmonisation of commercial quality standards applicable in international trade.[37] A second level of activity after 1954 was the mechanisation of agriculture, for which it created a joint Working Party with the FAO.

In the third place, 1947 saw the establishment of the Conference for European Economic Cooperation, which in 1948 became the Organisation for European Economic Cooperation.[38] The OEEC was the institution constructed in order to administer the Marshall Plan aid and, at the same time, work to achieve a closer union among Western European states.[39] It created first a technical committee for agriculture and then, in 1949, a permanent Food and Agriculture Committee, which were in charge of estimating the necessities of European agriculture and distributing American resources. The new 'politics of productivity' in the American aid after March 1950 brought about the establishment of the European Productivity Agency within the OEEC in 1953, with its own special American financing, and the start of specific programmes, aiming at multiplying agricultural yields, coordinated by the successive specialised commissions of the OEEC.[40] In the following eight years, thanks partly to the establishment of the Food and Agricultural Technical Information Services (FATIS) by the new American Foreign Operations Administration with the collaboration of the OEEC, hundreds of projects were launched in different fields.[41]

In 1954, as a consequence of the failure of the Pool vert, the OEEC reorganised its agricultural activities.[42] It established a Food and Agriculture Directorate under the Ministerial Committee for Food and Agriculture with a much more ambitious programme under four headings: trade expansion; assessment and policy recommendations on prices, production, distribution and consumption; productivity enhancement; and policy coordination.[43] Increasing the productivity of European agriculture was the field where the OEEC could boast higher success: international and intra-European trade increased, but the general free-trade principles of the OEEC faced strong internal opposition when it came to agriculture. National delegates were backed within the organisation by new international agricultural lobbies, especially after 1954. A long debate among ministers in 1955 concluded in a breach of the rules concerning the participation of non-governmental organisations in the OEEC and the admission of producers' associations as partners, thanks to the support especially of the French and the Belgian representatives.[44] In the first plenary meeting of the agricultural commission and the farmers' and agro-industrialists' organisations in 1956, producers argued that the organisation of agriculture through price and income support policies had to be coordinated via multilateral international agreements. The OEEC would provide in the years to come a relevant negotiating framework for the different projects of defining some kind of coordinated or even common agricultural policies and for multilateral trade agreements in Western Europe, but in itself did not lead to any changes in that direction.

Finally, in 1952, the United Kingdom proposed and NATO accepted the creation of a food and agriculture planning committee within the military organisation: 'in any future war the food problems confronting the NATO countries in the opening year of the war will be much more serious than in 1939', explained the British delegation in order to back its proposal.[45] The committee produced its first report in 1954. It underlined the need for a systematic planning of rural civil defence, rationing and industrial inputs distribution, and made explicit references to the creation of channels of public consultation with food processors and distributors wherever they did not exist. Moreover, it explained the advantages of a regional organisation of agriculture, since the transition to a war agriculture would be much easier if 'a group of neighbouring countries such as France, Belgium, the Netherlands and Luxembourg, could plan their [agricultural] production and trade regionally rather than nationally'.[46] Before then, and especially after this year, the Council of NATO discussed various reports on the agricultural situation in the Western Bloc as well as in the 'enemy countries' and made several policy recommendations to its members. NATO kept alive the old military preoccupation with food in times of war, fostering the idea of a certain level of self-sufficiency or autarky at a European level. In 1953, it encouraged its members to adopt measures for stockpiling of fertilisers and wheat, sugar and fats, whenever there were surpluses.[47] Moreover, the military organisation read technological change in the European countryside under its own geo-strategic light and made suggestions from this point of view. When in 1955, the General Secretary of the OEEC talked in the First Meeting of the Ministerial Committee on Food and Agriculture on the trade 'restrictions ... for reasons other than balance of payments difficulties, that is to say, for political, social and strategic reasons', he was no doubt echoing NATO recommendations, given the close links of both organisations in economic and social analysis.

The existence of four different permanent commissions or committees in Europe dealing with agriculture signified that the risks of overlapping and resource waste were very great. In February 1956, a meeting was held to try to coordinate the actions of the civil organisations.[48] The OEEC attempted to differentiate between purely technical matters, to be handled by the FAO and its European delegation, and technical questions derived from economic approaches, in which the OEEC could take the lead. Besides the fact that these distinctions were very vague and did not really avoid a clash among organisations, there remained the problem of the UNECE, where different countries – including the Communist ones – met. In any case, from 1956 onwards there was at least a yearly conference of the international agricultural organisations in Europe, in order to draw together the agendas of meetings and activities.

The upsurge of intergovernmental agencies and commissions led to a parallel growth of transnational non-governmental organisations. Both these and the national organisations that set them up were manned by people who very often held political and State posts. In West Germany, local leaders of the *Bauernverband* headed at the same time territorial party organisations, especially of the Christian Democratic CDU.[49] The situation was similar in other countries such as the Netherlands, France, Belgium, Italy and Sweden, where the leaders of agricultural organisations had a strong position in political parties as well as an official recognition that entailed their presence in consultative councils.[50] These national organisations established transnational associations. In 1946, a new International Federation of Agricultural Producers (IFAP) was launched. The IFAP that had been started by the British National Farmers' Unions, included American, Commonwealth and Western European associations and favoured international multilateral agreements by product.[51] It was recognised by the OEEC, the ILO and the FAO as representative of farmers' interests and granted consultative status. From this position it promoted the different product councils and international product agreements, starting with the 1949 International Wheat Agreement. In 1948 it established a Working Party on the European Recovery Programme which would very soon become a kind of Western European section of the IFAP.

At the same geographic level, the Confédération européenne de l'agriculture – direct successor to the CIA in personal and ideological terms – started its work in 1948. Launched by German, Swiss and French Christian and conservative agrarian organisations, it had a stronger political commitment to family farming and a more open protectionist tendency, which would make a significant contribution to framing the prevailing ideas behind agricultural policy in the years to come.[52] Besides this active cultural role, the CEA played in the 1950s a growing role in the successive projects of European agricultural integration and was turned into an associated partner by most international organisations, which is why at the end of the decade it brought together a very large number of Western European lobbies.[53]

Therefore, by 1950 a dense transnational and international grid of organisations which connected Western European countries among themselves, and their empires, and with the USA, had been set up. They were heterogeneous in nature and especially different in political terms, but all shared a general commitment to technological capital-intensive change, on the basis of collaboration among public scientific services, agribusiness and agriculturalists. In the following ten years, this grid would have a large influence on the development of European agriculture.

International agricultural politics and agricultural policies

Despite the efforts of the first Directors-General of the FAO, the 1940s and 1950s did not bring about any international global regulation of food trade: national governments, especially the American and the British ones, did not want to give up their economic power to supranational agencies. Since agriculture was also left out of the General Agreement on Tariffs and Trade (GATT), there were no formal rules concerning agricultural trade and therefore no external limits to national agricultural policies. International and transnational organisations did instead four other things concerning trade.

In the first place, they demanded intergovernmental product agreements, undertook preparatory work, and convened meetings and conferences to foster collective discussions. By the early 1960s, though, there were only four agreements (on wheat, on sugar, on coffee and on olive oil) and these agreements had not really managed to attain the promised price stability, nor of course advanced the ambitious mission of a world freed from hunger.[54]

Second, if malnutrition and starvation were not seriously fought at an international level, there remained an international commitment to food aid and the international endorsement of the creation of national food reserves to face scarcities and, eventually, partake in international campaigns. In 1954, the United States Congress passed the Public Law 480, which recognised the paradox of the coexistence of agricultural surpluses and malnutrition, and enabled US food aid to be used for international development and relief purposes. By the late 1950s, American aid represented nearly one-third of the total world wheat trade: 'instead of the New Internationalist vision of global coordination and of boosting local knowledge and centres of production, the logic of food aid was to turn food producing developing countries into importers of American wheat surpluses'.[55] In 1954, the FAO adopted its Principles of Surplus Disposal, which were guidelines, not legally binding, for the use of surplus agricultural production to support recovery and development abroad.[56]

The third feature of trade policy was that international organisations (especially, as we have seen, the OEEC, through its product working groups, together with the FAO and the UNECE) tried to advance the harmonisation of productive and commercial quality standards. In the second place, they produced massive amounts of statistical data and also recommended in an active way the production of commodities that were or could be scarce in international markets. Finally, they established an international vocabulary that contributed to the increase in international trade, in the mid-term, through the lowering of transaction costs.

Last, but not least, international and transnational organisations had a very relevant role in the agricultural side of the European integration process, which from 1962 was translated into the Common Agricultural Policy. The variety of failed schemes of the 1950s, described in detail by Noël and integrated by Milward in a process he calls 'Europeanisation of agricultural protection', would eventually have a huge impact on world agricultural trade inside and outside the member states of the EEC, but that falls beyond the chronological limits of this book.[57]

Since they fell very short of their initial programme regarding agricultural trade, we might be tempted to deny the relevance of the new institutions created at a world or regional level after 1945. It was not, though, their only formal aim. Advancing agricultural knowledge, 'rationalising' farm management, and renovating farm technology stood high on the list of priorities of the FAO, its European Commission for Agriculture, the UNECE or the OEEC Food and Agriculture committees. They all fostered the externalisation of farm inputs (fertilisers, machinery, pesticide, high-yield varieties), motorisation, and a permanent connection between farms and agricultural research services. A more productive agriculture demanded, in their view, a new management of farms and the professionalisation of farmers. All the agricultural organisations contributed to the formation of local experts and the granting of scholarships to send them to the USA or other European countries. Experts were to apply the new diffusion methods through the development of a renovated agrarian extension, based on the USA model. In 1949 the FAO organised an International Conference on Agricultural Information, the first of a long series of conferences, courses and visits aimed at importing the American institutional scheme.[58] Between 1953 and 1960, the European Productivity Agency alone financed 160 projects for all the OEEC countries, 20 per cent of which were developed in the field of farm management and advisory work and 50 per cent in courses on the marketing of various products.[59]

Notwithstanding the public discourse on development aid, most of the conferences of the period 1946–1960 took place in Western Europe and North America, in countries which had constructed large institutional schemes and monopolised the bulk of agricultural research by 1960. Hence, they favoured the exchange of models, the homogenisation of vocabulary and the introduction of benchmarks, and they launched collaborative projects.[60] For instance, right from the start of the OEEC and the FAO in the 1940s, high-yield varieties (especially of maize for animal feed) became a priority: transatlantic research and experience in this field was the initial step of the process that eventually led to the 1960s green revolution.[61] The FAO and the OEEC supported the development of national research structures, with the help of successive US agencies, providing them with models of research institutions and their connection with extension services. Even though American capitalist farming was frequently presented as the opposite of European rural society, research showed a clear bias in favour of capital-intensive technology, very different from the one which had been developed by early agricultural services in Europe.[62]

International and supranational organisations were powerful instruments in the legitimisation and even naturalisation of agricultural exceptionalism: even the agricultural commission of a large economic organisation like the OEEC demanded special treatment for agricultural professional organisations, without which, it argued, no policy success could be expected. In a more contradictory and complex way, they proclaimed the social and economic advantages of family farming. The UN and FAO guidelines for structural policies were directed in the developing countries towards redistributive land reform, which was seen as a means of consolidating a propertied peasantry and promoting productivity increases.[63] In relation to Western Europe, and besides the agrarian reform in Southern Italy (see Chapter 3), they stressed land consolidation and land reclamation, presented as well as devices to combine family agriculture and the achievement of optimal sizes for estates. Neither in Europe nor in the developing countries did this pro-peasant policy imply any reconsideration of technological policies, notwithstanding the contradictions that could arise between the ideal of the family farm and the race to frame a self-accelerating rate of technical change in order to increase production and lower costs in agriculture. With the end of food deficits in Western Europe, national agricultural policies tended to become palliative social policies, even though, given the structural policy in favour of 'viable farms' and motorised agriculture, they tended to be biased against small farms.[64] Only in the context of this shared set of values, however contradictory, can we understand, first, the development of national agricultural policies and, then, because of their cost, the diverse attempts at their Europeanisation, which finally succeeded at a more limited level in the Common Agricultural Policy.[65]

Technology and discourses were framed by national political and cultural elites in permanent interaction. We are told that many of the 'most influential professionals' working at the FAO in the 1950s and 1960s came from the UNRRA.[66] Many of its early leaders had been working in the LoN. A relevant part of its administrative staff had been at the IIA. These links backwards continued to work forwards. In recent years, historians who study the process of European integration have found in its early stages the formation of a 'trans- and supranational polity'.[67] This polity was integrated by technicians, civil servants, lobbyists and politicians who sat on the European and transatlantic meetings of the various organisations we have examined. For instance, Mansholt, a key figure in various European initiatives for a supranational agricultural policy, was closely involved in development of the FAO, became a good friend of leading figures of the USA Department of Agriculture and was the first European commissioner for agriculture.[68] He is an outstanding example of how the growing amount of formal and informal links and relationships fostered the foundation of networks of technicians, high civil servants, politicians and lobbyists on both sides of the Atlantic and beyond it. They were the ones who shaped a supranational consensus on the different levels we have referred to: the desirable special treatment for agricultural production in international trade; the existence of a correct type of technical progress which included the 'rationalisation' of farm management, motorisation and the externalisation of inputs; and the construction of agricultural policy as a palliative welfare policy to compensate for the social effects of the modernisation of the countryside. It seems that rent-seekers profited from this environment by obtaining protection well beyond the level that would have come from a mere palliative welfare policy.[69] Domestic political considerations and international strategic reasons had a major weight in creating financial mechanisms that multiplied support to rural societies in the West, even though they were not very effective in stopping the decline of agriculture or the rural exodus.

Concluding remarks

When we analyse the different Western European agricultures and the agricultural policies applied in the years of reconstruction and in the 1950s, we discover different pathways but as well common trends and a common analysis of desirable tendencies, conveyed in a very similar language.

Agronomists, politicians and agrarian elites had shared, at least from the 18th century onwards, readings and, increasingly, personal experiences abroad (formal education in renowned schools such as Grignon Gembloux, Wiehenstephan or Tharandt; conferences; exhibitions) that contributed to the birth of transnational tendencies in agronomy and agricultural economics. In addition to these links, from the late 19th century onwards and especially in the interwar period, a new generation of international institutions was born. They configured a strong reference for national discourses and offered new instruments to the working together of agricultural 'intellectuals' and 'politicians'. The understanding of agriculture as an exceptional sector which, on one hand, had a special value for economic and extra-economic reasons and, on the other hand, could not survive if it was not subject to specific regulations, became a shared view of these official and unofficial networks. After the experience of total war, the agricultural prices instability of the 1920s and, especially, the Great Depression in the 1930s, three discourses in relation to food and agriculture took shape. Autarky, international coordination and organisation of agriculture were the key terms with which they identified.

In the postwar period and under the leadership of the USA, international global and regional organisations multiplied their number, size, in terms of budget and staff, as well as their will to intervene in agricultural realities, at a world level. They inherited the discourses and proposals of the interwar agencies and policies. The FAO and the UNRRA were thought out by new internationalists who in general terms accepted the idea of a supranational authority to regulate food, and therefore agriculture, under a regime which combined the advantages of free trade with the guarantee of an international division of labour, to achieve a balanced nutrition all over the world. However, the deep mistrust of any form of supranational authority neutralised the original FAO project. The organisation, and its regional agencies like the ECA, kept the idea of some sort of international regulation to end hunger and stabilise agricultural markets but, in practice, limited its programmes to fostering technical and structural changes through specific measures.

Bipolarity in international relations had a deep impact during the first postwar years in the new food order, which some authors call the American food order. In Europe, the Cold War reduced to a minimum the activity of the United Nations Economic Commission for Europe (UNECE) and was behind the creation of the OEEC, which first administered the allocation of Marshall Plan aid and then became a fundamental instrument in economic cooperation, including agriculture. The 'colossal exercise in planning' of the New Deal exerted a direct influence through American funding and policy recommendations on the OEEC.[70] This organisation collaborated with the FAO in a vast undertaking to raise productivity in the European countryside, combining two approaches: on one hand what we could call a cultural programme to transform peasants and farmers into entrepreneurs and to push civil servants and technicians to participate in an active way in the 'modernisation' of farms, and, on the other hand, a technical programme that included the diffusion of American innovations, the development of basic and applied research institutions, and the creation of an active agrarian extension system.

Neither the American government nor European governments abandoned their protectionist position in relation to agriculture, a clear success of the discourse on the organisation of agriculture. However, the FAO and the OEEC were active instruments in favour of multilateral agreements and, actually, they contributed to the Europeanisation of agricultural protection by the end of the 1950s. Protectionism was promoted as well by NATO, which saw food as a strategic weapon and rural society as a possible source of manpower and as a potential political problem, wherever it was affected by structural unemployment. In a sense, the autarkic views of the interwar period had a certain continuity, showing their interdependence with military approaches.

Apart from creating a highly active flow of technology, knowledge, models and even cultural proposals, and apart from facilitating the expansion of agricultural trade via technical agreements and via the creation of negotiating spaces, international agricultural organisations did something more: they created a community of international technicians and economists who shared a language and instruments to deal with agricultural problems. Without this polity, already well established by the end of the 1950s, the construction of the CAP or the launching of the Green Revolution would have been delayed and would have probably taken a different shape.

Notes

1 Western Europe is understood throughout the text as capitalist European countries, those that by the end of the period under consideration belonged to the OEEC.
2 A.S. Milward, *The European Rescue of the Nation-State*, London: Routledge, 1992.
3 A.-C. L. Knudsen has also used the term 'exceptionalism' with a similar meaning. See, for instance, her 'Ideas, welfare, and values: Framing the Common Agricultural Policy in the 1960s', in K.K. Patel, *Fertile Ground for Europe? The History of the European Integration and the Common Agricultural Policy since 1945*, Baden-Baden: Nomos, 2009, pp. 61–78.
4 A very short biography of Lubin and his role in the development of the IIA appears in J.M. Wu, 'David Lubin as mediator. His letters, his library', in Anderson, K.L. and Thiery, C. (eds), *Information for Responsible Fisheries: Libraries as Mediators: Proceedings of the 31st Annual Conference. Rome, Italy, October 10–14, 2005*, Fort Pierce: International Association for Aquatic and Marine Science Libraries and Information Centres, 2005, pp. 283–290.
5 On its activities before the First World War: Institut International d'Agriculture, *Quelques aspects de l'activité de l'Institut International d'Agriculture*, Rome: Imprimerie Carlo Colombo, 1941.
6 A. Hobson, *The International Institute of Agriculture*, Berkeley, CA: University of California Press, 1931.
7 Institut International d'Agriculture, *Quelques aspects de l'activité …* 1941.
8 Ministère du Commerce, de l'industrie et des colonies. Exposition universelle internationale de 1889. Direction générale de l'exploitation, *Congrès international d'agriculture tenu à Paris du 4 au 11 juillet 1889 sous la présidence de M. Jules Méline*. Paris: Imprimerie générale Lahure, 1889.
9 Séance du 25.III.26, in SAF, *Séances du Conseil, Comptes-rendus*, Bibliothèque de la SAF, Paris.
10 F.G. Von Graevenitz, 'L'Europe comme modèle de l'Office du Blé? Les origines et les conséquences nationales de l'organisation internationale des marchés agricoles (1927–1939)', in A. Chatriot, E. Leblanc, É. Lynch (eds), *Organiser les marchés agricoles. Le temps des fondateurs*, Paris: Armand Colin, 2012, p. 56.
11 On French reluctance and the final acceptance of the new CIA: G. Nöel, 'La participation de la France aux stratégies d'organisation internationale de l'agriculture', *Économie Rurale*, 184-186, 1988, 63-70. On the membership and other traits of the CIA : F.G. Von Graevenitz, 'L'Europe comme modèle de l'Office du Blé ? …'
12 P. Clavin, *Securing the World Economy: The Reinvention of the League of Nations, 1920–1946*, Oxford: Oxford University Press, 2013, p. 85.
13 On the Italian turning point of 1935: Alexande Nützenadel, 'Dictating Food: Autarchy, Food Provision and Consumer Politics in Fascist Italy, 1922–1943', in F. Trentman and F. Just (eds) *Food and Conflict in Europe in the Age of the Two World Wars*, Basingstoke: Palgrave Macmillan, 2006, pp. 88–108. On Acerbo's appointment, it must be said that the presidency of the IIA corresponded to a person appointed by the Italian government. The economist and demographer Giuseppe de Michelis (1925-33) and the aristocratic politician Ludovico Spada Veralli Potenziani (1933–35) were the first presidents appointed by Mussolini: they had strong connections with the fascist regime but not a high political profile. The same cannot be said of the rural economist Giacomo Acerbo, former president of the Italian Chamber of Deputies between 1926 and 1929 and minister of Agriculture between 1929 and 1935, who held the presidency of the IIA until the Italian armistice in 1943. A short biography of Acerbo in *Dizionario Biografico degli Italiani* – Volume 34 (1988), by Antonio Parisella (www.treccani.it/enciclopedia/giacomo-acerbo_%28Dizionario-Biografico%29/).

14 M. Rieul Paisant, *La Commission internationale d'agriculture (Union internationale des associations agricoles) et son role dans l'économie européenne*, Paris, l'Académie d'agriculture de France, 1936.
15 F. Trentman, 'Coping with Shortage: The Problem of Food Security and Global Visions of Coordination, c. 1890s–1950', in Trentman and Just (eds) *Food and Conflict in Europe*, pp. 13–48. Trentman explains that this new project of international coordination in the field of food emerged out of 'three main building blocks: experiments in transnational governance, new ideas of citizenship, and nutritional politics' (p. 27).
16 On the nutrition approach and its impact: S. Turnell, 'F.L. McDougall: Éminence grise of Australian Economic Diplomacy', *Australian Economic History Review*, volume 40, issue 1, March, 2000, pp. 51–70, and P. Clavin, *Securing the World Economy*.
17 The Société d'Agriculteurs de France backed the efforts of its government to stop the ILO from tackling rural matters and then exercised pressure: SAF, Séances du Conseil, Comptes-rendus, 1921–1939.
18 Hartman was an American military officer commissioned to prepare a report on the IIA after the entrance of the Allied troops in Rome. On his report, see Luciano Tosi, *Alle origini della Fao. Le relazioni tra l'Istituto Internazionale di Agricoltura e la Società delle Nazioni*, Milan: Franco Angeli, 1989, p. 246.
19 J.H. Perkins, *Geopolitics and the Green Revolution: Wheat, Genes, and the Cold War*, New York: Oxford University Press, 1997.
20 Organización de las Naciones Unidas para la Agricultura y la Alimentación, *Primer informe anual del Director general a la asamblea de la FAO*, Washington, 5 de julio de 1946 (typed manuscript in Biblioteca del Ministerio de Agricultura, Madrid: 13511).
21 Definition by the Secretary-General in International Emergency Food Committee, *Report of the International Emergency Food Committee for the Council of the FAO at its Second Session*, Washington, FAO, 1948, p. 9.
22 J. Reinisch, 'Internationalism in relief: the birth (and death) of the UNRRA' in M. Mazower, J. Reinisch and D. Feldman (eds), *Post-War Reconstruction in Europe: International Perspectives, 1945–1949*, Oxford: Oxford University Press (Past and Present Supplement 210/6), 2011, pp. 258–289.
23 J. Reinisch, 'Internationalism in relief: the birth (and death) of the UNRRA', p. 285.
24 A description of the Conference and its achievements from the optimistic perspective of those in favour of the nutrition approach can be found in K. Evang and F.L. McDougall, articles on 'The United Nations Conference on Food and Agriculture, Hot Springs, Virginia, 18 May – 3rd June, 1943', *Proceedings of the Nutrition Society*, volume 2, issue 3–4, September 1944, pp. 163–176.
25 The guidelines of Orr world food policy in Lord Boyd Orr, *As I recall. The 1880's to the 1960's*, London, McGibbon & Kee, 1966, pp. 171–172 (full text in www.fao.org/library/library-home/lord-john-boyd-orr/lbo-full-text/es/).
26 Lord Boyd Orr, *As I Recall*, 1966, p. 161.
27 A. L. S. Staples, *The Birth of Development: How the World Bank, Food and Agriculture Organization, and World Health Organization Changed the World, 1945–1965*, Kent (Ohio): The Kent State University Press, 2006, p. 104.
28 R. Jachertz, 'To keep food out of politics: The UN Food and Agriculture Organization' in F. Marc, K. Sönke, Corinna R. Unger (eds), *International Organizations and Development, 1945–1990*, Basingstoke, Hampshire: Palgrave-Macmillan, 2014.
29 I have used the Spanish version: P.L. Yates, *Un propósito ambicioso. Diez años de cooperación internacional en la lucha contra la miseria*, Rome: FAO, 1955.

30 J. Abbot, *Politics and Poverty: A Critique of the Food & Agriculture Organization of the United Nations*, London: Routledge, 1992, p. 36.
31 H. Santa Cruz, *La función de la FAO en el bienestar rural*, Rome: Organización de las Naciones Unidas para la Agricultura y la Alimentación, 1959.
32 D.J. Show, *Food and Agricultural Institutions*, Abingdon: Routledge, 2009, p. 96.
33 *Rapport de la huitième session du Comité Européen d'Agriculture ténue à Rome, Italie, 7–11 mai 1956*, Rome: Organisation des Nations Unis pour l'Alimentation et l'Agriculture, 1956.
34 Ö. Appelqvist, 'Rediscovering uncertainty: early attempts at a pan-European post-war recovery', *Cold War History*, 8, 3, August 2008, pp. 327–352.
35 G. Myrdal, 'Twenty years of the United Nations Economic Commission for Europe', *International Organisation*, 22, 3, Summer, 1968, pp. 617–628.
36 NATO Archive, Brussels and on-line documents, AC_127-D_33_ENG.
37 Economic Commission for Europe. Committee on Agricultural Problems, *Four decades of work to the benefit of the food economy of the ECE region*, Geneva: United Nations, 1988.
38 The agricultural and agro-industrial agreements of the CEEC to measure the deficit in various means or production (tractors, fertilisers, pesticides …) in OECD Archive, CEEC.
39 On the origins of the OEEC: A.S. Milward, *The Reconstruction of Western Europe, 1945–51*, London: Methuen, 1984.
40 The politics of productivity in David W. Ellwood, *Rebuilding Europe: Western Europe, America and Postwar Reconstruction*, London: Longman, 1992, pp. 181–182. On the EPA: Bent Boel, *The European Productivity Agency and Transatlantic Relations, 1953–61*, Copenhagen: Museum Tusculanum Press: University of Copenhagen, 2003.
41 See on the initial steps of the FATIS and other American aid-programmes: 23rd session of the Food and Agriculture Committee on the 31 October, 1953 (OECD Archive, OECD-0030).
42 Pool vert (in English, Green Pool) is the term coined to define the common agricultural market which was negotiated after 1950, on the basis of the French Pfimlin Plan and the Dutch Mansholt Plan: see G. Thiemeyer, 'The failure of Green Pool and the success of the CAP. Long term structures in European integration in the 1950s and 1960s', in K.K. Patel, *Fertile Ground for Europe? The History of the European Integration and the Common Agricultural Policy since 1945*, Baden-Baden: Nomos, 2009.
43 The documents pertaining the creation of the new directorate in OECD Archive, OEEC-264.
44 See the various documents on this question in 1955 and 1956 and the first meeting of deputies of 1956 (OECD Archive, OEEC-265).
45 The proposal presented in the meeting of the Financial and Economic Board, 02.04.1952 (NATO Archives, FEB-R_52_3-ENG-DRAFT). The quote comes from the British memorandum, 09.06.1952 (NATO Archives, C-M_52_29_ENG).
46 The first report of the Committee, 16.03.1954 (NATO Archives, C-M_54_19_ENG) and its discussion in the Council, 24.03.1954 and 9.4.1954 (NATO Archives, C-R_54_9_ENG and C-R_54_14_ENG).
47 Progress Report by the Chairman of the Committee on Wartime Commodity Problems, 16.11.1953 (NATO Archives, C-M_53_149-ENG).
48 *Rapport de la huitième session*, p. 20.
49 K.K. Patel, 'Europeanization *à contre-cœur*', in K.K. Patel, *Fertile Ground for Europe? The History of the European Integration and the Common Agricultural Policy since 1945*, Bade-Baden: Nomos, 2009, pp. 139–160.
50 G. Nöel, *Du Pool Vert à la politique agricole commune. Les tentatives de Communauté agricole européenne entre 1945 et 1955*, Paris: Economica, 1988, pp. 32–38.

51 Federation of Agricultural Producers, *Report of the Second Annual General Meeting of the International Federation of Agricultural Producers held in Paris, France, from 19th–28th May*, 1948.
52 Confédération européenne de l'agriculture, *CEA: historique, organisation, activite. Ouvrage publié à l'occasion du dixième anniversaire de la CEA, 1948–1958*, Brougg: Secrétariat-général de la CEA, 1958. The influence of ideas like the ones expressed by the CEA in the framing of the CAP in K.K. Patel, 'Interest and Ideas. Alan Milward, the Europeanization of Agricultural Production, and the Cultural Dimensions of European Integration', in F. Guirao Francés, M. B. Lynch, S. M. Ramírez Pérez (eds), *Alan S. Milward and a Century of European Change*, Abingdon: Routledge, 2012, pp. 405–421.
53 Confédération Européenne de l'Agriculture, *Assemblée générale de la Confédération Européenne de l'Agriculture CEA du 5 au 10 octobre 1959 à Palerme (Italie). Activité des Organisations internationales officielles (FAO, OECE, OIT, Communauté Économique Européenne, CEE, Conseil de l'Europe etc.) et relations de la CEA avec ces organisations*, Confédération Européenne de l'Agriculture, 1959.
54 D.J. Shaw, *World Food Security: A History since 1945*, Palgrave-Macmillan, 2007, pp. 65–76.
55 F. Trentman, 'Coping with Shortage', p. 35.
56 D.J. Shaw, *World Food Security*, pp. 55–57.
57 G. Nöel, *Du Pool Vert à la politique agricole commune* and A. Milward, *The European Rescue of the Nation-State*, pp. 224–317.
58 On the interaction of FAO experts and American extension agents in Spain: C. Gómez Benito, *Políticos, burócratas y expertos. Un estudio de la política agraria y la sociología rural en España (1936–1959)*, Madrid: Siglo XXI, 1995, pp. 204–218.
59 Final reference report on activities of the European Productivity Agency in the Agriculture and Food Sector, 1960, OECD Archive, OCDE_0072.
60 Nevertheless, by 1987, the linkages between the national research systems of the developed countries were weak (V.W. Ruttan, 'Towards A Global Agricultural Research System', in V.W. Ruttan and C.E. Pray, *Policy for Agricultural Research*, Boulder, CO: Westview Press, 1987, p. 75): therefore we should not exaggerate the level of collaboration achieved in previous decades.
61 See the 'Report on hybrid maize in OEEC countries', by Jenkins, Watkins and Ferguson, 1949, in OECD Archive, OECD-0029.
62 J. Harwood, *Europe's Green Revolution and Others Since: The Rise and Fall of Peasant Friendly Plant-Breeding*, London: Routledge, 2012.
63 American authorities were behind the pro-land reform policies of the UN. See: U.S. Department of State, *Land Reform: A World Challenge*, Washington: GPO, 1952, and U.S. Inter-agency Committee on Land Reform Problems, *United States Policy Regarding Land Reform in Foreign Areas*, Washington, DC: GPO, 1951. On the UN, see the reports *Progress in Land Reform* published in 1954 and 1957.
64 A.C. Knudsen, *Farmers on Welfare: The Making of Europe's Common Agricultural Policy*, Ithaca, NY: Cornell University Press, 2009. The contradictions of family protection in G. Laschi, 'La politica agricola comune: gli agricoltori e il processo di integrazione europea', *Rivista di Storia dell'Agricoltura*, LIII, 1, 2013, pp. 179–190.
65 A global view of the deep forces behind the origins of the CAP in G. Thiemeyer, 'The failure of Green Pool …'.
66 J. Abbot, *Politics and Poverty*, p. 55.
67 W. Kaiser, B. Leucht and M. Rasmussen (eds), *The History of the European Union: Origins of a Trans- and Supranational Polity*, Abingdon: Routledge, 2009.
68 On Mansholt: J. van Merrënboder, 'Commissioner Sicco Mansholt and the creation of the CAP', in K.K. Patel, *Fertile Ground for Europe? The History of the European*

Integration and the Common Agricultural Policy since 1945, Baden-Baden: Nomos, 2009, pp. 139–160.
69 M. Spoerer, 'Agricultural protection and support in the European Economic Community, 1962–92: rent seeking or welfare policy?', in *European Review of Economic History*, 19, 2015, pp. 195–214.
70 The impact of the New Deal on reconstruction policies in A. J. Williams, 'Reconstruction before the Marshall Plan', *Review of International Studies*, 31(3), July 2005, pp. 541–558.

3 Political stability, modernization and reforms during the first years of the Cold War

Emanuele Bernardi

The Marshall Plan

For the Western European economies, the Cold War was perhaps a unique phase of development, inspired by capitalistic principles embedded with social and political aims. In the years immediately following the Second World War, people working in agriculture still formed a significant part of the total labour force, ranging from 23 per cent in Germany to 30 per cent in France and 43 per cent in Italy. Yet in 1950 agriculture produced only 10 per cent of national income in Germany, 15 per cent in France, and 32 per cent in Italy.[1]

The various aid programmes organized from the end of the war to the end of the 1950s influenced in many ways the recovery and the trajectories of the future European agriculture. The best known of these aid programmes was, without doubt, the European Recovery Program (ERP, otherwise called the 'Marshall Plan', 1948–1951). Even if confronting Communism was not the only task of the ERP, certainly it was one of the main features of the beginning of the Cold War.[2] Inspired by the philosophy of raising productivity and with the aim of promoting in the sixteen countries involved the intensification of the use of raw materials (water, minerals, wood, petroleum, etc.), the European Recovery Program began one of the most complex processes of transformation of agriculture that the economic history of Europe had until then known, helping to trigger an unprecedented increase in production throughout the second half of the twentieth century.

The years between 1945 and 1947 were difficult: economic, food and political crises seemed to take place in Europe and to advantage Soviet expansionism.[3] After the war, all governments maintained food rationing and control measures, to avoid unrest. The western Communist parties, especially the Italian, French and Finnish, became political forces able to influence national policies (see Table 3.1).[4]

American economic aid was instrumental in social and political stabilization. Announced in June 1947 after Great Britain's withdrawal from Greece and Turkey, and then discussed in Paris, the project of an international economic plan for all Europe with the United States in a dominant position led to the refusal of the Union of Soviet Socialist Republics (USSR) and, then, of its

Table 3.1 The post-war Communist vote

Nation	Year of voting	Communist electorate (%)
Austria	1945	5.4
Belgium	1946	12.7
Denmark	1945	12.5
Finland	1945	23.5
France	1945	26.0
West Germany	1949	5.7
Italy	1946	19.0
Norway	1945	11.9
Holland	1946	10.6
Sweden	1944	10.3

Source: Spagnolo, *La stabilizzazione incompiuta*, p. 38

allied nations (Poland, initially, had been interested) to be involved. Together with the Truman doctrine of 'containment', declared in March 1947, the Marshall Plan appeared to be a menace to the Soviet sphere of influence. In September, Stalin and Molotov therefore decided to create the Cominform, for coordinating and controlling the Communist parties in Italy and France as in other nations. One of its main objectives was to oppose the Marshall Plan, in order to fight for the Soviet cause and resist the American message of a capitalist society. It called upon all the socialist governments and Communist parties to follow the Soviet experience of collectivization.[5]

The Marshall Plan, which was anti-Communist in a progressive and co-operative way, encouraged moderate and reformist policies. These required that European agriculture should be 'modernized' and developed to increase production and productivity, so increasing commerce both inside the OEEC (Organization for European Economic Cooperation) area and with the United States, and thus contributing to the balance of payments. In estimating the aid that the participating countries would need from the United States and in fixing production goals to reduce the 'dollar gap', it is interesting also to note that the necessity of maintaining a certain level of trade between Western and Eastern nations for crucial commodities such as food, coal and timber was recognized.[6] Modernization and reforms meant many things at the same time. Financial stability had to be reconciled with the 'battle' against unemployment, low yields and backwardness, that was one of the main features of the appeal of Communism. At the same time, aid had to mean *business*. A well-known American business publication provided details of the investment opportunities that existed for US companies; its title could hardly be more significant: 'How to do Business under the Marshall Plan'.[7] Each government of ERP countries had to elaborate a four-year production programme, coordinated in Paris with the other OEEC nations, and ask for the imports necessary to fulfil the objectives of the programme. Traditional nationalisms had to be overcome through the construction of a political

Europe and a unified European market, which was, of course, open to trade with the USA.

An ad hoc organization, the Economic Cooperation Administration [ECA] was created for the administration of the aid. The ERP funds were of two kinds: loans and grants (they formed the 'counterpart funds'). An ECA mission sent to all the nations assisted had to control, and to negotiate, the use of the funds. The Food and Agriculture Chief in Washington was Dennis A. FitzGerald, while Benjamin Hur Thibodeaux was sent to Paris. Both of them had experience in the field, accumulated during the war years, and both were in contact with agro-food companies.

Reclamation and irrigation projects, research and experimentation, mechanization, the supply of high-quality animals (such as the Missouri mules sent to Greece) and of high-yield crops such as hybrid corn, fertilizers, and extension services, were some of the features of the ERP programme for the primary sector.[8] It was also involved in promoting land consolidation (as in France, the so-called *remembrement*, or in the Netherlands) and division (in Italy and, to some extent, Germany).[9] The breakdown of ERP expenditure in Italy (70 billion lire, from counterpart funds) for 1949 is shown in Table 3.2.

Market prices for the foodstuffs, especially cereals, imported by European countries decreased. This affected Italy and France mainly in the first two years of the programme and West Germany for the whole period of the ERP (see Table 3.3).

This was a well-chosen policy. The positive impact of food imports on social and financial stability made that kind of aid, together with other of donations, very useful in restoring not only the level of consumption but also the balance of payments. The other imported agricultural products, such as cotton, tobacco, machinery and fertilizers, contributed to a faster recovery of

Table 3.2 Utilization of the ERP *lire* fund for agriculture (Italian law no. 165 of 23 April 1949: 70,000 million *lire*)

- Reclamation and irrigation, 42,620 (60.8 per cent).
- Grants for land improvement works, 12,500 (1.4 per cent).
- Agrarian credit for improvement, 6,000 (8.5 per cent).
- Intensification of pest and parasite control, 1,300 (1.85 per cent).
- Research and experimentation, 780 (1.1 per cent).
- Professional education of farmers, demonstration activities, 700 (1 per cent).
- Contribution to purchases of draft cattle and machinery by direct cultivators and co-operatives, 900 (1.28 per cent).
- Integration of government share of a fund for the establishment of small landed property, 2,000 (2.85 per cent).
- Provisions to expand vine culture, 300 (0.42 per cent).
- General expenses, 800 (1.14 per cent).

Source: E. Bernardi: *La riforma agraria in Italia e gli Stati Uniti*, Bologna: il Mulino, 2005, p. 212

Table 3.3 Foodstuffs as a percentage of the total imports through ERP aid[10]

	1948	1949	1950	1951
France	23.4	12.0	4.4	n.d.
Italy	34.7	31.2	7.1	1.5
West Germany	72.2	41.5	4.9	29.8

the countries assisted by the ERP, and, at the same time, also permitted the building of strong commercial and political relations between those nations and the USA.

Another important aspect of the ERP was the Technical Assistance Program. The idea behind the programme was to promote an 'exchange' of knowledge to facilitate productivity intensification and the growth of Europe–US trade relations. The principle of 'exchange', however, was not conceived on an equal basis, but on the idea of the superiority of the American system of production, compared to Europe. It was assumed that this could – and should – become the model for the 'free world' to imitate, in order to counter the attraction of Communism. On 20 January 1949, in his inaugural address, President Harry Truman gave a global dimension to that vision. The fourth item of foreign policy (consequently known as 'Point IV') was:

> Fourth, we must embark on a bold new program for making the benefits of our scientific advances and industrial progress available for the improvement and growth of underdeveloped areas. ... The United States is preeminent among nations in the development of industrial and scientific techniques. The material resources which we can afford to use for assistance of other peoples are limited. But our imponderable resources in technical knowledge are constantly growing and are inexhaustible. I believe that we should make available to peace-loving peoples the benefits of our store of technical knowledge in order to help them realize their aspirations for a better life. ... Our aim should be to help the free peoples of the world, through their own efforts, to produce more food, more clothing, more materials for housing, and more mechanical power to lighten their burdens.[11]

In the specific context of the Cold War, technicians (agronomists, agricultural economists, engineers, etc.) played an important role in the international relations dialogue between the United States and individual European nations, at different levels, both economic and diplomatic. Knowledge of the complexities of different areas and their rural societies became instrumental in disseminating new farm and crop technologies. The 'triangle' between American companies, ECA missions and technicians involved in scientific research programmes was one of the mechanisms guiding the ERP. The networks established among the technicians also lasted for the whole Cold War, creating a little explored yet particularly significant world in the history of the twentieth century.[12] Building acceptance of the American economic model and way of life was one of the main tasks of the ERP propaganda campaign in the countryside. Numerous Marshall Plan films focused on modern agricultural methods. Communism and tradition were the two main 'evils' to fight. These films stressed the use of tractors, and better livestock and husbandry, with the overall theme of introducing scientific methods into the practice of farming. Several exhibitions were organized to show American modernity and abundance in order to convince farmers and peasants, in France, Italy, Austria and Turkey, etc.[13] The story of development was at the core of the Marshall Plan, and throughout the Cold War era.[14]

One of the most significant allies of the USA in the strategy of reconstruction and stabilization of Europe during Cold War – and less well known because the primary documents are lacking – was the Vatican and the Catholic Church. After some initial resistance to accepting the logic of the two 'blocs' (East and West), and despite the existence even within the Catholic world of anti-American currents, Pius XII gave the support of the Catholic Church to the Marshall Plan and then to programmes inspired by 'Point IV'. The Marshall Plan seemed to respond perfectly to the growing concerns of the Vatican hierarchy about the risks of instability in an impoverished and war-torn Europe. The president of the United States, the Protestant Harry Truman, and the representative of the Catholic Church, Pope Pius XII, found themselves converging on objectives and actions, despite the diversity of means and plans. The agricultural classes were considered bastions of peace, order and democracy. These were values that had to be defended by pursuing the moral unification of the West, in an alliance against atheistic communism, although that did not prevent a different assessment of the capitalism system.[15]

Despite the resistance of some influential Protestant circles, the Marshall Plan, in fact, retrieved the relationship between Washington and the Vatican. In a meeting in September 1948 with the US ambassador to Italy, the Substitute Secretary of State, G.B. Montini, informed him that the Moscow government was using the Orthodox Church 'as a political tool to undermine the Vatican, whose favorable attitude toward the Marshall Plan … has been particularly affected by Stalin'. Montini reaffirmed this support, repeating three times that the Marshall Plan 'must succeed for the good of mankind'. It was 'the most important contribution to the cause of peace, economic and moral rehabilitation of Europe and indirectly the whole world'.[16] This relationship was at least ambiguous, because it was based on two opposing ideas of society, modernity and tradition, between the American way of life, based on democracy, consumption, individualism and competition, and the 'top-down' welfare model of the Catholic Church led by Pius XII, a child of a relationship interwoven with Fascism, more likely to consider favorably Franco's regime in Spain than to embrace Republican democracy.[17]

The American administration did not recognize the Vatican State diplomatically until the Reagan presidency. The reconciliation of capitalistic productivity and charity would appear problematical with the implementation of the ERP. But in the event, bridging the gap between two different conceptions of aid and of capitalism was less difficult than historiography might suggest, as a result of the constraints imposed by the Cold War. In the context of a fierce ideological conflict, development was understood in a bipolar way, antithetical to materialism and Marxist collectivism. On 28 June 1949, the Holy Office, excommunicating Communists, invited Catholics to engage in social reform in the light of the values that would distinguish them from Marxist principles. Economic development, progress and social justice, technological modernity and the defence of Christianity had to find a single road, differentiated from that of the Marxist left, both socialist and Communist. 'The Vatican', the CIA observed, 'is putting pressure on the Catholic parties of Europe to design a positive social reform program, especially now that the Papal decree forbids Catholics to follow the socio-economic program of the Communists'.[18]

Put in a difficult position by the launch of the ERP and the Vatican attitude, the western Communist parties reacted to the American plan along the 'guideline' produced by the Cominform. They tried to explain how it would have limited national sovereignty, spoiled the agriculture economy in favour of multinational companies, prevented governments from carrying out structural reform, and prepared for a new war against the USSR, where agriculture had been instead changed to operate on a 'democratic' basis.[19] They also accused the Vatican of favouring a capitalistic and reactionary society. An international pacifist movement ('Partisans for peace'), coordinated between Rome, Paris and Moscow, was organized.[20]

Within the western Communist parties, an ongoing debate developed between those who wanted the party and unions or syndicates to encourage peasants to occupy even the cultivated fields, and those on the other hand who defended the crops; between those who promoted the struggle to provoke legislative reforms and those who argued instead for disruptive actions in order to maintain a constant tension in the countryside. Anti-Americanism was not simply organized sabotage by one side or radically conservative positions on the other. The opposition in Italy was probably less ideological than in France, since the Italian Communist Party (PCI), inspired by the analysis of Antonio Gramsci, was able to organize a broad front of industrial workers, peasants and sharecroppers, middle class (small farmers), even Catholics. Some of its leaders recognized that ERP funds were having a significant impact on some areas of the peninsula (as in the Emilia Region), but it was too little – they said – in the face of the loss of sovereignty and the 'imperialistic' plan's economic contradictions.[21]

Land reforms during the Cold War: the Italian case

For the Truman administration, maintaining an independent, individualistic, landowning peasantry offered the best chance of preventing Sovietization. As the Communist Revolution in China (1949) showed, and some economists tried to explain later, land reform could be as important in the modernization process as it was for the political stability of democratic nations. Land reform was part of the agrarian reform programme discussed for Italy, Germany, Spain and Portugal as it was for Japan, Korea, China and the nations of the Soviet Bloc.[22]

What should be emphasized is that modernization was not conceived in a conservative manner. Fascism and Nazism were two totalitarian regimes able to modernize their own economies from a technical point of view too.[23] But the Marshall Plan tried to favour modernization while trying to stabilize democratic governments and processes. It was against old nationalisms and protectionisms and, at the same time, the Communist 'menace'. Denazification, defascistization and anticommunism stayed together, sometimes entering into conflict. Land reform shifted, very quickly, from being a denazification and ruralization measure (as in the extreme case of the 'Morgenthau plan' in Germany), to being a Cold War weapon.

Technical modernization was therefore linked with social reforms, among which the 'landownership question' was important. Modernizing production techniques, raising productivity and modifying landed property were just as much the concerns of European governments' economic policies as of American diplomacy and technocracy abroad. This attitude was based on a cultural paradigm that recognized individual property but also attached great importance to state intervention, far from *laissez-faire*. Not only in the United States (given the influence of the New Deal experience), but also in Great Britain and other European nations, the state was still the main policy actor in the agriculture and food sector, even though the context of world trade policies was different from the interwar period.[24] This cultural factor went with the aim of reforming land patterns for political stabilization. The connection was weakened, but not defeated, by the risks of a war between East and West caused by the Korean conflict in the 1950s, when rearmament, military control of Communist parties and the reinforcement of Europe were considered more important than reform and civil aids.

While France decided to raise productivity through land consolidation (as laid out in the Monnet plan) and Spain under Franco's regime adopted a limited plan of colonization, land reform in Italy, in the earth of the Mediterranean theatre and near the 'front line' between East and West, with a strong Communist Party (PCI) allied to Socialist Party (they received 30.98 per cent of the vote in the 1948 election when they stood together in a 'Front') is probably, for Europe, the most interesting case. Even if it was a minor ally of United States, the internal political situation of Italy was particularly significant for all Western Europe.[25]

Italian agrarian reform was an issue that frequently appeared in the pages of international newspapers. A public debate started from the Italian election on 18 April 1948, when Alcide De Gasperi and his victorious Christian Democrat Party (DC, with 48.51 per cent) committed themselves to land reform, trusting in the USA for political and economic support. Would the De Gasperi government be able, many journalists asked, to contain a strong left sustained by Moscow and, at the same time, make reform of its own backward economic and social structure? The Catholic reformers could cite the words of Pope Pius XII spoken in 1944, in continuity with the basic teachings of the social Christian 'school' and of the encyclicals *Rerum Novarum* and *Quadragesimo anno*, which justified expropriation and exalted the small farmer as the highest representative of the religious and moral values of the nation.[26] An interventionist attitude animated some American monsignors, too. Father Luigi Ligutti, executive director of National Catholic Rural Life Conference in Des Moines and permanent observer for the Holy See at the UN Food and Agriculture Organisation (FAO) from 1948, was deeply convinced of the necessity of a reform, even direct to ecclesiastic properties.[27]

At the same time the conservatives, who were represented in the Christian Democrat Party as well as among big landowners and industrialists, could cite other words of the Pope. At a meeting with the Confederazione Coltivatori Diretti (a syndicate of small landowners very close to DC), in November 1948, for example, Pius XII asked for agrarian reform to be based on 'accurate and weighted preliminary measures' because otherwise it would have been reduced 'to be a pure demagoguery' and then 'instead of beneficial, useless and harmful, especially today when humanity must still fear for his daily bread'.[28] Looking at the future policy of the Italian Government, the Holy See was very interested in social reforms, but expressed some apprehension to the US administration about threats of reform which involved expropriation. Moreover, the Vatican Secretariat asked the Ministry of Agriculture for accurate information on land reform projects and agricultural contracts, fearing that they could also affect church property (which included around 460,000 hectares of land) and enter into conflict with the Lateran Pact of 1929, accepted in the Constitution of the new Italian Republic.[29]

While the government parties discussed the extent of the reform during 1948 and 1949, international attention on this topic increased, probably because of the impact of the victorious peasant revolution in China, and of the increasing social conflict inside the peninsula. Land reform became a global question. If we look and count, it appears amazing how many articles were dedicated to the topic, just in 1949, about Italy; we find influential journalists such as Joseph Alsop, Anne O'Hare McCormick and Arnaldo Cortesi, writing many articles in the *New York Times, Times, New York Herald Tribune, The Economist, Manchester Guardian*, and *Le Monde*.[30] The Communist Party and some of those journalists, from different points of view, accused the ECA Mission of being conservative, of slowing down an important reform. The technicians of the Marshall Plan, faced with an expropriative and redistributive land reform, were in fact very careful. They wanted to favour social reforms but, they asked, what exactly did 'agrarian reform' mean? They thought, in fact, that their main objective was to modernize techniques to increase productivity, to transform Italian agriculture *without* thinking about such a political question as the structure of landed property. They were involved in several 'development plans', mainly in the South area of Italy (the so called 'Mezzogiorno'), but with the creation of a large number of small farms they feared a drop in production after land redistribution. The ECA's view on agrarian reform was expressed confidentially in twelve points in 1949:

1. Land reclamation and improvement
2. Irrigation
3. Reforestation
4. Extension service to provide information and technical help to individual farmers
5. Improved farm techniques
6. Improved seeds
7. Market studies
8. Modernization and mechanization
9. Farm housing
10. Extension of fertilizer use
11. Improved herds and breeding
12. Division of unproductive land.[31]

It was evident that land reform was a small and unimportant part in the overall design followed by the American technicians. However, it was not possible to evade the problem. At the end of that year, after several bloody clashes in Sicily and Calabria (Crotone town) between police forces and peasants organized by the PCI (but also with some Catholic and socialist forces among them) who were occupying and dividing private lands, the American Ambassador in Rome decided to meet Alcide De Gasperi, President of the Council of Ministers. The Italian Government had tried to use the ERP against unemployment in order to weaken the Communist electoral base, in areas such as the 'red' Emilia region. And all the reclamation projects in the Centre and in South Italy had been approved with an eye on problems of public order, unemployment, poverty or low consumption.[32] But this was not sufficient. Social and political stability in Italy seemed to be in danger. And it was felt that the Italian government's slowness could undermine the West in general:

> At a private conversation with the Prime Minister today I took occasion to tell him that as a result of the press reports of the trouble in Calabria and Sicily over the occupation of lands there by the peasants the question of land reform in Italy had received great interest in the US on the part of government officials and the press. I also told him that each one of the groups of Senators and Congressmen that came here raised the question among the first on which they desired information. In response to my inquiry regarding the progress being made toward accomplishing these reforms the Prime Minister said that he and government officials principally concerned are now working intensively on proposed law for reform. Aside from difficulties of equitable formula which would make possible

wider distribution of land available for farmers, his greatest obstacle was finding funds necessary for required improvements to the land and building roads and other public works absolutely essential to newly opened areas. He said the government was determined to proceed as rapidly as possible now to the passage of a basic law through parliament and that the counterpart funds already allocated for land improvement particularly in the south would be of considerable assistance in the new program. .... Mr. De Gasperi stated definitely that the Italian Government fully realized the necessity for making immediate start on the land reform program, both from the point of view of the needs of the agricultural communities in the south, particularly Calabria and Sicily and also from the point of view of the general political situation in Italy ....[33]

The Secretary of State, Dean Acheson, made a similar point to the Italian Ambassador in Washington, Alberto Tarchiani, referring to what had recently happened to China, fallen under the Mao Zedong's Communist regime:

During a discussion with the Ambassador on various subjects, I [Acheson] expressed interest in learning the progress his Government was making in the matter of land reform. He [Tarchiani] referred to the legislation now pending in the Italian Parliament for land reform in Calabria. The primary difficulty was financial, since it was necessary to find funds not merely to compensate the present owners but for roads, houses and irrigation on the large undeveloped areas of poor land involved. The total amount for land reform in all Italy would not be less than 500 billion lire. His Government and particularly the Prime Minister were fully conscious of the importance from the political as well as the economic point of view of effective action. I reiterated the importance which this Government attached to such action and cited the failure to find a solution of this problem in China as one of the major reasons for the present plight of that country ....[34]

The growing instability of public order in the Italian countryside, and the difficulties encountered by the Italian government in responding to the ongoing conflict through an expansive economic policy, also attracted the attention of the British administration, which may have been presiding over a declining empire but was still interested in Mediterranean affairs.[35] The Labour government of Clement Attlee did not just observe, but intervened officially with De Gasperi, the ECA mission and the US Embassy in Rome. The Foreign Office expressed its opposition to a repressive policy, expressing its support for land reform directed against private and ecclesiastical property and inspired by the cooperative principle, able to give a crisp response to the land reform movement. While the American observers frequently compared the Italian situation to that of China, the British found similarities between what was happening in Southern Italy and what had happened from the mid-nineteenth century in Ireland. Even the British Ambassador in Rome, Victor Mallett, met De Gasperi.

The President of the Council, impressed by the attention given by the British press to the agrarian question, discussed the recent events in the South, reaffirmed his government's intention of intervening in the area of Calabria and assured the Ambassador that the movements were not being 'a serious threat to the stability of public order'.[36]

The pressure placed on the Italian government by a difficult social situation influenced the technicians of Marshall Plan, too. At that point in time the ECA in Washington and in Paris had just arrived at the conclusion that agricultural production in the ERP nations was lagging behind the rate of improvement needed to reach the desired goals by 1952/53. Consequently, they felt that agricultural investments had to be given a special emphasis by each mission within the framework of a total investment programme.[37] On 18 December, at the inauguration of reclamation works in Calabria (Bassa Valle del Neto), the Italian ECA Mission for the first time declared itself ready to back a land reform law directed against private property that would help to ameliorate the peasants' life.[38]

In the New Year of 1950, and in the middle of a new government crisis, German and French politicians also focused their attention on the question of the Italian reforms. It was an important test for the Christian Democratic parties' leaders. First, in January, a worried Konrad Adenauer asked the Italian ambassador in Bonn for news about the difficult situation in which De Gasperi found himself within his own party.[39] Then, in March, Maurice Schumann dedicated a long article to the 'véritable révolution pacifique' represented by the Italian reform: as with Italy, France needed a policy for employment and housing, too. Social justice was as important as freedom.[40] British diplomats and politicians of the Labour government continued to press the Italian government not to abandon the structural reform of landownership in favour of rearmament. They also argued for the realization of reclamation projects (as in Sardinia) in preference to the 'simple' solution of emigration to other European nations.[41]

The land reform laws approved at last by the Italian parliament between May and October 1950 (the so-called 'extract' law, and the two laws for Calabria and Sicily) sought to expropriate over 700,000 hectares of land in a few years.[42] The ECA granted the funds for the work necessary for settlement on the new small farms, followed by the 'Cassa per il Mezzogiorno' (fund for the South), but at the end decided not to finance the expropriations directly. Credit at low rates and extension services to the new settlers were essential for the future of the farms; on this point all the interested observers, from religious figures to ERP technicians and American syndicates involved in land reform abroad, were agreed.[43] The American administration (Department of State, Embassy in Rome and the CIA) and the British government also followed the Vatican attitude to the political impact of land reform, paying attention to the electoral effects on the Communist party and on the parties of the right.[44] From this point of view, local reactions in the South did not seem positive for the DC, which suffered losses on the left and on the right.[45] Showing how many different interests were concerned with landownership in Italy, this reformist policy exempted ecclesiastical and charity properties. Private American and British landowners in Italy complained of being paid too little by the Italian government for their expropriated lands and asked for an official intervention to amend the law. To the several letters of protest received, in some case from influential and noble people, the American and English embassies replied that it was impossible to interfere with Italian affairs.[46]

During the Korean War: civil economy versus rearmament

The growing tensions between the USA and USSR in Asia after the Korean War led to a new phase in American strategy towards Communism. The ECA and the Marshall Plan gave way to the Mutual Security Agency (MSA, 1951–1953), which would handle new endowment funds of US 7.5 billion. It had an increased focus on productivity growth and land consolidation, directing technical assistance in the civil as well as the military sector. The need for such initiatives was boosted by further reductions in trade from the USSR to Western European countries and the prospect of a food emergency situation. The Korean War was from this point of view a real watershed. Output growth was closely intertwined with military requirements; and problems of agricultural overproduction, which had returned to plague the US economy, acquired an increasingly clear strategic value in the context of an unprecedented international tension with the USSR, which meanwhile proceeded to a new phase of 'revolution from above' in satellite countries.[47]

The strategy developed for Italy became part of a global policy. Rearmament, a productivity drive and reforms went problematically together. *United States Policy Regarding Land Reforms in Foreign Areas*, 9 March 1951, was the first official statement of the Department of State, communicated to all interested countries. It laid down a broad definition of land reform:

> Land reform is concerned with improvement of agricultural economic institutions, i.e. agricultural land ownership and tenancy, land rents, taxation of agricultural land or income from land, and also agricultural credit and producer marketing. Agricultural technology, physical problems of land utilization and development, conservation of resources, methods and levels of productivity, and problems of rural industries will be included insofar as they are relevant to the institutional problems enumerated above.[48]

In many instances, land reform was considered necessary for the full development and use of modern science and technology in agriculture. But the two main objectives of the American position paper were political: the first was 'to improve agricultural economic institutions in order to lessen the causes of agrarian unrest and political instability'. A secondary objective was to disengage *land reform* from the complex of ideas exploited by Soviet Communism, by making clear to the various peoples and governments of the world that genuine land reform can be achieved through their own governmental processes, and that steps in the direction of accomplishing the basic objective will receive U.S. support, as appropriate.[49]

Thus, the USA reaffirmed the anti-Communist scope of the reform and rejected the Soviet idea of collectivization, despite the agreement made at the United Nations in November 1950.[50] The Departments of State, Intelligence, Labor, Interior, Agriculture, and ECA/MSA all decided to participate in an Interagency Committee on that issue, and a Conference on World Tenure Problems was finally held at the University of Wisconsin (Madison) in October 1951.[51] At FAO's headquarters, for the first time in Rome, Secretary of State Dean Acheson explained his Department's position in a well-known statement:

> One more word. You are talking here, you are working here dealing with resolutions on the subject of land reforms. That is a matter which we in the Department of State have believed is absolutely foremost in our whole international relations. It is in this matter of the reform of the ownership and utilization of land, with its attendant circumstances that go with it, because landownership reform alone is not enough. Along with it have to go institutions for credit, proper taxation and things with which you are far more familiar than I. It is in this front in which we really meet and grapple with the misleading slogans of communism, and therefore we in the Department of State have from the very beginning urged that this matter of land reform should become a primary objective within our own country, in our international relations and in those areas of the world which are now the battleground between freedom and communism. And so far as we have been able to affect the ebb and flow of this battle, I think our Government and our Department have thrown their full weight into the fight to help in tipping the scales toward the most progressive and rapid action possible.[52]

Because of the necessity of a rapid rearmament of its allies, the United States therefore considered land reform less important than before, but still useful for the stabilization of European countries like Italy, Spain and Portugal. The Office of Foreign Agriculture Relations (OFAR) recapitulated this in its recommendations for Italy in October 1952:

> In accordance with our policy declaration, which should be communicated to the highest level of the Italian Government, attention should be drawn to the importance the United States attaches to questions of land tenure and to the imperative need for vigorous and intensified action in order that real social and political benefits may be derived from the effort

and sacrifice involved. Obviously if the Italian Government were to temporize until its hand is forced by violence and disorder, all measures taken, far from helping the situation, might be turned into weapons of attack upon the security and existence of democracy in Italy.[53]

Conversely, for Spain under Franco's dictatorship, the OFAR argued that:

> While from the economic and social viewpoint the need for land reform is as great in Spain as it is in Italy, the question in Spain is not as in Italy an immediate political problem. Support of conservative groups, the dictatorship's monopoly of force, popular fear of another Civil War, the lack of a commonly accepted alternative to Franco, and a disunited opposition are among the factors giving stability to the present regime. This stability is not likely to be threatened by the slow pace of the land reform program. At the same time, agrarian discontent over the persistence of land tenure problems might well be exploited by extremist groups in the event of a future breakdown of public order.[54]

The 'reformist choice' was much weakened in the Asian context. For Korea, the National Security Council stated that 'land reform measures, nationalization and socialization of industries and other matters which have a serious impact upon individuals should be left in status quo'.[55] And in Japan the 'reverse course' was launched, while land reform acquired a huge political relevance in Latin America.[56]

On 11 June 1951, at the FAO, Secretary of Agriculture Clarence J. McCormick described a new policy of American interventionism in the critical areas of the world. If the improvement of international agricultural cooperation had been one of the most obvious successes of recent years, he said, 'the immediate defense of the progress of free peoples should take precedence on the progress that we intend to achieve in the future'. The United States was therefore prepared to give direct assistance, economic or military, to the countries that needed to strengthen the structure of their agriculture, even without consultation with the other allies.[57] In the context of the Atlantic alliance, civilian power and investments were to be not only affected but also undermined by the demands of new funds for the military sectors. Even the Italian Minister of Agriculture, in a secret meeting held on 16 June 1951, associated his sphere of competence with emergency situations. 'The agricultural sector', he said, 'assumes an importance in the defence of the country equal to that of Defence, as it cannot be a defence against external violence, under the pressure of food needs'.[58] Great Britain, interested in the possible uses of the American surplus, tried to get consent from the State Department and NATO to prepare import programmes for agricultural products needed to support the first 12–18 months of a future war.[59]

These were anything but impromptu reflections. They were the result of a mentality forged by war, hallmark of Western Europe. The spectre of hunger and sense of national vulnerability associated with the will to resist any attack from the outside, marked a substantial conceptual continuity, from the Second World War to the Cold War, which inspired the national food policy. Agricultural production was raised, but in 1951 Western Europe was still importing 30 per cent of its food. With the Korean War, food and economic growth as the means of political and diplomatic containment of communism were not enough. The reduced food assistance programmes and cooperation projects were joined by organic rearmament and military planning in view of a new phase of confrontation with the USSR.

At the same time, the United States developed a 'food diplomacy' policy, trying to take political advantage of its overproduction and of instability in the Eastern nations. The 'Food for Peace program' is one of the best-known food aid policies after the Marshall Plan, but for Cold War history, the German case is more interesting. An offer was made by the Eisenhower administration to East Germany in the summer of 1953, following a difficult harvest and a situation of food shortage exacerbated by an internal uprising. As with land reform, food was clearly a political weapon. The proposal to send United States government foodstuffs to East Germany were described in such a way by the CIA:

> The value of the proposal is that the Soviets, whatever their reply, would be placed at a psychological disadvantage. Soviet refusal to accept food would highlight the contradictions between Soviet peaceful pretension and Soviet actions and would increase Soviet Zone resentment and anti-Communist solidarity following East German riots. Soviet agreement would afford willingness to assist them, and the food alone would have an excellent propaganda impact.[60]

As with the Marshall Plan, finally the USSR decided not to accept the American offer, since it was evident that both of the two leading states (USA and USSR) had to show their own capacity to assist their allied nations.

Some conclusions

In societies and economies beginning to industrialize, the agricultural population was still relevant to electoral consensus and political stability, because *food* had a big stabilization function and would remain a strategic tool during the Cold War. Food production and consumption were important aspects of the Cold War.

Even in the face of a profound political struggle, in the end the allocation of ERP funds does not seem to have followed a discriminative logic towards areas or social classes with a strong appeal to the Communists. On the contrary, the mobilization activities and propaganda of Communist parties were motives for political and economic counteraction. Finally, there was an imbalance in the allocation of the ERP funds, in favor of industrial activities:

a fact probably better explained by focusing more on the subordination of agriculture to industry, than by considering only the ideological conflict existing in the European countryside. In general, Europe and Euro-Atlantic relations were marked from the start by the challenge of governing political conflicts through social reforms as well as by military measures: on that field, the Western area tested its own ability to build and implement a social policy that was expansive, not conservative, which could characterize and distinguish the Catholic and Socialist progressive forces from the Communists.

The state would continue to be the main driver of the European economy. The Pool vert would show all the existing difficulties in initiating an effective European cooperation in a strategic sector such as food. It would take several years before becoming the Common Agricultural Policy and even during the 1960s every European state would continue to have its own regulatory functions.[61]

Notes

1 M. Tracy, *Government and Agriculture in Western Europe, 1880–1988* (3rd edn), London: Harvester Wheatsheaf, 1989, p. 220.
2 M. Del Pero, *Libertà e impero. Gli Stati Uniti e il mondo (1776–2006)*, Roma-Bari: Laterza, 2008; F. Romero, *Storia della guerra fredda. L'ultimo conflitto per l'Europa*, Turin: Einaudi, 2009; S. Pons, *La rivoluzione globale: Storia del comunismo internazionale (1917–1991)*, Turin: Einaudi, 2012; D. Ellwood, *The Shock of America: Europe and the Challenge of the Century*, Oxford: Oxford University Press, 2012.
3 This point has been controversial and at the centre of a long historiographical debate. Two are the principal opposite interpretations: A.S. Milward, for example (*The Reconstruction of Western Europe, 1945–51*, London: Methuen, 1984) underplays the relevance of scarcity in Europe (except in West Germany) and therefore its relevance to the origins of the ERP; after the opening of the Soviet Archives, John Lewis Gaddis (*We Now Know: Rethinking Cold War History*, New York: Oxford University Press, 1997) maintains instead the thesis of a real 'red menace' and of the powerful legacy of the American model. For a point of the discussion, see Michael F. Hopkins, 'Continuing Debate and New Approaches in Cold War History', *The Historical Journal*, Vol. 50, No. 4 (December 2007), pp. 913–934.
4 C. Spagnolo, *La stabilizzazione incompiuta. Il piano Marshall in Italia (1947–52)*, Carocci, Rome, 2001, p. 38.
5 V. Mastny, *The Cold War and Soviet Insecurity: The Stalin Years*, New York/Oxford: Oxford University Press, 1996, pp. 27–29, 57–58; V. Zubok and C. Pleshakov, *Inside the Kremlin's Cold War From Stalin to Khrushchev*, London/Harvard, MA: Harvard University Press, 1996, pp. 104–108; A. Di Biagio, 'The Marshall Plan and the Founding of the Cominform', in F. Gori and S. Pons (eds), *The Soviet Union and Europe in the Cold War 1943–53*, London: Macmillan, 1996, p. 213.
6 W. Diebold, Jr, 'East–West Trade and the Marshall Plan', in *Foreign Affairs*, 26 (July), 1948, pp. 709–722. 'It is enough to point to three conclusions about east-west trade as it relates to the Marshall Plan: first, eastern supplies are very important to the Western European countries; second, whether these supplies are likely to be forthcoming is an extremely complex question; and third, the assumptions on which present calculations rest are precarious, so there is a considerable risk that the recovery program of the western countries will fall seriously short of its goal unless

American aid is increased to compensate for any failure of supplies from the east' (ibid., part IV).
7 'How to do business under the Marshall Plan', in *Kiplinger Magazine*, 5, May 1948, pp. 5–16.
8 For the diffusion of this technology in Italy, see E. Bernardi, *Il mais "miracoloso". Storia di un'innovazione tra politica, economia e religione*, Rome: Carocci, 2014.
9 See, for example, 'ECA in Action on the Food and Agriculture Front', *Journal of Farm Economics*, Vol. 31, No. 2 (May, 1949), pp. 317–336. For France, I. M. Wall, *The United States and the Making of Postwar France, 1945–1954* Cambridge, New York, Port Chester, Melbourne, Sydney: Cambridge University Press, 1991; for Denmark, V. Sorensen, *Denmark's Social Democratic Government and the Marshall Plan, 1947–1950*, Copenhagen: Museum Tusculanum Press, 2001, for Germany, U. Kluge, 'West German Agriculture and the European Recovery Program, 1948–1952', in J. M. Diefendorf, A. Frohn, H. J. Rupieper (eds), *American Policy and the Reconstruction of West Germany, 1945–1955*, Cambridge, New York, Port Chester, Melbourne: Cambridge University Press, Publications of the German Historical Institute, 1994, pp. 155–174.
10 Cf. Spagnolo, *La stabilizzazione incompiuta*. p. 134.
11 Truman's Address is at www.trumanlibrary.org/whistlestop/50yr_archive/inagural20jan1949.htm. The first three courses of action were: continue to give unfaltering support to the United Nations and related agencies; second, continue programmes for world economic recovery (ERP, plans for reducing the barriers to world trade and increasing its volume, etc.); third, strengthen military 'freedom-loving nations against the dangers of aggression' for a common defense.
12 For a single case, see 'Manlio Rossi-Doria negli Stati Uniti, 1951–1952', in *QA*, n. 2, 2010, pp. 7–83.
13 See, for France, B. A. McKenzie, *Remaking France: Americanization, Public Diplomacy and the Marshall Plan*, Oxford: Berghahn Books, 2008, p. 102 et seq.; D. Ellwood, 'E.R.P. Propaganda in Italy: Its History and Impact in an Official Survey', 274–302, in E. Krippendorff (ed.), *The Role of the United States in the Reconstruction of Italy and West Germany, 1943–1949*, Berlin: John F. Kennedy-Institut für Nordamerikastudien, Freie Universität Berlin, 1981.
14 For Asia and the *Green Revolution*, N. Cullather, *The Hungry World: America's Cold War Battle against Poverty in Asia*, Cambridge-London: Harvard University Press 2010; in general, O. A. Westad, *The Global Cold War*, Cambridge: Cambridge University Press, 2005.
15 See on Pius XII, for example, A. Riccardi (ed.), *Pio XII*, Bari: Laterza, 1984; E. Di Nolfo, *Dear Pope, Vaticano e Stati Uniti: La corrispondenza segreta di Roosvelt e Truman con Papa Pacelli (dalle carte di Myron Taylor)*, Rome: Iniziative Editoriali Avanzate, 2003, docc. nn. 134, 237, 288.; P. C. Kent, *The Lonely Cold War of Pope Pius XII: The Roman Catholic Church and the Division of Europe, 1943–1950*, Montreal: McGill-Queen's University Press, 2009.
16 Cited in A. E. Ciani, *The Vatican, American Catholics and the Struggle for Palestine, 1917–1958: A Study of Cold War Roman Catholic Transnationalism*, unpublished Ph.D. thesis, The University of Western Ontario, 2011, pp. 153–4.
17 Ellwood, *The Shock of America: Europe and the Challenge of the Century*, pp. 365–366.
18 CIA, Office of Reports and Estimates, working paper, 27 September 1949, in National Archives Records Administration (NARA, Washington), CREST.
19 E. Agarossi and V. Zaslavsky, *Stalin and Togliatti: Italy and the Origins of the Cold War*, Washington, DC, Woodrow Wilson Center Press, c.2011.
20 P. Brogi, *Confronting America: The Cold War Between the United States and the Communists in France and Italy*, University of North Carolina Press, Chapel Hill, NC, 2011.

21 Brogi, *Confronting America*; D.W. Ellwood, 'The Limits of Americanization and the Emergence of an Alternative Model: The Marshall Plan in Emilia-Romagna', in M. Kipping and O. Bjarnar (eds), *The Americanization of European Business*, New York–London: Routledge, 1998, pp. 149–166.
22 For an overall picture, see M. Rossi-Doria, 'Riforme agrarie', in *Enciclopedia agraria italiana*, X, Reda: Rome, 1980, pp. 502 and ss.
23 See, for example, L. Fernandez-Prieto, J. Pan Montojo and M. Cabo (eds), *Agriculture in the Age of Fascism. Authoritarian Technocracy and Rural Modernization, 1922–1945*, Turnhout: Brepols, 2014.
24 F.G. von Graevenitz, 'From Kaleidoscope to architecture. Interdependence and in integration in wheat policies 1927–1957', in K. K. Patel (ed.), *Fertile Ground for Europe? The History of European Integration and the Common Agricultural Policy since 1945*, Baden-Baden: Nomos, 2009, p. 37; P. Brassley, Y. Segers, Leen van Molle (eds), *War, Agriculture, and Food: Rural Europe from the 1930s to the 1950s*, New York and London: Routledge, 2012.
25 K. Mistry, *The United States, Italy and the Origins of Cold War: Waging Political Warfare, 1945–1950*, New York: Cambridge University Press, 2014.
26 In *Le encicliche sociali dei Papi. Da Pio IX a Pio XII (1864–1956)*, Rome: Studium, 1956, pp. 781–795.
27 D. S. Bovee, *The Church & the Land: The National Catholic Rural Life Conference and American Society 1923–2007*, Washington, DC: The Catholic University of America Press, 2010, pp. 180 and 194.
28 See 'Udienza del Santo Padre di coltivatori diretti', Minister of Foreign Affairs to the Presidency of Council and to the Agriculture Minister, 28 November 1948, in ACS, PCM 1948–50, 18.2/12441.
29 E. Bernardi, *La riforma agraria in Italia e gli Stati Uniti. Guerra fredda, Piano Marshall e interventi per il Mezzogiorno negli anni del centrismo degasperiano*, Bologna: il Mulino-Svimez, 2006, p. 166; Memorandum of the Archbishop in Milan, transmitted to A. De Gasperi and G. Andreotti, 10 March 1949, in Istituto Luigi Sturzo Archive (Rome), G. Andreotti, b. 237.
30 For example, see: J. Alsop, 'Matter of fact. Land reform remains Italy's great need', in *New York Herald Tribune*, 28 January; 'De Gasperi takes the plunge', in *Manchester Guardian*, 18 April; 'Land reform plan for Italy, division of estates', in *Times*, 19 April; 'De Gasperi's land reform', in *The Economist*, 23 April; B. McGurn, 'Land reform in Italy, redistribution of farmlands tops the list of contemplated economic changes', in *New York Herald Tribune*, 7 June; A. O'Hare McCormick, 'Land reform in Italy leaves big problems', in *New York Times*, 24 April; C.L. Sulzberger, 'Italy's Agrarian Reform still await implementation', in *New York Times*, 24 August; 'Land reform in Italy – plans for the breaking up of the large estates', in *Time*, 26 September; 'Land hunger', in *Time*, 19 December; A. Cortesi, 'Eca unit in Italy asks land reform as aid to peasants', in *The New York Times*, 19 December; 'La grève générale de vingt-quatre heures est un échec', *Le Monde*, 2 December. Cfr. F. Nunnari, *La riforma agraria italiana e la stampa estera tra informazione e guerra fredda 1948–1952*, in G. Bonini (ed.), AA.VV., *Riforma fondiaria e paesaggio. A sessant'anni dalle leggi di riforma: dibattito politico-sociale e linee di sviluppo*, Soveria Mannelli (CS): Rubbettino, 2012, pp. 65–81.
31 Letter from L. Dayton to J.D. Zellerbach, 8 February 1949, in NARA, RG (Record Group) 469, Mission to Italy, Food and Agriculture Division (FAD), Subject Files 1948–57, b. 3, f. 'Land reform'.
32 Bernardi, *La riforma agraria in Italia e gli Stati Uniti. Guerra fredda, Piano Marshall e interventi per il Mezzogiorno negli anni del centrismo degasperiano*, pp. 221–234 and passim.
33 Telegram from J.C. Dunn (USA Embassy in Rome) to Secretary of State (Washington), 28 November 1949, Secret, in NARA, RG 59, Decimal File 1945–49, 865.61/11-2849.

34 'Memorandum of conversation', 5 December 1949, confidential, NARA, RG 59, Lot File 54 D 328, b. 3, f. 'Land'. See J.L. Harper, *L'America e la ricostruzione dell'Italia (1945–1948)*, Bologna: il Mulino, 1987.
35 E.H. Pedaliu, *Britain, Italy and the Origins of the Cold War*, London: Palgrave-Macmillan Press, 2003. The Attlee government had been against the Italian participation to the North Atlantic Pact, signed in 1949.
36 Telegram from V. Mallett (British ambassador in Rome) to Foreign Office, December 1949, in The National Archives (London), Public Record Office, Foreign Office, 371/79452, 323463. 'The President of the Council spoke to me at considerable length about his projects for agrarian reform, which he noted were arousing great interest in the British press. ... As was well known there were great divisions of opinion among the Government majority and De Gasperi himself had to steer a course which would reconcile all except the extremists among his coalition followers. The problem of South Italy was not a new one and could not be solved in five minutes but he was resolutely determined to tackle it.'
37 In an interesting cable, sent from the Office of the Special Representative in Paris (A. Harriman) to the ECA Administrator (P. Hoffman), 12 November 1949, for the agriculture ECA called 'for more aggressive action and participation ... in formulation production programs than considered appropriate heretofore' (NARA, RG 469, E-56, b. 4, f. 'Programming Division').
38 Bernardi, *La riforma agraria in Italia e gli Stati Uniti*, pp. 277–278.
39 F. Babuscio Rizzo (Bonn) to C. Sforza (Rome, Minister of Foreign Affairs), 17 January 1950, in Ministero degli Affari Esteri, *I Documenti Diplomatici Italiani. Undicesima Serie: 1948–1953 Volume III* (10 July 1949–26 January 1950), pp. 611–612.
40 M. Schumann, 'Une révolution sociale', in *L'Aube*, 16 March 1950. About this article, see Jean-Dominique Durand, 'Alcide De Gasperi nella storiografia e nella cultura politica francese', in M. Garbari (ed.), *Alcide De Gasperi e la storiografia internazionale. Un bilancio*, Atti del convegno internazionale (Trento, 7–8 May 2004), Trento: Soc. di Studi Trentini, 2005.
41 Ministero degli Affari Esteri, *I Documenti Diplomatici Italiani. Undicesima Serie: 1948-1953 Volume V* (1 November 1950 – 25 July 1951), p. 411.
42 T. Bianchi, 'Riforma agraria ed economia dello sviluppo: lezioni internazionali dall'esperienza italiana', in *Meridiana*, n. 49, 2004, p. 241. The Marshall Plan funds were also used for the formation of small farmers' properties through market and subsidies. In this way, in few years, were transferred over 1 million hectares: see E. B. Shearer and G. Barbero, 'Public Policy for the Promotion of Family Farms in Italy: The Experience of the Fund for the Formation of Peasant Property', *World Bank Discussion Papers*, n. 262, 1994.
43 Memorandum from Msgr. L.G. Ligutti, 'Land reform, credit and extension work in Italy', July 1951, transmitted from J. Patton (President National Farmers Union) to W.C. Foster (ECA Administrator), 1 August 1951, in NARA, RG 469, Assistant Administrator for Programs, FAD, Land Reform Advisor, V. Webster Johnson, Subject Files 1950–53, b. 2, f. 'National Farmers Union'.
44 For Great Britain, see, for example, 'Vatican views on agrarian reform in Italy', 1950, in TNA, PRO, FO 371/89739.
45 CIA, Office of Reports and Estimates, Western Europe Division, 'Weekly Summary', working paper, 17 May 1950, in NARA, CREST; 'The electoral results of land reform', from O. Horsey to Department of State, 30 July 1952, in NARA, RG 469, E-164, b. 2, fasc. 'Land reform – Italy'.
46 See 'Annual Rome Consular Conference', 4 April 1951, in NARA, RG 166, Narrative Reports 1940–54, b. 32, f. 'Italy-Agriculture 1945-54'.
47 S. Pons, *La rivoluzione globale: Storia del comunismo internazionale (1917:1991)*, Turin: Einaudi, 2012, p. 236.

48 Foreign Relations of the United States, *I, 1951, National Security Affairs: Foreign Economic Policy*, Washington, DC: US Government Printing Office, 1979, pp. 1666–1670.
49 Ibid.
50 United Nations–FAO, *Land Reform: Defects in Agrarian Structure as Obstacles to Economic Development*, 1951; see also 'Land reform is ours', in *The New York Times*, 12 September 1951: 'Genuine land reform that preserves human dignity and individual values is demonstrably our policy: it is demonstrably not the Communist policy; and it is up to us to see that the whole world never forgets that this is so'.
51 D. FitzGerald, 'Land reform and economic development', 10 October 1951, at the Wisconsin Conference on World Tenure Problems, in NARA, RG 469, E-62, b. 1, f. 'Agriculture – land reform'; see also K.H. Parsons (ed.), *Land Tenure: Proceedings of the International Conference on Land Tenure and Related Problems in World Agriculture, Held at Madison, Wisconsin, 1951*, Madison, WI: University of Wisconsin Press, 1956.
52 'Statement by Secretary Acheson Before FAO Meeting at Rome', 29 November 1951, in *The Department of State Bulletin*, 11 February 1952, pp. 200–201. The FAO Conference stressed that 'the improvement of agrarian structures was not only essential to economic progress, but would contribute to human freedom, dignity and consequently would secure social stability and further peaceful democratic development'.
53 'Urgent land reform problems in Western Europe', J.H. Richter (OFAR) to the Chairman of the Interagency Committee on Land Reform Problems, 29 October 1952, in NARA, RG 469, FAD, Land Reform Advisor, V. Webster Johnson, Subject Files 1950–53, b. 1, f. 'Inter Agency Intelligence Committee Land Reform Policy'.
54 Ibid. See also 'Land reform in Spain. First draft of report to the Inter-agency Committee on Land Reform Problems', 23 September 1952, in NARA, RG 469, Assistant Administrator for Programs, FAD, Land Reform Advisor, V. Webster Johnson, Subject Files 1950–53, b. 3, f. 'Spain'.
55 Memorandum for National Security Council, 'Directive for the Occupation of North Korea', 31 October 1950, in www.trumanlibrary.org/whistlestop/study_collections/korea/large/documents/pdfs/ci-4-3.pdf.
56 J. Dower, *Embracing Defeat: Japan in the Wake of World War Two*, London: Penguin Press, 1999.
57 'L'inizio del consiglio della Fao. Importanti dichiarazioni del Delegato americano', in *Notiziario dell'ufficio stampa e informazioni del comitato nazionale italiano Fao*, 11 June 1951.
58 'CIR meeting', 16 June 1951, in M. Ferrari-Aggradi Archive, Rome. For Italian commerce after Korean war, see A. Castagnoli, *La guerra fredda economica: L'Italia e gli Stati Uniti 1947–1989*, Roma-Bari: Laterza, 2015.
59 See the documents about 'wheat stockpiling programme' in TNA, FO 371/94191.
60 In www.foia.cia.gov/sites/default/files/document_conversions/5829/CIA-RDP80 R01731R003300300003-4.pdf. See also C. Ostermann, *The United States, the East German uprising ff 1953, and the limits of Rollback*, Cold War International History Project, Working Paper No. 11, Washington, DC, December 1994, in http://wilsoncenter.org/sites/default/files/ACFB6C.PDF.
61 A.S. Milward, *The European Rescue of the Nation-State*, London: Routledge, 1992, pp. 197–280.

4 International agricultural markets after the war, 1945–1960[1]

Ángel Luis González Esteban, Vicente Pinilla and Raúl Serrano

The volume and composition of international trade is dependent on many variables: differences in national factor endowments, preferences, technology, income, prices, transport costs, etc. Two of these are, however, of crucial importance: the set of national trade policies implemented in different countries and the international framework regulating the design and execution of those policies. As will be explained, both national trade policies and the international set of regulations after the Second World War were extremely dependent on the domestic agricultural aims pursued at that time by the industrialised countries, particularly by the United States. In analysing world agricultural trade trends in the postwar period, a special mention of the so-called farm adjustment problem is necessary.

International flows of agricultural trade

To understand the evolution of international trade in agricultural and food products after 1945, it is essential to understand that the Great Depression of the 1930s had severely affected this trade. From 1929 to 1934 its volume diminished by 13 per cent in absolute terms, although a slight recovery in the latter years of the decade resulted in an annual negative growth rate of 1.2 per cent for the 1930s as a whole. Average international prices fell by approximately 50 per cent, which particularly affected countries producing agricultural goods; the value of international agricultural trade declined even more sharply than its volume.[2] But probably the most serious legacy of the years of depression was the general spread of protectionism worldwide. A remarkable increase in tariffs and also the use of other unconventional measures to protect domestic agriculture was one of the most important legacies of the depression for postwar years.

The Second World War profoundly affected world trade in general and both agricultural production and its commerce. The effects of the war varied greatly: on one hand, the war zones, mainly Europe, were the most affected. They reduced their imports and suffered massive devastation of their agriculture; elsewhere, other regions were only indirectly affected by the conflict, since their traditional export markets were radically reduced.[3] Thus, the volume of exports of agricultural and food products from South America fell overall by 42 per cent throughout the war.[4]

The return to the pre-war trade level occurred in a relatively short time. According to our estimates, between 1934 and 1938, and 1948 and 1950, international agricultural trade had contracted by 4.4 per cent, which means that the recovery after 1945 was quite fast, considering that its fall during the war was very important. By 1951, the pre-war volume of trade had been exceeded. Thus, in 1952–1954 it was already 9.2 per cent higher than in 1934–1938 (Table 4.1).

In the 1950s and 1960s, agricultural trade underwent spectacular growth. By 1963 its volume had more than doubled the level of 1951, with annual average growth of 4.2 per cent for the years 1951–1955 and 7.3 per cent for 1955–1960. Income growth, through its impact upon effective demand, was the principal reason for this expansion. This fundamental role of income in explaining agricultural trade expansion was no different than for general trade.[5] However, its income elasticity has been estimated as being predictably low (approximately unity), which is logical given the type of products in question.[6] To be precise, the lower elasticity than that of manufactured goods explains, in part, why growth in the volume of agricultural trade was significantly lower in those years than total trade, beginning a trend that would continue in subsequent decades.

In addition, due to a combination of supply and demand factors, such as increased production and the low income elasticity of farm products, prices of agricultural and food products rose less than total trade prices; between 1951 and 1961 real agricultural prices fell approximately 20 per cent.[7]

As a result the share represented by agricultural trade in total trade had already contracted in the 1950s and 1960s, but would fall rather faster from the 1970s due to the further deterioration in their real prices.

In the second half of the twentieth century the North–South pattern forged in the period of the first globalisation was gradually replaced by a trade pattern based principally on exchanges of manufactures between developed nations. In the case of agricultural trade, flows of processed goods between high-income countries grew significantly. However, these changes did not begin to become truly important until the mid-1960s. In the 1950s, European agricultural

Table 4.1 International trade in agricultural and food products, 1938–1954 (in thousands of $US at 1925 prices)

	1934–38	*1948–50*	*1952–54*
U.S. dollars (thousands)	14,157,433	13,531,753	15,462,611
Index numbers	100	96	109

Source: Authors' calculation, based on the Food and Agriculture Organization of the United Nations, *Yearbook of Food and Agricultural Statistics 1955*, Vol. IX, Part 2, Rome, 1956. This estimate includes 55 products for which the International Institute of Agriculture provided information in the 1930s.

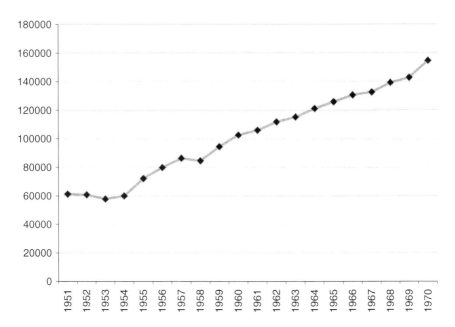

Figure 4.1 International trade in agricultural and food products, 1951–1970 (in millions of $US, 1980)

Source: R. Serrano and V. Pinilla, 'Causes of world trade growth in agricultural and food products, 1951–2000: A demand function approach', *Applied Economics*, 42, 27, 2010, pp. 3503–3518. In this estimate are included more than 125 products for which the FAO provides information on its *Trade Yearbook*.

exports gained weight in the world total, with respect to the interwar period, while its share of imports remained stable.[8] This means that the increase of agricultural trade in Europe tended to be largely a result of flows within the continent itself. From the mid-1960s, and largely as a result of successful European integration, the continent gained appreciably in importance regarding world agricultural trade. In the 1960s, access to new technologies made self-sufficiency possible, reduced the volume of imports from non-European Community partners and even allowed EC countries to become net exporters of agricultural products. The fall in European imports, especially bulk products, in relative terms is a clear example of this process. The counterpoint was the rise in food imports in Asia, which was undergoing a far-reaching process of industrialisation, demographic growth and urbanisation. Thus, Asian imports of farm products and foodstuffs grew in general, and the share of the continent increased in all product categories (bulk products, plantation products, high value foodstuffs and processed agricultural products).[9]

In the case of exports, changes in the geographical constitution of trade flows were even more marked. Governments in the developed nations provided agriculture with more support than any other sector, while many developing nations discriminated against farmers. This was especially the case in South America, where many countries opted early on for policies based on industrialisation and import substitution, which severely penalised their agro-export sectors. As a result, the continents that were most dependent on the export of bulk products (Africa, Oceania and South America) saw their share in world agricultural trade fall. Thus, both Africa and South America experienced a progressive decline in their relative share of the regional distribution of exports.

The counterpoint of this decline was the increasing share of high-income nations, and in particular the rise of European exports, which grew from 32 per cent of the world total in the 1950s to 40 per cent in the 1970s. This growth in the share of European exports was basically achieved by the bulk and processed products groups, while the region consolidated its already dominant position in high-value foodstuffs (around 70 per cent of world exports).

The historical framework: a postwar overview

In the immediate aftermath of the Second World War, the main concern throughout Western Europe was to raise agricultural production as rapidly as possible.[10] Agricultural systems in Europe and Asia had been devastated during the war or lacked huge amounts of essential supplies. World food production per capita with respect to the pre-war level had fallen by 15 per cent,[11] and only the United States was in the position to provide the food supplies required by the rest of the world.[12] The Marshall Plan significantly contributed to the economic recovery of Western European countries, and the world soon witnessed a boom in global production. By 1950 agricultural production in Western Europe had already exceeded its pre-war level.[13] Rapid growth and tariff reductions led to an even faster rate of growth in international trade. However, world trade in agricultural products expanded less rapidly, as the previous section underlines, and the share of agricultural products in world trade declined during the 1950s. The low demand elasticity for agricultural products and food, their meagre share in intra-industrial trade and the high degree of protectionism to which they were subjected were the principal causes of their relatively slow growth.[14] To a great extent, the high level of agricultural protectionism was the consequence of the domestic agricultural policies implemented over the period.

In contrast to the case of manufactured products, no European government dared to liberalise its domestic market for agricultural products after the war. Under the stimulus of the wartime experiences of food shortages, European countries 'set as paramount the aim of increasing total output to achieve, whenever possible, self-sufficiency and to raise farmer's incomes'.[15] The United States, struggling with the farm income problem, 'largely ignored its responsibilities for the development of sound world trade policies for farm products, and lent its power and prestige to the distortion of the principles of liberal trade in the establishment of the GATT'.[16] The Cold War and growing ideological confrontation also made international cooperation in agriculture increasingly difficult.[17] This led to a marked change in the pattern of agricultural trade: a growing concentration of trade among developed countries, a significant part of this occurring within regional blocs, the growing dependence of less developed countries and centrally planned economies upon the developed countries for more of their food imports, and a diminishing concentration of trade among centrally planned economies.[18]

The farm adjustment problem and the conformation of postwar agricultural policies in the USA and Europe

Trends in agricultural trade after the Second World War cannot be understood without examining both national trade policies and the domestic agricultural aims behind those policies. A powerful coalition of forces assembled after the war to create a stable regime of global agricultural policy referred to as the 'Cold War Regime', the 'Aid Regime', the '2nd Food Regime' or the 'U.S. Food Regime'.[19] This new world organization reflected the enormous political, economic and agricultural power of the United States.[20] To a great extent, it was also the expression of a political economy equilibrium within the United States itself, one which reflected its particular agricultural situation.

Throughout the 1930s, the United States had seen how food surpluses accumulated while farmers went bankrupt and millions of consumers went hungry. As Lamartine Yates pointed out, 'here were reversed the gloomy predictions of Malthus, with practical consequences as gloomy as he ever predicted'.[21] President Herbert Hoover (1929–1933) even said that the farm issue was the most important problem the nation was facing.[22] The grave agricultural situation in 1933, when Roosevelt entered the White House, led to the approval of the Agricultural Adjustment Act (AAA) with the ultimate goal of raising the purchasing power of most agricultural products to their 1909–1914 parity ratio.[23] The AAA marked the beginning of the end for *laissez-faire* in agriculture.[24] The farm income problem – that is to say, gains in agricultural efficiency and output were not matched by a comparable advance in farm incomes – was soon perceived as structural rather than temporary, and intervention measures were undertaken in order to raise and stabilise agricultural income. The theoretical nature of the problem was thoroughly discussed after the war, since many other industrialised countries were facing a similar situation. The continuing disparity between farm incomes and incomes in other sectors inevitably became a major concern of governments, and therefore a major determinant of their agricultural trade policies.[25]

The farm adjustment problem was characterised as 'a persistent tendency for the aggregate supply of agricultural commodities to grow faster than the aggregate demand for them, so that agriculture is burdened constantly with an excess supply of labour, even when business is expanding and there are brisk job opportunities in non-agricultural industries'.[26] According to Earl Heady, the problem of agricultural surplus[27] creation was the result of: (1) the low-income elasticity of demand for farm products; (2) the determination of the prices of farm capital inputs by economic forces in the non-farm sector; (3) the continual decline in the price of capital inputs relative to the price of labour, and (4) technological exogenous shocks.[28] As far as agricultural policy is concerned, there was a conflict between the need to adapt supply to demand and the desire to give farmers a 'fair income'.[29] The idea that low farm incomes were due at least in part to deficiencies in the structure of agriculture itself and to the existence of barriers to the outflow of labour from agriculture[30] became increasingly accepted over the 1950s.[31] However, policy developments in the rich countries over the period following the Second World War tended to ignore the supply side and were mainly focused on raising farm returns via price supports (i.e. acting on the 'demand side' and assuming that incomes were primarily determined by demand).[32] One paradoxical outcome of those policies was to encourage production, thus aggravating the problem of surpluses.

The farm problem and the notion of an equitable income for those engaged in agriculture were at the heart of most policy statements in postwar industrialised countries.[33] However, agricultural policy was also driven by other considerations. As Johnson has pointed out, some of them were national self-sufficiency or autarky for food, reducing balance of payments difficulties, and benefits to consumers in the form of an assured source of supply and stable prices.[34] For instance, British agricultural policy after the war was strongly influenced by the fear of a continuing balance of payments problem. Many other European countries also tried to achieve a certain degree of self-sufficiency in food after the experience of the war. However, as food shortages disappeared, price supports were maintained and even reinforced, thus revealing that the objective of sustaining higher incomes in agriculture was the major driving force behind policymaking.[35] Of course, national farm policies strongly reflected private and public interests underlying their national political economy systems. In the US case, there is no doubt that postwar agricultural policy was deeply influenced by the farm lobby (in fact, it reflected a powerful coalition of interests within agriculture itself).[36] By strengthening these coalitions of interests, the Second World War contributed to the consolidation of state-directed agriculture both in the United States and in Western Europe.

During the Second World War, the position of supply management as the fundamental core of the United States's national agricultural policy became entrenched in two ways: (1) an expansion of the number of commodities eligible for price supports, together with an increase in the support levels for the pre-eligible commodities and (2) the elimination of alternative agricultural policies such as rural reform.[37] The weakening of the ideas defended during the New Deal by agencies such as the Bureau of Agricultural Economics (BAE) or the Farm Security Administration (FSA) meant that agricultural policy would be biased in favour of the largest and wealthiest farmers.[38] Importantly, the fact that interventionist policies expanded during the war, when wartime demand eliminated surpluses and raised farm prices, thus solving the problems that farmers had faced over the previous twenty years, clearly shows the political power of agricultural interests within the state. In 1945, the wheat, corn and cotton sectors joined forces to favour the extension of price support policies, and it would not be until the 1950s that the corn sector would start advocating more market-oriented policies.[39]

The wartime years in Europe were characterised by even stronger state intervention.[40] Britain entered the war with a prepared plan for maintaining food supplies: the Ministry of Food became the sole buyer and importer of all major agricultural products, price controls were imposed, existing stocks of the main products were requisitioned and rationing was introduced.[41] In France, prices of foodstuffs were officially fixed and progressively raised in the course of the war, and the philosophy of the *retour à la terre* gained acceptance as the conflict developed. Highly interventionist policies were set in motion by many other Western European governments. Some of these policies were abandoned after the war, but the main elements of state intervention were maintained or even reinforced in all major European countries when the conflict was over.[42] Moreover, it has been said, for countries such as Britain, that 'the war years were pivotal in the acceptance of state-directed agriculture at a time when the farms of Britain were, in Churchill's words, 'the front line of freedom'.[43] The experience of the Second World War 'cemented the idea of a "National Farm" in both the popular and the governmental psyche'.[44] In the immediate postwar years an increase in agricultural production was considered necessary all over Europe, both to meet food shortages – for instance, in France agricultural production by 1945 had fallen to two-thirds of its pre-war level[45] – and to relieve the balance of payments. European countries enthusiastically embraced the Marshall Plan in 1947, which served as an outlet for US agricultural surpluses while alleviating food shortages in Europe.[46] Britain maintained fixed prices and government purchase of foodstuffs with the aim of raising net farm output to 50 per cent above pre-war levels. In France, the Monnet Plan for 1947–50 introduced a campaign to modernise French agriculture and raise its productivity. Germany, Norway and Sweden also announced policies to expand agricultural output.[47] From 1939 onwards, Spain also introduced a system of mandatory prices at which farmers had to sell some essential commodities, such as wheat or oil, to ensure supplies to the population. However, the result was disastrous, as intervention prices were too low. In a context of international isolation and difficulties in importing inputs, intervention did not boost production and also encouraged the development of a significant black market.[48]

However, European price support measures were not removed once the immediate problem of food shortages had been solved. In Britain, 'the guarantees given during the war were put on a permanent basis by the Agriculture Act of 1947'.[49] In Germany, imports of food were still being subsidised in 1949, but different policy measures were implemented in order to keep up German prices as soon as the food situation eased and world prices declined.

French aims of self-sufficiency were soon transformed into the objective of developing exports of basic agricultural goods, and export subsidies were established. Spain developed policies to support farmers somewhat later, beginning in the 1960s, through subsidies and price support policies.[50] As in the case of the United States, some European farmers became fairly affluent through subsidies, the larger part of them going to the biggest farmers who probably needed them least.[51] There is no doubt that agricultural interest groups such as the German Farmers' Union or the *Fédération Nationale des Syndicats des Exploitants Agricoles* (France) played an important role in the configuration of such interventionist policies after the Second World War. However, as mentioned above, those policies tended to encourage production and therefore contributed to aggravate the problem of surpluses and falling agricultural prices. By the 1950s the farm income problem was far from being solved in industrialised countries.

On the other hand, the farm problem was not shared by developing countries. For instance, Latin American countries at that time were mostly following industry-driven development strategies, which often had an anti-agricultural bias and affected trade, reducing their agricultural exports.[52] The intention was to provide cheap food for urban workers in order to foster industrialisation. However, 'the emphasis on increased food production and self-sufficiency, clearly at odds with the anti-agricultural bias', often created ambiguous policy settings in many countries.[53]

National agricultural aims affected world farm trade via the limits imposed on their own national trade policies, and the configuration of the international trade framework (where the 'national interest' of the United States was crucial).[54] Overall, agricultural protectionism in the highly industrialised countries was a major factor restricting world trade in such products.[55]

Policy instrument types and trade repercussions

As mentioned above, there were two different, yet complementary, approaches for tackling the farm income issue: (1) agricultural reform focusing on the supply side (regrouping of small holdings into larger units, action to facilitate the 'inevitable' movement of labour from farms into other occupations or into retirement[56]), and/or (2) applying some kind of price support measure. The latter was the overwhelmingly preferred way of raising farm income in rich countries. There were, however, many diverse forms of intervention directly affecting farm returns, all of which had different effects in terms of efficiency costs, income distribution, governmental resources required and, of course, trade. After the Second World War, industrialised countries pursued different aims regarding the prices received by farmers for their sales of many commodities: fixed prices, target prices, minimum prices, guaranteed average prices, etc. Each of these was achieved through the combination of different policies and the implementation of diverse institutional mechanisms. For example, the pursuing of fixed/target/minimum prices often required the control of imports and exports (i.e. the implementation of tariff or non-tariff barriers, quantitative restrictions or prohibitions, etc.). In some countries and with some commodities, limiting output was also part of the scheme.[57] Some of the price support aims required specific policy measures in order to be implemented, and others admitted a certain degree of flexibility in the choice of instruments.

Whatever the case, all the above forms of price support had an impact on trade, but some of them were far more distortive than others. For example, the deficiency payment system, frequently used to maintain guaranteed average prices, is often said to be the least harmful: it allows prices to be determined by the free market and it provides a means of reconciling support for farmers with the free entry of food imports.[58] However, the system was liable to stimulate increased production (at the expense of imports) insofar as the guaranteed prices were set as levels above international prices. Limiting output is also a policy distorting trade: 'it is almost inevitable that a nation that attempts to limit the output of a crop or product that it normally exports, and uses price support as the primary means for transferring benefits to farmers, will sooner or later resort to export subsidies'.[59] As mentioned previously, the pursuit of target/fixed/minimum prices often requires the implementation of complementary trade-distorting measures, and they are usually more distortive than those required for the pursuit of guaranteed average prices. Therefore, the aim of raising farm income through price supports was not compatible with the liberalisation of international agricultural trade.

Trade policies

Trade in manufactured products was gradually liberalised after the Second World War, but the same was not true for agricultural products. As has been stated, many forms of domestic intervention were implemented and maintained all over Europe and the US after the war. The aim of raising farm income was the main driver of such policies and, therefore, a major determinant of trade policies. 'It is not possible to have free international markets for agricultural products and tightly controlled and managed domestic markets'.[60] In fact, the agricultural trade measures that each country adopted were 'an adjunct of its domestic farm policies. In most cases, a specific trade restrictive or interfering device has been adopted, not for its particular benefits, but because it is a device that will make it possible for a domestic measure to function.'[61]

> If a nation adopts a farm program that establishes the domestic price for a product above the world market price, it must have some technique for preventing imports from entering its market and making it impossible to support the domestic price at the specified level. And if a nation sets a support price for a product that it exports at a level above the world market price, it discovers that if no action is taken exports fall to zero. Thus in order to maintain its 'fair share' of the world market, or for some other

equally transparent reason, it resorts to an export subsidy ... Agriculture surely stands out as the most important single case in which the governments of most industrial countries are willing to permit domestic policy considerations to over-ride so completely their interest in achieving the advantages from increased international specialization in production.[62]

International agricultural trade after the Second World War was, therefore, greatly distorted by trade policies that were an adjunct of domestic farm policies. Intervention was widespread among industrialised countries, and was actually permitted by the set of international rules regulating trade. Those rules were, in turn, shaped mostly by the agricultural interests of the United States.

GATT

After the Second World War plans were made to establish an International Trade Organization (ITO). Its charter was drawn up in Havana, 1947, but the Organization never became a reality (mainly because the US Senate refused to ratify it).[63] However, the trade provisions of the Havana charter and the tariff reductions negotiated in parallel were signed by 23 countries (including the US) and formed the General Agreement on Tariffs and Trade (GATT). Those provisions became 'the legal basis for the conduct of trade policies of all countries which were and later became contracting parties of that agreement'.[64] The basic principles of the GATT were: most favoured nation treatment (trade benefits conferred on one country should be extended to all other suppliers); national treatment (imports should be treated no less favourably than domestic products); prohibition of all forms of protection except customs tariff; and reciprocity and transparency.[65]

Although it is frequently said that agriculture remained largely outside the GATT, agriculture 'has always been fully in the GATT, in the sense that all the provisions of the Agreement have applied to agricultural products'.[66] However, it is also true that special rules were applied to agricultural trade and agricultural protectionism was largely untouched.[67] In fact, 'not only did agriculture receive special treatment in the GATT, but the special treatment also appears to have been tailored to the US farm programs then in existence'.[68]

Opposition to special treatment for agriculture came from certain countries whose agricultural policies did not require the use of protective measures or export subsidies (for instance, Australia) and developing countries which had an interest in promoting manufacturing but were denied the means to protect their domestic industries with similar measures to those allowed for agriculture.[69] However, the US 'was prominent amongst the GATT member countries who insisted on agricultural commodities being accorded exceptional treatment under the GATT'.[70] As a result, the following protective devices were eventually either not covered by the original GATT or were included without any provision for regulating their use:[71]

1   Variable import levy protection. These were periodically adjusted to raise the price of imports to a level as least as high as the domestic price, thus giving domestic producers the most complete form of protection from outside competition. They were scarcely in use at the beginning, but later, since their use was not considered in the GATT, they became the main instrument of protection in the new European Community.
2   Voluntary export restraints (VER), or voluntary restraint agreements (VRA) which were, of course, not voluntary.[72] They were mainly used because the exporting country was threatened with import controls expected to be less favourable.
3   The use of producer subsidies was not forbidden. Their application, whether to stimulate domestic production at the expense of imports or to facilitate the disposal of surpluses at a price lower than that prevailing in the domestic market, was only required to be reported by the contracting parties (Article XVI). When this article was extended in 1955, in recognition of the harm that export subsidies could cause to the interests of competing exporters, an exception was made for agricultural products (Article XVI:3). This exception stated vaguely that subsidies should not be used to obtain a 'more than equitable share' of world trade. Of course, the interpretation of 'equitable share' would be the subject of many subsequent disputes.[73]
4   Quantitative restrictions on both exports and imports were permitted in defined circumstances (Article XI:2). Quantitative import restrictions 'could be applied only if measures were in force to restrict the production or marketing of the like domestic product or a product which is a close substitute'.[74] This was clearly designed to fit the American case, because the US was the only major agricultural producer with acreage and marketing controls (in addition to price supports).[75] However, it seemed insufficient for the United States, because Section 22 of the Agricultural Adjustment Act (AAA) allowed the government to use quantitative restrictions on any agricultural commodity for which a domestic support or other government programme existed (regardless of whether there were output restrictions or not). That is why in 1951 the United States Congress declared that 'No trade agreement could be applied in a manner inconsistent with Section 22'.[76] Moreover, in 1955 the US obtained the famous Section 22 waiver that allowed it to apply import quotas to agricultural products without adopting measures to restrict domestic output. Importantly, this waiver applied only to the US and not to other members of the GATT.[77] It has been said that this waiver 'sanctified the full range of US interference in agricultural trade'.[78]

The US-backed exceptions looked 'like a laundry list of the trade complaints of American producers'.[79] In general, GATT rules relate to how governments may intervene to protect domestic markets, and the idea is that governments bring their practices into line with these rules. However, 'for agriculture the process was exactly the reverse. The GATT rules were written to fit the agricultural programmes then in existence, especially in the United States. Since then, the rules have been adopted or interpreted to fit various other national agricultural policies.'[80]

The position of the United States regarding agricultural liberalisation in the postwar years may be somewhat surprising from a historical point of view. After all, powerful agricultural interest groups had historically been advocates of free trade policies, including US wheat producers, which had dominated world markets since the 1860s, and cotton growers in the South.[81] Almost all sectors of US agriculture supported expanding trade after the Second World War, but opposition existed to the reinstitution of free agricultural markets because of the fear that surpluses and falling prices would reappear.[82] The historically unprecedented hostility to free trade that prevailed within the cotton–wheat coalition after the war was a major factor influencing GATT and intimately shaped it to reflect the domestic policy aims of the United States's farming bloc. Importantly, all major Western European countries agreed with the special treatment conferred on agriculture by the GATT.[83] By allowing agricultural protectionism, a permissive international trade framework would better serve the European aims of increasing the revenues of farmers, improving the balance of payments, reducing dependence on the dollar area and achieving food security. Therefore, the negotiations towards European integration throughout the 1950s were not obstructed by the international trade framework.[84]

From shortages to surplus disposal

At the end of the war, the objective of raising farm income was shared by most industrialised countries.[85] However, they had different positions regarding other policy aims, such as the need to increase agricultural production or to solve balance of payments problems. The choice of policy instruments for tackling the farm income issue was, therefore, deeply influenced by national factors such as the level of self-sufficiency in agriculture or the government's willingness or ability to finance specific price support programmes. Political economy equilibria and policy outcomes were different in each country, but they followed a similar pattern over the years following the Second World War: the emphasis changed from raising production at all costs to achieving selective expansion, raising agricultural efficiency and, in some cases, finding ways of getting rid of surpluses. Of course, this pattern accompanied the general tendency of shortages to become surpluses in world markets. European countries suffered a serious lack of agricultural supplies and farm inputs in the aftermath of the war. In France, essential transportation and storage facilities had been destroyed and much agricultural acreage remained inaccessible. Italian farmers could not transport their crops to markets because one third of all railways had been destroyed.[86] Bread was rationed for the first time in the UK in 1946.[87] Desperate conditions led to food riots in Germany and other European countries in 1948. However, all over Europe the shift in emphasis became apparent from about 1953, as agricultural production caught up with demand.[88] In the UK, fixed product price guarantees were supplemented by production grants or input subsidies and minimum guaranteed prices for cereals (backed by deficiency payments) were introduced in 1953.[89] The Labour government also restrained the output of certain products to prevent surpluses from increasing. In France, agricultural surpluses began to reappear from 1950 onwards and the aim of self-sufficiency changed into a new plan for developing exports of basic agricultural products.[90] Export subsidies were soon implemented in products such as wheat and sugar. While traditionally importer countries such as Germany were not particularly troubled by surpluses, other European countries such as Belgium soon had to rely on export subsidies in order to dispose of the excess production of certain products (eggs, butter, etc.). Other European countries also had to take measures in order to control overproduction (rice in Italy, the dairy sector in Switzerland, etc.). Nevertheless, as mentioned earlier, it was in the United States where the problem of surpluses first reappeared and led to major policy interventions.

The motivation for export subsidies in the United States arose because world prices were usually lower than American prices, which had been artificially inflated by price supports. In order to keep exports flowing from American ports, the government had to pay trade companies for the difference between wheat prices inland and the gateway price at which foreign customers would buy it at the ports.[91] Export subsidies started to be USDA's principal tool for maintaining exports of US wheat in 1949 and they were fully established when Public Law 480 was approved in 1954.[92] Under PL 480 (the 'food for peace' law), government-owned surplus commodities were shipped directly to recipient governments in the developing world, and 'payment was accepted for the food in nonconvertible local currencies that could only be spent by the US embassy inside the local economy'.[93] Export subsidies, in the form of international food aid, 'became the third pillar of supply management policy', the other two being price supports and production controls.[94] American food alleviated hunger all over the world, but at the same time it helped the US government to dispose of its grain surplus when commercial markets were stagnant and became a convenient tool for American foreign policy.[95] However, as already mentioned, the United States was probably the first, but not the only, country that produced significant grain surpluses and aimed to dispose of them abroad: several countries participating in the process of European integration soon intended to do the same. Of course, this is not to say that EU/US interests have been synonymous. They indeed 'constituted very large and significant agricultural powers in global terms, and have disproportionately influenced and dominated the discourse', but 'they have played agricultural brinkmanship too many times to secure the deal each wanted'.[96] This dynamic has indeed marked the evolution of international agricultural policy and trade since the 1950s.

The level of agricultural protectionism

In order to measure protectionism in agricultural markets the Nominal Protection Coefficient (NPC) can be employed, as an indicator of the degree to which domestic prices exceed border prices for the same products – i.e. it measures the degree of protection resulting from the distortions produced by both sectorial and trade policies. To measure the degree of protectionism in agricultural markets we have calculated an aggregate index of the NPC. This coefficient is defined as follows:

$$NPC_i = \frac{P_{di}}{P_{bi}}$$

where P_{di} are producer prices and P_{bi} border prices. The index was constructed from a representative sample of 13 countries and 20 homogeneous agricultural products.[97] Both the producer and border prices were calculated using FAO Statistical Yearbooks.[98]

To construct an aggregate index of the NPC, we first calculated protection coefficients for each product, weighting the share in the coefficient of each country by its weight in the world trade in each product in 1961. Second, to calculate the total NPC of agricultural trade we weighted the share of each product group by its weight in agricultural and food trade in 1961.

The NPC, despite its simplicity, nevertheless quantifies trade barriers, both tariff and non-tariff, which are difficult to measure in the long term. However, it does not reflect other factors, such as production subsidies, which also distort agricultural trade. A second deficiency, according to Tyres and Anderson, is its extreme sensitiveness to fluctuations in international prices; in particular, the value of this coefficient falls significantly when prices increase rapidly.[99]

Turning to long-term evolution, and as the graph in Figure 4.2 shows, the level of protection in agricultural markets increased between 1951 and 1970, in contrast to the sharp decrease which occurred in the case of manufactures. The initially severe international protection of agricultural products was even heavily increased, throughout the 1950s. It must be emphasised that the decreasing trend reflected by the indicator for the 1960s appears to be more a result of falling international prices than of a reduction in protection.

To take into account other factors which also distort agricultural trade we can use the nominal rate of assistance (NRA), defined as 'the percentage by which government policies have raised gross returns to producers above what they would be without government intervention (or lowered them, if the NRA is below zero)'.[100] Reasonably reliable estimates exist of the impact of these polices on agriculture in a significant group of European and developed countries since 1955. The figures are telling: the NRA was positive in weighted average terms in the developed world at least since 1955, the first year for which data are available. Thus, developed countries' public policies increased farm incomes by 44 per cent in Western Europe, 39 per cent in

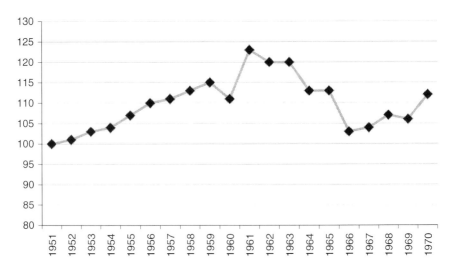

Figure 4.2 Evolution of the Nominal Protection Coefficient, 1951–1970 (1951 = 100)
Source: R. Serrano and V. Pinilla, 'Causes of world trade growth in agricultural and food products, 1951–2000: A demand function approach', *Applied Economics*, 42, 27, 2010, pp. 3503–3518.

Japan and 13 per cent in the US in the years 1955–59. In later years, support to farmers grew considerably, especially in Western Europe and Japan.[101]

Conclusions: disarray in world agriculture and the new food regime

The above described set of national and international policies led to a major 'disarray' in world agriculture.[102] The farm subsidies operating in rich countries tended to distort production and trade, causing 'too much food to be produced in regions not well suited to farming ... and too little to be produced in the developing countries of the tropics, where agricultural potential is often more bountiful'.[103] On one hand, agricultural trade was severely restricted by import control measures, but on the other hand it was actually expanded by the use of export subsidies and restitutions. On average, agricultural trade experienced considerable growth throughout the 1950s and 1960s, although this growth was significantly lower than that of industrial products. The Harberler Report[104] considered agricultural support schemes to be the principal culprit of reduced agricultural trade, and 'recommended that countries refrain from using trade policy to achieve domestic agricultural stabilization'.[105]

The disarray in world agriculture was visibly significant because of the distortions in prices and trade, the large cost imposed upon taxpayers and consumers, the uneconomic expansion of farm output in the industrial countries and the associated effects upon the developing countries.[106] Some of the principal features of the new postwar food regime were, according to Friedmann,[107] grain surpluses, sustained mainly for domestic reasons by the American government; American policies, particularly food aid, designed to dispose of these surpluses abroad; an increase in the American share of world grain exports; a consequent downward pressure on world prices and on grain production in other countries; 'cheap food' policies in developing countries and the opening of new grain markets in those countries. The international agricultural trade framework that was shaped by the GATT after the Second World War reflected the interests of a powerful coalition of forces within US agriculture. Importantly, this international framework did not obstruct negotiations for a Common Agricultural Policy (CAP) in Europe, which can be considered as the culmination of interventionist agricultural policies.[108]

Notes

1 This work has been partially supported by the Ministry of Science and Innovation of the Spanish Government, projects ECO 2012–3328, ECO 2015-65582, HAR2013-40760-R and ECO2012–36290-C03-01 and the Department of Science, Technology and Universities of the Government of Aragon and the European Social Fund (Agrifood Economic History and COMPETE research groups). Ángel Luis González Esteban gratefully acknowledges aid from the Ministry of Science and Innovation of the Spanish Government. The usual disclaimers apply.
2 G. Aparicio, V. Pinilla and R. Serrano, 'Europe and the international agricultural and food trade, 1870–2000', in P. Lains and V. Pinilla (eds), *Agriculture and Economic Development in Europe since 1870*. London: Routledge, 2009, pp. 56–57.
3 P. Brassley, 'International Trade in Agricultural Products, 1935–1955', in P. Brassley Yves Segers, Leen Van Molle (eds), *War, Agriculture, and Food: Rural Europe from the 1930s to the 1950s*, London: Routledge, 2012.
4 V. Pinilla and G. Aparicio, 'Navigating in Troubled Waters: South American Exports of Food and Agricultural Products, 1900–1950', *Revista de Historia Económica-Journal of Iberian and Latin American Economic History*, 33, 2, 2015.
5 S.L. Baier and J.H. Bergstrand, 'Do free trade agreements actually increase members' international trade?', *Journal of International Economics*, 71, 2007, pp. 72–95; D. Irwin, 'Long-run trends in world trade and income', *World Trade Review*, 1(1), 2002, pp. 89–100.
6 R. Serrano and V. Pinilla, 'Causes of world trade growth in agricultural and food products, 1951 –2000: A demand function approach', *Applied Economics*, 42, 27, 2010, pp. 3503–3518.
7 R. Serrano and V. Pinilla, 'Terms of trade for agricultural and food products, 1951–2000', *Revista de Historia Económica-Journal of Iberian and Latin American Economic History*, 29, 2, 2011, pp. 213–243.
8 Aparicio *et al.*, 'Europe and the international agricultural and food trade'.
9 R. Serrano and V. Pinilla, 'The evolution and changing geographical structure of world agri-food trade, 1950–2000', *Revista de Historia Industrial*, 46, 2011, pp. 95–123.
10 M. Tracy, *Agriculture in Western Europe*, New York: Praeger, 1964, p. 225.
11 FAO, *The State of Food and Agriculture 2000*, Rome: Food and Agriculture Organization of the United Nations, 2000.
12 The United States was the only contender nation to end the war in a healthy economic state. American incomes had risen and its farmers had higher productivity than any country. In fact, rather than experiencing shortages, soon after the War the

United States would have to deal again with the problem of agricultural surpluses and low farm prices. See L. Collingham, *The Taste of War: World War II and the Battle for Food*, New York: Penguin Press, 2011; P. McMahon, *Feeding Frenzy: The New Politics of Food*, Great Britain: Profile Books, 2013.

13 M. Martín-Retortillo and V. Pinilla, 'Patterns and causes of the growth of European agricultural production, 1950 to 2005', *Agricultural History Review*, 63, I, 2015, pp. 112–139.

14 R. Serrano and V. Pinilla, 'The long-run decline in the share of agricultural and food products in international trade: A gravity equation approach of its causes', *Applied Economics*, vol. 44, 32, 2012, pp. 2199–2210; 'Changes in the structure of world trade in the agri-food industry: The impact of the home market effect and regional liberalization from a long-term perspective, 1963–2010', *Agribusiness: An International Journal*, 30, 2, 2014, pp. 165–183.

15 G. Federico, *Feeding the World: An Economic History of Agriculture, 1800–2000*, Princeton (NJ): Princeton, University Press, 2005, p. 198.

16 D.G. Johnson, *World Agriculture in Disarray*, London: Macmillan, 1987, p. 24.

17 FAO, *The State of Food and Agriculture 2000*, p. 114.

18 K.A. Ingersent and A.J. Rayner, *Agricultural Policy in Western Europe and the United States*, Northampton: Edward Elgar, 1999, p. 123; S.C. Schmidt, H.D. Guiter and A.B Mackie, 'Quantitative dimensions of agricultural trade', in Agricultural Extension Service (ed.), *Speaking of Trade: Its Effect on Agriculture*, St Paul: Agricultural Extension Service, University of Minnesota, 1978, p. 76; R. Serrano and V. Pinilla, 'Agricultural and food trade in European Union countries, 1963–2000: A gravity equation approach', *Économies et Sociétés, Série Histoire économique quantitative*, AF, 43, 1, pp. 191–219, 2011.

19 R. Almas and H. Campbell, 'Introduction: Emerging challenges, new policy frameworks and the resilience of agriculture', in R. Almas and H. Campbell (eds), *Rethinking Agricultural Policy Regimes: Food Security, Climate Change and the Future Resilience of Agriculture*, Bingley: Emerald, 2012.

20 R. Patel, *Stuffed and Starved: Markets, Power and the Hidden Battle for the World Food System*, London: Portobello, 2007, p. 89.

21 P.L. Yates, 'Food and Agriculture Organization of the United Nations', *Journal of Farm Economics*, 28(1), 1946, pp. 54–70.

22 B. Winders, *The Politics of Food Supply: US Agricultural Policy in the World Economy*, New Haven, NJ and London: Yale University Press, 2009.

23 A. Olmstead and P. Rhode, 'The transformation of northern agriculture from 1910–1990', in S.L. Engerman and R.E. Gallman (eds), *The Cambridge Economic History of the United States, Volume 3. The Twentieth Century*, New York: Cambridge University Press, 2009, pp. 639–742.

24 G.D. Libecap, 'The Great Depression and the Regulating State: Federal Government Regulation of Agriculture', in M.D. Bordo, C. Goldin and E.N. White (eds), *The Defining Moment: The Great Depression and the American Economy in the Twentieth Century*, Chicago: University of Chicago Press, 1998, pp. 181–226.

25 Tracy, *Agriculture in Western Europe*, p. 231.

26 T.W. Schultz, *Food for the World*, Chicago: Chicago University Press, 1945.

27 An official definition of surplus was provided in 1949 by the Food and Agriculture Organization (FAO): 'supplies of food and agricultural commodities for which no effective demand exists at current price levels, on the basis of payment in the currency of the producing country'; S. Marchisio and A. di Blasé, *The Food and Agriculture Organization (FAO)* Boston, MA: Dordrecht, 1991, p. 26.

28 E. Heady, *Agricultural Problems and Policies of Developed Countries*, Oslo: Bodenesforlag, 1966.

29 Tracy, *Agriculture in Western Europe*.

30 Low agricultural mobility could be due to: '(1) lack of non-farm employment opportunities; (2) lack of industrial employment skills; (3) attachment to the rural way of life; (4) unacceptable costs of migration; (5) lack of knowledge about alternatives'. See Ingersent and Rayner, *Agricultural Policy in Western Europe and the United States*, p. 171.
31 P.L. Yates, *Food, Land and Manpower in Western Europe*, London: Macmillan, 1960; Tracy, *Agriculture in Western Europe*.
32 Johnson, *World Agriculture in Disarray*, p. 32.
33 Ingersent and Rayner, *Agricultural Policy in Western Europe and the United States*.
34 Johnson, *World Agriculture in Disarray*. At least in the case of the United States over the Cold War period, another farm policy objective has often been mentioned: to exercise what has been called 'food power' ('to seek coercive advantage by manipulating – or threatening to manipulate – the volume and timing of their food exports'; R.L. Paarlberg, *Food Politics: What Everyone Needs to Know*, Oxford: Oxford University Press, 2010.) This aim, however, can be understood as secondary, or as one corollary of the surplus-stimulating policies already implemented.
35 As explained in the chapter written by Emanuele Bernardi in this book, higher incomes in agriculture were perceived by many European governments as an instrument to achieve social stability.
36 Winders, *The Politics of Food Supply*.
37 The term *Supply Management Policy* refers to the set of agricultural policies comprising price supports and production controls initiated in 1933 – when the Agricultural Adjustment Act (AAA) was approved – and whose major aim was to boost farm income.
38 Winders, *The Politics of Food Supply*.
39 It is widely acknowledged that producers who dominate their respective world markets are more likely to favour free trade than those that face competition. See H. de Gorter and J. Swinnen, 'Political Economy of Agricultural Policy', in B. Gardner and G. Rausser (eds), *Handbook of Agricultural Economics*, vol. 2, 2002, pp. 1893–1943. Shifts in the world economy over the late 1940s and the 1950s were characterised by an overall expansion of the livestock sector. Meat consumption was increasing enough to prevent corn surpluses on the scale that cotton and wheat were experiencing. The corn segment in the United States dominated world markets, and corn producers soon perceived that supply management policy was negatively affecting their interests. According to Winders, that is the reason why they started to advocate market-oriented policies, even when they had supported supply management in its initial stages. Winders, *The Politics of Food Supply*.
40 P. Brassley *et al.* (eds), *War, Agriculture and Food: Rural Europe from the 1930s to the 1950s*, London: Routledge, 2012.
41 Tracy, *Agriculture in Western Europe*; B. Short, C. Watkins and J. Martin (eds), *The Front Line of Freedom: British Farming in the Second World War*, British Agricultural History Society, 2006.
42 G. Federico, 'Natura Non Fecit Saltus: The 1930s as the Discontinuity in the History of European Agriculture', in P. Brassley *et al.* (eds.), *War, Agriculture, and Food: Rural Europe from the 1930s to the 1950s*, London: Routledge, 2012, pp. 15–32.
43 Short, *The Front Line of Freedom*.
44 D. Harvey and M. Riley, '"Fighting from the fields": developing the British "National Farm" in the Second World War', *Journal of Historical Geography*, vol. 35, 2009, pp. 495–516.
45 Tracy, *Agriculture in Western Europe*.
46 A. Magnan, 'Food Regimes', in J.M Pilcher (ed.), *The Oxford Handbook of Food History*, 2012, Oxford Handbooks Online. Scholars usually agree that postwar US food aid

policies were also largely motivated by its fear of the expansion of communism. For instance, see J. McGlade, 'More a plowshare than a sword: the legacy of US Cold War agricultural diplomacy', *Agricultural History*, 83(1), pp. 79–102.
47 Tracy, *Agriculture in Western Europe*, pp. 231.
48 E. Clar and V. Pinilla, 'The contribution of agriculture to Spanish economic development', in P. Lains and V. Pinilla (eds), *Agriculture and Economic Development in Europe since 1870*, 2009, London: Routledge, pp. 311–332; T. Christiansen, *The Reason Why: The Post Civil-War Agrarian Crisis in Spain*. Zaragoza: Prensas Universitarias de Zaragoza, 2012.
49 Tracy, *Agriculture in Western Europe*, p. 254.
50 Eva Fernández, 'Las políticas redistributivas de la España no democrática: del objetivo industrializador al sostenimiento de los ingresos de los agricultores (1950–1975)', *Investigaciones de Historia Económica*, 4, 12, pp. 11–42.
51 Tracy, *Agriculture in Western Europe*.
52 Roy Hora, 'La evolución del sector agroexportador argentino en el largo plazo, 1880–2010', *Historia Agraria*, 58, 2012, pp. 145–181; R. Serrano and V. Pinilla, 'The declining role of Latin America in global agricultural trade, 1963–2000', *Journal of Latin American Studies*, 48, 1, pp.115–146, 2016.
53 FAO, *The State of Food and Agriculture 2000*, p. 117.
54 Here, the national interest can be understood as a balance of five institutional and economic factors: strength of national lobbies, relative benefits and costs, public interest (viewed as the Pareto optimal set of measures for each country), electoral system and the style of government; P.B. Philipps, *Wheat, Europe and the GATT: A Political Economy Analysis*, New York: St Martin's Press, 1990.
55 GATT, *Trends in International Trade: Report by a Panel of Experts*, Geneva: GATT, 1958, p. 87.
56 Tracy, *Agriculture in Western Europe*, p. 251.
57 It is generally assumed that small reductions in output would result in much larger price increases, since the elasticity of demand for crop products is low.
58 Tracy, *Agriculture in Western Europe*.
59 Johnson, *World Agriculture in Disarray*, p. 34.
60 D.E. Hathaway, *Agriculture and the GATT: Rewriting the Rules*, Washington, DC: Institute for International Economics, 1987, p. 133.
61 Johnson, *World Agriculture in Disarray*, p. 20.
62 Johnson, *World Agriculture in Disarray*, p. 20.
63 Ingersent and Rayner, *Agricultural Policy in Western Europe and the United States*.
64 D.A. Sumner and S. Tangermann, 'International Trade Policy and Negotiations', in B. Gardner and G. Rausser (eds), *Handbook of Agricultural Economics*, vol. 2, 2002, pp. 1999–2005.
65 Summer and Tangermann, 'International Agricultural Policy and Negotiations'; P. Moser, *The Political Economy of the GATT: With Application to US Trade Policy*, Grüsch: Rüegger, 1990.
66 Summer and Tangermann, 'International Agricultural Policy and Negotiations', p. 2003.
67 Ingersent and Rayner, *Agricultural Policy in Western Europe and the United States*.
68 Hathaway, *Agriculture and the GATT: Rewriting the Rules*, p. 187.
69 Hathaway, *Agriculture and the GATT: Rewriting the Rules*.
70 S. Harris, A. Swinbank and G. Wilkinson, *The Food and Farm Policies of the European Community*, Chichester: John Wiley & Sons, 1983, p. 275.
71 Ingersent and Rayner, *Agricultural Policy in Western Europe and the United States*. Besides GATT statements regarding specific protective devices, there were also GATT rules related to the practice of state trading. In reality, none of the provisions were enforced and states that used state trading entities were essentially free to

Agricultural markets after the war, 1945–1960 83

operate without regard to the rules normally applied to trade (Hathaway, 1987). For instance, 'a country using state trading in a product can limit imports, and thus maintain high internal prices without resorting to overt import quotas … On the export side, state agencies can be used to sell products abroad at prices well below domestic prices without resorting to export subsidies'; Hathaway, *Agriculture and the GATT*, p. 111.

72 Hathaway, *Agriculture and the GATT*.
73 Hathaway, *Agriculture and the GATT*.
74 Hathaway, *Agriculture and the GATT*, p. 108.
75 G. Rausser, *GATT Negotiations and the Political Economy of Policy Reform*, New York: Springer, 1995, p. 6.
76 Ingersent and Rayner, *Agricultural Policy in Western Europe and the United States*.
77 Ingersent and Rayner, *Agricultural Policy in Western Europe and the United States*, p. 126.
78 Rausser, *GATT Negotiations and the Political Economy of Policy Reform*, p. 7.
79 Rausser, *GATT Negotiations and the Political Economy of Policy Reform*, p. 6.
80 Hathaway, *Agriculture and the GATT*, p. 104.
81 Winders, *The Politics of Food Supply*.
82 A.J. Matusov, *Farm Policies and Politics in the Truman Years*, New York: Atheneum, 1967; W.W. Wilcox, *The Farmer in the Second World War*, Ames: Iowa State College Press, 1947.
83 L. Coppolaro, 'The Six, Agriculture and the GATT. An International History of the CAP Negotiations, 1958–1967', in K.K. Patel (ed.), *Fertile Ground for Europe?: the History of European Integration and the Common Agricultural Policy since 1945*, Baden-Baden: Nomos, 2009, pp. 201–219.
84 G. Thiemeyer, 'The failure of the green pool and the success of the CAP: Long term structures in European agricultural integration in the 1950s and 1960s', in K.K. Patel (ed.), *Fertile Ground for Europe?: the History of European Integration and the Common Agricultural Policy Since 1945*, Baden-Baden: Nomos, 2009, pp. 47–59.
85 Federico, *Feeding the World*.
86 J. McGlade, 'More a plowshare than a sword'.
87 Collingham, *The Taste of War*, p. 472.
88 Tracy, *Agriculture in Western Europe*.
89 Ingersent and Rayner, *Agricultural Policy in Western Europe and the United States*, p. 130.
90 Tracy, *Agriculture in Western Europe*, p. 274.
91 D. Morgan, *Merchants of Grain*, New York: Viking Press, 1979.
92 Morgan, *Merchants of Grain*.
93 R.L. Paarlberg, *Food Politics: What Everyone Needs to Know*, Oxford: Oxford University Press, 2010.
94 Winders, *The Politics of Food Supply*.
95 R.C. Eggleston, 'Determinants of the levels and distribution of P.L 480 food aid: 1955–79', *World Development*, 15(6), 1987, pp. 797–808; Paarlberg, *Food Politics: What Everyone Needs To Know*.
96 R. Almas and B. Muirhead, 'The Evolution of Western Agricultural Policy since 1945', in R. Almas and H. Campbell (eds), *Rethinking Agricultural Policy Regimes: Food Security, Climate Change and the Future Resilience of Agriculture*, Bingley: Emerald, 2012, p. 25.
97 These products accounted for approximately 42 per cent of international trade in 1961. The countries are: Australia, Germany, Belgium–Luxembourg, Canada, China, Egypt, France, India, Italy, Japan, Portugal, Spain, the United Kingdom and the United States. The product groups are: wheat and wheat flour, rice, barley, maize, potatoes, tomatoes, onions, apples, oranges, bananas, bovine meat, pig meat, poultry meat, fresh cow's milk, eggs, tobacco, soybeans, linseed, cotton, wool.

98 Producer prices in domestic markets are data from FAO production handbooks (for the period 1950–1973), and the FAOSTAT database (for the period 1990–2004). For the period 1974–1990, the series were provided directly by the FAO Statistical Office, since they are not published. Border prices were calculated using the database compiled from the FAO and FAOSTAT yearbooks, dividing the value of imports/exports by their quantities for each country in the sample.
99 R. Tyres and K. Anderson, *Disarray in World Food Markets: A Quantitative Assessment*, Hong Kong: Cambridge University Press, 1992.
100 K. Anderson, *Distortions to Agricultural Incentives. A Global Perspective, 1955–2007*, Washington/New York: Palgrave Macmillan and the World Bank, 2009.
101 Anderson, *Distortions*.
102 Johnson, *World Agriculture in Disarray*.
103 Paarlberg, *Food Politics: What Everyone Needs to Know*, p. 104.
104 GATT, *Trends in International Trade*.
105 Almas and Muirhead, *The Evolution of Western Agricultural Policy Since 1945*, p. 32.
106 Johnson, *World Agriculture in Disarray*.
107 H. Friedmann, 'The Political Economy of Food: The Rise and Fall of the Post War International Order', *American Journal of Sociology*, vol. 88, 1982, pp. 248–286.
108 Negotiations for a Common Agricultural Policy for Europe over the 1950s were not uncritically embraced by US officials and farm lobbies. However, Washington adopted a pragmatic policy and decided to negotiate in the framework of the CAP rather than opposing the process of European integration (L. Coppolaro, 'The six, agriculture and the GATT'). It has been pointed out that the benefits of a politically united and capitalist Europe for the United States outweighed the costs of a custom union (M. Spoerer, '"Fortress Europe" in long-term perspective: agricultural protection in the European Community, 1957–2003', *Journal of European Integration History* 16(2), pp. 143–162. In addition, negotiations resulted in corn and soy products being exempted from European import controls and, as a result, the United States became essentially the sole supplier of feedstuffs such as corn and soybeans. See Winders, *The Politics of Food Supply*.

Part II
Market regulation and the motives behind it

Figure P2 The small-scale pig trade in 1962 (courtesy of the Archives of Rural History, Berne)

5 The policy of wheat self-sufficiency and its impact upon rural modernization in Greece, 1928–1960*

Socrates D. Petmezas

The purpose of this chapter is to present the gradual orientation of Greek agricultural policy from liberalism towards public intervention and protectionism in the markets and production of wheat, during the interwar and immediate postwar period. It is impossible to dissociate interwar from postwar development, since the fundamental policy choices were made in the 1930s and were later fully materialized and implemented. Wheat, the main subsistence product in the country, set the pattern of intervention in the postwar years in the markets for the other major subsistence and domestically consumed products. In the mid-1920s, the liberal government reluctantly adopted such a decisive policy shift because of the growing nutritional deficit and financial strain felt from rising wheat imports. I shall show that the nutritional deficit has certainly been a persistent long-term characteristic of the Greek agricultural economy, but it was greatly accentuated during the extremely distressful early interwar years, consequently forcing the administration into action. The *modus operandi* was copied from the accumulated experience acquired during the long war period (1914–1922). The initially more timorous and piecemeal approach of the liberals made ample use of the National Bank and its privately owned financial and storehouse infrastructure. Under the conservative and – later – dictatorial governments, in the last years of the interwar period, this decentralized approach was changed to a more comprehensive and permanent system of intervention. The Ministry of Agriculture implemented its policy by combining two institutional vehicles. The intervention into wheat markets was organized through a Special Organization, using, initially, the services of the National Bank and, subsequently, dependent on the Agricultural Bank and the Unions of Agricultural Cooperatives. The intervention in wheat production necessitated a more ambitious and long-term project of publicly financed and organized Agricultural Research Institutes and extension services. This project was fully put into practice well after the end of the Second World War, and proved to be effective in increasing wheat production and putting a definite end to the nutritional deficit.

Greece has long been an agricultural economy, whose main exports were a few distinctively Mediterranean and highly income elastic agricultural products. Its foreign trade balance in agricultural products was usually positive, in spite of the fact that its overall trade balance was *always* negative due to large imports of manufactures and a persistent high volume of income transfers balancing the current and capital accounts. The country produced enough foodstuffs to feed the rapidly growing population indirectly, through commercial exchange. Exports of labour-intensive agricultural products fully paid for the chronic deficit in cereals and other land-intensive agricultural and livestock products. Agricultural exports accounted for more than 60 per cent of the total value of Greek exports until 1960, and just four products were responsible for this figure (currants, tobacco, wine and olive oil). Wheat and cereal imports were responsible for one-third of the total value of Greek imports, until the postwar period. It was ironic that a country with a chronically surplus agricultural foreign trade was heavily dependent on the imports of basic foodstuffs to assure the nutrition of its population.[1]

Of course, territorial, demographic and geopolitical transformations greatly influenced the aggregate figures, the level of the cereal (and nutritional) production deficit, and the composition of exports, but they did not change the labour-intensive character of Greek agriculture and its foreign trade composition which was chronically in surplus, in cash terms, but nutritionally in deficit. Seen from a different angle, we can say that Greek commercial agriculture produced mainly export goods in large quantities, while the subsistence sector was trailing behind. Any dichotomy of a commercial versus a subsistence sector is, of course, simplistic and schematic. The subsistence sector offered labour services and products to, and received income and products from, the commercial sector, and thus there was an intimate interdependence between the two, but it is useful to examine them separately, especially when the effects of economic policy and public intervention are concerned.

In fact, public intervention in agriculture had followed a different path and rationale depending on whether it was aimed at the subsistence or the commercial sector of the agricultural economy. The commercial and export sector usually did not seek public support or state-sponsored banking credits.[2] During the 19th century currant exports were the main engine of growth of the Greek economy, and the successive Greek governments refrained from any kind of policy intervention in agriculture, save for a policy of modest tariffs on wheat imports, after 1884, destined to offer slightly higher prices to grain-exporting large landowners.[3] Liberalism, mitigated by pragmatism, was the avowed economic doctrine of the Hellenic political elite. Import and export tariffs were generally low and they were mostly meant to secure fiscal income.[4] State intervention in agricultural markets was seen as inappropriate and unnecessary. The only domain in which the state regularly intervened, as the country gradually expanded territorially, was the distribution of land, formerly held by Ottoman Muslim landlords, to their Christian cultivators, thus securing the formation of small and medium-sized landowners loyal to the Greek nation-state.[5]

Only after a severe and chronic crisis affected a particular agricultural export sector, such as currants after 1893 or tobacco after the Great Depression, was there a concentrated public intervention effort. The current crisis was the first and formative case of intervention in Greek agriculture by the public and private sectors. In fifteen years (1893–1908) a full range of modes of intervention was put in place, from the public regulation of the stock sold on world markets to a system of guaranteed low prices and cheap credit to producers, and to the foundation of dedicated industries using the unsold surplus. Both civil servants and executives of the private banking sector familiarized themselves with all these measures.[6] The long war decade that followed (1912–1922) forced the same people and institutions to intervene urgently in the production, marketing and distribution of agricultural goods, and gave them new opportunities for familiarizing themselves with methods and means of public and private intervention in agricultural markets and institutions.

The structure of the ministerial administration itself remained unchanged until 1910, when the new reformist governments of the Liberals gradually expanded the number of ministries and, more importantly, intensified the internal specialization of public administration. Meanwhile, in the early 1920s, schools and faculties of higher education in Agronomy, Veterinary and Forestry were finally established in Athens, and the newly founded University of Thessaloniki, producing a growing number of agronomists and veterinary doctors who were employed by the public or private institutions engaged with the agricultural economy.[7] This accumulated personnel, experience and expertise was put into practice in the interwar period, when a large-scale public effort to achieve wheat (and nutritional) self-sufficiency was undertaken. In fact, this effort began just after the First World War and lasted until the late 1950s, when finally the task was accomplished. It constituted a radical policy shift towards intervention and protectionism, and had a marked impact on the process of modernization of agriculture.

During the 19th century, foreign trade, almost exclusively depending on currant exports, had thus enabled rural Greece to feed its rapidly growing population, keep most of its rural demographic surplus in the countryside, and achieve a satisfactory rate of growth. In the long run, territorial expansion and demographic growth exacerbated the contradiction of a nutritionally deficient agricultural export economy.

Thus, the cereal deficit of Greek agriculture increased steadily until the Second World War (see Table 5.1). It was only after the War and the traumatic experience of war famine that imports declined and finally reversed, in 1958, to net wheat exports.[8] The per capita level of estimated wheat consumption steadily grew, from about 100 kg in 1860s to little less than 150 kg in the early interwar period. If we add the per capita volume of other grains produced and consumed by subsistence farmers, then the per capita grain consumption may have been as high as 200 kg per capita.[9] In effect, as time passed wheat substituted for other cereals (mostly maslin, rye, barley and maize), which were mainly consumed as alternative cereals for bread by subsistence farmers.[10] As the urban proportion of the population increased and the commodification of agricultural production expanded, wheat (imported or home-produced) displaced other

Table 5.1 Estimation of wheat production and imports (kg per capita)[11]

Yearly average	Wheat production	Net wheat imports	Wheat consumption	% of imports	Other grains consumed*	Total grain consumption
1851–1863	84.2	21.4	102.1	21.0	83.0	185.1
1865–1880	78.9	49.5	124.5	39.7	72.0	196.5
1882–1911	74.6	62.8	146.2	43.0	55.7	202.2
1914–1922	60.0	49.3	109.4	45.1	46.8	156.2
1923–1932	50.8	84.9	135.7	62.5	37.9	178.6
1933–1940	113.3	56.8	170.1	33.4	49.2	219.3
1947–1952	111.5	57.9	166.9	34.7	42.2	209.1
1953–1958	181.9	31.3	210.4	14.49	41.0	251.4
1959–1962	203.0	1.3	204.4	0.6	38.2	242.6

*The volume of grains consumed equals to the production of 100 per cent of wheat, maslin and rye, 80 per cent of maize and sorghum, and 25 per cent of barley (mainly used for fodder in rural Greece).

secondary cereals, and a growing part of the rural consumption of bread depended on imported wheat. Import dependence reached its highest level in the early interwar period (1923–1932), when almost two-thirds of wheat consumption was imported (see Table 5.1). This was happening while the impoverished country faced serious strains in balancing its current accounts. It was thus not surprising that successive Greek governments and independent academics considered that the time was ripe for an ambitious coordinated policy shift, aimed at expanding cereal output and reducing import dependency.

Greek dilemmas from the First World War to the Great Depression: wheat self-sufficiency as a target of financial policy

In late 19th- and early 20th-century Greece, a country burdened with the service of a large sovereign debt, the public discussion on self-sufficiency in wheat primarily had a financial rationale: economizing on valuable foreign exchange. Increasing output was the means to this end. Experts argued for the expansion of arable land and of its yields, because labour was abundant and its supply was never considered as a possible constraint on output. Yields were expected to rise moderately through the expansion of the tilled area and as a result of more meticulous work by farmers.[12] The only concrete protection policy was the imposition (in 1884, 1892 and 1906) of gradually higher tariffs on wheat imports which mildly protected the interests of large landed estate owners in Thessaly, without unduly increasing the price of bread in the cities. Its impact was considered unsatisfactory for wheat producers, and their advocates insisted upon the need to raise tariffs more.[13]

The First World War, unpredictably, forced the Greek public administration to intervene in markets for imported foodstuffs to ensure the regular provision and consumption at affordable prices, of staple products like wheat.

It is nonetheless crucial to emphasize that the public administration did not and, most probably, could not fulfil these operations alone. It was the private National Bank of Greece that was mandated (by Law 528/Dec. 27, 1914) to purchase all necessary provisions and sell them, against a legal commission, to certified private wholesalers and retailers who were to distribute them to the public (consumers or flour industries) at fixed prices, under the inspection of the appropriate public authorities. The Greek government guaranteed the National Bank against any loss due to currency depreciation or to any other commercial misfortune. The National Bank, through its network of offices and its Privileged Anonymous Society of General Warehouses (PAEGA), was capable of undertaking this task until the end of the war.[14] Nonetheless, it was made more difficult by the dislocation of the public service due to internal discords among the governing elite.

In fact, during the First World War, Greece was torn apart in a latent civil war between the liberals, who favoured the Allied powers, and the royalists who, unable to side with the central powers, favoured neutrality. In December 1916, the royalist government had given the Allies sufficient cause to force a military embargo of Greek ports for a few weeks. This act, coming on top of growing difficulties imposed on the cereal import trade by the war, in conjunction with a diminishing national production and growing strains on the internal transport system, led to a shortage of foodstuffs, which plagued the country throughout the following year, 1917.[15] The growing demand for provisions by the Allied armies in Macedonia further exacerbated the problem. The country, reunited under the victorious liberals in mid-1917, suffered from a shortage of wheat and cereals until the end of the war. In response to this problem, both royalists and Liberals when in government chose to centralize and monopolize the collection, trade and distribution of cereals and other provisions.[16] The new Ministry of Purveyance and Autarky, established in February 1917 and dissolved in June 1923, controlled the import and procurement of cereals and other provisions, and their sale to certified merchants and other intermediaries.[17]

An important aspect of state intervention in the productive sector was the complete control it exercised upon the process of production, pricing and distribution of bread. The domestic flour industries were legally obliged to mill for a fee the grain imported or collected by the services under the financing and supervision of the National Bank. They were then forced to supply the bakers with the necessary flour at relatively low fixed prices. Of course, the quality of baked bread sold at fixed prices was pitiful, inflation rose faster than wages and the black market flourished, but at least the basic consumption of the population was assured, in spite of the competition for wheat with the large Allied armies in Macedonia. This regime of quasi-state monopsony over wheat imports and flour production lasted more than eight years and ended after the war in 11 June 1923, by which time the Greek Treasury owed the National Bank 440 million drachmas (or 4 per cent of the GDP of that year), which it paid in full five years later.[18]

This experience of nutritional insecurity during the First World War was not forgotten, but it did not enter prominently into the interwar debates on cereal self-sufficiency. The debate was still primarily about financial (and monetary) stability: nutritional self-sufficiency if obtained would reduce imports in value by 30 per cent, trim down the trade deficit and depreciate foreign exchange. Financial stability – i.e. the depreciation and stabilization of foreign exchange – was the magic word for a country that was plagued by high inflation, a dearth of foreign exchange and a large unserviced sovereign debt whose exact size was, until 1928, a matter of negotiation in parallel with the exact amount of war reparations.[19]

In effect, the situation in cereal agriculture was extremely precarious in the 1920s. The territorial expansion of the country into the ethnically diverse and economically less developed northern provinces, dominated by archaic share-cropping agriculture, had added a supplementary budgetary burden and an additional source of social conflict. Abrupt population growth and massive flows of exchanged ethnic populations weighed heavily upon an agricultural structure caught in a process of painful reconversion due to radical land reform and population resettlement.[20] Land reform and refugee settlement in the northern countryside had a short-term, but severe, impact upon agricultural (especially cereal) output due to the forced readjustment of the active population, and livestock and natural resources. This impact was particularly felt in the newly annexed northern provinces, but unfortunately the older provinces of the kingdom in southern Greece were not spared. The income crisis that followed the chronic stagnation of international demand for currants (c.1893–1910) had forced the farmers to intensify their crop rotation at the expense of fallow, without any compensating use of fertilizers. Between 1911 and 1914, and 1923 and 1926, average cereal yields regressed by a stunning 45 per cent, while arable land had only marginally expanded (see Figure 5.1).[21] The situation was not different in the northern provinces, where average yields were higher, and many conservative agronomists later blamed the land reform, although yield regression was universal and was not restricted to the provinces that experienced land reform and refugee settlement. Making things worse, there was a series of disappointing low cereal harvests in the last years of the 1920s due to adverse weather conditions. Wheat and grain production thus attracted the most urgent governmental attention in the mid-1920s.

The protection of domestic wheat production under the Liberals

The administration initially envisaged increasing import tariffs, but they did not offer adequate protection for the grain producers and could not increase the price paid for their wheat. The cause of this failure was allegedly the excessive bargaining power of the wheat traders. Merchants in the domestic wheat markets (as in most other domestic agricultural products) had all the advantage of scale, organization and asymmetric information.[22] They were in a position

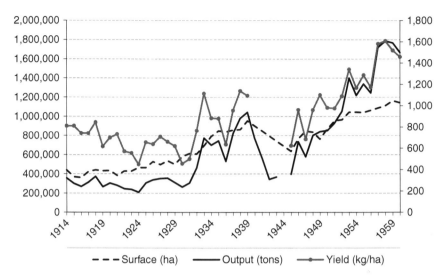

Figure 5.1 Wheat area cultivated, production (left axis) and yields (right axis)

to impose excessively low prices on grain producers and were not interested in any long-term amelioration of quality or output. Contrary to this situation, it was thought that if domestic wheat prices were stabilized (and thus predictable), grain producers would be motivated to assume the cost and effort needed to expand their yields, resulting, in the long run, in the expansion of domestic wheat output. Since tariff protection was considered an insufficient motivation, the only way of influencing the market price in the short term was to combine tariffs with fixed guaranteed prices offered to producers after harvest.[23] Such a policy demanded, initially at least, large outlays of capital to buy and warehouse the wheat sold by grain producers. Subsequently, it was important that this volume of stored wheat should be securely and promptly disposed of. It was thus of paramount importance to find a large, regular and solvent buyer. The flour industry (the unique purveyor of wheat flour for internal commercial consumption) was once again the only possible partner.

Additionally, of course, in the long term it was imperative that the productivity (and income) of the average grain producer increased. This could be achieved when the cost of production per unit area was reduced and grain yields increased.[24] Consequently, there were two ways to achieve a favourable influence upon the wheat market and production: on one hand, to intervene in the wheat market and make a long-term association agreement with the processing industries, and, on the other, to cut down costs by offering free extension services, low-cost inputs and cheap credit to the producers.

Public intervention in the grain sector initially aimed at securing satisfactory minimum prices to wheat producers, and the regular and profitable sale of the collected surplus to the flour industry. A special policy operation, with enough capital, expertise and storage capacity, concentrated on this short-term task. In the long run, a more ambitious and costly intervention was organized under the guidance of the Ministry of Agriculture to produce yield increases in the medium term and lower input costs in the long run.

To achieve the first task, the Ministry of Agriculture created, in 1926, a permanent Central Committee for the Protection of Domestic Wheat (KEPES), composed of high civil servants and the representatives of the interested parties (the National Bank, the Association of Flour Industries, the regional Unions of Agricultural Cooperatives in the wheat-producing areas).[25] KEPES, whose mission was renewed by law every year, was ordered to offer guaranteed prices to domestic wheat producers, build warehouses and provide additional assistance such as high quality selected seed at reasonable prices to domestic producers. The first such agreement, struck in August 1927, between the Greek state, the National Bank, the PAEGA and the Association of Flour Industries, provided that the bank would finance the purchase and the PAEGA would assure the collection and storage of what would henceforth be called 'collected wheat'. Finally, and most importantly, the flour industry would be obliged to mix domestic and imported wheat to the ratio of at least one-sixth of domestic wheat in the total volume milled.[26] Later, in 1932, KEPES was transformed into a permanent legal entity, with its own personnel, and expanded its activities and mission. It financed the construction of cooperative warehouses and the distribution of seed to producers, while it also extended its mission to other grains (barley etc.). KEPES also financed two applied research institutes of the Ministry of Agriculture – namely, the Institute for Crop Improvement (IKF) and the Centre for Testing Agricultural Machinery (SDGM) – which offered extension services to wheat producers.[27]

In fact, KEPES offered to wheat producers a secure outlet for their production at minimum guaranteed prices according to the quality of the product, thus helping them to secure a minimal income as a return for their investment in inputs. At the other end of the productive chain, KEPES was also particularly cautious in protecting the smaller flour producers who could only compete through a lower price of wheat. In fact, high (fixed) prices of wheat offered a modicum of protection to smaller and less competitive flour millers against larger competitors who could have profited from massive input purchases at lower negotiated prices. Of course, this policy put the burden of higher bread prices on the domestic urban consumers, but it had the advantage of protecting a strategically important and, in the short run, non-competitive sector of the agricultural industry.

KEPES officially started to intervene in the market in 1927, but it was only in 1931 (when yields and domestic output were still disappointingly low) that a small but substantial part (4 per cent) of domestic production was purchased at fixed prices (see Figure 5.2).[28] During these first years, before the Great Depression made itself felt in Europe in the summer of 1931, guaranteed prices were lower than market prices, offering only price stabilization. In the next few

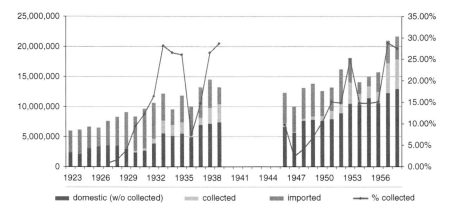

Figure 5.2 Domestic wheat consumption (in hl)

years (1932–35), under the constraint of falling international prices and the worsening income crisis of the agricultural population, KEPES offered substantially higher guaranteed prices, which were above the domestic market price (of mostly imported wheat) and thus provided a kind of income support to wheat producers.[29] The proportion of domestic wheat in the total of wheat used by the flour industry rose to 28 per cent.

Dictatorship, wars and economic reconstruction: full-scale state intervention and protectionism

In the final years of the 1930s, the percentage of wheat collected by KEPES stabilized at a quarter of the increasing domestic production. Since world prices had recovered, the fixed guaranteed prices remained below the higher market prices, which were heavily influenced by the prices of imports.[30] Meanwhile, after a contested referendum in November 1935, which abolished the Second Hellenic Republic and re-established the monarchy, a *coup d'état* in August 1936 brought a royal dictatorship under Ioannes Metaxas to power. The new dictatorial government squeezed the market price of flour and the income protection of wheat producers. It also made the strategic choice to expand the role of cooperatives (closely supervised by the Agricultural Bank) in the collection and warehousing of collected wheat.[31] The cooperative warehouse construction programme, which had proceeded slowly up to that point in time, was intensified.[32]

This decision coincided with a clear reorientation of the policy and regulations of the Ministry of Agriculture, which became more centralized and dirigiste. This authoritarian and productivist policy reorientation left little space for either local initiatives or the unimpeded function of free market forces. It was inspired and embodied by high civil servants like the charismatic general secretary of the Ministry of Agriculture, Babis Alivizatos, a politically controversial personality but certainly one of the most brilliant Greek agricultural economists.

KEPES now relied upon the Agricultural Bank (ATE) and the regional Unions of Agricultural Cooperatives, which were also controlled by the dictatorial government. The Agricultural Bank (founded in 1929) was a public non-profit credit institution that became the main and most successful vehicle of public intervention, penetrating through its offices deep into rural society. It offered cheap agricultural credit, mid and long-term investment loans, extension services and cheap inputs (fertilizers, seed, herbicides etc.).[33] Until the late 1930s, the newly founded Agricultural Bank shared its regional offices and employees with the older National Bank. In that way the National Bank was able, through these shared offices and personnel, to exert an indirect and latent influence to (and profit from) the activities of the Agricultural Bank. This ambiguous situation gradually finished by 1937 when the creation of an exclusive network of ATE offices was almost completed. The financing of the wheat collection had already been taken over by the Agricultural Bank in 1930.[34] It was much later, though, in 1939, that the Privileged Anonymous Society of General Warehouses (belonging to the National Bank) was excluded from the collection of wheat, which was taken over by the National Confederation of Unions of Agricultural Cooperatives (ESSE).

Finally, in 1940, the dictatorial government decided that a 'Consortium of Unions of Agricultural Cooperatives for the Administration of Domestic Wheat' (KESDES) was to be founded and entrusted with the task of supervising the collection of wheat at guaranteed prices, always with the support of the Agricultural Bank. The KESDES brought together 58 unions of agricultural cooperatives and delegated its powers to the 'Central Service for the Administration of Domestic Wheat' (KYDES), which substituted itself for KEPES.[35] Just before entering the war in October 1940, state-controlled institutions (KYDES, ESSE and ATE) had gained complete control over the collection, storage and marketing of domestic wheat, while the country had finally achieved a relatively high level of per capita consumption and domestic production of wheat (see Table 5.1).

In the following decades the Agricultural Bank and Cooperative Unions became the backbone of the Greek system of intervention into the agricultural markets. It is important to emphasize that the Agricultural Bank exerted a very strong supervisory influence upon agricultural cooperatives, whose elected administrators had become in effect a kind of unofficial, decentralized and self-administered branch of public administration. The ruling parties, in the anti-communist postwar regime, had furthermore used the cooperatives to extend their political influence and legitimacy. It can safely be argued that the postwar parliamentary regime adopted the basic premises laid down by Alivizatos and the authoritarian Metaxas dictatorship.

In the last years of the 1930s, wheat production had grown substantially, even though imports still counted for two-thirds of the demand of domestic flour mills and more than one third of total domestic production in 1939. The progress made was reversed during the Second World War, and the civil war that followed. The danger of famine due to nutritional deficiency materialized when the British Royal Navy blockaded occupied Greece and the German High Command refused to share the provisions of the occupation army with the endangered Greek population. The winter of 1941/42 and the spring of 1942 was a catastrophic period. In the cities, there were a quarter of a million deaths caused by famine.[36] The Quisling government used the KYDES, renamed to 'Central Service for the Administration of Domestic Production' (KYDEP), to expand the system of wheat collection to other products in order to feed the population and the occupation armies.[37] It proved an almost impossible task, and the population survived thanks to the black market and the resistance forces that, in the summer of 1944, fought to achieve a partial control of the grain production in the countryside. Meanwhile, the Greek government had re-enacted the interwar policy of collection of wheat and grain in fixed guarantee prices, and their delivery to flour industries who were again, since the beginning of the war in 1940, obliged to process the collected wheat and sell the flour in low fixed prices to the bakers. The population itself received food stamps rationing its basic subsistence needs (such as bread etc.).[38] In October 1944, the German army evacuated Greece and the liberated country found itself in a desperate situation, which was only averted thanks to massive imports of American aid in the form of wheat and flour.

Thus, the end of German occupation and the war did not mark the end of Greek food supply problems, and the rationing system continued until the end of February 1953.[39] Throughout that time, the KYDEP was in charge of the effective collection of wheat (as well as other grains and oilseeds) and followed a policy of offering prices that were somewhat lower than the average market price. Its purpose was to stabilize prices without actually raising the market price paid by the consumer. The state monopsony of wheat and the quasi-monopoly of flour continued and the flour industries were effectively milling (against a fixed fee) imported and 'collected' domestic wheat, under the direct control of the public administration.[40] Both the collected and the imported wheat (mostly a part of free American aid, after the war)[41] were under state control and were either used by the flour industry or distributed to farmers in wheat-deficient provinces. In effect, the public administration had become the largest grain trader in the country and practically the main regulator of the income of impoverished farmers and small grain producers, living in remote mountainous villages and the islands during or immediately after the conflict that started in 1947. The Civil War (1947–1949) had debilitating effects upon cereal production, in particular because a significant number of farmers were evacuated and temporarily lived in camps, awaiting the end of military operations in their mountainous villages.[42] Once again the system, corrupted and inefficient as it was, offered cheap rationed bread to the population, which had to resort to the black market to buy additional or better quality products. When food rationing finally ended, direct supervision and control over the flour industries

98 Socrates D. Petmezas

also ended. Flour industrialists were now simply obliged to mix a part of domestic collected wheat with the imported or domestic wheat bought in the free market (see Table 5.2).[43]

In late February 1953, a few weeks before definitively pegging the devalued drachma to the dollar, food rationing and state supervision of the flour industries ended, but the official policy of intervening in the grain market through the KYDEP and fixing the price of bread continued. The system was still destined to stabilize prices (which differed according to the quality of the product) at a level somewhat lower than that of the domestic market. It was not a state monopoly: merchants could buy freely in the market provided they offered satisfactory prices, above the guaranteed prices to producers. The KYDEP did not buy all the production offered by a producer. There was a limit to the volume of grains purchased from farmers, proportionate to the size of their farm or their debt owed to the Agricultural Bank. Small owners were offered higher guarantee prices. In fact, there was a clear desire to advantage smaller and more vulnerable producers (with a landed property of under 3 ha), who were actually subsistence farmers. This policy was ever more pronounced and in 1958, once wheat self-sufficiency was achieved, KYDEP decided to stop offering guaranteed prices to those considered as large producers (tilling more

Table 5.2 The KYDEP system of the collection of wheat in tons (1953–1957)[44]

In tons	1953	1954	1955	1956	1957
Domestic production of wheat	1,400,000	1,219,000	1,337,000	1,245,000	1,720,000
State collection of wheat	348,258	180,622	197,493	183,374	495,185
Provision of wheat to flour industries	517,018	675,122	777,053	836,241	707,238
Domestic collected wheat	348,000	180,622	197,493	183,080	362,445
Domestic free market wheat	61,018	165,000	194,560	169,500	205,774
Imported wheat	108,000	329,500	385,000	483,661	139,019
Domestic wheat consumption	1,508,000	1,548,500	1,722,000	1,728,661	1,859,019
% of domestic free market wheat	4.0%	10.7%	11.3%	9.8%	11.1%
% of imported wheat	7.2%	21.3%	22.4%	28.0%	7.5%
% of domestic collected wheat	23.1%	11.7%	11.5%	10.6%	26.6%
Farmers involved in wheat collection			153,183	179,035	203,030
Average volume per farmer (kg.)			1,270	1,094	2,439
Estimated average size of farm (in ha)			2.5	2.1	4.8

than 8 ha).[45] Of course, price stabilization and cheap provision of inputs or extension services were of major importance to medium-sized competitive wheat producers in the lowlands, even if they did not directly profit from guaranteed prices to the extent that small farmers did.

In the mid-1950s, the years that led to the achievement of wheat self-sufficiency, the collection of wheat rose, fluctuating between 180 and 500 thousand tons, or 15–30 per cent of the total volume of the domestic crop (see Table 5.2). Meanwhile, the local subsistence consumption of the crop (seed of the next year included) by the agricultural population was estimated at 900,000 tons. The rest was sold to grain traders and ended in the local flour industry. It fluctuated less abruptly between 60 and 200 thousand tons or 4–15 per cent of the total output (see Figure 5.3). It is clear that public intervention in the market simply siphoned off the excess volume in order to preserve the level of domestically offered prices. The intervention system was fully operational, and it rapidly proved its efficiency. In fact, by the late 1950s the country had become nutritionally self-sufficient. This was as much the result of direct intervention into the wheat market as of amelioration of the structure of production.

Public intervention in wheat production: extension services and the rise of wheat yields and output

The creation of KEPES was not designed to address the problem of the relatively low profit margins in Greek wheat production. This was the task of various newly founded public 'institutes of applied research' of the Ministry of Agriculture, which were meant to offer extension services to farmers. They were modest in institutional terms, but had a positive effect on cereal production. All these initiatives shared a productivist rationale aimed at increasing the

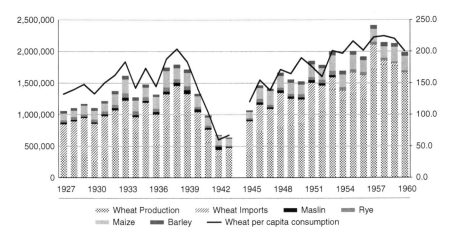

Figure 5.3 Production of cereals and imports of wheat in tons, 1927–1960

growth of wheat and cereal output. There was almost no question of economic efficiency, which is understandable in the autarkic economic context of the 1930s.[46] The increase of cereal yields and the expansion of the tilled land were the primary variables the administration tried to influence. They were not concerned with increasing labour productivity, which would have resulted in the release of labour from cereal agriculture and its addition to the latent rural unemployment or, worse, to the already unemployed urban labour force. The majority of the specialists who called for an end to the wheat deficiency of Greek agriculture believed that the best solution would be the intensification of the wheat cultivator's labour.[47] As at the beginning of the 20th century, the acquisition of more efficient equipment (iron ploughs and harrows), the use of rainwater and other sources of irrigation, a careful selection of seed and a more meticulous seeding, manuring and weeding were the fundamental proposals of the agronomists.[48] Farmers were given the same advice in the interwar period, and state policy was reoriented to increasing yields, through the provision of chemical fertilizers and selected seed, and expanding the seeded area. This depended on the implementation of a large public programme of land reform and water management (drainage of marshes, river flood management and irrigation projects) that would eventually produce an additional 200,000 ha of land and protect another 100,000 until the early 1950s.[49] In fact, these were methods that did not economize on labour, but on land. The agronomists and economists knew that emigration was not an option and that the urban or the industrial economy of Greece was unable to absorb the rural labour surplus.

In the 1930s, the agronomic research and extension services had made significant progress in providing seeds better suited to Greek farms. The Institute for Crop Improvement (IKF) of the Ministry of Agriculture (founded in 1925), headed by John Papadakis, one of the most talented Greek agronomists, specialized in research on seeds. Among many locally produced hybrid seeds, his Γ-32920 has proven to be the most successful.[50] The imported 'Mentana' and 'Canberra' varieties also proved to be instrumental in the growth of wheat yields. A number of institutional interventions had facilitated this development. In 1931 five pilot centres for the Improvement of Wheat Cultivation were founded in five rural counties which specialized in cereal agriculture. They were supposed to act as examples of the best practices in cereal agriculture and to provide assistance and counselling to farmers.[51] One should not exaggerate the short-term impact of any of these initiatives, but it is clear that in the long run their cumulative effect was important. Other such institutes provided additional applied research and extension services in the cultivation of fodder and pulses, and in soil surveys, etc. These institutes generally used the Agricultural Bank to extend their services to farmers: chemical fertilizers, selected seeds, herbicides were distributed through the bank offices, while a denser network of agronomists and veterinary surgeons employed in the agricultural office of each prefecture was meant to offer its services to farmers.

Yields rose substantially before and after the war (Figure 5.1), but it was in the 1950s that the use of chemical fertilizers and selected seeds gave the best results. In 1937, one quarter of the tilled surface was sown with selected imported wheat seed[52] while in 1957, ameliorated selected seeds (half of them being the Γ-32920) were used on three-quarters of the land.[53] Yields rose from 710 kg per hectare in 1927 to 1,010 in 1939 and 1,610 kg per hectare in 1958, while the sown area increased from 498,000 ha in 1927, to 953,000 and to 1.111,000 in 1958. Thanks to the increasing use of chemical fertilizers, fallow was abandoned for more intensive crop rotations. In fact, in 1959 the wheat area peaked and began to decline while yields (and fertilizer consumption) continued to rise with increasing speed.

During the 1930s and the 1950s, the main source of agricultural growth was the more intensive use of land. Then, in the 1960s the sources of growth of Greek agriculture were gradually modified. Fixed capital investment in agriculture (both public and private) rose rapidly, but it did so faster in the 1960s than in the 1950s (see Table 5.3). In the 1960s, the rise in fixed investment was directed mostly to machinery, equipment and the means of transportation, while in the previous decade buildings and land improvement absorbed the largest part of capital outlays. The number and horsepower of tractors grew at a very high annual rate over the whole period 1953–1971. In effect, in the 1960s, capital was more intensively used and this, in conjunction with emigration, finally led to a substantial increase in labour productivity. Meanwhile, in the 1960s the programme of land reclamation had substantially reduced the fragmentation of the small family farms and helped to optimize the use of labour in the countryside. The adoption of labour-saving techniques was clearly related to the rapid decline in the active rural population in the 1960s and 1970s. In the late 1950s, the Greek countryside was still overpopulated and its agriculture mostly labour intensive. A rural exodus had already begun after the war, but it was only in the 1960s that a substantial part of the rural population emigrated to the city or abroad, paving the way for a substantial reconfiguration of farm structure and regional specialization.

As wheat self-sufficiency was finally achieved in the mid-1950s, the government, satisfied with price stabilization and the rise of the yields, had already

Table 5.3 The growth of factors of production in agriculture (1951 = 100)[54]

	Active agricultural population	Cultivated land		Chemical fertilizers (tons)	Fixed investment (in constant drs)			
		Irrigated	Total		Land amendment	Buildings excluding houses	Machinery, equipment and transport	Tractors (HP)
1929		74	100	15				
1953	100[a]	100*	100*	100	100	100	100	100
1962	143**	215	103	208	416	354	726	434
1971	96	328	99	343	805	611	964	1,862
1981	71	398	99	522	277	364	1,912	4,785

[a]1951, *1950, **1961

decided to spend its limited budget investing in the structural transformation of farms rather than in intensifying a policy of income subsidies to poorer farmers through higher guaranteed prices. Having opted to favour industrialization, the basic question was how to facilitate low food prices and low wages, a steady (not 'excessive') flow of rural people to the urban/industrial sector, and a substantial rise in investment in agriculture (in the form of land consolidation, large and small-scale land improvement and irrigation projects, fixed investment in machinery, equipment and construction etc.).[55] Emigration, especially after the bilateral agreement with West Germany in 1961, helped evacuate, in less than ten years, a large part of the latently unemployed labour, mainly originating from mountainous provinces and centres of declining export agriculture (tobacco). This acknowledged that specialization would entail radical regional differentiation and growing income discrepancies between the modernized and highly productive agriculture in the plains and littorals and the stagnating rural economy in the rest of the country.

Conclusion

The first experience of successful public intervention into the market and the production of a major subsistence product – wheat – culminated in the early postwar period when Greece finally achieved nutritional self-sufficiency. This postwar achievement can only be seen as the final result of a radical policy shift towards public intervention in the marketing and production of wheat and later in other basic subsistence crops, which was initiated earlier in the interwar period, when the successive liberal Greek governments, under the pressure of massive population exchange, crushing foreign debts and a disappointing economic performance, were forced to re-enact the wartime experience of control of the market and provision of wheat and flour. Initially, privately owned institutions like the National Bank and its affiliate companies (PAEGA) and the Union of Flour Industrialists were called upon the task. It was after the World Depression, which led to financial default and economic introversion, that the authoritarian royal governments built a more ambitious system of public institutions designed to intervene in the marketing and the production of wheat. This included a comprehensive system of guaranteed prices to producers and of long-term contracts for the industrial processing of the collected wheat. The Agricultural Bank and the National Confederation of Unions of Agricultural Cooperatives (the latter harnessed by the state, through the Agricultural Bank) became the main institutions which took upon themselves the long-term mission of intervention into the market. Other dedicated public institutions of agronomic research and extension services were founded and gradually expanded their influence with the aim of intervening in the production of wheat. They were given a productivist goal (the growth of cereal yields and the intensification of rotations), which was consistent with the labour-intensive factor endowment of the country and the protectionist international environment.

Nutritional self-sufficiency was finally achieved, in the late 1950s, when the countryside was gradually coming under the spell of massive emigration and rural exodus. In the next two decades, this development led to a radical modification in the factor endowments of Greek agriculture, towards a relatively more labour-saving productive structure. It was followed by a decisive and gradual policy shift, away from interwar interventionism and protectionism, towards a more market-friendly orientation, fully compatible with the strategic choice made at the same time to push for association with the European Communities.

Notes

* This research, hosted on the Institute for Mediterranean Studies/FoRTH, was co-financed by the Hellenic Republic and the European Union–European Regional Development Fund, in the context of the OP Competitiveness and Entrepreneurship (OPC II) and the ROP Attica, ROP Macedonia–Thrace (programme regions at the centre of development). I feel obliged to thank George Gassias for his cooperation in bibliographic and archival research and Carin Martiin for her valuable comments and helpful suggestions.
1 Socrates Petmezas, 'Agriculture and economic development in Greece, 1870–1973', in Pedro Lains and Vicente Pinilla (eds), *Agriculture and Economic Development in Europe since 1870*, London and New York: Routledge, 2009, pp. 353–374.
2 Costas Kostis, *Αγροτική Οικονομία και Γεωργική Τράπεζα. Όψεις της ελληνικής οικονομίας στο Μεσοπόλεμο (1919–1928)*, Morphotiko Idryma Ethnikis Trapezas: Athens, 1987, Chapters 7–8.
3 Cf. Giorgos N. Mitrophanis, *Η κίνηση των τιμών του σταριού στην Ελλάδα. Εξωτερικό εμπόριο και κρατική παρέμβαση (1860–1912)*, Morphotiko Idryma Ethnikis Trapezas: Athens, 1991, pp. 74–84.
4 Taxation and tariffs were primarily destined to cover the financial exigencies of the state budget in 19th-century Greece and should not be seen as instruments of a rational developmental policy aiming at economic growth. In that sense Cameralism rather than Liberalism was the predominant economic theory behind the decisions of the 19th-century Greek governments, see Michalis Psalidopoulos, 'Οικονομική σκέψη και πολιτικές', in Costas Kostis and Socrates Petmezas (eds), *Η ανάπτυξη της Ελληνικής Οικονομίας τον 19ο αιώνα*, Alexandreia Publications: Athens, 2006, pp. 337–377.
5 Alexis Franghiadis, 'Land tenure systems, peasant agriculture and bourgeois ascendancy in Greece', Ehdem Eldem and Socrates Petmezas (eds), *The Economic Development of Southeastern Europe in the 19th Century*, Alpha Bank Historical Archive: Athens, 2011, pp. 101–135; Socrates Petmezas, *Προλεγόμενα στην ιστορία της ελληνικής αγροτικής οικονομίας του Μεσοπολέμου*, Alexandreia Publications: Athens, 2012, pp. 165–182.
6 Socrates Petmezas, 'El comercio de la pasa de Corinto y su influencia sobre la economía griega del siglo XIX (1840-1914)', in José Morilla-Critz et al. (eds) *Impactos exteriores sobre el mundo rural mediterráneo: del imperio romano a nuestros días*, Ministerio de l'Agricoltura: Madrid, 1997, pp. 523–562.
7 Dimitris Panayiotopoulos, *Γεωργική εκπαίδευση και ανάπτυξη. Η Ανώτατη Γεωπονική Σχολή Αθηνών στην Ελληνική Κοινωνία, 1920–1960*, Ellinika Grammata: Athens, 2004.
8 Violetta Hionidou, *Famine and Death in Occupied Greece, 1941–1944*, Cambridge University Press: Cambridge and New York, 2006.
9 Spyros Chassiotis (*Η σιτάρκεια της χώρας. Μέτρα ριζικά και μέτρα πρόχειρα και δυνατά σήμερον. Πώς θα σωθώμεν εκ της σιτοδείας*, Athens, 1917, p. 9) considered that the

average cereal consumption was 230 kg per capita. Panagiotis Gennadios (*Μέτρα δια την σιτάρκειαν της χώρας*, Vassiliki Georgiki Etaireia: Athens, 1917, p. 9) gives a relatively lower estimate of 205 kg per capita. In the immediate postwar period, it has been estimated that the rural population consumed 200 kg of cereals per capita, while the urban population 91–104 kg, see *Σίτος: προκαταρκτική εισήγησις*, Epitropi Ereunis kai Organoseos Oikonomikou Programmatismou-Vasiki Epitropi Protogenous Paragogis, vol. II: Athens 1959, pp. 97–98.

10 I have calculated the estimated wheat consumption in Greece by adding production and net imports of wheat and flour. I have also added net imports of grain and flour of other cereals as well (they are usually insignificant in size). The estimated annual volume of cereal production are published in George Kostelenos, Socrates Petmezas *et al.*, *Ακαθάριστο Εγχώριο Προϊόν 1830–1939*, Morphotiko Idryma Ethnikis Trapezas-KEPE: Athens, 2007, Table 2–I in accompanying CD–ROM. Data on exports were collected from the annual publication of the Greek Foreign trade (1858–1940). In the interwar, one-fifth of the production of barley and four-fifths of the production of maize and sorghum were consumed by men (mostly by the farmers themselves), the rest being used as fodder crop, see Chryssos Evelpidis, *Η γεωργία της Ελλάδος: οικονομική και κοινωνική άποψις*, Logos: Athens, 1944, p. 90. For a comparable estimate, see *Σίτος: προκαταρκτική εισήγησις*, Athens, 1959, p. 97 ff.

11 *Σίτος: προκαταρκτική εισήγησις*, pp. 95–97.
12 Gennadios, *Μέτρα δια την σιτάρκειαν της χώρας*.
13 *Υπόμνημα του Θεσσαλικού Γεωργικού Συλλόγου περί ενισχύσεως της σιτοπαραγωγής*, Larissa, 1904, pp. 10–12.
14 The bank was the majority shareholder of the Privileged Anonymous Society of General Warehouses, which controlled the largest share of storing and warehousing facilities in Greece until well into the postwar period. PAEGA had already played a leading role in the regulation of the currant surplus production.
15 George Leon, *Greece and the First World War: From Neutrality to Intervention, 1917–1918*, Columbia University Press: Boulder, CO, pp. 163–184.
16 Theodosios Melas, *Δια την αύξησιν της παραγωγής του σίτου*, Athens, 1921, p. 33.
17 On the disappointing inefficiency and endemic corruption of the Greek public servants employed in this ministry, cf. Leon, *Greece and the First World War*, pp. 168–173.
18 s.v. George Kofinas, 'Επισιτισμός', in *Μεγάλη Ελληνική Εγκυκλοπαίδεια*, Athens, vol. 11, 1931, pp. 413–414.
19 Mark Mazower, *Greece and the Inter-War Economic Crisis*, Clarendon Press: Oxford and New York, 1991, pp. 100–112.
20 Petmezas, *Προλεγόμενα*, pp. 157–158.
21 Petmezas, *Προλεγόμενα*, pp. 136–141.
22 *Τα μέτρα προς επαύξησιν της εγχωρίου σιτοπαραγωγής. Τεύχος πρώτον: Εισήγησις και γνωμοδότησις*, Ethniko Typografeio: Athens, 1934, p. 24; *Τα μέτρα προς επαύξησιν της εγχωρίου σιτοπαραγωγής. Τεύχος δεύτερον: Υπομνήματα ειδικών*, Ethniko Typografeio: Athens, p.15; Babis Alivizatos, *Κράτος και γεωργική πολιτική*, Ethniko Typografeio: Athens, 1938, pp. 370–371; *Επί του γεωργικού προβλήματος της χώρας: (γνωμοδοτήσεις-εισηγήσεις-εκθέσεις)*, Pyrsos: Athens, 1939, pp. 173–174.
23 *Τα μέτρα προς επαύξησιν της εγχωρίου σιτοπαραγωγής. Τεύχος δεύτερον*, p. 14; *Επί του γεωργικού προβλήματος της χώρας*, pp. 181–182.
24 In an agricultural economy endowed with limited land and plentiful rural labour, and without a substantial demand for labour from the urban sector, the rise of labour productivity was an economic impossibility. As a result, all efforts went towards maximizing yields and the cash returns to the land and minimizing cost per unit area, Nikolaos Anagnostopoulos, *Σιτοκαλλιέργεια και σιτάρκεια εν Ελλάδι*, Elliniki Georgiki Etaireia: Athens, 1930, p. 31.

25 Mazower, *Greece and the Inter-War Economic Crisis*, pp. 88–91.
26 Agreement of 27/08/1927, see *Τα μέτρα προς επαύξησιν της εγχωρίου σιτοπαραγωγής. Τεύχος πρώτον*, pp. 24– 25. The Treasury guaranteed that it would cover all losses of the National Bank.
27 On the applied research institutes of the Ministry of Agriculture and other such institutions, see *Γεωργική έρευνα, Epitropi Ereunis kai Organoseos Oikonomikou Programmatismou-Vasiki Epitropi Protogenous Paragogis*, vol. II: Athens, 1959.
28 Data for Figure 5.2: *Αγροτική Τράπεζα Ελλάδος. Το έργον μιας δεκαετίας (1930-1939)*, Athens, 1940, pp. 121– 122; *Επί του γεωργικού προβλήματος της χώρας*, pp. 177–178; Aristidis Klimis, *Η αγροτική οικονομία προ και μετά την ίδρυσιν της ATE: Εξελίξις 1924–1954, διαρθρώσεις-προβλήματα, κατευθύνσεις*, Athens, 1961, p. 102.
29 On the income crisis of the interwar agriculture in Greece, see Kostis, *Αγροτική Οικονομία και Γεωργική Τράπεζα*, pp. 131–139.
30 Petmezas, *Προλεγόμενα*, pp. 370–380.
31 In fact, cooperatives had always been under the indirect control of banks that were active in agriculture (the National Bank, initially, and then the Agricultural Bank) since they were the most efficient way to reduce the transaction costs of agricultural credit, cf. Kostis, *Αγροτική Οικονομία και Γεωργική Τράπεζα*, pp. 185–194; Petmezas, *Προλεγόμενα*, pp. 212–215.
32 Alivizatos, *Κράτος και γεωργική πολιτική*, pp. 379–380; George Daskalou, *Από την διαρκή ανάπτυξη στην χρεωκοπίαν της ΚΥΔΕΠ και στην κάμψη της ελληνικής γεωργίας*, Sygchroni Ekdotiki: Athens, 2003, p. 255; *Σίτος: προκαταρκτική εισήγησις*, p. 116.
33 On the foundation of the Agricultural Bank and its role, see Petmezas, *Προλεγόμενα*, pp. 208–212.
34 Agricultural Bank of Greece, *Αγροτική Τράπεζα Ελλάδος, Το έργον μιας δεκαετίας (1930–1939)*, Athens, 1940, pp. 121–122 (on financing KEPES to buy wheat at guaranteed prices) and pp. 199–201 (on the number of its branch offices).
35 Daskalou, *Από την διαρκή ανάπτυξη στην χρεωκοπίαν*, pp. 27–28; Evelpidis, *Η γεωργία της Ελλάδος*, p. 153.
36 Mark Mazower, *Inside Hitler's Greece: The Experience of Occupation, 1941–1944*, Yale University Press: New Haven, CT, 1993, Chapter 3 (pp. 64–67).
37 Daskalou, *Από την διαρκή ανάπτυξη στην χρεωκοπίαν*, pp. 28–29.
38 On grain production in Greece, during the German and Italian Occupation, and on the struggle for control over its consumption by the Quisling government, the different armed resistance organizations and the British military mission, see Giannis Skalidakis, *Η Ελεύθερη Ελλάδα. Η εξουσία του ΕΑΜ στα χρόνια της Κατοχής (1943-1944)*, Asini Publ.: Athens, 2014.
39 On the British rationing system and its perseverance until 1952, see Chapter 6.
40 Until February 1948, flour mills were effectively taken over by the government, which only paid a rent, proportional to the volume of wheat milled, to their owners. From March 1948, and for the next five years, the management of the flour industries was given back to their owners who were paid a fixed fee for every ton of imported or collected domestic wheat milled. They were supposed to produce a certain volume of flour for every ton of wheat received and allowed to keep the product exceeding the minimum output. The flour received by the public administration was either sold at low prices to the bakers or distributed to small-owner and impoverished farmers to complement their income deficit, s.v. S. Zymarakos, 'Αλευροβιομηχανία', *Οικονομική και Λογιστική Εγκυκλοπαίδεια*, vol. 1, Athens, p. 83.
41 On the impact of the Marshall Plan and free American aid, see cf. [Roger Lapham] *Το σχέδιον Μάρσαλ στην Ελλάδα: Ο πλήρης απολογισμός της βοηθείας του σχεδιασμού Μάρσαλ προς την Ελλάδα: Ιούλιος 1948– Ιανουάριος 1952*, Athens 1952, pp. 99–102. More generally on the Marshall Plan in Greece, see George Stathakis, *Το δόγμα Τρούμαν και το σχέδιο Μάρσαλ Η ιστορία της αμερικανικής βοήθειας στην Ελλάδα*, Athens, 2004.

42 Angeliki Laiou, 'Population movements in the Greek countryside during the civil war', in Lars Baerentzen *et al.* (eds) *Studies in the History of the Greek Civil War, 1945–1949*, Museum Tusculanum Press: Copenhagen, 1987, pp. 55–104.
43 Flour industries long remained under a regime of lenient supervision and speculative corruption, and were repeatedly accused of profiteering from an inefficient and mismanaged regime of routine provision of collected wheat at predictably low prices, cf. *Προβλήματα της πολιτικής σίτου*, EBEA: Athens, October 1958, pp. 25–28.
44 *Σίτος: προκαταρκτική εισήγησις*, pp. 121–129.
45 *Προβλήματα της πολιτικής σίτου*, pp. 29–30.
46 The main introduction in the official and authoritative 'Memorandum on the growth of domestic wheat output' prepared by Al Kouklelis, head of a special committee of the High Economic Council, following a specific request by the prime minister, Eleutherios Venizelos, makes no reference to the need for a rise in labour productivity or in economic efficiency. He only addressed the questions of expanding the tilled area and raising yields, cf. *Τα μέτρα προς επαύξησιν της εγχωρίου σιτοπαραγωγής: Τεύχος πρώτον*, p. 11.
47 For the debate in 1931–1932, between the aged George Kyriakos, later the Minister of Agriculture in Metaxas government, and John Papadakis, young and brilliant agronomist in charge of the Institute for Crop Improvement, on the question whether state policy should favour wheat self-sufficiency or the expansion of speculative agricultural products, see Mazower, *Greece and the Inter-War Economic Crisis*, pp. 241–250.
48 Chassiotis, *Η σιτάρκεια της χώρας*; *Τα μέτρα προς επαύξησιν της εγχωρίου σιτοπαραγωγής. Τεύχος πρώτον*, pp. 15–16; *Τα μέτρα προς επαύξησιν της εγχωρίου σιτοπαραγωγής: Τεύχος δεύτερον*, pp. 19–21.
49 Petmezas, *Προλεγόμενα*, pp. 243–245.
50 *Σίτος: προκαταρκτική εισήγησις*, pp. 42–43.
51 *Τα μέτρα προς επαύξησιν της εγχωρίου σιτοπαραγωγής. Τεύχος δεύτερον*, pp. 25–48; Epaminondas Kypriadis, *Η οργάνωσις της σιτοπαραγωγής μας Επιτακτική ανάγκη επιστημονικωτέρας και εντονωτέρας εργασίας. Μελέτη*, Athens, 1931; Alivizatos, *Κράτος και γεωργική πολιτική*, pp. 348–350.
52 Alivizatos, *Κράτος και γεωργική πολιτική*, pp. 338–342.
53 *Σίτος: προκαταρκτική εισήγησις*, p. 44.
54 Petmezas, *Προλεγόμενα*, Tables 6.10–6.13.
55 Petmezas, *Προλεγόμενα*, pp. 283–298.

6 British agriculture in transition
Food shortages to food surpluses, 1947–1957

John Martin

The period 1947 to 1957 constitutes a period of profound change in the state's relationship with agriculture. The Labour Party which, in the General Election of July 1945, had secured an overwhelming majority in the House of Commons, initially continued with the wartime system of controls and directives. This was a prelude to the 1947 Agriculture Act, landmark legislation which committed the government to ensuring 'stability and efficiency' for British farmers. For the first time since the imposition of the Corn Laws in 1815, the government had decided to protect British agriculture from foreign competition in peacetime. This was accompanied a few months later by the introduction of a five-year plan, which further increased guaranteed prices and laid the foundations for what critics had considered the 'feather bedding' of farmers. The return of the Conservatives to power in 1951 led to a fundamental shift in this approach, with food rationing and the other controls administered by the Ministry of Food being gradually dismantled in favour of re-establishing pre-war Marketing Boards, and radically reforming the system of state support. This was followed, in 1957, by a new Agriculture Act which transformed the system of state support in line with the Conservatives' prevailing free market philosophy. Given these significant shifts in policy directives, it is tempting to endorse the narrative that the explanation for these changes reflects the fundamentally different ideological aspirations of the Labour and Conservative administrations.

An alternative scenario implied by Michael Tracy is that these differences are more explicable in terms of the international food situation, that it was the immediate postwar food shortages that compelled the Labour government to treat farmers in the way it did.[1] Even by 1947/48, more than two years after the end of military hostilities, world food production was still 7 per cent below its pre-war levels.[2] Extrapolating this line of argument would suggest that it was the more abundant supply of food and the emergence of potential surpluses in the 1950s which explains the Conservative government's more benign approach to increasing agricultural production. According to this interpretation, both Labour and Conservative attitudes to agriculture were a pragmatic response to the extent to which food shortages or surpluses prevailed. This chapter will reappraise this prevailing narrative. In particular, its focus will be the 1947 Agriculture Act, the postwar agricultural expansion programme, the impact of the 1947 winter and the reasons for the Conservative government's new approach to agriculture which culminated in the 1957 Agriculture Act.

The Labour government and the 1947 Agriculture Act

Following the General Election of 1945, the Labour Party, headed by Clement Attlee, had been swept to power on the back of a populace keen for social reform, and the desire for a better and more egalitarian society. Consequently, its programme of reform included the establishment of the Welfare State and the nationalisation of the 'commanding heights of the British economy'. Under the circumstances it was not surprising that the Labour government wanted not only to retain but to build upon the control over agricultural markets which had prevailed during the Second World War.[3]

After the cessation of Lend-lease which, until VJ Day, had effectively bridged the gap in the British accounts, the newly elected Labour government rapidly found itself heavily dependent on massive dollar loans to sustain its balance of payments. In 1945, Britain had an unprecedented current account deficit amounting to £10,000 million.[4] In contrast, exports amounted to little more than 30 per cent of their pre-war levels, while shipping earnings had been substantially diminished. In terms of the country's capital account, about one quarter of its pre-war investments had been sold, with large debts having been accumulated in the form of sterling balances. Keynes considered the country's position similar to that of a 'financial Dunkirk'.[5] The ensuing crisis brought the pound under constant attack, causing industrial production to fall and construction to be virtually suspended.[6]

While the overall impact on the balance of payments was anticipated by the government, the way lend-lease was abruptly terminated was more of a shock; even more surprising was the dollar shortage caused by the difficulty of securing a loan from America. The initial idea that funds would be provided as a free gift was gradually and rather begrudgingly replaced with the acceptance that it would take the form of an interest-free loan to a loan-bearing interest. According to the Chancellor of the Exchequer, Hugh Dalton, these terms were then replaced by 'strings so tight that they might strangle our trade and, indeed, our whole economic life'.[7]

The Labour government had little option but to embark on an export drive while at the same time restricting domestic consumption by intensifying wartime rationing controls, particularly those on food, nearly 50 per cent of which still originated from overseas. In stark contrast to the post First World War crisis, when world food surpluses had led to unprecedented collapse of agricultural prices in 1921, immediately after the Second World War, food shortages now prevailed. These shortages and high prices made it even problematic for Britain to import food, even if the necessary finances could be found.

The postwar food shortages primarily reflected the fact that world agriculture, with the exception of North America, had been acutely disrupted by the prolonged military conflict. It was, however, the convertibility crisis of 1947 which resulted from a run on the pound sterling, which was convertible into dollars. In a desperate attempt to protect Britain's currency reserves, the government restricted the imports of a wide range of items, including meat and wheat.[8]

The outcome was that, by 1947, food consumption patterns in Britain were not only considerably worse than those during the food shortages and rationing controls of the Second World War, but even those of the depressed conditions of the late 1930s. Rations of meat, bacon and ham as well as fats were reduced to all-time lows, well below those which had prevailed during the darkest days of the Second World War. According to research undertaken by Ina Zweiniger-Bargielowska, the average daily calorie intake of an individual had declined from 3,275 calories in 1937 to 2,307 in 1947.[9] As the Minister of Food in 1945 had claimed, 'The Ministry would be responsible for the procurement and subsequent distribution of all foods of importance in the national diet, and for the operation of such modified controls as might be necessary to reform the system of food distribution.'[10] Given the prevailing food shortages it was, therefore, considered that producers did not need the protection they had enjoyed under the Marketing Board system which had prevailed in the 1930s, when food surpluses were the order of the day. In Labour circles there was also the lingering fear that if they were to revive the powers of Marketing Boards along their pre-war lines, such a strategy would necessitate fundamental changes in government policy and allow the boards, which they considered to be producer controlled, to become an integral and permanent part of the system of state support.[11]

Following on from the widely acclaimed success of the wartime state-directed food production campaign, which had saved the country from the malnutrition and starvation which had engulfed many of the other combatants, it was not surprising that the wartime system of the state control of agriculture should be continued in peacetime.[12]

In spite of the fact that the Labour government decided not to implement its historic commitment to land nationalisation, its agricultural policy enshrined in the 1947 Agriculture Act still represented a major departure for farming in peacetime. This Act was considered one of the most significant reforms in the national protection of agriculture, the rationale for its implementation being an integral part of the Labour's government policy of social reform and, in particular, the creation of the modern welfare state.[13] The last major effort to protect British farming from foreign competition during peacetime had been the introduction of the 1815 Corn Laws. With the exception of the First World War period and its immediate aftermath, when the state had control in peacetime, agriculture had continued to be exposed to external free markets forces (rapidly decreasing its value and role within the food production system of the United Kingdom).

The Labour administration embarked upon an agricultural policy whereby the private sector was sponsored, rather than being directed by the state, through a complex system of assured markets and guaranteed prices. The 1947 Agriculture Act was specifically intended to provide 'a sure and sound foundation for the industry and for future production of the food which was needed',[14] concentrating on two key pillars of improvement – production and price protection of agricultural produce. As a result, farmers were ensured of guaranteed prices for their produce, the levels of which were regularly reviewed, through a process of negotiation with the National Farmers' Union, known as the annual farm price review. Initially, these discussions were dominated by the objective of ensuring food security for Britain, with the emphasis on the maximization of production as the principal goal of agricultural policy.[15]

It was the financial legacy of the war which at this time severely constrained the policy options open to the Attlee government, ensuring that it was more or less inevitable that it would be forced to control imports, promote exports and to seek aid from the US. The alternative to seeking such support was what Keynes deemed 'starvation corner' and involved radical reductions in civilian consumption levels, but this was not feasible on political grounds. However, there had been considerable scope for alternatives. The balance of payments problem was not simply one of being able to pay for essential imports. An important issue was that of the scale of government overseas expenditure and the level of foreign investment. The extent of the country's overseas expenditure was, and still remains, a controversial issue. According to Keynes, imports were being efficiently controlled; the problem was that 'the current and prospective demands upon us for politically and military expenditure overseas have already gone far beyond the figure which can, on any hypothesis be sustained'.[16]

While the extent of the country's overseas commitments was widely debated, both by the Labour Party and Parliament, the level of overseas investments was not widely known, and therefore not subjected to political scrutiny. It was not until Cairncross's seminal work that the significance of this was finally appreciated. His analysis showed that between 1947 and 1949, capital outflow amounted to £1,500m, significantly in excess of the amount received from the American loan. Indeed, in 1947, the figure was £643 million. As Cairncross was subsequently to lament, 'Given the straits to which the British economy was reduced in 1947, when it was necessary to ration even bread and potatoes, an outflow of capital equal to about 8 per cent of national income … is an extraordinary event, it was certainly not the purpose for which the American and Canadian loans were procured.'[17] There was, though, reluctance within government circles to heed Keynes's warning about the implications of Britain's efforts to retain its position as a great power in the world, even though these reservations were, in principle, supported by a paper compiled by the Balance of Payments Working Party.[18] Concerns about the gravity of the impending crisis were also noted in the (unpublished) Economic

Survey for 1946, and the normally restrained reports produced by the Bank of England.[19] Under the circumstances, it is not surprising that the tenure of Attlee's government is best remembered as a paradoxical period, particularly in terms of the ways its euphoria for reform was juxtaposed with its drab, demoralising and increasingly stringent austerity measures.

Given the prevailing official constraints on agricultural imports, farmers were in a particularly favourable position in terms of their bargaining power. Collectively, they could literally have held the country or, to be more precise, the newly elected Labour Party, to ransom. Whether or not this would have materialised in practice is a moot point, but it was certainly perceived by some in the Labour Party that it was essential to keep the farmers on side. As the 1947 Agriculture Act noted:

> The following provisions of this part of the Act shall have effect for the purpose of promoting and maintaining, by the provision of guaranteed prices and assured markets for the produce mentioned in the first schedule of this Act, stable and efficient agricultural industry capable of producing such part of the nation's food and other agricultural produce as in the national interest it is desirable to produce in the United Kingdom, and of producing it at minimum prices consistently with proper remuneration and living conditions for farmers and workers in agriculture and an adequate return on the capital invested in the industry.[20]

More importantly, it was accepted that the annual price-fixing arrangements for agricultural commodities, which were an integral part of the legislation, were to be determined in the negotiations taking place exclusively between the officials and the representatives of the farming interest. There was no attempt to incorporate the interests or views of the agricultural workers.

The legislation provided guaranteed prices and was designed to encourage farmers to increase production. However, the 1947 Act enhanced the power of the government in the price-fixing system by specifying that these were to be determined 'by a Minister ... in the light of the Minister's conclusions from reviews'.[21] While this in theory allowed for a degree of flexibility in price changes, it meant that in practice the Marketing Boards had little control over pricing policy, even in respect of the individual commodities for which they were responsible. As a result, while they might offer advice, they could not enact change without the support of the Minister of Agriculture.

One of the most important consequences of wartime control and the 1947 Agriculture Act was its impact on the farming community. According to the Farmers' Rights Association, during the wartime state-directed food production campaign, a new morality had emerged, transforming the yeomen of Britain, the traditional custodians of the countryside, into 'yesmen' who were concerned with short-term economic advantage and unquestioning compliance.[22] While there is clearly a degree of exaggeration in this rather simplified and generalised view, there is little doubt that the experience of wartime control did ensure that farmers were considerably more responsive to the directives issued by the state. During the war, farmers had been expected to endorse without question the official orthodoxy of high input farming. This was further underpinned with the 1947 Act, which had directly linked the amount of state support each farmer received to the level of output and productivity of their farm. Farmers were, in effect, encouraged to become technical specialists, implementing the most economically effective ways of maximising food production.

An important but isolated exception to this general trend was promulgated by Eve Balfour, whose seminal work, *The Living Soil*, first published in 1943, subsequently came to be regarded as the classic contemporary text of the organic movement.[23] However, it was not until the 1970s that organic farming finally began to be considered a serious alternative to the high output, high input system of farming which had evolved in response to the food shortages of the Second World War and its aftermath. Indeed, the leading authority on the subject, Philip Conford, has shown that the war was essentially a major setback to those who desired to promote organic farming.[24]

In explaining the motives for the Labour Party's sympathetic treatment of farmers, it is tempting, but not completely convincing, to endorse Self and Storing's view that this reflected the Labour government's belief that this strategy would enhance their political support in rural constituencies which had historically returned Conservative candidates. Their analysis suggests that there were nearly fifty rural constituencies dominated by the farming interest, where a relatively small swing in favour of the Labour party would ensure that their candidate was elected. As Desmond Donnelly, MP was subsequently to lament, 'we have sold our birthright to the land [common as opposed to private ownership of the land] for a mess of pottage, and we have not had the pottage so far'.[25]

A more convincing explanation is that the support for agriculture was a reflection of the prevailing food shortages and the fear that, unless the farmers were kept on board in supporting the agricultural expansion programme, the impact of possible food shortages on the electorate would have been catastrophic for the future aspirations of the Labour government. By 1947, the food supply situation was even more precarious than it had been during the war. In 1946, the Labour government had rationed bread, a strategy which Churchill had refused to even contemplate during the Second World War and which had last been implemented in 1802. These reforms, and the change in the relationship between the state and agriculture that occurred as a result of them, were influenced by a number of factors, the most overlooked being the impact of the 1947 winter. In Britain, the food situation was so desperate that, in July 1946, the Labour government had taken the unprecedented step of rationing bread in peacetime.[26] Such a policy was not, however, simply a response to the prevailing shortage of food but, as Zweiniger-Bargielowska has shown, an attempt to draw America's attention to the country's precarious financial position as a result of the Second World War.[27]

The 1947 winter

One of the key factors contributing to the difficulties experienced by the Labour government was the abnormally bad winter of 1947, which is commonly regarded as a major watershed or 'annus horrendous' in the career of the postwar Labour government. As Hugh Dalton, the Chancellor of the Exchequer, noted in his memoirs, the fuel crisis which accompanied the winter constituted 'certainly the first really heavy blow to confidence in the Government and in our post war plans. This soon began to show itself in many different and unwelcome ways. Never glad, confident morning again.'[28] The Minister of Agriculture, Tom Williams, who was more personally involved in the food crisis, described it as 'as a disaster of the first magnitude'.[29]

The winter of 1947 was considered by historians to be one of the worst winters of the twentieth century, only to be rivalled by the weather experienced during the winter of 1962–63. Robertson concurred with this viewpoint in his work *The Bleak Midwinter, 1947*, stating that it 'constituted a kind of crisis … making that winter a strong contender among meteorologists for the title of the worst winter on record'.[30] The first three months of 1947 represent one of the most severe spells of weather experienced in this country since possibly the early seventeenth century. Following the first snowfalls on 22 January and the initial cold spell of the weekend of 24–26 January 1947, the period through February and into the middle of March established a number of weather records which stand today, despite subsequent inclement periods during the early part of 1963 and 1979, and December 1981 to January 1982. One of the most depressing of these records was the never-ending dullness, with the vast majority of British inhabitants being denied the merest glimpse of the sun for virtually all of February. The effects of the cold were compounded by a severe wind-chill factor, and snowfalls were not only prolonged and extensive, but also deep by normal standards.[31]

Essentially, the bad winter of 1947 highlighted the fragile nature of the farming infrastructure. As a result of the freezing conditions which made it difficult to riddle potatoes stored in outside clamps and to transport them to urban centres, not only were there widespread potato shortages, but in some areas distributors were forced to implement a quasi-rationing scheme.[32] Canada's export of bacon and pig meat to Britain increased to around 3,140,000,000 pounds to support the large loss in production occurring due to the poor weather across Europe.[33] Self and Storing concluded that, without clear incentives to produce, farmers could essentially hold the country to ransom in times of poor harvests through threats of reducing production if prices did not favour them, particularly in times of crisis like 1947 when food production was at an all-time low. The reduced levels of agricultural output due to the 1947 winter had a profound impact on the Labour administration. Faced with the possibility that food shortages could completely destabilise their regime, price increases were agreed by the Cabinet with the intention of stimulating production and getting results immediately.[34] In the case of potatoes, for example, a 6 per cent increase was granted, while other cereals also received increases. Not surprisingly, the most generous increases were given to hill sheep farmers who had borne the brunt of the winter.[35]

Another factor of a more international nature was pivotal in altering the relationship between the state and agriculture within Britain in the late 1940s – namely, the international food shortages that were occurring within Western Europe and across North America. Evidence of these shortages can be seen within a House of Commons Debate, in which a Member of Parliament sums up the production of food across Europe, stating 'we are living in an age of shortage, and these shortages will continue for some considerable time', going on to highlight that American production of wheat had dropped to only 40 per cent of its pre-war total.[36] This equated to food production totals being lower in 1947 than that of pre-First World War levels, which by December 1947 had arrived at what *The Times* described as 'worrying' levels creating 'fears' over a potential period of extended malnutrition due to low production.[37]

Therefore, it can be seen that these shortages prompted a drastic need to reform the agricultural system for benefits in production, as without this it would bring a further severity not only to the country's food intake but also to the dollar crisis. Evidence to support the presence of this realisation among British politicians at the time can be seen within this debate on 6 December 1947, in which MPs noted that without an increase in food production 'more dollars will have to be spent to keep the country going', indicating a realisation of the severity of the situation.[38] Following Hugh Dalton's resignation in the autumn of 1947, he was succeeded by the more austere Stafford Cripps, who enforced a further reduction in domestic consumption in an effort to boost exports by allowing Britain to trade itself out of the crisis and to stabilise the pound sterling.[39] Under these circumstances it was essential to restrict, as far as possible, the importations of high priced feeding stuffs which had to be paid for using scarce dollars.

In spite of the country's wartime efforts to increase food production, it was still a considerable way short of self-sufficiency with regard to fats, meat, grain and dairy products. The sterling area, which effectively meant the empire, could alleviate some of these difficulties without draining Britain's precarious dollar reserves, but fats had to be acquired from non-sterling sources, of which the United States was the most important supplier. In an attempt to alleviate this situation, the government developed plans for draconian rationing restrictions on civilian diets. Anticipating a tough winter, coupled with the prevailing food situation in Europe and America, John Strachey, the Minister of Food, emphasised that enforcement of food orders was 'of terrific importance to this country' in securing Marshall Aid as a precondition of the recovery programme.'[40] There was little improvement even after after the introduction of Marshall Aid in 1948 and the devaluation of 1949. These external considerations, coupled with Labour's commitment to achieving full employment and maintaining the greater social equality achieved during the war, gave the Attlee government little option, in spite of its unpopularity, but to continue with food rationing. In an effort to at least partly alleviate the food shortages, the government embarked upon a plan to encourage further increases in agricultural output by increasing agricultural prices in excess of those already granted by the Agriculture Act 1947.

The Five Year Expansion Plan

A second important agricultural reform introduced by the Labour government in the late 1940s, which was said by Whetham to have altered the farmers' relationship with the state, was the Five Year Plan.[41] Its key aim was to increase food production.[42] Higher outputs of meat, eggs and milk by around 20 per cent were intended to provide both a stable supply of food and higher incomes that could then be used in the further restoration of the farming infrastructure. The House of Commons debate noted that this was estimated to be around £40 million per annum.[43]

The plan worked on the basis of the 1947 Agriculture Act by attempting to increase prices of goods through a chain system, beginning with what was known as 'fodder goods'. This would increase meat product prices in the attempt to raise production among farmers through the appeal of increased revenue.[44] Farmers would be encouraged to take advantage of the grants and subsidies which had been put in place through the 1947 Act. It would remedy what Self and Storing had identified as the unwillingness of farmers to borrow money from banks.[45]

The plan was successful and, importantly, it can be seen as a direct result of the 1947 winter, as these subsidies were put in place to keep farmers on the side of the state. With higher, more generous prices came the appeal of increased production and the elimination of the possibility of refusal to produce in times of crisis among the agricultural community. But the benefits of higher prices were not really that substantial. Whetham notes that some of the additional money was diverted into personal consumption rather than infrastructure improvements.[46]

By the end of June 1947 the Agricultural (Emergency Payments) Bill, intended to authorise measures for the relief of farms which had suffered loss from blizzards and floods, received its second reading without a division in the House of Commons.[47] Acreage payments and hill sheep subsidies were to be paid as quickly as possible, while in addition it was proposed that hill sheep farmers, if they desired, should receive an advance on their 1948 subsidy payments. In order to alleviate the effects of reduced numbers of livestock on farms during the next two to three years, the subsidy was to be paid not on the number of sheep on the holdings at the end of each year, but on the numbers retained on the farm in December 1946 before the blizzards struck.

The introduction of higher prices for agricultural produce precipitated an infamous speech by Stanley Evans, MP, Parliamentary Secretary to the Minister of Food, in April 1950, when he accused British farmers of being 'feather bedded'. Not only did he argue that farmers were receiving considerably higher prices for their produce, but that inefficient, high cost producers were now able to survive free from the threat of dispossession.[48] His allegations received short shrift from the Labour government who rapidly dismissed him from office.[49] The 1949 Agricultural Marketing Act expanded on the 1947 legislation, implementing some of the recommended changes in legislation proposed by the Lucas Committee Report. The Act focused on 'regularising and encouraging the formation of producer boards and by providing an alternative much milder device for safeguarding the public interest'.[50] These producer boards, while very similar to the Marketing Boards of the 1930s, were to be controlled by the Minister of Agriculture, who had the power to refuse the legislation proposed. This was in order to enable the 'Minister to consider the matter before a board takes action which might conceivably be contrary to the public interest.'[51] These producer boards also had to accept the appointment of one-fifth of the members of each board by the Minister in the hope of keeping consumer interests involved when drafting agricultural marketing policy.[52]

While the 1949 Act did not endorse the main proposal of the Lucas Commission — namely, to remove government from the day-to-day issues of agricultural marketing policy, the changes implemented were an important step in re-establishing the powers of the Marketing Boards. The Labour government continued to resist the re-establishment of the powers of the marketing boards, but this had the effect of alienating both the Farmers Union and the Marketing Boards. This was particularly evident in terms of the return of the Milk Marketing Board's powers. According to Major Guy Lloyd, MP for Renfrewshire East, 'many millions of pounds could be saved to the taxpayer if this was done, that, generally speaking, distribution would be better and prices lower, or is this just another Social theory being persisted in'.[53]

Return of the Conservatives to power

The 1950 General Election resulted in the return of the Labour Party to power, but its 146 majority in the 1945 General Election had now been reduced to a mere 3.[54] Difficulties in governing with such a small majority and the ongoing conflict in Korea compelled Attlee to call another election in October 1951, with the result that Churchill's Conservative government was returned to power. This erosion of support was, to a significant extent, the inevitable reflection of the electorate's disillusionment with the on-going period of austerity and continued rationing of food in particular. The Conservatives had campaigned on the policy of 'set the people free' from the bureaucracy of red tape and officialdom. The Conservative administration quickly lifted quantitative restrictions on food imports and although duties were still in place, these were still at levels established in the 1930s, the value of which had been eroded by postwar levels of inflation.

Like their Labour predecessors, the Conservatives wished to encourage further increases in agricultural production, but their programme to achieve this objective was considerably less ambitious and fundamentally different. The target was to increase net output to 60 per cent above its pre-war level. However, taking into account the expansion which had taken place in the late 1940s, this amounted to a rise of less than 2 per cent per year between 1952 and 1956. Contrary to the Labour administration, the Conservatives declined to set specific targets for individual commodities, instead issuing general guidelines for expansion. It was anticipated that a large part of the increased output was to be achieved by an expansion in beef and sheep production as a result of more efficient use of grassland.[55]

The increase in agricultural output was facilitated by the outbreak of myxomatosis in 1953 which devastated the rabbit population.[56] Measuring the extent to which the decline in the rabbit population contributed to increasing agricultural output is problematic, with estimates varying widely. However, according to the Myxomatosis Advisory Committee, the loss or potential loss to agriculture and forestry was between £45 and £60 million each year.[57]

Another factor in 1953 was the re-emergence of the pre-war Marketing Boards, such as the Milk Marketing Board. By this time, however, milk output was already exceeding demand, with surplus production, as in the past, being diverted to the manufacturing sector. As a result, the government imposed standard quantities in order to limit Exchequer liability. Other Marketing Boards, such as the Potato Board, were also re-established in 1953 in an effort to disseminate more productive and efficient methods. It is tempting to endorse the proposition that this shift in approach simply reflected an ideological stance on the part of the Conservative administration. However, it was also motivated by pragmatic considerations and, in particular, changes in the international food situation. Following the end of the Korean War, stockpiles of food in the US, Canada and other food-exporting countries began to increase. Those in the United States had increased as a result of its postwar support system, while competition increased between food-exporting nations, such as Denmark, which resumed its long-established pig meat exports to the UK, and Sweden and Finland, both of which dumped domestically produced food surplus to their own requirements, much of which had been produced at high cost. This change had led to the government's main policy objective for agriculture, which shifted from a focus on further expansion at almost any cost, to the promotion of more efficient methods of production.[58]

As Table 6.1 shows, by the harvest of 1953–54, agricultural output was estimated to be 56 per cent above the pre-war levels as compared with the planned 60 per cent increase. With prices on the international markets continuing to fall, the costs of agricultural support, which were by then amounting to about £200 million per year, were beginning to cause concern.[59] As the 1954 Annual Review noted:

> In future home agriculture cannot be asked to produce a given amount of a commodity irrespective of cost ... it is evident that home agriculture cannot be completely insulated from world market conditions ... account must be taken of long term trends in market prices.[60]

118 *John Martin*

Table 6.1 Production of the major agricultural commodities

	Pre-war	1946/7–48	1950/1–52/3	1954/6–56/7
	Averages of June/May agricultural years			
	⟵ Million tonnes ⟶			
Wheat	1.7	2.0	2.4	2.8
Barley	0.7	1.9	2.0	2.7
Potatoes	5.0	10.1	8.7	7.2
Sugar-beet	2.8	4.0	4.7	4.8
	Hundred thousand tonnes meat equivalent			
Cattle and calves	5.7	5.1	6.1	7.9
Sheep and lambs	1.9	1.3	1.6	1.9
Pigs	4.2	1.7	4.4	6.6
Poultry meat	0.8	0.7	0.8	1.1
	Thousand million litres, gross production			
Milk	8.1	8.6	9.9	10.8
	⟵ Hundred million dozen ⟶			
Eggs	4.4	3.4	5.4	6.4

Source: Asher Winegarten and M. Acland-Hood, 'British Agriculture and the 1947 Agriculture Act', *Journal of the Royal Agricultural Society of England*, Vol. 139 (1978), p. 83.

This was to be achieved in two main ways: first, by further shifting the system of support from guaranteed prices to the provision of grants and subsidies intended to encourage more efficient methods of production; output expansion would from now on be selective, focusing on commodities such as beef and home-produced animal feeding stuffs. In contrast, further expansion of milk, pigmeat and wheat, which were already in over supply, were to be discouraged.

This shift in focus was also accompanied by restoring the powers of the Marketing Boards. These were considered to be the most effective way of dealing with the intricacies of rapidly changing markets, and encouraging technological advancement would enable British farmers to compete with low-cost overseas producers, of which Commonwealth supplies were increasingly important. There were, however, practical difficulties associated with restoring the Marketing Boards, not least because the government needed the agreement of the National Farmers Union.[61] In the case of the Milk Marketing Board (MMB), which was the largest and most influential of the pre-war boards, the plans included a proposal for the Board to be granted statutory powers to fix the prices of any product that used 'milk as a raw material.'[62] These proposals were discussed in a White Paper issued in November 1953 before the proposals became law on 1 April of the following year.[63]

In spite of fact that the 'structure of the dairy industry … required [the MMB] to collect milk from large numbers of what were often widely dispersed farms',[64] nevertheless the MMB was instrumental in improving the quality of milk and 'reducing the margin between the price paid to the producer and that paid to the consumer.'[65] Its success showed that a market monopoly worked

Table 6.2 Price review determinations, 1949–1957 (£ million)

Agreed annual changes	Changes in factor costs* Review commodities	Changes in price review determination	Amount of over- or under-recoupment
1949	40.5	30.5	(10)
1950	37	19.5	(17.5)
1951	75.75	43.25	(32.5)
1951**	16	16	–
1952	41	39	(2)
1953	22.25	15.5	(6.73)
1954	(6.75)	(33.25)	(26.5)
1955**	33.5	27	(6.5)
1956	36.75	25.25	(11.5)
1957	37.75	14.15***	(23.5)

*For example, changes in wage rates, in prices per tonne of fertilisers, feeding stuffs and so on, as opposed to changes in costs which reflect changes in the quantity used as well as the price of the requisite or service. From 1955 onwards, changes in the price of feed for fat pigs and eggs are not included: the 'feedingstuffs formula' automatically adjusted the producers' guaranteed price to take account of changes in feed.
**Special Review. In 1957 a Special Review was held concurrently with the Annual Review.
***Includes adjustment to crop prices for 1957 harvest made at 1956 Review (£3.5 million)

Source: A. Winegarten and M. Acland-Hood, 'British Agriculture and the 1947 Agriculture Act', *Journal of the Royal Agricultural Society of England*, Vol. 139 (1978), p. 82.

successfully under a producer-controlled board with consumer interests being represented by board members who had been specifically appointed by the Minister of Agriculture.[66]

The achievements of the MMB helped to speed up the reintroduction of other Marketing Boards, particularly the Potato Marketing Board, which in 1955 embarked upon an ambitious plan to stabilise potato production by means of a quota system on the number of acres each registered grower could plant, with fines being imposed on those who exceeded them. During years when yields were higher than average and market prices fell below support prices the Board would purchase ware potatoes (potatoes intended for human consumption) and dispose of them for animal feed, the financial deficit being borne by the Exchequer. While its efforts to regulate production were rather mixed, it played an important role in disseminating more efficient methods of production as well making efforts to arrest the long term decline in potato consumption.[67]

The Hops Marketing Board established at the same time operated a similar quota based system to the PMB based on its estimates of the amount of hops required by the brewing industry. As a monopoly purchaser of hops the Board was able to exercise complete control over a niche market amounting to about 600 producers.

Less successful was the British Wool Marketing Board, which attempted to coordinate the marketing of domestically produced wool. Faced with a multiplicity of different breeds and a predominance of small flocks, the Board

120 *John Martin*

experienced difficulties in coping with imported of standardised wool and the growing competition from artificial fibres. Even more problematic was the British Egg Marketing Board (BEMB) established in 1957 at a time when the country was in danger of being flooded with home-produced eggs which now accounted for 95 per cent of consumption. Unlike the PMB and Hops Board, it had no power to compel producers to use its facilities or to impose restrictions on supply. Its marketing activities, however, contributed to the long-term rise in egg consumption.[68]

The 1957 Agriculture Act

By the mid 1950s, the problem was no longer that of world food shortages, but more of surpluses. By 1956, for example, in the case of wheat, the estimated stocks of the world's four major grain-exporting countries – the United States, Canada, Argentina and Australia – amounted to an estimated 46.2 million tons as opposed to a mere 13.5 million tons in 1952.[69] Collectively, wheat stocks amounted to nearly one year's total production of these countries.[70] With considerably more than half of these stocks being in the US, it is not surprising that the country was embarking on an export drive as a means of disposing of some of its surplus stocks.[71] An increase in inventories of a similar magnitude was also evident in the case of other food stocks such as grains, cheese and butter, and it was accompanied by a similar response.

It was the emergence of international food surpluses which could be easily imported into Britain, now that imports restrictions had been largely lifted, which effectively kept market prices for most agricultural commodities well below the guaranteed prices. The result was that the deficiency payment scheme proved increasingly costly for the Exchequer and in turn the British taxpayer. As Table 6.3 shows, by 1956–1957 the cost of the price guarantee system had risen to £163.7million as compared with £139.6 million three years earlier.[72] In an effort to limit the liability to taxpayers, coupled with the financial retrenchment induced by the Suez crisis, the 1956 Annual Price Review resulted in a rather acrimonious disagreement with the NFU.[73]

Within government circles it was, however, accepted that more fundamental reform was required, even possibly involving the repeal of the guaranteed price system which had been implemented by the 1947 Act. In an

Table 6.3 Government subsidies to agriculture (£ millions)

	Price guarantees	Production grants	Research and advisory	Total
1954–5	139.6	50.4	7.3	197.3
1955–6	142.7	58.1	7.6	208.4
1956–7	163.7	70.8	7.9	242.4
1957–8	203.2	76.8	8.6	288.0

Source: Hansard, 621, No. 97, 12 April 1960, pp. 123–4.

effort to reassure farmers about the state's long term commitment to the agricultural sector and to prevent a repeat of disillusionment which had been precipitated by the repeal of the Corn Production Act in 1921, the Conservative government provided long-term assurances, restricting the level to which prices could be changed annually, which were enshrined in legislation. As a result, the 1957 Agriculture Act committed the government to 'maintain the total value of the guarantees at not less than 97.5 per cent of the total value in the preceding, after allowing for cost changes, ... and to maintain the guaranteed price for each commodity at not less than 96 per cent of that determined after the preceding annual review'.[74] The aim of the legislation was to facilitate further agricultural expansion while at the time making efforts to restrict the level of financial assistance in line with the ongoing restrictions in civil investment.

Conclusion

With the benefit of hindsight, it is very easy to exaggerate the magnitude of these political differences, ignoring the extent to which pragmatic considerations in terms of food security influenced the way that agriculture was managed. During the late 1940s the world food situation, coupled with Britain's precarious financial condition and the Labour government's commitment to overseas expenditure and the level of foreign investment, ensured that food shortages in Britain were the order of the day. Under the circumstances, it is not surprising that the Labour administration passed the 1947 Agriculture Act and, more importantly, embarked on a state-directed plan to increase agricultural production. However, shortly after the Conservatives had been returned to power, food surpluses began to emerge and attention focused on ways of improving the economic efficiency of agriculture while at the same time trying to limit the rising cost of Exchequer support. The 1947 Agriculture Act still remained the basis of the state's approach to supporting agriculture and subsequent legislation in the form of the 1957 Agriculture Act merely helped to modify rather than fundamentally transform the state's relationship with the agricultural sector. The differences in approach between the Labour and Conservative governments, as Michael Tracy has implied, was more explicable in terms of the degree to which the country was able to achieve food security rather than in terms of fundamental ideological differences between the two main political parties.

Notes

1 M. Tracy, *Agriculture in Western Europe*, London: Granada, 1964, p. 235.
2 United Nations Department of Economic Affairs, *Economic Report: Salient Features of the World Economic Situation 1945–47*, Lake Success, NY: UN Publications, 1948, p. 3.
3 The Labour Party's approach to agriculture was in stark contrast to the volte-face which had taken place in 1921, when the wartime system of controls had been

abruptly repealed, and farmers had once more been left at the mercy of overseas competition. In the 1920s, as the world economy was faced with unprecedented food surpluses, there was little need for the British government to placate the agricultural interest by continuing with its wartime system of financial support. At that time the prevailing economic orthodoxy had ensured that financial retrenchment was the order of the day.

4. M.W. Kirby, *The Decline of British Economic Power*, London: Routledge, 1981, p. 8.
5. Keynes first mentioned the term in July 1945 and it was mentioned again in a seminal paper on 'Our Overseas Financial Prospects', which was a precursor for the US loan negotiations. See J.M. Keynes, *Collected Writings*, Vol. 24, London: Macmillan, 1979, pp. 64 and 410.
6. For an authoritative account, see A.K. Cairncross, *Years of Recovery: British Economic Policy 1945–51*, London: Routledge, 1985, pp. 121–164.
7. Hugh Dalton, *Memoirs, 1945–1960: High Tide and After*, London: Muller, 1962, pp. 74–75.
8. David Kynaston, *Austerity Britain 1945–51*, London: Bloomsbury, 2007, p. 228.
9. Ina Zweiniger-Bargielowska, *Austerity in Britain: Rationing Controls and Consumption 1939–1955*, Oxford: Oxford University Press, 2000, pp. 125 and 218.
10. House of Commons debates, 23 March 1948, vol. 154, cc1016.
11. *The British Farmer*, 31 December 1948, pp. 8–10.
12. For a detailed critique of the wartime success of agriculture, see J. Martin, *The Development of Modern Agriculture: British Farming since 1931*, Basingstoke: Macmillan, 2000, pp. 36–66; P. Brassley, 'Wartime productivity and innovation, 1939-45', in Brian Short et al., *The Frontline of Freedom: British Farming in the Second World War*, Exeter: British Agricultural History Society, 2006, pp. 36–55.
13. N. Whiteside, 'Creating the Welfare State in Britain, 1945–1960', *Journal of Social Policy*, Vol. 25, No. 1, 1996; British Agricultural History Society, Trowbridge, 2007, pp. 83–103.
14. House of Lords, '*Agriculture*', (10 December 1947), Vol. 153, cc112–53, Hansard Archive.
15. K.A. Ingersent and A.J Rayner, *Agricultural Policy in Western Europe and the United States*, Cheltenham: Edward Elgar Publishing, 1999, p. 130.
16. Keynes, *Collected Writings*, pp. 465–466.
17. Cairncross, *Years of Recovery*, p.153.
18. TNA CAB129/7 CP(46)Balance of Payments Working Party, '1946 Import Programme'.
19. L. Pressnell, *External Economic Policy: Vol 1, The Post War Financial Settlement*, London: HMSO, 1987, pp. 358–360.
20. Agriculture Act 1947, Chapter 48, pp. 10 and 11, Geo. 6, p.7.
21. Agriculture Act 1947, Chapter 48, pp. 10 and 11, Geo. 6, p. 7.
22. Farmers Rights Association, *The New Morality*, p. 5.
23. J. Martin, 'Balfour, Lady Evelyn Barbara [Eve]', in H.C.G. Matthew and B. Harrison, *Oxford Dictionary of National Biography*, Oxford: Oxford University Press, 2004.
24. See, for example, Philip Conford, 'The Organic Challenge' in Short et al, *Frontline of Freedom*, pp. 67–77.
25. P. Self and P. Storing, *The State and the Farmer*, London: Allen & Unwin, 1971, p. 201.
26. I. Zweiniger-Bargielowska 'Bread Rationing in Britain July 1946–July 1948', *Twentieth Century British History*, 1993, 4 (10), pp. 57–85.
27. Zweiniger-Bargielowska, 'Bread Rationing', pp. 57–85.
28. Dalton, *Memoirs, 1945–1960: High Tide and After*, p. 205.
29. A.J. Robertson, *The Bleak Midwinter, 1947*, Manchester: Manchester University Press, 1989, p. 128.

30 Robertson, *Bleak Midwinter*, p. vii.
31 Robertson, *Bleak Midwinter*, p. 10.
32 *HC Deb 19*, February 1947, vol. 433, cc1181–3.
33 J.G. Gardiner, 'Food from Canadian Farms, Variety of Agricultural Products', *The Times*, October 1947, p. 4.
34 *Farmers Weekly*, 2 May 1947, p. 23; for a detailed account of the threat posed by the farmers to the success of the Labour administration, see Self and Storing, *The State and the Farmer*, pp. 20–28.
35 *Farmers Weekly*, 2 May 1947, p. 23.
36 House of Commons, *World Food Situation*, 6 February 1947, Vol. 432, cc1986–2087, Hansard Archive.
37 'Fears Over Food Shortages', House of Lords', *The Times*, 11 December 1947, p. 2 Times Digital Archive.
38 House of Commons, *World Food Situation*, 6 February 1947, vol. 432, cc1986–2087, Hansard Archive.
39 For a detailed personal account of his resignation, see H. Dalton, *Memoirs*, pp. 276–286.
40 PRO, MAF 100/56, Enforcement Review, vol. 1, no. 3 (November 1947). Extracts from an address to the Divisional Enforcement Officers Conference, 26 November 1947.
41 E.H. Whetham, 'The Agricultural Expansion Programme, 1947–51', *Journal of Agricultural Economics*, Vol. 11, No. 3, 1955, pp. 313–319.
42 House of Lords, *Economic Situation*, 6 August 1947, Vol. 151, cc1035–99, Hansard Archive.
43 House of Lords, *The Agriculture Bill*, 14 July 1947, Vol. 150, cc494–628, Hansard Archive.
44 Martin, *The Development of Modern Agriculture*, p. 73.
45 Self and Storing, *The State and the Farmer*, pp. 20–28.
46 E.H. Whetham, 'The Agricultural Expansion Programme, 1947–51', *Journal of Agricultural Economics*, vol. 11 (3), 1955, p. 317.
47 *Farmers Weekly*, 27 June 1947, p. 26.
48 For a detailed review of Stanley Evans's allegations, see A.G. Street, *Feather Bedding*, London: Faber & Faber, 1954, p. 11.
49 K.O. Morgan, *Labour in Power, 1945-51*, Oxford: Oxford University Press, 1984, p. 305.
50 Self and Storing, *The State and the Farmer*, p. 93.
51 House of Commons debates, 15 June 1955, vol. 193, cc115–118.
52 Self and Storing, *The State and the Farmer*, p. 93.
53 House of Commons debates, 17 May 1950, vol. 475, c1212.
54 H.G. Nicholas, *The British General Election of 1950*, London: Macmillan, pp. 283–305.
55 MAF 265/44 *Notes on Beef and Milk Production in Relation to Proposed Expansion 1952–6*.
56 J. Martin, 'The Wild Rabbit: Plague, Policies and Pestilence 1931–55', *Agricultural History Review*, vol. 5 (2), 2010, p. 21.
57 *Report of the Advisory Committee on Myxomatosis*, London: HMSO, 1954, p. 5.
58 Ingersent and Rayner, *Agricultural Policy*, 1999, p. 131.
59 *Annual Review and Determination of Guarantees*, London, HMSO, 1954, p. 3.
60 *Annual Review and Determination of Guarantees*, London, HMSO, 1954, p. 3.
61 House of Commons Debates, 2 July 1953, cc 606–713.
62 House of Commons Debates, 24 November 1953, vol. 521. cc306–26.
63 House of Commons Debates, 24 November 1953, vol. 521, cc306–26.
64 Martin, *Modern Agriculture*, p.77.
65 House of Commons Debates, 2 July 1953, vol. 528, cc 1467–85.

66 For a different view, see L. Whetstone, *The Marketing of Milk: An Empirical Study of the Origins, performance and future of the Milk Marketing Board*, London: Institute of Economic Affairs, 1970.
67 G.C. Allen, *Agricultural Marketing Policies*, Oxford: Blackwell, 1959, p. 284.
68 Allen, *Agricultural Marketing Policies*, p. 308.
69 Food and Agriculture Organisation of the United Nations (hereafter FAO), *The State of Food and Agriculture 1957*, Rome: FAO, 1957, p. 3.
70 FAO, *The State of Food and Agriculture 1957*, p. 31.
71 FAO, *The State of Food and Agriculture 1957*, p. 51.
72 Note that the latter payment also includes subsidies borne by the Ministry of Food. Hansard, 621, No. 97, 12 April 1960, col1. 23–4; G. McCrone, *The Economics of Subsidising Agriculture*, London: George Allen & Unwin, 1962, p. 46.
73 Self and Storing, *The State and the Farmer*, pp. 73-4.
74 Cmnd 109, *Annual Review and Determination of Guarantees 1957*, London: HMSO, 1957, p. 5.

7 From food surplus to even more food surplus

Agrarian politics and prices in Denmark, 1945–1962

Thomas Christiansen

Introduction[1]

The present book covers the change between 1945 and 1960 from a situation of food shortages to food surplus. In this context, the Danish case is an exception, since there was no food shortage departure point.

The agrarian sector emerged from the Second World War in relative good shape compared to other war-affected countries. It still rested on a production model introduced in the late 19th century built around the import of plant-based inputs and export of animal products, mainly in the form of meat, butter and eggs to the UK and Germany. The export earning capacity of the agrarian sector was a fundamental factor in the modernisation of the Danish economy, as export earnings were used to import, for example, energy, industrial products and inputs for the agrarian sector.

However, the model had been threatened in the 1930s due to restrictions on international trade. To alleviate this, the government initiated a close collaboration with a heterogeneous mix of interest groups, regulated consumer and farm prices, and introduced export quotas. The interest groups entered this arrangement reluctantly as ideologically it was a big step away from the traditional liberal organisation of the agrarian economy. Yet, it became clear for the interest groups that co-operation was a necessity during the crisis. The outbreak of the Second World War, and especially the German occupation of Denmark on 9 April 1940, further complicated the situation for the agrarian sector, but this was relieved by high prices paid by Germany during the occupation.

The following sections will describe the post-1945 conditions for the Danish agrarian sector, and the recurrent theme is that restrictions on international trade in agricultural products often made it difficult to sell the substantial surplus production abroad, and that the limited domestic market was never in a situation to consume all that was produced. The 1945–62[2] period can be divided in three subperiods, based on the main political approach to the agrarian sector:

- The immediate postwar years (1945–50), when the government tried to alleviate a difficult economic situation by continuing the pre-war

practices while hoping that the conditions in the international markets would improve.
- A brief recovery period (1950–58), when the economic situation for the agrarian sector improved and state intervention and support was rolled back.
- A return to more difficult circumstances (1958–62), when economic support was required again, this time including a fundamental change of the policy paradigm, with the introduction of direct cash transfers to the farmers.

1945–1950: Continuation of pre-war practice and politics

When analysing the Danish postwar agrarian policy it is important to take into account the export-oriented nature of the agrarian sector. From the late 19th century, Danish agriculture had developed a production model, in which a part of domestic crop production, together with large amounts of imported fodder, were used to produce an important surplus of animal output, which was exported mainly to two markets, the UK and Germany.[3] The exports to the UK were facilitated by the free trade policy, while the exports to Germany were helped by the proximity to the important markets in northern Germany.[4] The importance of the agrarian sector can be seen in that agrarian exports constituted close to 80 per cent of the value of all exports in the 1920s and 1930s, and although this diminished after the war, the figure was still close to 50 per cent as late as in 1960.[5]

This state of affair had three consequences. First, the predominant role of the agrarian sector as earner of foreign currencies meant that a reduction of agrarian exports would have serious repercussions for the entire economy, as lack of foreign currencies would have severe consequences for the ability to import e.g. raw materials and energy, which could not be produced domestically. Second, production of basic foodstuffs always surpassed domestic demand by a large margin. Third, any agrarian policy would have to take the export conditions into consideration. With this in mind, it is fair to say that the immediate post-1945 conditions resembled the pre-war situation, and the agrarian policy was also a continuation of pre-war practices. On the other hand, the conditions during the German occupation were a break from the pre- and postwar situation, both with regard to the production and export conditions and agrarian policy.

When the Second World War ended, the Danish agrarian sector was in relatively good shape compared to other European countries. Denmark had hardly experienced any warfare, and although occupied by Germany from April 1940 to May 1945, the occupation had brought much less havoc than in most other countries. The agrarian sector had not been exploited by Germany, farmers were not forced to reduce their livestock, and the civil population had not starved.[6] With regard to the political situation, a national coalition government was formed at the time of the occupation, which was in place until August 1943, when it resigned due to unacceptable German demands.[7] For the rest of the occupation, there was no government as such, and the day-to-day administration of the ministries was led by the permanent secretaries. During the entire occupation there was a German plenipotentiary in Denmark, but many parts of the relationship between the Danish and the German governments was handled through the ministries of foreign affairs.[8]

These circumstances had important consequences for the agrarian sector. The main pre-war exports markets were the United Kingdom and Germany, but with the German occupation in April 1940 all trade with the UK was cut off. This meant that all exports were directed to Germany and to a lesser degree other occupied countries, and that there was a complete stop between 1941 and 1945 of imports of cereals and oilcakes.[9] Nevertheless, the agrarian sector emerged relatively unharmed from the occupation period, although there was a marked difference between the development of crop and animal production. The cultivated area and total crop output remained fairly stable (Tables 7.1 and 7.2), but there was a significant decline in the production of milk, butter, pigmeat and eggs, while the production of beef and cheese hardly changed (Table 7.3). This last is reflected in a rather sharp decline in the number of pigs and poultry (Table 7.4), while the decline in milk production was related to the lack of protein fodder, rather than a decline in the number of cows.

During the occupation, negotiations on exports were handled by representatives from Danish farmers' organisations and German officials, who knew and trusted each other from the pre-war years and had a common interest in maintaining a high and stable production level. When reductions were required, both parties were interested in reducing the amount of pigs rather than cows, as Germany was more interested in buying butter than pig meat, while it would be easier and faster for the farmers to re-establish a normal stock of pigs than of cows in the postwar years.[10] It should also be noted that the decline in production was mainly absorbed by a reduction in exports, and the average calorific intake during the war as well as the immediate postwar years was 90–95 per cent of the pre-war average of 3.370 calories per person.[11] Hence, neither the war years nor the postwar years were characterised by food scarcity in Denmark.

Table 7.1 Cultivated area (1,000 hectares)

Years	Cereals and pulses	Root crops	Grass and green fodder	Seeds and industrial crops	Fallow areas etc.	Total
1936–40 av.	1,348	524	1,291	51	34	3,248
1941–45 av.	1,337	539	1,202	90	39	3,168
1946–50 av.	1,298	561	1,172	92	24	3,123
1951–55 av.	1,329	578	1,102	90	12	3,099
1956–60 av.	1,413	578	1,024	85	9	3,100
1961–65 av.	1,570	461	926	105	5	3,062

Source: Danmarks Statistik, *Statistiske undersøgelser, Nr. 22, landbrugsstatistik 1900–1965, bind 1.* Copenhagen, Danmarks Statistik, 1968, pp. 8, 9, 131.

128 *Thomas Christiansen*

Table 7.2 Vegetal output (1,000,000 crop units*)

Years	Cereals	Root crops	Grass and green fodder	Total
1936–40 av.	4,201	3,469	4,172	11,842
1941–45 av.	4,305	3,373	4,068	11,746
1946–50 av.	4,501	3,571	4,068	12,140
1951–55 av.	5,071	3,888	4,225	13,184
1956–60 av.	5,433	4,284	3,805	13,523
1961–65 av.	6,779	3,681	4,175	14,635

Source: Danmarks Statistik, *Statistiske undersøgelser, Nr. 22, landbrugsstatistik 1900–1965, bind 1.* Copenhagen, Danmarks Statistik, 1968, pp. 20–21.

*A "crop unit" is used as a standardised way of calculating the size of the total harvest according to the fodder value of the harvested crops. One "crop unit" equals 100 kg barley, 120 kg oats, 110 kg mixed grain, 100 kg other cereals, 100 kg sugar beet dry matter, 110 kg turnip dry matter, 100 kg potato dry matter, 230 kg lucerne hay, 250 kg normal hay, and 500 kg straw.

Table 7.3 Animal output (1,000,000 kg)

Years	Milk	Butter	Cheese	Beef	Pigmeat	Eggs
1936–40 av.	5,206	180	33	189	344	122
1941–45 av.	3,811	124	35	146	193	47
1946–50 av.	4,609	144	56	159	246	91
1951–55 av.*	5,225	168	84	194	466	135*
1956–60 av.	5,277	167	104	238	573	150
1961–65 av.	5,313	162	119	262	719	107

Source: Danmarks Statistik, *Statistiske undersøgelser, Nr. 25, landbrugsstatistik 1900–1965, bind 2.* Copenhagen, Danmarks Statistik, 1969, pp. 23–24, 64–67, 80–81, 86–87, 119–120, 142–143.

*There is a minor discontinuity in calculation in the number of eggs in 1955.

Table 7.4 Number of animals (1,000)

Years	Horned cattle	Pigs	Chickens
1936–40 av.	3,227	3,200	28,657
1941–45 av.	3,087	1,768	14,851
1946–50 av.	3,002	2,193	22,333
1951–55 av.	3,112	4,107	23,485
1956–60 av.	3,286	5,521	25,005
1961–65 av.	3,412	7,642	26,030

Source: Danmarks Statistik, *Statistiske undersøgelser, Nr. 25, landbrugsstatistik 1900–1965, bind 2.* Copenhagen, Danmarks Statistik, 1969, pp. 8, 9, 131.

It is also important that farmers received good export prices during the occupation, although most of the payments were made through a clearing account in the Danish National Bank, which in the end was never honoured by Germany.[12] Consequently, the agrarian sector as a whole experienced much better earnings during the occupation than in both the 1930s and the immediate postwar years, in spite of the occupation, the loss of the main export market, and the lack of imports of cereals and oilcakes. For the five-year period from 1940/41 to 1944/45, the average rate of return on invested capital in the agrarian sector was 6.98 per cent compared to 2.82 per cent for the five-year period from 1935/36 to 1939/40. This also compares favourably to the three first postwar years, where the average rate of return on invested capital was 3.23 per cent.[13] Against this background we will now take a look at the agrarian politics of the immediate postwar period, the most notable feature of which is the very large degree of continuity with the 1930s.

Given the export-oriented nature of Danish agriculture, the sharp reduction in international trade in the 1930s hit Danish exports hard and led to a significant decline in terms of trade of the agrarian sector and an increase in the indebtedness among farmers.[14] The agrarian crisis policy selected to handle this situation was made of four main components.

The first two components were that farmers could obtain cheap state loans, as well as deferment of payments on loans.

The third component was introduced in 1931 in the form of a number of 'commodity export boards', the purpose of which was to balance the interests of producers, industry and commerce in a situation where international trade was restricted and mainly managed through bilateral trade agreements. The task of the boards was to act as centralised agencies which managed the exports of the relevant commodities to ensure better prices and avoid internal competition between Danish export companies. Moreover, in case of discrepancies between domestic and international prices, income was transferred from producers selling in the privileged market to producers selling in the unprivileged market. For example, if export prices were higher than domestic prices, revenue was distributed from producers selling in the export market to producers selling in the domestic market. Funds for this were collected through export tariffs, which were sent back to the agrarian sector. From November 1932 the boards formally acted on behalf of the Ministry of Agriculture, but they were in reality run by representatives from interest groups related to the agrarian sector, the industries and commerce, while government officials acted as secretaries to the boards. The advantage for the ministries was that they gained access to expertise and manpower, while the interest organisations had influence on the day-to-day working of the system. Initially, the boards were expected to be a temporary measure, but they remained in place in their original form until approximately 1950, when they were removed from the realm of the Ministry of Agriculture and the responsibility was given over to the Agrarian Board.[15]

The last component of the agrarian crisis policy was a number of 'commodity arrangements'. These were introduced in January 1933 as a part of the landmark 'Kanslergade-agreement', which was a political compromise between the government and Venstre that tried to balance on one side the agrarian export interest and on the other side the interest of the working class and the home market business community.[16] The main characteristic of the arrangements was that when required, Parliament approved, for example, a 'pig arrangement', a 'butter arrangement' or a 'cereal arrangement', which often ran for six to twelve months. The nature of a commodity arrangement would depend on the specific yearly situation, with the guiding principle being that the agreement supported minimum prices in time of over-production and included consumer subsidies and/or maximum prices in times of insufficient supply. Hence, as a general rule, producers were supported prior to and after the war, while consumer subsidies were the norm during the occupation and the immediate postwar period, although examples of producer subsidies can also be found in the late 1940s. It is noteworthy that although the arrangements included economic incentives for farmers to behave in a certain way, the legislation never included production quotas or similar instruments. The individual farmer was always free to produce as he saw fit. The system of commodity arrangements was also thought of as a temporary measure, but this type of regulation ended up being in place for approximately twenty years. All in all, this means that while the administrative system as such continued to be the same from 1933 to 1950, the price policy during the occupation – and in some cases also the immediate postwar years – was, generally speaking, a break in the pre-/postwar continuity.

The arrangements and the boards were continuously discussed and questioned by interest groups and political parties. Consequently, throughout the period, new arrangements and boards were introduced and existing ones were adjusted on an ad hoc basis,[17] and the effort was not managed according to a coherent plan.[18] Nevertheless, the four main political parties accepted the boards and arrangements, although with varying degrees of enthusiasm, probably due to the often close connection between the parties and the interest groups represented in the boards.[19]

Returning to the 1945 situation, the agrarian sector faced difficult circumstances with declining prices compared to the war years, and continued constraints on international trade. Nevertheless, the sector managed to increase both crop and animal output in the late 1940s, not least through the rapid recovery of the pre-war pig numbers, but the commodity arrangements continued to be used for the rest of the decade.[20] The number of boards and the frequent changes to the price and support schemes makes it impractical to describe all the postwar measures, but some examples will illustrate the working of the political and the administrative process.

Exports to the UK were resumed in 1945, and two things were of great importance for the agrarian sector: the exchange rate between Danish kroner and the pound, and the prices the British were willing to pay for the products. The government[21] fixed the exchange rate at 19.36 kroner to the pound, which was below the pre-war level, and then went on to negotiate export prices with the British counterparts. The agreement reached in July 1945 caused dissatisfaction in the agrarian sector, given that the agreed prices for the May to October period were set 10 per cent below those paid by

Germany until May 1945, and a further reduction would be implemented from November 1945 onwards.[22] To compensate for this development, both a 'butter arrangement' and a 'pigmeat arrangement' were introduced in September 1945. In the case of butter, farmers were paid 4.00 kroner/kg, which was 10 per cent below the price level in May 1945, while the consumer price was set at 3.89 kroner/kg, with the difference being paid for by the state and a tariff on non-UK exports. The 'pig arrangement' was made according to similar principles with farm prices set 10 per cent below the May 1945 level at 2.59 kroner/kg, while the consumer price in the domestic market was set to 2.40 kroner/kg, with the difference being paid by the state.[23] Finally, a 'cereal arrangement' included the provision that the entire output should be handed in to the state, to avoid cereals suitable for human consumption being used as fodder. The measure was extended in March 1946, although it was contested by both the agrarian sector and Socialdemokratiet.[24]

In spite of an increase in animal production, the overall situation in 1945/46 was a decline in earnings for the farmers in comparison with the war level. A revision of the treaty with the UK was obtained in July 1946, which led to a minor increase in the prices for butter, pigmeat and eggs.[25] However, this was insufficient to maintain farm income, and a producer subsidy was introduced in the summer of 1946, which covered butter, pigmeat and eggs, and ensured prices at a significantly higher level than in the export markets.[26]

The price policy and the export relation with the UK continued to take several turns during 1947. First, in February 1947 the British government agreed to purchase larger amounts of Danish products and at the same time to pay higher prices for butter, pigmeat and eggs.[27] Second, a bad harvest in 1947 led to the Danish government introducing a consumer subsidy on butter and pigmeat. Producer prices were set to the average export prices, while consumer prices were fixed below this level, with the difference being paid for by the state.[28] Finally, when the agreement from February 1947 had to be renegotiated in September 1947, relations with the UK deteriorated, leading to a short-lived export stop to the UK from October 1947,[29] and an equally short-lived redirection of exports to other European markets until a new agreement was made with the British in early 1948.[30] The government wished to maintain the 'cereals arrangement' for another year, in spite of its unpopularity in the agrarian sector. In Parliament the consensus favoured a continuation of regulation and the arrangement was prolonged.[31]

The pattern from the previous years was repeated in 1948, in the form of new negotiations with the UK and new regulation of the domestic prices. With regard to the first issue, the social democratic government achieved a new agreement with the UK in January 1948, which was valid for six months and included a 40 per cent increase in the export prices for pigmeat and 33 per cent in the case of eggs.[32] This was followed by a new agreement in September 1948, which was valid for three years for pigmeat but only for one year for butter.[33] Simultaneously, consumer prices were gradually aligned with the export prices. In May 1948, the domestic butter price was fixed at the same level at the average export prices, and the same happened for milk, cream and pigmeat in late 1949 when the consumer subsidy was removed, except for poor consumers who received food coupons for pigmeat.[34] A final twist in the development of the export prices in the immediate postwar years was the devaluation in September 1949, when the exchange rate for the US$ was increased from 4.79 kroner to 6.92 kroner, parallel to the devaluation of the pound to the US$. This increased import prices for some agrarian inputs, but in this case the sector was not compensated.[35]

By the late 1940s, public and political opinion had grown dissatisfied with the system of intervention and this was all the more so because the lack of foreign reserves in the postwar years meant that the governments also intervened in the distribution of other products through a rationing system. The reasons for introducing rationing for a given commodity could either be that this was in short supply, as in the case of coffee, or that the government wanted to reserve a large proportion of the domestic production for export, as in the case of butter, which was rationed in spite of the enormous surplus production.[36]

All in all, the intervention system was never popular, but for a long time considered unavoidable, and similar measures were used by governments led by both Socialdemokratiet and Venstre.[37] The continuity of the measures has been interpreted in two different ways in the historical literature. On one hand, there has been an interpretation which has stressed the apparent consensus between the two principal political forces Socialdemokratiet and Venstre. On the other hand, more recently there has been a tendency to focus more on the political differences between Socialdemokratiet and Venstre and, consequently, interpreted the policy as a compromise between two opposed views of the desired development of the Danish society.[38]

The continuous intervention in producer and consumer prices was made on an ad hoc basis, where interventions in one subsector were likely to produce consequences in other subsectors. This balancing act was delicate, so at any given point in time, one or more interest groups would be dissatisfied with their relative position. Farmers growing cereals would argue for higher cereal prices, while those specialising in pig breeding would oppose. At the national level, high export prices would be an advantage, but consumers would be hurt and argue for a dual price system. Yet, a dual price system would require some sort of compensation to those farmers forced to sell in the domestic market where prices were often lower. And so on. However, the high degree of involvement of relevant interest groups in its administration helped the day-to-day working and acceptance of the system, and its longevity apparently reflects a high degree of mutual trust among the representatives from the state and the various interest groups, in spite of the underlying ideological differences. Yet by the late 1940s, as the economy of the agrarian sector as well as the general economic situation improved, the time was ripe for a change.

Table 7.5 Number of farms by size, 1946–66

Years	< 5 ha	5–9.9 ha	10–29.9 ha	30–59.9 ha	60–119.9 ha	>120 ha	Total
1946	45,933	55,640	80,136	21,908	3,534	996	208,147
1951	42,922	55,165	82,019	21,401	3,390	938	205,835
1956	39,143	53,998	81,125	20,721	3,238	865	199,090
1961	37,163	54,478	81,393	19,693	2,916	877	196,520
1966	21,779	40,102	79,001	20,870	3,605	949	166,306

Source: Danmarks Statistik, *Statistisk Årbog*. Copenhagen, Danmarks Statistik, various years.

1950–1958: At the crossroad between liberalisation and intervention

We have seen that in the immediate postwar years the economic situation for farmers deteriorated in comparison with the war years.[39] Yet from 1949 onwards, the economic situation improved somewhat and the years from the late 1940 to the mid-1950s were the last period when the agrarian sector as a whole obtained acceptable earnings without receiving massive state subsidies.

The sector also continued a modernisation process, which included a decline in the number of farms (Table 7.5), and an increase in the use of land for cereals at the cost of root crops, grass and green fodder.[40] The last reflects a pronounced decline in the number of work animals due to mechanisation.

Simultaneously, there was a continued increase in the number of pigs, which more than doubled in a decade from some 3 million in 1950 to more than 7 million in the early 1960s, while the number of cattle only increased slightly in the same period.[41] The result of the structural changes in crop production were an increase in cereal output, but a stagnation in the production of root crops, grass and green fodder.[42] With regard to animal output there was a sharp increase in the production of pigmeat, a minor increase in the production of beef and dairy products, and first an increase and then a decline in the production of eggs.[43] This happened against a background where international trade in agricultural products continued to be regulated by bilateral agreements, but the prices that could be obtained were much better in the early 1950s than in the 1930s and the immediate postwar years. This is reflected in the average rate of return on invested capital in the agrarian sector, which reached 8.28 per cent for the 1949–1954 period.[44] Yet the fact that international trade liberalisation, introduced in the late 1940s and early 1950s, did not cover agrarian products soon turned out to be a major problem for the Danish economy.

From 1949/50, there was increasing pressure for the abolition of the commodity arrangements and only a few were continued until 1951/52. A transformation also took place in the case of the commodity export boards. From early 1949, and as a part of the political discussion on a general reduction in the intervention system, the future of the boards was discussed intensively.

The conclusion was that they were still required although not necessarily as a part of the Ministry of Agriculture. They were needed because international trade in agrarian products was still regulated by bilateral agreements, which meant that the agrarian sector needed an organisation to conduct the negotiations with trading partners as well as to coordinate the trade domestically. Hence, new commodity export boards were set up within the realm of Landbrugsrådet in 1949/50, basically taking over the role of the former boards.

As already mentioned, the early 1950s was the last period where the classic production model in Danish agriculture, which had been successful since the 1880s, worked without major subsidies. By the mid-1950s, the model ran into a number of structural issues and unfavourable conditions in international trade, in spite of the fact that in the early 1950s the OEEC had reached the conclusion that the Danish agrarian sector had the highest productivity in Europe both with regard to land and labour.[45] Given this condition, a liberalisation of international trade in agricultural products was in the interest of the Danish agrarian sector. Yet, one of the main structural issues was related exactly to the conditions in the international markets.

During the 1950s the Danish position in relation to the creation of the European Economic Community was a topic of much political debate, and one of the main points under consideration was the conditions for agrarian exports. The discussion on market integration was also a political discussion about the preferred development model for the country. By the mid-1950s, the division line was running between, on side side, Landbrugsrådet and Venstre, which favoured an affiliation to the EEC based on a continued strong position for the agrarian sector. On the other side, Socialdemokratiet, the small-scale farmers and Radikale Venstre, as well as the Industrial Council (Industrirådet) and Konservative Folkeparti favoured a focus on the export to the UK within a larger and more loose market integration where the industrial sector was not exposed too quickly to competition from, especially, German exports.[46]

The establishment of the EEC left Denmark in a difficult situation as the two main export markets were respectively a member (West Germany) and a non-member (UK).[47] This was all the more the case since the agrarian policy of the EEC was a severe blow to the aspirations of Danish agriculture, given the EEC external tariff barriers and focus on supporting the farmers within the EEC to the detriment of the farmers in exporting countries.[48] Moreover, the EEC protectionist policy came at a point in time when both the Danish and British population were relatively well fed, meaning that it could not be expected that the demand for food in these markets would increase significantly, even for animal products.[49] The export problem was not solved by joining EFTA in 1960[50] and the contemporary conception of this situation was that efficient Danish agriculture was undeservedly left as a reserve supplier to the EEC-market.[51]

The second main issue was related to the internal structure of the sector. With limited opportunities for increasing exports and declining relative prices in relation to the rest of the economy, the sector was in a situation where increased productivity without an increase in total production was required, if earnings were to be maintained without state subsidies. A contemporary evaluation argued that productivity should increase with respect to capital and labour and the sector should focus on animal production.[52] Yet, a number of issues made it difficult to go in this direction sufficiently fast to maintain adequate earnings. Danish agriculture was characterised by a large number of family owned small and medium farms mostly engaged in mixed farming. It had been a policy throughout the 20th century to increase the number of small-scale farms through state intervention and support, and as late as 1949 new legislation established tight restrictions on ownership.[53] By the 1950s this model of ownership was entering into a crisis. The smallest of the farms were no longer viable as economic platforms for a family, and nominally small-scale farmers increasingly earned their main living as salaried workers outside the sector.[54] For the medium-scale farms, the process was slightly different. Traditionally, they had been run by a family with a limited number of hired hands, but a large exodus of farm workers began after 1945.[55] This meant that an increase in the productivity of labour had taken place after the war and many medium-sized farms were by the late 1950s operated only by the owner and his family. This process accelerated modernisation and mechanisation, but by the late 1950s the medium-scale farms were also facing a situation in which larger average units were needed to maintain a viable economic situation. Yet the restrictions on farms merging meant that the number of farms remained fairly stable during the 1950s, with the exception of those with less than 5 ha,[56] and any increase in the productivity of labour for the small and medium scale would therefore have required a change in the legislation. Another option would have been to increase the productivity of capital in animal production through investment in production facilities in the form of, for example, better housing and milking machinery. As in the case of improving the productivity of labour, an increase in the productivity of capital would also have required larger average farms, as well an improvement in credit facilities.[57]

All in all, the 1950–58 period is characterised by two opposite tendencies. On one side a return to a pre-1930 situation with an agrarian sector based on small- and medium-scale farms producing animal products for export markets and a decline in intervention in the domestic market. On the other side, a crisis of that same model, given the problems of finding new markets and the limits on productivity growth in the small- and medium-scale farms. The consequence of the second tendency was that the rate of return on invested capital in the agrarian sector, which was 8.28 per cent for the 1949–1954 period, declined sharply to an average of 3.71 per cent for the 1955–1962 years, and reached the lowest level in thirty years in 1962 at 0.9 per cent.[58] The remarkable thing is that the last trend materialised itself so forcefully and so fast that the agrarian policy changed for good around 1960.

1958–1962: A change of ground rules

On the production side, the late 1950s and early 1960s witnessed a continuation of the trends from the previous years – i.e. that cereal output increased at the cost of root crops and grass, pig meat production continued to grow rapidly, while cow-related output was more stagnant, and the production of eggs continued its decline.[59] The combined effects of the structural problems described above were acknowledged by the main political parties by the late 1950s, and hence the agrarian sector started to receive more and more support from 1958 onwards, which will be described briefly.

From 1958, the state started compensating the farmers for regional land taxes if their profits fell below 4.5 per cent, but with a maximum compensation of 45 million Danish kroner per year. From 1961, the maximum limit was cancelled and the regional land taxes for farmers were entirely paid by the state. On top of that, a law was passed in 1963 – retroactively implemented for 1961 onwards – exempting farmers from tax on the added value of normally used farmland. A new cereal arrangement was approved in 1958, which included minimum farm prices for wheat and rye, a monthly storage supplement to be paid to the farmers until the harvest was sold, and the compulsory use of Danish bread cereals in cereal mills. With regard to fodder cereals, an import duty was introduced, which, however, would be cancelled in the case of falling export prices for pigmeat. The import duty was returned to the agrarian sector as cash pay outs in the form of cow subsidies, subsidies to poultry breeders etc. Also, from 1958 the margarine industry and the agrarian sector entered a voluntary agreement about the market for rapeseed. This was replaced by legislation in 1961, and in both cases the industry promised to use rapeseed equalling at least 10 per cent of the fat consumption, and to pay a premium to *Rapsfonden* (Rapes Fund), which then made a cash payout to the farmers cultivating rapeseed. At the same time the industry was allowed to pass the cost directly on to the consumers through an increase in consumer prices.

From 1959, new commodity arrangements were gradually introduced for animal products to ensure that domestic prices were at least as high as export prices. Domestic minimum prices were guaranteed for butter and other dairy products with the exception of cheese. At first this was done with the help of the state, but this was replaced in 1961 by a voluntary agreement administered by the dairies. Likewise, in 1961, minimum domestic prices were introduced for pork, followed in 1962 by measures for beef, veal, chicken and eggs.

A major turning point took place in May 1961, when an agreement between the government and the agrarian sector introduced direct cash transfers from the state to the farmers. It was divided in four groups, with the largest being a 250 million Danish kroner yearly payout to the *Landbrugets Rationaliseringsfond* (Agrarian Rationalisation Fund), which distributed money to individual farmers as 'cow subsidies', 'property subsidies' and reimbursement of regional taxes. Other cash transfers included subsidies for export promotional activities, partial reimbursement of the cost of artificial fertilisers and a grant to the *Mejeribrugets Rationnaliseringsfond* (Dairy Rationalisation Fund).[60]

Within the area of export control and consultancy support, the cost of the export controls for agrarian products was covered by the state from April 1961 and at the same time six new state consultants were employed abroad to facilitate Danish exports. Moreover, the state increased the subsidies for the consultancy work carried out by the associations of agrarian economics.[61]

Some of these initiatives were well-tested policies while others were new. Here, the agreement introducing direct cash transfers from the state to the farmers was a landmark which meant that the agrarian sector entered into the welfare system of income transfers, a true ideological turning point.[62] All in all, by the early 1960s the sector and the political system opted for limited internal reforms, as well as direct and indirect support to the sector, while waiting for a final clarification of the relationship between Denmark and the EEC.

Conclusions

The period from 1945 to the early 1960s was a period where the production model in Danish agriculture, which had been introduced in the 1880s, was almost continuously under pressure. In the immediate postwar years, the governments reacted with a reuse of the crisis management methods of the 1930s, while the improvement of the situation around 1950 led to a relaxation of intervention and a return to a more liberal approach. Finally, from 1958 onwards, the agrarian sector entered into a new economic crisis and state subsidies were introduced including cash payouts to struggling farmers. This was the result of a process in which the classic production model was no longer economically viable unless the sector either received substantial state subsidies and/or there were profound structural changes in the form of concentration of ownership, mechanisation and specialisation.

The main pressure on the model came both from rigid structures and – not least – the continuous postwar restrictions on international trade in agrarian products, which hindered the efficient Danish agriculture from benefiting from its comparative advantages in the international markets for animal products. To put it another way, somebody had to pay for the protectionist policies of other European countries, and Denmark, being a large net exporter, paid the price. This was a problem for the Danish economy as a whole, and economic growth in the 1950s was below the European average and characterised by a 'stop and go' rhythm determined by recurrent problems of lack of foreign reserves.

With this in mind, it is clear that the Danish case is an exception to the overall topic of the present book, which covers the transition from food shortage to food surpluses in postwar Europe. This transition had already taken place in the late 19th century when Danish agriculture transformed itself into a main supplier of animal products to Germany and the UK. Seen in this light, market regulation was a defensive act, a way of riding out troubled times, before it hopefully would be possible to return to 'normal' conditions – i.e. free export possibilities to the UK and (West) Germany. In spite of the ideological differences between Socialdemokratiet and Venstre, the actual market regulation was made much along the same lines by both parties, and there was close cooperation between the main agrarian organisations and the social democrat Kristen Bording, who was Minister of Agriculture from 1924 to 1926, from 1929 to 1945, and from 1947 to 1950.

Three other factors were probably also instrumental in the acceptance of the agrarian policy. First, the very close connection between Socialdemokratiet and the trade union movement was probably important for the acceptance of the policy among the urban population. Second, the equally close connection between Venstre, the farmer organisations and the co-operative movement, which was dominant in the meat and dairy industries, was probably equally important for the acceptance of the agrarian policy in the industrial sector related to agrarian products. Third, it was a notable part of the agrarian policy that it did not determine directly what the farmers were allowed to grow or produce. To put it another way, the continuous disagreements between the four main political parties and their connected interest groups – i.e. trade unions, the co-operative movement, trade and farmer organisations – were at a high level an ideological disagreement, but in daily life were more disagreements about the details of the specific regulations, such as the level of the guaranteed producer price or the level of consumer subsidies, than about whether regulation was required or not in the years of crisis.

In a recent overview, Jan Pedersen has a short discussion about whether the intervention system was economically efficient and whether an alternative would have been viable. Theoretically, he says, there was probably no doubt that the continued support of a surplus production in animal products came at a cost. However, in the 1930s, and maybe also after the war, a faster release of manpower from the agrarian sector as a result of a faster structural change could not necessarily have been absorbed in the rest of the economy, leading to growing unemployment. Whatever the case, he states, it was probably not in the mind of the politicians at the time that a fast and significant change to the agrarian sector was a possibility, because the general perception of the countryside was so strongly attached to the concept of the family-driven farm.[63] To this conclusion it can be added that in the 1940s and 1950s, the political power of the farmer interest groups was strong enough to block any such 'heresy' and the discussion of structural reforms had to wait until the 1960s. In the meantime, the policy initiatives of the late 1950s and early 1960s stabilised the sector in a situation where rapid structural changes would otherwise have been required to ensure its survival in both the international and domestic markets.

A final point should be made about the relationship between Danish postwar agrarian policies and EEC agricultural policy. As is clear from the above, the fundamental difference is related to the dissimilarity in the departure point, respectively a situation in Denmark of a large surplus production oriented towards the export markets, and a situation of food shortages during and after the Second World War. In this situation, the goal of promoting production within the EEC included the raising of tariff barriers and economic support

Agrarian politics and prices in Denmark, 1945–1962 139

to the farmers. The various postwar Danish governments also at times resorted to economic support in the form of minimum prices and direct cash transfers, but as a defensive reaction to hostile international conditions. Hence, the use of similar instruments within the agrarian sector should not obstruct the fundamental difference in the respective trade policies of the EEC and Denmark.

Notes

1 There is limited foreign language scientific literature on Danish agriculture. In English, H.C. Johansen, *The Danish Economy in the Twentieth Century*. London: Croom Helm, 1987, gives an overview of the 1920–1980 economic development, including the agrarian sector. More recently, P.J. Pedersen, 'Postwar growth of the Danish Economy', in N. Crafts and G. Toniolo (eds), *Economic Growth in Europe Since 1945*, Cambridge: Cambridge University Press, pp. 541–575, covers the postwar period. I. Henriksen, 'The contribution of agriculture to economic growth in Denmark, 1870–1939', in P. Lains and V. Pinilla (eds), *Agriculture and Economic Development in Europe since 1870*. Oxford: Routledge, 2009, pp. 117–147, focuses on the pre-Second World War agrarian development, while nothing has been published in English specifically about the Danish agrarian sector in the 1945–1960 period. J. Pedersen, *Danmarks økonomiske historie 1910–1960*. Copenhagen: Forlaget Multivers, 2009, is the most recent overview of Danish economic history between 1910 and 1960 in Danish, while agrarian history is described in E.H. Pedersen: *Dansk Landbrugs Historie, vol. 4*. Copenhagen: Landbohistorisk Selskab, 1988. H. Kryger Larsen, S. Larsen and C.-A. Nilsson 'Landbrug og industri i Danmark 1896–1965. Nye beregninger af BFI inden for de varefremstillende sektorer' in *Historisk Tidsskrift*, vol. 110, Hæfte 2, 2010, pp. 358–401, contains new calculations of the Brutto Factor Income for industry and agriculture.
2 1962 is the end point of the analysis, due to the introduction of new policy instruments in the early 1960s.
3 Calculated by value, the two main agrarian export products were butter and pigmeat. The pigmeat exports were based on the successful breeding programme of the 'Land race pig', which was specially suited for bacon production. A total of 80–90 per cent of the butter production and 50–60 per cent of the pigmeat production was exported in the pre-war years. Danmarks Statistik, *Statistisk Årbog*. Copenhagen: Det Statistiske Departement (various years). See Henriksen 'The contribution of agriculture' for a description of the contribution of agriculture to economic growth 1870–1939. See Johansen, *The Danish Economy*, and Pedersen, *Danmarks økonomiske historie* for the development of the agrarian sector within the general economic development after 1910.
4 From the late 1870s Germany introduced a number of tariffs on agrarian imports, which hit Danish exports. Yet, from the mid-1890s, exports reassumed driven by an increase in demand following rapid industrialization. S. Aa. Hansen, *Økonomisk vækst / Danmark, bd. 1*, Copenhagen, Akademisk Forlag, 1984, pp. 212, 276.
5 Det Landøkonomiske Driftsbureau, *Landbrugets Økonomi i 50 år*. Copenhagen: Landhusholdningsselskabets Forlag, 1968, p. 134.
6 M.R. Nissen, *Til fælles bedste*. Copenhagen: Lindhardt og Ringhoff, 2005, pp. 177–178, and S. Aa. Hansen, *Økonomisk vækst i Danmark, bd. II*. Copenhagen: Akademisk Forlag, 1974, p. 106.
7 From 1929 to 1940 the Danish government was formed by the Social Democratic Party (Socialdemokratiet) and the Social Liberal Party (Radikale Venstre). After the occupation, the Liberal Party (Venstre), the Conservative Party (Konservative

140 Thomas Christiansen

Folkeparti), and several 'non-political personalities' entered the government, but the social democrat Thorvald Stauning continued as prime minister until his death in May 1942. Stauning was followed by the social democrat Vilhelm Buhl from May to November 1942, and then by Eric Scavenius, who was independent but connected to Radikale Venstre from November 1942 until August 1943. T. Kaarsted, *De danske ministerier, 1929–1953*. Copenhagen: Pensionsforsikringsanstalten, 1977.

8 See Kaarsted, *De danske ministerier, 1929–1953*, pp. 131–260.
9 Det Landøkonomiske Driftsbureau, *Landbrugets økonomi*, p. 140.
10 Nissen, *Til fælles bedste*, pp. 14, 40–62, 168, 178 and 224–234.
11 Nissen, *Til fælles bedste*, p. 189.
12 During the war Germany build up a large trade deficit with Denmark that was recorded in a clearing account between the two countries in the Danish National Bank. Germany never honoured the deficit, meaning that the National Bank de facto paid the farmers for a large part of the exports to Germany during the war.
13 Det Landøkonomiske Driftsbureau, *Landbrugets økonomi*, pp. 96–97. Det Landøkonomiske Driftsbureau – i.e. the Agrarian Economical Office – helped farmers with economic management and collected standardised statistics on farm profitability. In the postwar years, balance sheets from approximately 1,000 farms were used to calculate the average rate of return on invested capital, and the data was used as reference point within the agrarian sector and among politicians. A short history of the institution is in Det Landøkonomiske Driftsbureau, *Landbrugets økonomi*, pp. 7–31 and 75–81. Yet, while the trends regarding income can be used, the precision of the numbers is more questionable. In 1947 the social democratic Minister of Trade, J.O. Krag, insisted that the government should not use data from Landøkonomisk Driftsbureau at face value for the negotiations with the UK. R. Mariager, *I tillid og varm sympati*. Copenhagen: Museum Tusculanums Forlag, 2006, p. 277. Henriksen also questions the validity of the calculations of the average rate of return on invested capital. Henriksen, 'The contribution of agriculture', p. 121.
14 Henriksen, 'The contribution of agriculture', p. 130, and Pedersen, *Danmarks økonomiske historie*, pp. 134–140.
15 The Agrarian Board – Landbrugsrådet – represented a number of agrarian interest groups and acted as the main interlocutor between the government and the agrarian sector.
16 Kaarsted, *De danske ministerier, 1929–1953*, pp. 33–37. J. Laursen, 'Indenrigspolitikkens fortsættelse med andre midler?' in *Den Jyske Historiker*, vol. 73–74, 1996, p. 59.
17 Export boards were established for bacon, breeding animals, butter, cereals, cheese, eggs, fats, fruit, horses, potatoes and poultry. The number of boards varied over the years. F. Just, *Staten, landbruget, og eksporten*. Esbjerg: Sydjysk Universitetsforlag, 1992.
18 Johansen, *The Danish Economy*, p. 48.
19 Just, *Landbruget, staten og exporten*. pp. 477–488.
20 See Tables 7.2, 7.3 and 7.4.
21 Socialdemokratiet continued to be the dominant party after the war. Between 1945 and 1968 all prime ministers were social democrats, with the exception of 1945–47 and 1950–53. Kaarsted, *De danske ministerier, 1929–1953*, and T. Kaarsted, *De danske ministerier, 1953–1972*. Copenhagen: PFA Pension, 1992.
22 Kaarsted, *De danske ministerier, 1929–1953*, pp. 294–295, Just, *Landbruget, staten og eksporten*, pp. 172–182, Mariager, *I tillid og varm sympati*, pp. 107–114.
23 Just, *Landbruget, staten og eksporten*, pp. 185–186. Det Landøkonomiske Driftsbureau, *Landbrugets Økonomi*, p. 42.
24 Kaarsted, *De danske ministerier, 1929–1953*, p. 334.
25 Mariager, *I tillid og varm sympati*, pp. 114–118.
26 Det Landøkonomiske Driftsbureau, *Landbrugets Økonomi*, p. 42.

Agrarian politics and prices in Denmark, 1945–1962   141

27 Det Landøkonomiske Driftsbureau, *Landbrugets Økonomi*, p. 42. Mariager, *I tillid og varm sympati*, p. 128. The food supply situation in the UK was especially precarious in 1947 due to a bad harvest. For further details see the chapter about the UK by Martin in the present book.
28 Det Landøkonomiske Driftsbureau, *Landbrugets Økonomi*, pp. 42-43.
29 Det Landøkonomiske Driftsbureau *Landbrugets Økonomi*, p. 43, Just, *Landbruget, staten og eksporten*, pp. 267–272, Mariager, *I tillid og varm sympati*, pp. 134–141.
30 Det Landøkonomiske Driftsbureau, *Landbrugets Økonomi*, p. 43.
31 Kaarsted, *De danske ministerier, 1929–1953*, p. 334.
32 Kaarsted, *De danske ministerier, 1929–1953*, p. 391, Det Landøkonomiske Driftsbureau, *Landbrugets Økonomi*, p. 43, Mariager, *I tillid og varm sympati*, pp. 278–282.
33 Mariager, *I tillid og varm sympati*, pp. 292–293.
34 Kaarsted, *De danske ministerier, 1929–1953*, p. 400.
35 Det Landøkonomiske Driftsbureau, *Landbrugets Økonomi*, p. 44.
36 In 1950, in a complicated parliamentary situation, the opposition parties passed a law for the abolition of butter rationing. Following this, the social democratic Prime Minister Hans Hedtoft resigned power, arguing that abolition of butter rationing was irresponsible since it would reduce exports and hence foreign reserves. Kaarsted, *De danske ministerier, 1929–1953*, pp. 430–432 and 440–442.
37 Pedersen, *Danmarks økonomiske historie*, p. 141.
38 There is an outline of the discussion in Laursen, 'Indenrigspolitikkens fortsættelse'. A notable example of the ideological differences between Venstre and Socialdemokratiet is the 1945 social democratic programme *Fremtidens Danmark* – i.e. *Denmark in the Future* – which included ideological arguments for a more comprehensive state control with the economy. *Fremtidens Danmark. Socialdemokratiets Politik.* Copenhagen: Socialdemokratisk Forbund, 1945. Yet, since Radikale Venstre found that *Fremtidens Danmark* was too left wing, Socialdemokratiet published a more centrist programme prior to the 1947 election. N. Wium Olsen, 'Tillidskrisen. Socialdemokratisk politik mellem fortid og fremtid 1943–1947', in H. Dethlefsen and H. Lundbak, H. (eds), *Fra mellemkrigstid til efterkrigstid*. Copenhagen: Museum Tusculanums Forlag, 1998, pp. 614–620.
39 N. Banke, 'Prispolitik og priskontrol efter krigen', *Nationaløkonomisk tidsskrift*, vol. 86, 1948, p. 13.
40 See Table 7.1.
41 See Table 7.4.
42 See Table 7.2.
43 See Table 7.3.
44 Det Landøkonomiske Driftsbureau, *Landbrugets økonomi*, pp. 96–97.
45 Milthers, 'Dansk landbrugs stilling i den internationale konkurrence', *Nationaløkonomisk tidsskrift*, vol. 90, 1952, p. 136.
46 J. Laursen, 'Mellem Fællesmarkedet og frihandelszonen. Dansk markedspolitik, 1956–58', in B. Nüchel Thomsen, *The Odd Man Out. Danmark og den Europæiske integration 1948–1992*. Odense: Odense Universitetsforlag, 1993, pp. 74–75. See also V. Sørensen, 'Between Interdependence and Integration: Denmark's Shifting Strategies', in A.S. Milward, F.M.B. Lynch, R. Ranieri, F. Romero and V. Sørensen (eds), *The Frontier of National Sovereignty: History and Theory 1945–1992*. London: Routledge, 1993, pp. 88–116 for the debate about market integration from 1950. For a description of the Danish situation in the international context, see A.S. Milward, *The Reconstruction of Western Europe, 1945–51*. Berkeley, CA: University of California Press, 1984, especially pp. 435–461.
47 Between 1950 and 1960 approximately 50 per cent of all Danish exports went to Germany (approximately 16 per cent) and the UK (approximately 33 per cent). Danmark Statistisk, *Statistisk Årbog* (various years).

48 Det Landøkonomiske Driftsbureau, *Landbrugets Økonomi*, p. 45.
49 K. Skovgaard, 'Landbrugets tilpasning til skiftende økonomiske vilkår', *Nationaløkonomisk tidsskrift*, vol. 95, 1958, pp. 57–59.
50 Laursen states that the adherence to EFTA, which only included supplementary guarantees for Danish agrarian exports to the other EFTA members, marked the definitive end of the era where the agrarian sector was the leading player in the Danish (export) economy. Laursen, 'Indenrigspolitikkens fortsættelse', p. 69.
51 Det Landøkonomiske Driftsbureau, *Landbrugets Økonomi*, p. 48.
52 Skovgaard, 'Landbrugets tilpasning', pp. 54–55.
53 Skovgaard, 'Landbrugets tilpasning', p. 55. See Henriksen, 'The contribution of agriculture', pp. 133–134 for a short description of the land policy from the 1890s to 1930.
54 Det Landøkonomiske Driftsbureau, *Landbrugets Økonomi*, p. 101.
55 The number of hired hands declined from 261,000 in 1945 to 130,000 in 1960. Det Landøkonomiske Driftsbureau, *Landbrugets Økonomi*, p. 143.
56 See Table 7.5.
57 Det Økonomiske Råd, *Strukturproblemer i dansk landbrug*. Copenhagen: Statens Trykningskontor, 1964.
58 Det Landøkonomiske Driftsbureau, *Landbrugets Økonomi*, pp. 96–97.
59 See Tables 7.2 and 7.3.
60 The agreement was reached after the farmers organised a production strike following growing economic problems and simultaneous conflicts in the labour market. Kaarsted, *De danske ministerier, 1953–1972*, pp. 198–202.
61 Det Økonomiske Råd, *Strukturproblemer*, pp. 33–36.
62 Kaarsted, *De danske ministerier, 1953–1972*, p. 202.
63 Pedersen, *Danmarks økonomiske historie*, pp. 140–142.

Part III
Technical change

Figure P3 Demonstration of milking machinery. Photo taken in Torrelavega (Cantabria, Spain) in 1959 by Feijoo (Mediateca, Ministerio de Agricultura, Alimentación y Medio Ambiente. Secretaría General Técnica, Spain).

8 Mechanisation and motorisation

Natural resources, knowledge, politics and technology in 19th- and 20th-century agriculture

Juri Auderset and Peter Moser

Introduction

When August Strindberg travelled around rural France in the 1880s in order to understand the development of French agriculture facing the rise of industrialisation and a first wave of globalisation, he was impressed by the fundamental changes in the landscape of the heavily industrialised Normandy. In industrial production, Strindberg observed, the steam engines literally 'fed themselves' into the earth's interior in order to access the longed for coal stocks.[1] In contrast to the vertical digging movements of the steam engine into the lithosphere, the 'organic motors' of draught animals used in agriculture moved horizontally, nourished by plants grown within the biosphere.[2]

Strindberg's observation is more than a vivid blending of topographical, metabolic and technological metaphors. It sketches an important analytical perspective on the resource basis of technological change and reminds us of the importance of distinguishing between mechanisation and motorisation, two terms often confusedly used when it comes to the analysis of 19th- and 20-century agriculture.[3]

Machines in agriculture were up to the middle of the 20th century basically powered by a rising number of draught animals (horses, cattle, dogs) whose upkeep was contingent upon plants and animals continuously reproduced in the process of production. As long as animal (and human) power remained the principal source of power for machines in agriculture, it was simply impossible to create the same growth rates in agriculture as in industrial production, whose rising volume and productivity in the 19th century can mainly be attributed to the steam engine, entirely depending on the consumption of mineral resources from the lithosphere.[4] The manifold attempts to introduce the steam engine in agriculture were, if not a downright failure, at least only a very partial success.[5] Generally speaking, its distribution and successful application was limited to activities in the farmyard like threshing, mostly activities which occurred due to the seasonality and cyclicity of all agricultural work, but not continuously. While the steam engine was the perfect solution for a spatially fixed, continuously operated production, it was rather ill suited for the improvement of the decentralised, cyclical, seasonally bound and weather-dependent production processes in agriculture. As Eduard David, the German socialist thinker, shrewdly observed in his book *Socialism and Agriculture*, the steam engine did *not* have the same revolutionary impact in agriculture as it had in industry, where it was possible to organise production 'in a continuing chain of mechanic operations'. In contrast, the temporal and spatial structures of the biotic resources used in agriculture rendered it impossible to convert temporally discontinuous and spatially dispersed patterns of (re)production into temporally synchronic and continuous and spatially concentrated, modularised sequences of production.[6]

While the thermo-industrial revolution enabled a continuous process of production in the industrial sector, it strengthened the cyclical production rhythms in agriculture.[7] Here, the industrially produced machines and equipment suitable for improving the production demanded not steam engines but draught animals such as horses, oxen, cattle and even dogs. They were all a much more suitable source of power in agricultural production than the steam engine. For almost a century, in agriculture they were conceptualised and installed as organic motors and produced comparable, but significantly different, results from the distribution of the steam engine in industry. Since they were biotic resources themselves, they shared many similarities with the living matter they were used to improve. Draught animals were adaptive and interacted with men who tried to improve and model them actively for their purposes through breeding, feeding and husbandry methods. Hence, mechanisation in agriculture went along with the creation, increase and improvement of draught animals. Farmers, farm labourers and farm women developed a great variety of methods for educating and training animals in their youth to work, often in co-operation with older, already 'learned' animals such as the mare in the case of foals.

Figure 8.1 A widely used draught-training method for horses and cattle in the 19th century

Copyright Picture: Archives of Rural History, Bern

Figure 8.2 Educating instead of breaking horses: men and animal in a co-operative educational enterprise for socialising foals into their future role as draught animals
Copyright Picture: Archives of Rural History, Bern

The number of draught animals in rural areas rose significantly in the second half of the 19th century, whereas they gradually disappeared in industry and the transport systems. Here, they were first replaced by steam and then by combustion engines.[8]

The simultaneousness of a continuous throughput of energy in industry and discontinuous rhythms of energy input, throughput and output in agriculture puzzled contemporaries as early as in the middle of the 19th century. While scientists and adherents of the industrial society advocated an outright industrialisation of the agricultural sector, the biotic resources resisted certain forms of this particular form of modernisation and, therefore, created tensions and frictions between the emerging industrial societies and their agricultural sectors.[9] Besides establishing endless ideological debates[10] they also turned out to be a productive force of intellectual differentiation and knowledge production that eventually generated an agrarian–industrial knowledge society whose actors were trying to meet the requirements of the agricultural reproduction, including seasonally bound use of biotic resources, with those of the lithosphere based industrial society.[11]

When the 'motor dreams', so popular in the middle of the 19th century, were shattered again and again when applied in agricultural practice, astute observers became convinced that engines fit for agriculture had to blend the diversity of skills so characteristic of the draught animal with the steadiness, speed and precision of the combustion engine.[12] The comparison of the combustion motor and the organic motor of the draught animal became the crucial interpretative pattern in the development of agricultural technologies.

It was not until the 1940/50s, however, that a complex interplay between the significant enlargement of energy resources, epistemic changes, technological innovations, political interventions and sociocultural dispositions led to the breakthrough of the combustion engine in agriculture. The long dreamed of, versatile, multifunctional, oil-fuelled tractor, equipped with power take-offs that transferred power directly to implements under tow, and endowed with rubber tyres that increased mobility between spatially dispersed fields and enabled a relatively flexible adhesion to changing soil conditions and terrains, was finally developed in a close co-operation between farmers, engineers and agronomists. Only the appearance of these versatile tractors enabled agriculture to participate in a significant way in the consumption of mineral resources – a precondition for the replacement of the now innumerable draught animals and the impressive growth of agricultural production and productivity in the post-war years.[13]

In the following sections we will explore the processes of mechanisation and motorisation from the middle of the 19th century to the 1960s by emphasizing the different potentials and limitations of mineral and biotic resources. It was basically this different resource basis in industry and agriculture which led to such notable differences between the patterns of mechanisation and motorisation in industry and agriculture and not, as historians have tended to argue, the assumed conservative character of the peasants, their sentimental and irrational veneration for the horse, their apparent dislike for technological innovations and their quasi-Luddite tendencies against progress.[14] A close reading of the sources suggests that the farming population by and large made quick, efficient and creative use of new technologies, if they were actually capable of improving the process of reproduction.[15] Farmers themselves were anxious to improve existing technologies or develop new ones. Since technological choices are always accompanied by contingencies, uncertainties and unintended consequences, farmers carefully reflected on the practical use of new inventions in order to minimise the high technology-induced risks. An implementation of new technology in agricultural practice, therefore, depended on many more aspects than the availability and transfer capacities of technology from the factory or the workshop to the farm.

To take the different resource basis in agriculture and industry seriously opens up, in a combination with an historic-epistemic approach, a new perspective for the history of mechanisation and motorisation that avoids the trap of technological or energetic determinism.[16] Our approach, therefore, emphasises the interactive relationships between the specific material conditions of energy use, the social force of historic epistemic cultures in shaping reality and the path dependencies and dynamics of technological change.[17] From this perspective, the mechanisation and motorisation of agriculture can no longer be narrated as the result of a smooth – albeit, compared to the industrial sector, late – 'victory of change and progress over traditionalism and apathy'.[18]

In order to underpin this alternative narrative of technological change in 19th- and 20th-century agriculture, we will first trace the attempts to introduce the steam engine in agriculture and then discuss how this failure shifted intellectual attention to the observation, analysis and improvement of draught animals that were increasingly conceived as organic or animal motors. Second, we will argue that the semantic spill-over of this metaphor not only had illustrative and heuristic effects, but also constitutive and epistemic ones.[19] From the 1870/80s onwards, self-propelled, motor-driven agricultural machinery was increasingly shaped after the specific capabilities of draught animals. Therefore, the tacit as well as the newly gained scientific knowledge of the animal body, its specific emotional, intellectual and physical capacities, its physiology, agility and multifunctionality became something like a blueprint for the invention of motor-powered agricultural machines. Third, we will focus on the causes of the gradually successful motorisation of agricultural production in the 1940/50s and the profound impacts it had far beyond the agricultural sector.

The failure of the steam engine and the rise of the draught animal

The steam engine was, according to Joel Mokyr, 'one of the most radical inventions ever made'.[20] If we take into account that the thermo-industrial revolution for the first time in history enabled actors to decouple the processes of production and reproduction in the industrial sector, it was probably even *the* most important invention. The disconnection of the production from the necessity to reproduce the consumed resources nurtured the vision that eternal growth was a concept that could be applied to the economic sphere. The steam engine, therefore, not only transformed a (temporary) abundance of coal into an affluence of kinetic energy, it also transcended the knowledge of the temporal and voluminous limits of an 'organic economy' and introduced the notion of an ever growing economy.[21] Not surprisingly, the steam engine became *the* central iconic symbol of the 'culture of technology' in the 19th century.[22] In a characteristic vison of the zeal for technological progress, the machine engineer M.A. Alderson argued in 1834 that the advantages of the steam engine lay in its capacity to overcome the physiological limits and the cyclical and land-bound patterns of energy use inherent in an animal powered economy:

> Animals require long and frequent periods of relaxation from fatigue, and any great accumulation of their power is not obtained without great expense and inconvenience ... To relieve us from all this difficulties, the last century has given us the steam-engine for a resource, the power of which may be increased to infinitude: it requires but little room – it may be erected in all places, and its mighty services are always at our command, whether in winter or in summer, by day or by night – it knows no intermission but what our wishes dictate.[23]

These 'machine dreams', which were, more precisely, motor dreams, were by no means an exclusively urban and industrial phenomenon.[24] Agricultural reformers, agronomists, scientists and farmers alike were fascinated by the tireless, continuous movements of the machines powered by steam engines day and night, weekdays and Sundays, summer and winter. In Switzerland, a commentator in an agricultural journal wrote in 1871 that the co-operation between agrarian sciences and technical engineering would lead to the day when the peasant would be nothing more than a 'controlling and intelligent conductor of machines which are subject to his will'.[25] Since the 1850s, when agronomists became convinced that agriculture should and could be modelled along industrial lines, agricultural journals regularly printed reports of 'successful' implementations of the steam engine in France and England.[26] But, significantly, these reports were rather based on public demonstrations than everyday practice, and they often illustrated more the aspirations of agricultural reformers, scientists, engineers and mechanics than the everyday reality in the fields.[27] Nevertheless, it became common to expect that the transfer of motorised technology from the industrial workshop to the field and barn of the farm would lead to similar effects here as in industry and that agriculture would soon be transformed from an 'empirical handicraft' into a 'science-based' industry, as the agronomist and farmer Albrecht von Fellenberg-Ziegler wrote in 1865.[28] The steam-based motorised technology in industry, therefore, set an ever moving 'horizon of expectation'[29] for the transformation, rationalisation and scientisation of agriculture into operation.[30]

When it came to adopting the steam engine into agricultural practice, however, it soon became evident that things were much more complicated. The 'progressivist fervour' was consistently brought down to earth when the steam-powered, newly developed machinery crystallised itself as rather unreliable because it was often not capable to adapt to the ever changing conditions.[31] Weather and topographical factors, seasonally and diurnally changing degrees of capacity utilisation and the limited possibilities of modularising and serialising work sequences with living animals and plants often turned the elegant efficient machine of industry into an inefficient monstrosity in agriculture.

Decentralised, soil-based agricultural production apparently required a different form of mobility and versatility from the centralised one in industry: 'Rather than the Copernican revolution of manufacturing whereby nature must circulate around the machine, nature in agriculture maintains its predominance and it is the machine which must circulate.'[32] Mindful observers of the agricultural development in industrial societies like Karl Kautsky and Eduard David had already come to similar conclusions in the late 19th century. In his *The Agrarian Question*, published in 1899, Kautsky wrote that the introduction of machinery in agriculture faced 'more obstacles than the mechanisation of industry'. Whereas 'the industrial workplace, the factory, is an artificial creation, adapted to the requirements of the machine', in agriculture 'most machines have to work in and adapt to natural surroundings'. Kautsky, one of the strongest supporters of a scientisation and industrialisation of agriculture, even admitted that it was 'often difficult, and occasionally downright impossible'.[33]

The only undisputed, truly successful application of the steam engine in 19th-century agriculture was the threshing machine.[34] Here, significantly, the power of the steam engine was not used to facilitate the *production process*, but, as in industry, for the *transformation* of a *product*: cereals into grain and straw.[35] Thus, the use of the steam engine proved to be advantageous only for stationary belt-work. For almost all other activities and especially the fieldwork, the diversity and the specific temporal and spatial structures of the tasks required a more mobile and flexible source of power. Thus, when steam engines were actually used beyond their fixed place in the farmyard, they had to be installed on wheels and pulled by animals in order to fulfil the requirements.[36] The steam engine, therefore, did not replace draught animals in agriculture – quite the contrary: for almost a century their numbers on the farms rose significantly. Because draught animals remained even on farms where tractors were bought too, in agriculture a hybrid energy system emerged which remained firmly within the biosphere and demanded a congenial co-operation between humans, animals and motors.

The problems created by the attempts to adjust the steam engine to agricultural conditions led not only to an increase in the numbers of draught animals but also to a new intellectual interest in them, which representatives of the emerging industrial societies had somewhat prematurely perceived as a 'pre-industrial' phenomenon.[37] Hence, agriculture not only witnessed a disenchantment in the attempts to motorise its production, but also a shift of the intellectual attention towards animals which could be bred, fed and trained to work in co-operation with human beings: horses, mules, donkeys, oxen, cows, bulls and dogs. Peasants, agronomists, veterinarians and engineers began to view the body and mind of draught animals increasingly as an 'epistemic

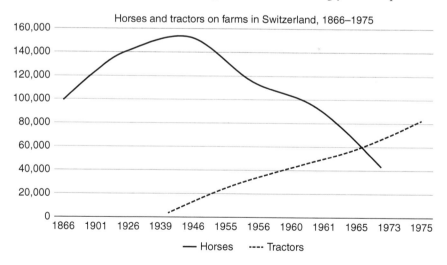

Figure 8.3 Horses and tractors in Swiss agriculture, 1866–1965

Source: Heiner Ritzmann-Blickenstorfer: Land-und Forstwirtschaft, in: Idem (ed.), Historische Statistik der Schweiz. Zürich 1996, pp. 513 and 575.

object', worthy of elaborate and sometimes expensive observations, studies and scientific experimentations.[38] Breeders began to collect data concerning the ancestry of the animals, kept records on their performance, applied information processing procedures, statistics and theories of inheritance for selective breeding and thus increased the average weight, height and pulling power of draught animals. Not surprisingly, this process led not only to the creation of 'new' breeds, but also to the disappearance of others.[39] Veterinarians and agronomists analysed the physiology, anatomy and motion of their bodies, and tried to improve their versatility and the relationship of energy incorporated in feed and exhausted by work. Farmers sharpened their long established hermeneutic culture of observation of the behaviour of the animals which mostly lived under the same roof, often crediting them with qualities so far reserved for human beings, such as character, memory and capacities to learn.[40] In short, the farm became a crucial site of observation and an important intersection of scientific and tacit knowledge production regarding the animal as an 'intelligent' and variable energy source for increasing and facilitating agricultural production.[41]

The heterogeneity and complexity of tasks to be done in agriculture produced a remarkable variety of energy structures on the farm: steam and stationary combustion engines were used along with electric, animal and human power.[42] But electricity, like steam, was a spatially (too) fixed source of energy for fieldwork; it too remained confined to the farmyard where it was introduced on a large scale in the first half of the 20th century. As a source of energy circulating in network structures, the distribution patterns of electrification depended heavily on the activities of electricity works and collective decisions made by local communities and regional political institutions.[43] As predicted by contemporary observers like Fellenberg-Ziegler, mechanisation alleviated many operations on the farm, but it also created a demand for new skills and knowledge, and it did not save labour to a significant extent. Instead, it shifted labour mainly from humans to animals who 'could push, pull or drive with their legs and feet by using the motion of walking or trotting' and thus convert their 'linear motion into the kind of power needed for the machine'.[44]

Animal motors and iron horses: the intellectual fascination for draught animals and their influence on technological change

The close interplay between men and the increasing number of draught animals and machines created a conceptual dialectic between the animal and the motor in many of the agricultural discourses on labour and technology in the age of the second industrial revolution. At the same time as the human body was increasingly conceptualised as a 'human motor', as Anson Rabinbach has shown, the animal body had become an animal motor in the eyes of the actors of the agrarian–industrial knowledge society.[45] In the language of thermodynamics, which governed much of the late 19th- and early 20th-century thinking on labour, productivity, technology and energy (and which linked discourses in physics, engineering, economics and agriculture), all productive activity was linked interchangeably in the concept of energy.[46] The implications of this spread of thermodynamics in scientific discourse were aptly summarised by François Jacob:

> The concepts of thermodynamics completely upset the notion of a rigid separation between beings and things, between the chemistry of the living and the laboratory chemistry. With the concept of energy and that of conservation, which united the different forms of work, all the activities of an organism could be derived from its metabolism ... the same elements compose living beings and inanimate matter; the conservation of energy applies equally to events in the living and in the inanimate world.[47]

At the same time it is important to remember that the two main laws of thermodynamics experienced a rather asymmetrical reception in scientific discourse. While the first law of thermodynamics stated that matter and force can be exchanged and converted but neither created nor destroyed, the second law of entropy, however, insisted on the irreversible dissipation of energy in the production process. While the first law in combination with the access to the resources in the lithosphere fitted perfectly into the concept of eternal growth and progress, the second was a rather uncomfortable and, therefore often ignored, reminder of the limits and costs of growth in an 'energy-rich economy'.[48] This asymmetric reception proved to be of crucial importance for the conceptual amalgamation of animals and motors, because it obscured the difference between living and inanimate matter, as François Jacob emphasises. Only from this rather reductionist point of view could humans, animals and motors equally be reduced to means of energy transmission.[49]

The levelling of the differences between living beings and inanimate matter in the thermodynamic concept of energy corresponded, not surprisingly, only partially with the experiences of the farming population which lived and worked in community with their animals.[50] The peasants were too well aware of the fatigue of their working companions, their need to rest, their intellectual adaptability and their changing performance capacities depending on the cycle of reproduction to be ignorant of the fundamental differences between motor and animal. The practical and tacit knowledge of the farming population rather supported the insight of the agronomists that draught animals and electric and combustion motors showed both similarities, but also striking differences. Therefore, the emerging discourse on the 'farm power question' was by no means structured by an antagonistic pattern, pitting the draught animal against the motor and operating in an either/or mode of discussion.[51] Rather, animals and motors were more and more conceptualised as complementary tools. Consequently, farmers and agronomists began to identify operations which should best be done with the help of animals and operations where the use of engines was more efficient. Franz Ineichen, a farmer and pioneer of motorisation in Swiss agriculture, brought this perspective to the point when he wrote in 1941 that every source of power on the farm was 'suitable for some tasks and causes trouble for others'.[52]

Both sources of energy, animals and motors, were identified as epistemic objects to be developed in order to meet the diversity of tasks, and the patchy temporal and spatial structures of agricultural work. This process of improvement occurred by mutual observations and conceptual transfers of insights. Just as the metaphor of the animal motor provided a means for thinking of the animal body in an analogy to the engine, the development of suitable agricultural technology drew on the animal body as a source for intellectual inspiration. Quite tellingly, the successfully implemented motorised machines were increasingly perceived as 'iron horses' or 'modern superhorses',[53] a metaphoric and semantic indicator that the machine–animal relation was not a cognitive one-way street, shaping solely the perception of the animal along the lines of the engine, but rather a dialectical process producing heuristic and epistemic effects in both directions.

This comparative cognitive pattern between animal and motor had profound implications on the specific development of technological innovations in agriculture in the first half of the 20th century, which received a first boost in the second half of the First World War, when a large proportion of the agricultural horses were required for military purposes. In Switzerland, the campaign for an 'advancement of a rational motorisation' began in 1916/17.[54] But the laborious and expensive attempts to find a tractor suitable to agricultural conditions were mainly unsuccessful, since they were still more or less the same technical 'monsters', 'leviathans' and 'behemoths' which Siegfried Giedion and other historians identified in North America around the turn of the century.[55] Only the new agricultural tractors, developed in the interwar period, successfully acquired some of the qualities the analytical eyes of agronomists and veterinarians so aptly captured in their close inspection of the animal body. The agronomist and promoter of motorisation of agriculture in Switzerland, Hermann Beglinger, set the pace of development when he declared in 1920 that the tractor of the future would have to correspond 'to a higher degree to the horse' than it had so far.[56]

From the 1920s on the language of motor-technology began to shape the perception of the animal more profoundly. Agronomists claimed that the capacity of the horse to keep its pulling power and speed constant despite an uneven road or wet soil was about the same thing as 'continuously variable transmission' and 'changing gears' in motor-technology.[57] The agile movements and speed variations of the animal body were captured with concepts such as 'motoring torque' and 'gears'. Hooves became 'pneumatic tyres' and were analysed with regard to their 'adhesion', and instead of trotting and galloping the horse had certain 'driving and guiding characteristics'. For the agronomist Emil Rauch it was clear that the horse 'changed gears' and raised the 'adhesion' depending on the conditions of the terrain and the tasks to be done, thereby showing an adaptability, agility and flexibility the tractor was not yet able to compete with.[58] In a sense, then, the animal became at least in the conceptual realm of agricultural technology something of a cyborg.[59]

This blurring of spheres had the reciprocal effect that the animal's body and mind became a model for the development of new and improved agricultural machinery. As long as the tractor showed such deficiencies regarding its adaptation to agricultural conditions, draught animals were kept even on those farms which had bought tractors. In the everyday experiences of the farming population, the specific capabilities of the animals continued to reveal the technological shortcomings of the tractors. Thus, the necessity to blend the speed, mechanical precision, steadiness and timeliness of the already existing tractors with the versatility and diversity of skills displayed by the animal became an intellectual driving force for the agro-technological improvers, whose developments of innovative technology were chiefly the result of a close co-operation between farmers, agronomists and engineers, as can be seen in the great variety of agricultural machines developed around the capacities of the draught animal.

In analogy to the animal body and mind, technological innovations were increasingly directed towards a multifunctional usability, combining different motors for specialised tasks within the same machine. In other words, the challenges of developing technologies suitable to agricultural conditions led many observers to the firm conviction that the longed for self-propelled, motor-driven universal and general-purpose tractor had to have the qualities of most draught animals too, in order to replace them eventually.

Figure 8.4 An industrial technique adapted to the power available on the farm: a partly motor-powered mowing-machine in the interwar years

Copyright Picture: Archives of Rural History, Bern

Extending the energy base: access to the lithosphere and the motorisation of agricultural production in the 1950s

The 1950s are characterised by an accelerated period of change in agriculture, based on an interplay of historical experience, new access to mineral resources, rapid technological development, shifting political conditions and the production of new as well as the marginalisation of hitherto 'useful knowledge'.[60] The old attempts to develop a tractor shaped along the multifunctional lines of the draught animal while simultaneously transcending its constraints, limitations and peculiarities made its breakthrough in the 1940/50s, and, therefore, created the conditions which enabled a broad and rapid diffusion of the now versatile motorised technology. Tractors were, of course, an important topic in agricultural discourses since the first decade of the 20th century, but their application remained mainly restricted to pulling purposes. This rather slow implementation of a technical innovation often frustrated contemporaries, and is often interpreted by historians as proof of an assumed conservative character of farmers when it comes to technology. Our reading suggests that this fractured process of technological implementation was a crucial experience for the actors involved; it created the cultural dispositions, knowledge and skills which eventually led to an accelerated adaptation of the more versatile tractors when they entered the stage in the postwar years. It was exactly the complex and unpredictable experiences with new technologies that created the epistemic breeding ground which enabled farm labourers as well as farmers to creatively cope with the challenges of the tractors and a whole range of other motor-powered machines in the 1950s. Now the 'monsters' of the early 20th century and the 'steel-horses' of the 1930s were finally turned into 'a power centre of the farm',[61] equipped with the crucial power take-off that eventually made it possible to multitask, the ultimate precondition for its superiority over the draught animal, as predicted in the early 1920s.[62]

It was this technological breakthrough that empowered agriculture to participate in a so far unprecedented degree in the consumption of mineral resources, making the reproduction of biotic ones superfluous to a large, but by no means total, extent. This access to the lithosphere 'liberated' farmers partially from the temporal and spatial restrictions bonded to the use of living matter and enabled agricultural production to catch up with growth rates which had characterised the industrial sector since the 19th century. Contrary to popular perception of a stagnating sector, Giovanni Federico recently pointed out that 'the productivity performance of agriculture during the postwar boom was outstanding. From 1967 to 1992, its rate of TFP (Total Factor Productivity) growth from 1967 to 1992 exceeded the rate in manufacturing in seven Western European countries out of eight and the average difference was 94 per cent'.[63] But the main causes for this economically extraordinary (and ecologically far-reaching if not disastrous) performance lay less in a new interventionist agricultural policy, as Federico and many others suggest,[64] than in a multitude of close epistemic, institutional, technological and political interactions within the new extending energy base of the 1950s. Certainly, the Second World War accelerated the already comprehensive state interventions with the newly emerging credit and knowledge institutions. And the re-creation of agriculturally relevant international institutions and the American-based technological improvement programmes after 1945 equally supported the implementation of the now technologically improved tractors and other motor-powered agricultural technology. But these institutional, technological and political factors only produced the profound changes in agriculture in the context of the rapidly extending energy base that characterised the 1950s as a decade of a hitherto unknown growth of production and productivity in agriculture. Particularly crucial for this age of transition, therefore, was the replacement of one natural resource, the reproducible plants and animals, by another, the consumable minerals which have a much bigger growth potential (in the short term) than the biotic ones. In other words, the extension of the energy base 'disintegrated' the energetically so far partly self-supporting farm while it integrated the agricultural sector into the growth paths typical of industrial-capitalist societies since the 19th century.[65]

A crucial factor for the growing output and productivity in agriculture was that the broad diffusion of the tractor and other motorised technology unleashed land so far used for the feed and upkeep of draught animals, and breeding bulls, which were replaced by the rapidly expanding technique of artificial insemination. Moreover, farm labourers were no longer needed to handle the draught animals and to do work which was now superfluous because of the multifunctional versatile tractor and the application of chemical aids in plant production.[66] Thus, the tractor not only facilitated work, but it also made labour superfluous and provided large land areas which were now used for producing food and commodities for the agro-food industry.[67] Whereas in the age of mechanisation the increasing number of draught animals simultaneously promoted and limited growth, in the age of motorisation agriculture for the first time was able to meet the growth expectations of industrial societies. The process of tractorisation integrated the sector into the industrial economy by 'disintegrating' the farm from its former partly energy independence.[68] The necessity to buy fuel, replacements, artificial fertilisers, seeds, semen, etc. exposed farmers to the hitherto unknown volatilities and uncertainties of the markets, and the disappearance of draught animals deprived them of a part of their reproducible means of production. In short, when capital and mineral resources replaced labour and biotic resources, the production was decoupled from its former self-supporting, but growth-restricting system of a partial reproduction in the process of production. The farm, in other words, was transformed from a semi self-supporting unit to a crucial, but still vulnerable, link in the chain of the growing agro-business. It was primarily the anxiety to safeguard the stability of agricultural production, still subject to changing weather conditions and cyclical and seasonal patterns of production, which promoted the new state interventionism of the 1950/60s, rather than the often more lamented than analysed farming lobby.[69] This process of disintegrating the farm by integrating the agricultural sector into the capitalist economy has often been reduced to the single aspect of labour being replaced by capital. While this interpretation is not entirely wrong, it nonetheless obscures more than it enlightens the fundamental changes which characterised agricultural production in the 1940/50s: the replacement of biotic resources by mineral ones.

The predominant view of these changes in the postwar years usually emphasises the financial costs for the taxpayer and the beneficial results of the process of rapid modernisation that turned food shortages into food surpluses. Contemporaries were fascinated by the new possibilities which opened up thanks to access to the lithosphere. The problems that went hand in hand with this appropriation of new energy stocks for agricultural production, however, were for the time being mainly concealed behind the veil of prosperity, emancipation from drudgery, unexpected growth of production and productivity, and rising living standards. To some extent, it might have been the unfamiliarity and the sheer speed of the changes in postwar agriculture which led many observers to endorse the unprecedented powers of production and, at the same time, to neglect the ecological problems associated with them.

As profound and far reaching as these changes undoubtedly were, it is important to remember that they did not free the agricultural sector from the growth restrictions of an organic economy entirely. Even in the age of a new wave of 'industrialisation', agriculture still used animals and plants that contested their industrialisation and commodification to a certain degree, and, therefore, reminded the public not only that there would be alternative forms of agricultural modernisation to the comprehensive attempts to industrialise it, but also that modernised agriculture is something quite different from simply industrialised agriculture. Nicholas Georgescu-Roegen had already realised this in 1960 when he wrote: 'For industrial uses man has been able to harness one source of energy after another, from the wind to the atom, but for the type of energy that is needed by life itself he is still wholly dependent on the most 'primitive' source, the animals and plants around him.'[70] The transition process of the 1950s, therefore, created the possibilities of gaining access to new sources of energy which were used to a large extent by the farming population, but it did not lead to an escape, from an industrial perspective, of the peculiar structures and growth restrictions of biotic resources.

Conclusions

The third agricultural revolution of the long 1950s, which Paul Bairoch aptly characterised as 'the industrialisation of the agro-food-chain',[71] was by no means the outcome of a historically inevitable process of technological change, but rather the historically contingent result of a complex interplay between resource-bound, epistemic, technological, political and institutional forces. The 1950s were indeed a caesura with regard to both the use of energy in agriculture and the epistemic framework in which the newly gained access to mineral energy was interpreted. The motorisation of agricultural production based on the access to a *store* of energy in the lithosphere unleashed an unprecedented potential of production thanks to the new knowledge created and accumulated by the actors of the agrarian–industrial knowledge society in their long enduring efforts to motorise agriculture. Significantly, this process went along with the marginalisation of the hitherto essential knowledge about the characteristics of the energy *flows* of biotic resources reproducible with the help of the photosynthesis. The long 1950s witnessed an epistemic shift away from an intellectual occupation with the temporal and spatial logics of living resources to a scientifically supported 'decontextualised rationality' that derived its concepts chiefly from industrial realities which were placed above agricultural realities.[72] Not surprisingly, therefore, the distinction between the characteristics of the reproducible biotic resources and the idiosyncrasies of the consumable fossil resources almost completely vanished from the discourses in agricultural science in that period.[73]

A historic-epistemic approach towards change and continuity in agriculture reveals that the practical outcomes of technological developments are by no means the result of a more or less 'frictionless'[74] diffusion process, nor can they be solely traced back to agricultural policies or institutional frameworks alone. Our approach rather suggests a preponderance of a multitude of close interactions of theory and practice; scientists and farmers both conceptualised 'their' object along the lines of the other. In the case of the key invention of the

Figure 8.5 Only the development of the power take-off and its perfecting in the 1950s made the tractor 'a power centre of the farm', enabling it to multitask

Copyright Picture: Archives of Rural History, Bern

tractor, technology not only transformed and conquered nature, as the standard progressivist narrative of technological change in agriculture maintains, but the understanding of the nature (and culture) of the animal shaped technological improvements in a reciprocal way. A history of technological change in agriculture, therefore, has to pay more attention to the social and epistemic interactions between humans, animals and motors – interactive relationships that have been hidden from history for all too long.

The peculiarities of technological change in agriculture are heavily influenced by the spatial and temporal characteristics of agricultural production. Farms, therefore, were (and still are) characterised by a hybrid energy resource system with the result that agriculture became (almost) like industry while it (partly) remained different. To identify and recognise this hybridity as an empirical fact enables us to do historical justice to the creative *bricolage* (Claude Lévi-Strauss)[75] that the farming population revealed in the use of different energy resources in their daily work – so aptly illustrated by the rise of draught animals in the age of steam and the simultaneous transformation of monster-tractors into steel horses first and then versatile, multifunctional oil-fuelled tractors equipped with power take-offs.

Notes

1 A. Strindberg, *Unter französischen Bauern Eine Reportage*, Frankfurt a.M.: Eichborn, 2009, p. 142.
2 This metaphor was used extensively in the discourses on animal labour; see e.g. E. David, *Sozialismus und Landwirtschaft*, Berlin: Verlag der Sozialistischen Monatshefte, 1903, p. 217.
3 See e.g. R.E. Ankli and A.L. Olmstead, 'The Adoption of the Gasoline Tractor in California', *Agricultural History*, 55(3), 1981, pp. 213–230, here p. 225; A.L. Olmstead and P.W. Rhode, 'The Agricultural Mechanization Controversy of the Interwar Years', *Agricultural History*, 68(3), 1994, pp. 35–53; W.J. White, 'The Unsung Hero: The Farm Tractor's Contribution to Twentieth-Century United States Economic Growth', *The Journal of Economic History*, 61(2), 2001, pp. 493–496.
4 E.A. Wrigley, *Energy and the English Industrial Revolution*, Cambridge: Cambridge University Press 2010, pp. 26–52.
5 R.M. Wik, 'Steam Power on the American Farm, 1830–1880', *Agricultural History*, 25(4), 1951, pp. 181–186, here: p. 182. Although Wik draws attention to the difficult process of adaptation, his account is heavily structured by assumptions of technological progress and peasant reluctance.
6 David, *Sozialismus und Landwirtschaft*, p. 217.
7 N. Georgescu-Roegen, *Energy and Economic Myths: Institutional and Economic Essays*, New York: Pergamon Press, 1976.
8 On the notion of the 'horse age', see R. Koselleck, 'Das Ende des Pferdezeitalters', in *Süddeutsche Zeitung*, 25 November 2003. On the gradual decline of horses in urban spaces, see A. Norton Greene, *Horses at Work: Harnessing Power in Industrial America*, Cambridge, MA: Harvard University Press, 2008.
9 P. Moser and T. Varley (eds), *Integration through Subordination: The Politics of Agricultural Modernisation in Industrial Europe*, Turnhout: Brepols, 2013.
10 S. Miller, 'Urban Dreams and Rural Reality: Land and Landscape in English Culture, 1920–1945', *Rural History*, vol. 6, 1995, pp. 89–102.

11 On the concept of an agrarian–industrial knowledge society, see J. Auderset and P. Moser, *Die Agrarfrage in der Industriegesellschaft. Wissenskulturen, Machtverhältnisse und natürliche Ressourcen in der agrarisch-industriellen Wissensgesellschaft im 19. und 20. Jahrhundert*, Vienna, Köln, Weimar: Böhlau (forthcoming).

12 This is a slight modification of a notion introduced by Herbert Sussman; see his 'Machine Dreams: The Culture of Technology', *Victorian Literature and Culture*, 28(1), 2000, pp. 197–204.

13 The technological evolution of the tractor, but not its impact on the consumption of mineral resources, is traced by A.L. Olmstead and P.W. Rhode, 'Reshaping the Landscape: The Impact and Diffusion of the Tractor in American Agriculture, 1910–1960', *The Journal of Economic History*, 61(3), 2001, pp. 663–698; G. Federico, 'Natura Non Fecit Saltus: The 1930s as the Discontinuity in the History of European Agriculture', in P. Brassley, Y. Segers and L. Van Molle (eds), *War, Agriculture, and Food: Rural Europe from the 1930s to the 1950s*, London: Routledge, 2012, pp. 15–32.

14 R.V. Scott, *The Reluctant Farmer: The Rise of Agricultural Extension to 1914*, Urbana, IL: University of Illinois Press, 1971; Wik, 'Steam Power on the American Farm', p. 185; G.B. Ellenberg, 'Debating Farm Power: Draught Animals, Tractors, and the United States Department of Agriculture', *Agricultural History*, 74(2), 2000, pp. 545–568, here: p. 562.

15 M. Finley, 'Far Beyond Tractors: Envirotech and the Intersections between Technology, Agriculture, and the Environment', *Technology and Culture*, 51(2), 2010, pp. 480–485.

16 On the problem of technological determinism, see P. Scranton, 'Determinism and Indeterminacy in the History of Technology', *Technology and Culture*, 36(2), 1995, pp. 31–53; D. Fitzgerald, 'Beyond Tractors: The History of Technology in American Agriculture', *Technology and Culture*, 32(1), 1991, pp. 114–126.

17 J.R. Kloppenburg Jr, 'Social Theory and the De/Reconstruction of Agricultural Science: Local Knowledge for an Alternative Agriculture', in G. Henderson and M. Waterstone (eds), *Geographic Thought: A Praxis Perspective*, New York: Routledge, 2009, pp. 248–265. On the concept of epistemic cultures, see C.K. Knorr, 'Epistemic Cultures: Forms of Reason in Science', *History of Political Economy*, vol. 23, 1991, pp. 105–122.

18 Scott, *The Reluctant Farmer*, p. 3.

19 On the role of metaphors in the history and sociology of science and knowledge, see J. Rouse, 'What are Cultural Studies of Scientific Knowledge?' *Configurations*, vol. 1, 1992, pp. 57–94; S. Maasen and P. Weingart, 'Metaphors – Messengers of Meanings: A Contribution to an Evolutionary Sociology of Science', *Science Communication*, vol. 17, 1995, pp. 9–31.

20 J. Mokyr, 'Editor's Introduction: The Economic History of the Industrial Revolution', in J. Mokyr (ed.), *The British Industrial Revolution: An Economic Perspective*, Boulder, CO: Westview Press, 1993, pp. 1–131.

21 Wrigley, *Energy and the English Industrial Revolution*, pp. 9–25.

22 H. Sussman, 'Machine Dreams', p. 197.

23 M.A. Alderson, *An Essay on the Nature and Application of Steam, with an Historical Notice on the Rise and Progressive Improvement of the Steam-Engine*, London: Sherwood, Gilbert & Piper, 1834, p. 44.

24 Sussman, 'Machine Dreams'.

25 J.F. Schneeberger, 'Die Landwirthschaft gegenüber der Industrie und dem Handel', *Landwirthschaftliche Zeitung*, 8(32), 1871, pp. 141–142.

26 Mittheilungen über Haus-, Land- und Forstwirtschaft für die Schweiz, 1858, p. 151; 1860, p. 87.

27 These reports more often included the message of the attendance of important persons such as the French emperor than precise information of the work actually

performed by steam engines; see e.g. Mittheilungen über Haus-, Land- und Forstwirtschaft für die Schweiz, 1860, p. 87.
28. A. Fellenberg-Ziegler, 'Die Aufgabe der Landwirtschaft in der Gegenwart', *Bernische Blätter für Landwirthschaft, 19*(21–23), 1865.
29. R. Koselleck, *Futures Past: On the Semantics of Historical Time*, New York: Columbia University Press, 2004, pp. 255–275.
30. Lutz Raphael translates the German word *Verwissenschaftlichung* as *scientization* (and not *scientification*) cf. L. Raphael, 'Embedding the Human and Social Sciences in Western Societies, 1880–1980: Reflections on Trends and Methods of Current Research', in K. Brückweh et al. (eds), *Engineering Society: The Role of the Human and Social Sciences in Modern Societies, 1880–1980*, London: Palgrave, 2012, pp. 41–56.
31. Fitzgerald, 'Beyond Tractors', pp. 114–126.
32. D. Goodman, B. Sorj and J. Wilkinson, *From Farming to Biotechnology: A Theory of Agro-Industrial Development*, Oxford, New York: Blackwell, 1987, p. 21.
33. K. Kautsky, *The Agrarian Question*. In two volumes, London, Winchester, MA: Zwan, 1988, p. 32.
34. See the account in *Bernische Blätter für Landwirtschaft*, 1865, p. 26. The exceptionally successful implementation of the threshing machine is highlighted by F. Dovring, *Land and Labour in Europe 1900–1950: A Comparative Survey of Recent Agrarian History*, the Hague: Nijhoff, 1956; Wik, 'Steam Power on the American Farm', pp. 181–186.
35. Goodman et al., *From Farming to Biotechnology*, p. 21.
36. Wik, 'Steam Power on the American Farm', p. 181.
37. Norton Greene, *Horses at Work*, pp. 164–165.
38. H-J. Rheinberger, *An Epistemology of the Concrete: Twentieth-Century Histories of Life*, Durham, NC: Duke University Press, 2010.
39. On the marginalisation and promotion of certain races, without explicitly dealing with the question of animal labour, see B. Theunissen, 'Breeding without Mendelism: Theory and Practice of Dairy Cattle Breeding in the Netherlands 1900–1950', *Journal of the History of Biology*, 41(4), 2008, pp. 637–676.
40. A. Günthart, 'Über das Gedächtnis des Rindes und seine Verwendung bei der Zugarbeit', *Die Grüne, Schweizerische Landwirtschaftliche Zeitschrift*, 13, June 1941, Nr. 24, S. 642–644.
41. A.E. Clarke, *Disciplining Reproduction: Modernity, American Life Sciences and the 'Problems of Sex'*, Berkeley, CA; Los Angeles, CA; London: University of California Press, 1998; S. Wilmot, 'Between the Farm and the Clinic: Agriculture and Reproductive Technology in the Twentieth Century', *Studies in History and Philosophy of Biological and Biomedical Sciences*, vol. 38, 2007, pp. 303–315; J-P. Gaudillière, 'The Farm and the Clinic: An Inquiry into the Making of our Biomedical Modernity', *Studies in History and Philosophy of Biological and Biomedical Sciences*, vol. 38, 2007, pp. 521–529.
42. A. Seufferheld, *Die Anwendung der Elekrizitität im landwirtschaftlichen Betriebe*, Stuttgart 1899; F. Ringwald, ‚Die Elektrizität im Dienste der Landwirtschaft', *Mitteilungen der Gesellschaft schweizerischer Landwirte*, 2, 1921, pp. 74–83. On the history of electrification, see e.g. P. Brassley, 'Agricultural Technology and Ephemeral Landscape', in D.E. Nye (ed.), *Technologies of Landscape: From Reaping to Recycling*, Amherst, MA: University of Massachusetts Press, 1999, pp. 21–39; D. Gugerli, *Redeströme. Zur Elektrifizierung der Schweiz 1880–1914*, Zürich: Chronos, 1996.
43. A. Nef, 'Vom Laufberuf zum Sitzberuf': Die Technisierung des Gutsbetriebs 'Schloss Gündelhart', Lizentiatsarbeit an der Universität Zürich, Zürich, 2003.
44. Norton Greene, *Horses at Work*, p. 190.
45. A. Rabinbach, *The Human Motor: Energy, Fatigue, and the Origins of Modernity*, Berkeley, CA: University of California Press, 1992.

46 Rabinbach, *The Human Motor*; P. Mirowski, *More Heat than Light: Economics as Social Physics, Physics as Nature's Economics*, Cambridge: Cambridge University Press, 1989; M. Osietzki, 'Körpermaschinen und Dampfmaschinen: Vom Wandel der Physiologie und des Körpers unter dem Einfluss von Industrialisierung und Thermodynamik', in P. Sarasin and J. Tanner (eds), *Physiologie und industrielle Gesellschaft: Studien zur Verwissenschaftlichung des Körpers im 19. und 20 Jahrhundert*, Frankfurt a.M.: Suhrkamp, 1998, pp. 313–346.
47 F. Jacob, *The Logic of Life: A History of Heredity*, New York: Pantheon, 1983, p. 194.
48 Wrigley, *Energy and the English Industrial Revolution*, pp. 26–52; N. Georgescu-Roegen, *The Entropy Law and the Economic Process*, Cambridge, MA: Harvard University Press, 1971.
49 T.S. Kuhn, 'Energy Conservation as an Example of Simultaneous Discovery', in M. Clagett (ed.), *Critical Problems in the History of Science*, Madison, WI: University of Wisconsin Press, 1959, pp. 321–356.
50 This failure corresponded partially with the experiences made in scientific studies on human labour; see F. Vatin, *Le travail, science et société: Essai d'épistémologie et de sociologie du travail*, Brussels: Ed. de l'Université de Bruxelles, 1999.
51 G.B. Ellenberg, 'Debating Farm Power: Draught Animals, Tractors, and the United States Department of Agriculture', *Agricultural History*, vol. 74, No. 2, 2000, pp. 545–568; Olmstead and Rhode, 'The Agricultural Mechanization Controversy of the Interwar Years'.
52 F. Ineichen Franz, 'Vergleichende Betrachtung über Traktoren und Zugtiere', *Der Motor in der Landwirtschaft, Spezialheft von Auto*, 15(21/22), 1941, pp. 64–67, here: p. 67.
53 On the metaphor of the 'iron horse', see Wik, 'Steam Power on the American Farm', p. 185; the 'superhorse' is mentioned in A. Benteli, 'Ein neuer Raupen-Traktor', *Schweizerische landwirtschaftliche Monatshefte*, vol.1, 1923, p. 21.
54 A. Sidler, 'Etwas über die Entwicklung und den gegenwärtigen Stand der Motorisierung der Landwirtschaft in der Schweiz', *Der Motor in der Landwirtschaft, Spezialheft von Auto*, 15(21/22), 1941, pp. 9–13. On the history of agriculture in Switzerland during the First World War, see P. Moser, 'Mehr als eine Übergangszeit: Die Neuordnung der Ernährungsfrage während des Ersten Weltkriegs', in R. Rossfeld, T. Buomberger and P. Kury (eds), *14/18: Die Schweiz und der Grosse Krieg*, Baden: Hier und Jetzt-Verlag, 2014, pp. 172–199.
55 S. Giedion, *Mechanization Takes Command: A Contribution to Anonymous History*, New York, 1948: Oxford University Press, p. 162; Wik, 'Steam Power on the American Farm', p. 186; Ankli and Olmstead, 'The Adoption of the Gasoline Tractor in California', p. 214.
56 H. Beglinger, 'Entwicklung und Stand des Motorpflugwesens in der Schweiz', *Landwirtschaftliches Jahrbuch der Schweiz*, vol. 34, 1920, pp. 210–243, here: p. 212.
57 Ineichen, 'Vergleichende Betrachtung über Traktoren und Zugtiere', p. 65.
58 E. Rauch, 'Pferd und Motor', *Neue Zürcher Zeitung*, Nr. 2568, 8 December 1949; U. Duerst, 'Zur Statik und Mechanik des Pferdes', in Probleme der schweizerischen Pferdezucht: Vorträge, gehalten an der Tagung der Schweizerischen Vereinigung für Tierzucht vom 23. und 24. March 1945 in Murten (=Schriften der Schweizerischen Vereinigung für Tierzucht, Nr. 6), Bern: Benteli, 1945, pp. 107–113.
59 D. Haraway, 'A Cyborg Manifesto: Science, Technology, and Socialist-Feminism in the Late Twentieth Century', in D. Haraway, *Simians, Cyborgs and Women: The Reinvention of Nature*, New York: Routledge, 1991, pp. 149–181.
60 On the notion of useful knowledge, see J. Mokyr, *The Gifts of Athena: Historical Origins of the Knowledge Society*, Princeton, NJ: Princeton University Press, 2002.
61 *Der Traktor*, Nr. 1, 1956, 6.
62 K. Wiesinger, 'Universal-Traktor', *Mitteilungen der Gesellschaft schweizerischer Landwirte*, No. 1, 1921, pp. 47–52.

63 G. Federico, 'Natura Non Fecit Saltus', p. 24.
64 Federico, 'Natura Non Fecit Saltus'. This view is generally shared as well by K.K. Patel, 'The Paradox of Planning: German Agricultural Policy in a European Perspective, 1920s to 1970s', *Past & Present*, vol. 212, 2011, pp. 239–269.
65 O. Howald, 'Betrachtungen zur Abgrenzung des Geltungsbereichs des Landwirtschaftsgesetzes von 1951', *Agrarpolitische Revue 1963/64*, pp. 459–464, here: p. 461.
66 P. Moser, 'Zugriff auf die Lithosphäre: Gestaltungspotenziale unterschiedlicher Energiegrundlagen in der agrarisch-industriellen Wissensgesellschaft', *Traverse*, 2013 (3), pp. 37–48.
67 A.L. Olmstead and P.W. Rhode, *Creating Abundance: Biological Innovation and American Agricultural Development*, Cambridge: Cambridge University Press, 2008, p. 11.
68 Howald, 'Betrachtungen zur Abgrenzung des Geltungsbereiches des Landwirtschaftsgesetzes von 1951', p. 461.
69 See e.g. M. Spoerer, '"Fortress Europe" in Long-term Perspective: Agricultural Protection in the European Community, 1957–2003', *Journal of European Integration History*, 16, 2010, pp. 143–162.
70 N. Georgescu-Roegen, 'Economic Theory and Agrarian Economics', in *Oxford Economic Papers*, New Series, 12(1), 1960, pp. 1–40.
71 P. Bairoch, 'Les trois révolutions agricoles du monde développé: Rendements et productivité de 1800 à 1985', *Annales E.S.C.* vol. 44, 1989, pp. 317–353.
72 See J. Kloppenburg Jr, 'Social Theory and the De/Reconstruction of Agricultural Science', p. 248.
73 J. Auderset and P. Moser, *Die Agrarfrage in der Industriegesellschaft*.
74 E.M. Rodolfo and A. Seshadri, 'Frictionless Technology Diffusion: The Case of Tractors', *American Economic Review*, 104, 2014, pp. 1368–1391.
75 C. Lévi-Strauss, *La pensée sauvage*, Paris: Plon, 1962, p. 26.

9 Technology policies in dictatorial contexts

Spain and Portugal

Daniel Lanero and Lourenzo Fernández-Prieto

The 1930s and 1940s were a time of agrarian fascism in the Iberian Peninsula. The influence of international fascism on agriculture and the rural world materialised in a series of core policies that were commonly adopted by the political regimes of various European countries within the fascist ideological sphere. These policies were characterised by economic intervention in every phase of agriculture, from production to commercialisation, preference for technical agricultural reform (colonisation policies), inclusion of the rural population in mass organisations, and a discourse that exalted the ethical and moral virtues of the rural world. The agricultural policy of the Portuguese Estado Novo operated within these parameters from its establishment in 1933 until the end of the Second World War. Similarly, in Spain this period began with the adoption of certain measures by rebel officers in the territories they controlled during the Civil War (1936–1939) and extended until well into the 1950s.

The Estado Novo and the Franco regime constitute two privileged historical laboratories for examining the transition from the scientific, technocratic and authoritarian modernising push of agrarian fascism to the agricultural modernisation paradigm implemented in Western Europe after 1945, which was adopted later by the Iberian dictatorships. The common elements and continuities between these models are much more relevant than a first glance would indicate.[1]

Broadly speaking, this panorama provides the backdrop to the 1950s, which is the stage we will address in this text in three sections. In the first and second sections, we analyse the evolution of agriculture and agricultural policies in Spain and Portugal, respectively, during that decade. Both sections give special attention to technological innovation processes and the role of key actors such as the technical agronomic elites within these dictatorships. The third section provides a comparative synthesis.

The 1950s: a decade of changes in Francoist agrarian policies

Spanish agricultural historiography consistently marks the early 1950s as a significant turning point in the economic policies of the Franco regime. This change in course is attributed to both the weakening (and eventual demise) of economic interventionist policies in the agricultural sector and the influence of a new Minister of Agriculture, Rafael Cavestany, who assumed the post in 1951. So much has been written on this agronomic engineer, agricultural landowner and fascist member of the FET-JONS single party that he has almost become a historiographic topic in his own right. Cavestany is recognised as the author of the Spanish agricultural modernisation programme, which he described in his book, *Una política agraria*[2] and which can be summarised in his well-known maxim 'fewer farmers and better agriculture'. However, continuity with 1940s fascist policies regarding agriculture, agronomic research and agricultural knowledge transfer did not disappear overnight.[3]

The novelty of the 1950s should be understood on three interacting planes. First, structural changes occurred in the agricultural sector as the Franco regime began to acknowledge agricultural autarky as a blind alley and gradually abandon it, in spite of political-ideological resistance from certain quarters. Second, the international political situation of the Franco government changed and foreign relations with the West were re-established early in the decade. Finally, a new legislative and institutional framework emerged for developing the envisioned agricultural policy model, designed in collaboration with international organisations.

The new international situation of Francoism and its effects on the agricultural sector

The Franco regime found itself in a very delicate international position during the Second World War and the years immediately following it. The dictatorship was excluded from the founding conference of the United Nations in San Francisco in the summer of 1945. In 1946, most Western states closed their diplomatic offices in Madrid. Most significantly, however, Spain was not included in the Marshall Plan, the massive US-driven postwar reconstruction and economic aid programme to Europe. However, the ongoing Cold War climate between the US and the USSR that began in 1947–1948 ensured the mid- and long-range survival of the Franco regime, though this did not involve an invitation to join NATO.

With the onset of the Korean War, Spain began its journey towards international recognition. Complex negotiations commenced between the Franco regime and the US government, which culminated in 1953 with the signing of the Pact of Madrid, involving military cooperation. The same year, Spain became a member of the United Nations Food and Agriculture Organization (FAO), and a member of the UN itself in December 1955. In 1958, Spain also joined the International Monetary Fund, the World Bank and the Organisation for European Economic Cooperation.

Incorporation into these political institutions also allowed Spanish agricultural experts, who had been isolated during the 1940s, to begin participating again in international scientific communities and forums. This, along with US technical assistance, became the primary channel for implementing in Francoist Spain the large-scale agricultural modernisation paradigm that had been underway in Western Europe since the end of the Second World War. International institutions greatly influenced the political-legislative implementation of the agricultural modernisation programme in Spain a decade later. The 1962 World Bank agricultural sector diagnosis for Spain (along with the corresponding action proposals) and its 1966 report in collaboration with the FAO were especially significant.[4] Their agricultural policy recommendations were taken into account by the regime, though some reticence was registered among its technical and academic elites. However, certain insurmountable limitations still applied to any international attempts at political rehabilitation of a dictatorship that had arisen from interwar fascism. In spite of its participation in European organisations responsible for fostering the coordination of State agricultural policies, the Franco regime was excluded from the 1957 Treaty of Rome.

The 1953 military cooperation agreement between the US and Spain included secondary dimensions such as cultural and economic cooperation based on economic incentives. To supervise the correct investment of economic cooperation funds, the US government established a special Economic Mission in Spain. Its activities included US technical assistance for Spanish agriculture that reached 5.5 billion Spanish pesetas between 1953 and 1964.[5] One of the main outcomes was the establishment of an Agricultural Extension Service (SEA) in 1955, modelled entirely after the US Cooperative Extension Service. Agricultural cooperation was complemented by the importation of agricultural machinery, chemical fertilisers and cattle. American aid improved the Spanish diet in a decisive way through the importation of cereals and soya oil.

The agricultural programme of the Cavestany Ministry: modernisation principles, policies and instruments

Inspired by a modernising ideal reaching back to the early 1900s, the Cavestany agricultural programme sought efficient agriculture with well-capitalised farms and adequate technology that would make them internally and economically similar in outlook to industrialised companies. State intervention would drive agricultural change through strong economic support, intense legislative activity and deep institutional reorganisation of the central agricultural administration. Along with two policies derived from agrarian fascism, reforestation and a new version of agricultural colonisation, land consolidation constituted a third and novel reference measure in the 1950s. Leaving aside reforestation,[6] the other two complementary structural reform measures shared the same modernisation logic as other agricultural activities intended to increase productivity.

Colonisation policies in the 1950s prioritised maximum extension of irrigation through the construction of large hydraulic infrastructures (dams and wells), leaving any social dimensions in the background. Between 1941 and 1950, irrigation had been applied to some 10,000 ha. In the following decade, irrigation reached almost 200,000 ha, which still fell far short of Cavestany's ambitions for increasing irrigated land by 50,000 ha per year.[7] Through irrigation and colonisation, agriculture contributed to regional industrialisation and the 'full use of the economic potential of the areas affected'.[8] Hydraulic policy became a decisive sphere for the transfer of new technologies and a key to the exponential growth in agricultural productivity from 1955 onwards.[9]

The objective of land consolidation was to end the tremendous plot fragmentation in the centre and north of Spain by establishing 'minimum farming units' that were adequate for motorised farming (decreasing the number of farm plots, opening roads, etc.). In spite of the creation of the *Servicio Nacional de Concentración Parcelaria* (National Land Consolidation Service) in 1952 and the legislative backing of these policies through laws in 1952 and 1955, land consolidation was only occasionally successful until the 1960s and reached its point of greatest impact in 1970s.

A similar tendency was evident in incentive schemes for farms that achieved a level of excellence set by the State. They were rewarded with technical consulting, better loan conditions or subsidies for acquiring inputs.[10] A more relaxed view of economic intervention and a significant increase in public investment in agriculture from the mid-1950s on had positive effects on private agricultural investment, which began to recover thoughout the remainder of that decade and became well established in the 1960s.[11]

The deep postwar production crisis of the 1940s was addressed in the 1950s through infrastructure policies and a new official price policy that sought to stabilise the internal food markets. Certain invervention measures that had been restricting the supply of agricultural products were eliminated and the fixed prices of others were increased. A system of minimum prices was established, alongside State guarantees of unlimited crop purchases of any quality. Owners reacted by returning to traditional dry crops (wheat, olives, vineyards) that were protected by price guarantees. These measures increased cultivated area, production, consumption and agricultural exports during the 1950s.[12] However, towards the end of the decade and beyond,

Table 9.1 Evolution of land consolidation in Spain (1953–1959)

Year	Thousands of hectares consolidated
1954	7.9
1955	12.2
1956	10.6
1957	21.7
1958	50.2
1959	68.6
1953–1959	171.2

Source: Ramón Tamames, *Estructura económica de España*, Madrid: Alianza, 1983

negative effects on the agricultural sector became evident as production surpluses accumulated, inflation increased, these subsectors demonstrated poor competitiveness and it became difficult to supply agricultural products for the new nutritional demands associated with growing per capita income. This took place in a context of technological standstill derived from the effects of the Civil War (1936–1939).

The motorisation of agricultural work expanded in relative terms during the 1950s, given that the starting point was negligible.[13] The classical explanation sees as a major factor the increased labour costs caused by renewed rural exodus.[14] Other authors argue that it was not the cost of labour, but the effects of decreasing official prices for agricultural products that forced farmers to improve productivity by using machinery.[15] Moreover, in contrast with the scarcity of the 1940s, fuel now became more available and the national agricultural machinery industry gradually began to grow.[16]

The lack of reliable statistics precludes a description (along the lines of Chapters 8 and 10) of the way in which tractors took over from work animals (mules, oxen and cows more than horses) in Spanish agriculture from 1940 to 1960. The Civil War particularly affected cattle; mules were used for military purposes and cows for army food provision, hence decreasing livestock reproduction. Some authors suggest a direct relationship between the scarcity of work animals and reduced postwar cultivated agricultural surface.[17]

Looking beyond the economic situation, political and institutional factors such as the end of Spain's international isolation led to increased imports, assisted by US aid and the stimulus of soft loans for motorisation through the *Servicio Nacional de Crédito Agrícola* (National Agricultural Credit Service). Paradoxically, interventionist restrictions on foreign currency in the 1950s limited tractor imports and thus the potential for agricultural motorisation.[18] Even so, it is important to highlight the direct relationship between agricultural structural policies and increased motorisation.

Agriculture in the 1940s suffered from constant scarcity in the provision of chemical fertilisers (especially nitrate-based), caused both by the regime's economic autarky policy and an international decrease in the production and trade of inorganic fertilisers.[19] In the 1950s, chemical fertiliser production gradually recovered thanks to State subsidies, foreign capital inflows (manufacturing permits and technical assistance) and the financial support of the USA.[20]

Table 9.2 Spain (1950–1964): number of tractors, tractors per cultivated ha and tractors per number of agricultural workers

Year	Tractors	Tractors/cultivated ha	Tractors/agricultural workers
1950	12,800	1.9	1/406
1960	56,800	9.9	1/85
1964	130,100	25.4	1/35

Source: Simpson, *La agricultura española*, p. 336

Table 9.3 Fertiliser consumption in kilograms per hectare in Spain (1930–1960)

Year	N	P_2O_2	K_2O
1930	3.8	11.0	1.7
1935	4.6	10.1	1.5
1945	0.7	5.2	2.0
1951	4.6	10.0	2.7
1955	11.0	15.0	3.4
1960	14.9	17.7	4.3

Source: Pan-Montojo, 'Spanish Agriculture, 1931–1955: Crisis, Wars and New Policies in the Reshaping of Rural Society', in Brassley, Segers and Van Molle (eds) (2012) *War, Agriculture, and Food: Rural Europe from the 1930s to the 1950s*. New York: Routledge, p. 79.

The bottlenecks that limited Spanish agricultural inputs were eventually overcome, generating positive effects on production that became especially visible in major crops during the second half of the 1950s.

In contrast, research and genetic improvements in herbaceous crops and cattle were virtually non-existent until 1965.[21]

Spanish cattle farms went through a time of transition in the 1950s. This subsector had been marginalised by agrarian policies and suffered intensely the effects of the postwar agricultural crisis.[22] Urbanisation and the gradual recovery of per capita income stimulated the demand for meat; by 1955, consumption in cities exceeded levels prior to the Civil War. Increased demand was met by an increase in production of the cheapest animal proteins (eggs and pork). The notable expansion of pig and poultry farms in the late 1950s paved the way for the type of industrial cattle farming that became dominant from 1960 to 1975.[23] In a parallel manner, the nutritional levels of the national population also improved during that decade. The end of food rationing in 1952 and recovery of production led first to an increase in consumption of basic products (cereals, potatoes, legumes) and later to greater consumption of calories from animal sources. In the 1960s, the Spanish diet diversified almost to the point of fitting the nutritional patterns of Western European countries.[24]

Table 9.4 Yields per hectare of the main Spanish agricultural products (1950–1959)

Years	Wheat	Barley	Rye	Corn	Must (a)	Olive oil	Potatoes	Sugar beet	Oranges
1931–1935	100	100	100	100	100	100	100	100	100
1950–1954	97	95	84	109	93	91	93	87	106
1955–1959	106	95	96	125	93	88	100	102	106

Note: (a) unfermented grape juice.
Source: Pan-Montojo, 'Spanish Agriculture, 1931–1955: Crisis, Wars and New Policies in the Reshaping of Rural Society', in Brassley, Segers and Van Molle (eds) (2012) *War, Agriculture, and Food: Rural Europe from the 1930s to the 1950s*. New York: Routledge, p. 80.

Table 9.5 Evolution of the consumption of animal products in the Spanish diet, 1935–1975 (kg per inhabitant per year)

Year	Meat	Milk	Eggs	% animal proteins (total)
1935	14	61	5	28 (88)
1952–53	14	56	5	25 (69)
1955–59	21	68	6	28 (-)
1960–64	26	68	9	32 (80)
1970	45	81	12	45 (80)
1975	61	95	16	52 (95)

Source: Domínguez, 'Las transformaciones del sector ganadero ...', p. 54.

Agricultural research and technical experts in the 1950s: from autarky to economic development

During the 1950s the Ministry of Agriculture was reorganised several times to accommodate new policy needs of the dictatorship, giving continuity to the *Instituto Nacional de Investigaciones Agrarias* (INIA; National Agrarian Research Institute) that had been created in 1939. In 1951, the Directorate General of Coordination, Credit and Agricultural Training was established.[25] Its broad range of responsibilities included vocational training in agriculture, credit management, agricultural insurance policies, propaganda through cinematography and the complex coordination with the *Organización Sindical Agraria* (Agrarian Trade Union).[26] This compulsory corporative structure had been designed by the dictatorship for the rural world and had relatively little political influence, but often interfered in the Ministry of Agriculture's spheres of action. So, the new Directorate General centralised organisations and autonomous services that were decisive in implementing the modernisation programme. Prominent among these was the *Servicio de Extensión Agraria* (SEA) or Agricultural Extension Service, created in 1955.[27]

The Director of the US Economic Mission in Spain was behind the creation of the SEA. Charles Fossum contacted Minister Cavestany, along with the Director General of Coordination, Credit and Training and the Head of the INIA. Fossum convinced them that their planned agricultural development model would never succeed because Spain lacked a true advisory service and he invited the Minister of Agriculture to the USA for a direct experience with the work of the US Cooperative Extension Service. Upon returning in September 1955, the ministry enacted the order to create an Agricultural Extension Service in Spain.

The SEA, in cooperation with the USA, was essential to the agricultural modernisation programme of the dictatorship. SEA activity began experimentally in areas subject to land consolidation. Within a fairly short period, the programme had extended throughout the country and the number of agencies had increased greatly. At first, the fledgling SEA focused almost exclusively on areas relating to production. The agents were primarily concerned with the transfer of new technology and consistently applied a main tenet of the SEA – that of working actively alongside the farmer to bring about change.

The most relevant aspect of the analysis of the reorganisation of the Ministry of Agriculture and its services is what it suggests regarding the redefinition of State intervention. Francoism gradually abandoned policies of intervention in agricultural production and commercialisation, which had in fact led the country to the brink of economic collapse. It began to pursue an ideal of efficient, modern, and profitable agriculture integrated within the overall Spanish economy, and implemented international recommendations mainly to ensure the political survival of the regime.

The reorganising efforts of the 1950s also affected agricultural research and training. The State had given very little priority to innovation in the prior decade, in spite of the establishment of the *Centro Superior de Investigaciones Científicas* (CSIC) (Spanish National Research Council) in 1939 and the creation of the *Instituto Nacional de Investigaciones Agrarias* (INIA). The INIA replaced the *Instituto de Investigaciones Agrarias* (IIA; Agrarian Research Institute) of the Spanish Second Republic. Leaving aside the sense of discontinuity in agronomic research through the creation of INIA and the expectations associated with every new State institution, research centres after the Spanish Civil War were marked by poor organisation, regression in lines of research, budgetary difficulties and scant material and human resources. Moreover, a considerable gap existed between research and the rural context it was intended to influence.[28] The consolidation of Francoism created a break with the institutional innovation structures that had existed in the previous liberal context. The only really significant undertaking in the 1950s was an inventory of the remaining research, experimentation and dissemination centres in order to determine which of them were still viable. New proposals were put forward for systematising this complex structure.[29] At that time, less than 10 per cent of the 1,500 registered agronomic engineers in the country worked within the INIA structure. Those that did, generally carried out more bureaucratic than scientific work.[30] Moreover, in the mid-1960s, a World Bank report warned of weak, inferior and uncoordinated scientific research in Spanish agriculture.[31]

Most of the active agronomic technical experts from the Second Republic had survived the political purges of the Civil War and the early 1940s.[32] The technical experts with the most advanced degrees dominated the agricultural sphere in the 1940s and 1950s. Agronomic engineers dictated agricultural policies and younger experts implemented the postwar agricultural modernisation paradigm. Under the dictatorship, complete trust in the efficiency of the new technological package was imposed on a rural world bereft of the old forms of association that had facilitated the incorporation of technological advances, a world increasingly disarticulated socially due to the rural exodus.

The new phase was symbolically launched in March of 1950 with the first National Conference of Agronomic Engineering at the Madrid School of

Agronomic Engineering. Extensive discussion and debate took place regarding agricultural policies in the first decade of the dictatorship and the crisis of Spanish agriculture.[33] The central topic was whether to maintain or abandon economic intervention policies for agriculture. The conference prepared the ground for the changes in agricultural politics we have been discussing and set the stage for Cavestany's arrival at the Ministry of Agriculture in 1951. It also gave agronomic engineers the opportunity to reclaim their authority, with regard to directing agricultural policy, over other actors with political interests in the rural sphere, particularly the *FET–JONS* single party and its satellite structures:[34] official trade unions, youth associations and rural women's organisations.[35] The corporative demands of the agronomists triumphed: all three Ministers of Agriculture between 1945 and 1965 were agronomic engineers (Rein Segura: 1945–1951; Cavestany: 1951–1957 and Cánovas: 1957–1965). The technocratic component of the dictatorship had triumphed over the political.

The end of the 1950s in Spain was marked by policy continuity under the leadership of Cirilo Cánovas (1957–1965). Agricultural policies stagnated in the early 1960s and the sector gradually moved towards a new phase of guided economic planning that was inaugurated by the Stabilisation Plan (1959) and expanded in the first Development Plan (1964–1967).

Portuguese agriculture in the 1950s: stagnation on the threshold of great change

The Estado Novo: economic modernisation and the agrarian question in the 1950s

In contrast with Francoist Spain, which departed from 'agrarian fascism' in the 1950s, the Portuguese *Estado Novo* maintained important continuities with agricultural policies that had been set in motion in the 1930s. In the final quarter of the nineteenth century, a great debate began that attempted to address the need for deep agrarian structural reform in order to move Portuguese agriculture beyond its centuries of backwardness. Essentially, agricultural property was extremely fragmented and even atomised to the point that the disproportionately large population found even subsistence farming difficult in the north. Meanwhile, the south struggled with under-population and large, inefficiently cultivated landholdings, especially in the Alentejo region.

However, it would be a mistake to think of Portuguese agriculture in the 1950s as completely synonymous with the past. The Second World War had greatly impacted on this economically peripheral country. One of the main political consequences was to strengthen the interventionist role of the State, which had been a clear tendency since the 1930s.[36] The Salazar regime emerged from the economic and social tensions of the Second World War intending to oversee an economic modernisation process sustained by national industrial development. It was led by an industrialist technocratic elite with engineer José Ferreira Dias, the sub-Secretary of State for Industry, as its most exalted representative. Industrialism became the official economic discourse of the *Estado Novo* and in the aftermath of the Second World War several alternative economic modernisation projects were postponed.

The main project affected was that of Rafael Duque, Minister of Agriculture (1934–1940) and later of Economy (1940–1944). In the second half of the 1930s, he launched an economic modernisation programme based primarily on updating Portuguese agriculture as the engine for national industrial growth. The three main axes of the programme were: 1) correcting the land ownership structure by dividing up the large southern properties and consolidating the northern smallholdings; 2) crop diversification and intensification, and 3) introducing industrial capital for food processing in order to create an agro–industrial sector in the Portuguese economy.[37]

In the southern regions, the campaign to correct land ownership regimes was summarised in four words: *irrigate, colonise, reorganise, modernise*. The aim was to establish economically viable family farms by dividing up and irrigating large, arid tracts of land. Duque saw internal colonisation and hydraulic agriculture as the only possibility for altering the land ownership structure. Duque's reform project was legislatively formalised and an institutional infrastructure was developed for its implementation. This involved the 1936 creation of the *Junta de Colonização Interna* (JCI; Internal Colonisation Board) and the 1937 Law on Hydraulic Agriculture with its corresponding 1938 Hydraulic Agriculture Plan.

The project ran head-on into a wall of opposition from the large national agricultural lobbies, large landowners in the south (from Alentejo, Ribatejo, Beiras, etc.) and even prominent northern landowners. They monolithically defended the interests of their productive sectors (wheat, wine, olive and cattle) against any insinuation of change in traditional Portuguese agriculture. Large landowners had been close to the core of the *Estado Novo* from its inception and were embedded in political power structures and institutions at every level, from governmental decision-making to rural parishes, by means of a dense clientelistic network. They constituted a key social and political pillar that the regime would never challenge.[38] The political and social influence of the large-scale landowners diminished slightly or was rechannelled in the final years of the dictatorship, when it was overcome by the irreversible and accelerated modernisation of economic structures from 1960 to 1974. This led to complete subordination of the rural world on every level.

The agricultural question faded into the background in the political debate of the 1950s. Industrialists opted for a pragmatic and voluntaristic post-war strategy. Industrial development, which ultimately did not depend on the agricultural sector, would drive the economic modernisation of Portugal. This formula avoided direct confrontation and permitted a peaceful coexistence with the political interests of the agricultural lobbies. This industrial pragmatism was eventually successful, but smallholders and day labourers paid the highest social cost of economic modernisation in the form of a massive rural exodus and the capitalisation of small-scale agriculture through emigrant remittances.

Though its most qualified leaders had been relegated to second-string politics, the modernising agrarian reformism of the 1930s was temporarily reactivated in the late 1950s within the framework and legislation of the Second Stimulus Plan, known as the *II Plano de Fomento* (1959–1964). This was a new product of the dictatorship's mid-range economic planning programme, which spanned from the early 1950s to the end of the regime in 1974. More than the restoration of the agricultural reform programme of the 1930s, the plan in the late 1950s involved 'a miscellaneous mix of the old context with what at that time was seen as the modern theory of economic development and certain contributions from industrialism'.[39]

The Second Stimulus Plan returned to the classical idea of dividing large southern landholdings while consolidating atomised properties north of the Tagus River. The large southern properties would be divided up under the subsidiary Alentejo Irrigation Plan, an enormous hydraulic project that largely succeeded in its aim of bringing irrigation to 162,000 hectares in eighteen years.[40] This was achieved to a large extent. In the north, the Plan sought to consolidate economically inefficient micro-farms into larger family farms that could provide a comfortable living, aided by motorisation and heavy consumption of inputs and other industrial goods. This land ownership restructuring project was complemented by a proposal to modify leasing legislation in favour of the tenants, who were farming families in the north and entrepreneurs in the south. The goal was to improve land-leasing contracts in order to stimulate capitalist agricultural initiatives.

The Second Stimulus Plan included an exhaustive report on the status of the agricultural sector. It was authored by Eugenio de Castro Caldas, a professor at the *Instituto Superior de Agronomía* (Higher Institute of Agronomy) who was well connected with the technical elites of the regime. He proposed a series of solutions for the main bottlenecks in Portuguese agriculture, all of which were to some extent related to imbalances in the land ownership structure. The report recommended reducing the agricultural area dedicated to wheat cultivation and converting less productive or more eroded lands into forest. It also proposed an increase in fruit production to satisfy domestic and foreign demand, while insisting on the need to improve livestock production levels. This in turn involved more irrigated land and more efficient farming of dryland fodder crops.

The sectorial objectives for agriculture established in the Second Stimulus Plan were not met. Once again, it collided with the interests of large agricultural pressure groups; once again, the regime settled the matter in favour of the latter and, once again, the structure of land ownership remained intact.[41]

Some signs along the road towards modernisation in Portuguese agriculture

In the 1950s continuity was maintained with the main lines of the Portuguese agricultural policies that had been defined in the 1930s (protection of traditional crops, colonisation, irrigation, reforestation). The old debate regarding the reform of agricultural structures remained at an impasse. Certain tendencies of the 1930–60 period reached their peak; they preceded the great crisis of transformation in the agricultural sector that occurred after 1960, which was fairly similar to the crisis of traditional agriculture in Spain.[42]

Between 1927 and 1960, total agricultural production grew at an annual rate of 2.43 per cent, in contrast with 0.77 per cent between 1902 and 1927. This growth has been explained as the result of three interacting factors: official protection of traditional crops (wheat, olive, vineyards), high levels of public investment in this sector and the beneficial effects of improved institutional provisions for the rural world, which we consider doubtful.[43] The production protection policy kept tax rates low and established fixed prices for traditional products, while others with more elastic demand (fruit, vegetables and legumes, animal products) remained outside official control. Thus, production increased in a more diversified manner, responding to changes in internal demand due to increased industrial activity and urbanisation. The *Estado Novo* invested heavily in the agricultural sector, especially between 1935 and 1950, when one third of all public expenditure went to agriculture.[44] The 1946 Law on Agricultural Improvement (which was revised in 1960) decisively ameliorated agricultural loan conditions for the motorisation of entrepreneurial and large family farms. Between 1934/38 and 1961, the ratio of tractors per hectare increased from 0.1 to 2.6, though it remained among the lowest in Southern Europe. Furthermore, the consumption of mineral fertilisers tripled from 10 to 35 kgs/hectare between 1934/38 and 1960/62.[45] Its actual impact was much greater in the 1960s, especially in the large southern properties. There, a new social group emerged to facilitate large-scale land leasing, which led to capitalised, intensively mechanised agricultural firms with a productive focus on fruit and milk, to meet the new demands of an expanding urban consumer market.

The onset of the rural exodus led to increased salaries for the farm workers and day labourers who remained, what favoured the motorisation of Portuguese agriculture. Mechanisation even intensified in the family-based agriculture of the north, thanks to remittances sent by Portuguese emigrants in other parts of Western Europe, the growing possibility of leasing agricultural machinery and credits fostered by the *Estado Novo* for northern landowners whose rents were decreasing due to the rural exodus.

A few initiatives emerged in the 1950s to create agricultural cooperatives within the entities of the *Organização Corporativa da Lavoura* (Corporative Farm Organization). This official corporative structure of the *Estado Novo* had been implanted in the rural context during the 1930s and membership was compulsory for all agricultural producers. Apart from specific initiatives by the local and provincial corporative entities, the main actors were generally the powerful *Organismos de Coordenação Económica* (Economic Coordination Organisations). They regulated for each subsector the price of produced and processed agricultural products in national and colonial markets. The *Junta Nacional do Vinho*

(National Wine Board), the *Junta Nacional do Azeite* (National Oil Board), and others promoted the formation of cooperatives at this time. A total of 163 cooperatives were created from 1947 to 1956, and 169 more from 1957 to 1966. Though most were olive, milk or wine cooperatives, some were concerned with cooperative consumption.[46] Other Economic Coordination Organisms such as the *Junta Nacional das Frutas* (National Fruit Board) invested in storage infrastructures, refrigeration or incentives to create agro-industrial complexes.

Along the northern coast, the *Federação de Grémios da Lavoura da Beira Litoral* (Beira Federation of Farmers' Guilds) demonstrated a clear entrepreneurial approach at the end of the 1950s. The small producers of the region vertically integrated milk production and processing through the local groups and the provincial Guild Federation. It led to the implementation of important technological innovations in the 1960s and 1970s, such as automated milking, product refrigeration and widespread artificial insemination techniques.[47]

Unlike the Franco regime in Spain, the Portuguese *Estado Novo* had less difficulty joining postwar international institutions. Portugal was included in the Marshall Plan in 1948. Under the Technical Assistance & Productivity Programme of the Economic Cooperation Administration (ECA), 25 projects were developed in Portugal between 1951 and 1956, with clear features of the US postwar modernisation paradigm.[48] These included soil conservation, improvement of milk quality, livestock health, cultivation of pasture and grazing lands, introduction of hybrid maize species, promoting fruit cultivation and agricultural extensionism. All of these initiatives sought to eventually improve agricultural productivity.

Procedures for technology transfer followed the lines established in other countries of Western Europe. US specialists and consultants visited Portugal to evaluate its agricultural sector, identify obstacles to modernisation and propose specific action plans for each problem. The US also regularly funded visits of Portuguese technical experts to the US for training in specific projects. The agricultural engineers and veterinarians involved in this programme were mainly from departments dependent on Sub-Secretariat of State for Agriculture – namely, the Directorate General for Agricultural Services, followed by Livestock Services, Forest Services (to a much lesser degree) and even some from corporative organisms. Although we know the basic details of these projects, we know nothing of their real impact on modernising Portuguese agriculture in the 1950s – whether they were carried forward by official institutions or were transitory experiments.

Agricultural technical elites were most affected during that decade by the creation of the institutionally unique *Centro de Estudos de Economia Agrária* (CEEA; Centre for Agro-Economic Studies),[49] the work of a group of agronomic engineers led by Mário de Azevedo Gomes and Henrique de Barros. Both prestigious professionals were known for their proximity to the political opposition movement. In September 1957 they presented their proposal to the President of the Calouste Gulbenkian Foundation, a philanthropic entity that actively supported artistic, scientific and educational activities under the *Estado Novo*. The CEEA began to function in January 1958 with the objective of contributing to the modernisation of Portuguese agriculture by promoting innovative agricultural practices based on scientific knowledge and new technologies.[50] The CEEA argued for a model of intensive, technologically well-equipped family farming that implemented entrepreneurial management methods and prioritised production for expanding internal markets. Agricultural extensionism would have been the ideal tool for taking this paradigm to farmers and bridging the gap detected by agronomists between farmers and State agricultural research centres studying genetics and phytopathology. However, the CEEA remained little more than a think-tank dedicated to agricultural issues and supplementary training for young agronomists.

Conclusions

In these pages we have sought to demonstrate how the agricultural policies of the Iberian dictatorships shared certain important features in the 1950s. Common points also existed in the evolution of the agricultural subsector within these national economies, though relevant differences became more apparent between 1960 and the oil crisis of the 1970s, which coincided with the end of these dictatorships.

Departing from the common base of agrarian fascism and its key policies in the second half of the 1930s, agriculture in Portugal and Spain tended toward marked divergence in the 1940s.[51] Portugal exhibited a continuity in agricultural policies from 1930 to the late 1950s that was only altered by the economic and social tensions surrounding the Second World War.[52] In contrast, Spanish agriculture suffered an acute crisis in the 1940s and only began to recover in the 1950s through the gradual abandonment of autarky and embracing of the US modernisation and development model.[53] Throughout that decade, the foundations were laid for the profound and accelerated structural transformation of the agricultural sector and rural world that took place in Spain during the 1960s.

Why did the agricultural autarky imposed by the Franco regime affect Spanish farmers so negatively? Why did production and domestic agricultural market protection in Portugal not have equally devastating effects? Certainty is elusive, but perhaps during the first third of the twentieth century Spanish agriculture had been more dynamic than Portuguese agriculture, which was defined by its colonial empire.[54] This was especially evident in Spain's greater integration of certain agricultural subsectors into international markets and receptiveness to external inputs (mineral fertilisers, machinery, etc.). Unlike Portugal, the political and commercial isolation of the Franco regime after 1945 enhanced the rigidity of the autarky ideal, the regime's insistence on solving its dysfunctionality through tighter regulation, and the extent of post-war effects. In contrast with autarkic novelties in Spain, and in spite of the fascist tendencies that marked the *Campanha do Trigo* (Wheat Campaign) (1929–1933), the protectionist policies of the *Estado Novo* for traditional agricultural subsectors displayed continuity with policies of the late nineteenth century.

In the 1950s, gradual convergence occurred in the agricultural policies of the Iberian Peninsula. The Franco regime and the *Estado Novo* adopted an economic modernisation model based on political support for industrial development. This had important demographic effects such as rural exodus and intensified urbanisation. Economic effects included the transition of the active population from agriculture to industry and services along with the eventual subordination of agriculture to industrial interests.

Agriculture became more modern and economically efficient. The political elites of both countries sought capitalisation of farms, especially the largest ones, through low-interest loans that facilitated initial input acquisition (mainly machinery). In the 1950s, both regimes also benefited from US agricultural technical assistance programmes. However, in the short term, agricultural production in the two countries evolved differently, as seen in the production data from 1954 to 1966. In Spain, production grew at an annual rate of 3.8 per cent, while in Portugal it only reached 1.2 per cent.[55] Both countries experienced similar changes in the internal structure of agricultural production. Land used for bread cereals was lost to animal farming; diets and nutrition changed with greater urbanisation, which led to increased diversification of crops (cereals, fodder, rice, fruits, vegetables, sugar beet, maize). Some of these new crops were closely linked to the extension of irrigation. Such changes appear to have occurred earlier and more intensely in Spain, while in Portugal traditional crops resisted change.[56] Why?

Although more comparative research is needed, we shall point out some interpretative hypotheses here.[57] After 1945, the Franco regime was in a much

Table 9.6 Active agricultural population as a proportion of total active population and Gross Agricultural Product (GAP) as a proportion of Gross Domestic Product (GDP) in Spain and Portugal (1930–1970)

Year	Spain		Portugal	
	Agricultural population (%)	GAP (%)	Agricultural population (%)	GAP (%)
1930	45.5	29	49(a)	30
1940	50.5	–	53(a)	29
1950	47.6	31	49(a)	31
1960	36.6	21	42	20
1970	22.8	11	26	12

Note: (a) includes fisheries
Source: Dulce Freire and Daniel Lanero, 'The Iberian dictatorships and agricultural modernisation after the Second World War', in Peter Moser and Tony Varley (eds), *Integration Through Subordination: The Politics of Agricultural Modernisation in Industrial Europe*, Turnhout: Brepols, 2013, p. 185.

Table 9.7 Agricultural output (percentage) in Spain (1931–1975)

	1931	1940–45	1950–55	1961–65	1971–75
Cereals and pulses	34.2	30.3	24.0	21.0	20.5
Wheat	16.5	13.8	13.7	10.7	7.1
Barley	6.3	6.7	3.5	3.4	6.6
Vineyards	6.0	10.5	14.5	9.7	5.3
Olive trees	5.7	7.8	10.1	6.5	3.4
Fruits	8.0	5.7	5.8	9.5	12.0
Vegetables	5.9	6.8	5.6	8.8	11.4
Roots	11.0	7.4	17.0	9.4	5.0
Raw materials	2.9	1.6	2.2	4.2	4.8
Fodder	2.6	2.4	1.2	3.8	3.3
Meat	11.4	8.6	5.8	11.5	17.7
Milk	6.9	12.2	8.3	9.3	12.2
Eggs	5.0	6.0	4.2	5.7	4.3
Wool	0.6	0.8	1.2	0.5	0.2
Total agriculture	100.0	100.0	100.0	100.0	100.0
Crops	76.2	72.4	80.5	73.0	65.6
Livestock	23.8	27.5	19.4	26.9	34.4

'Economic development, 1870–1973', in Pedro Lains and Vicente Pinilla (eds), *Agriculture and Economic Development* ..., 317.

Table 9.8 Agricultural sectoral growth (constant prices, per cent) in Portugal (1930–1973)

	1930–50	1950–60	1960–73
Wheat	2.10	−1.54	0.38
Maize	−0.04	−1.01	0.67
Rye	1.61	−2.04	−0.26
Rice	7.99	0.68	0.80
Wine and spirits	1.40	2.04	0.11
Olive oil and olives	2.11	8.90	−5.36
Beans and potatoes	3.99	−1.80	0.28
Meat	2.61	1.71	−0.73
Milk		2.27	2.15
Eggs, wool, etc.		1.92	1.92
Vegetables		2.70	−0.76
Cork	3.11	3.65	0.59
Wood		0.66	3.81
Resins		14.48	−7.79
Total	2.45	1.81	0.44
Vegetable		0.80	0.56
Animal		1.85	0.35
Forest		4.62	0.30

Source: Lains and Pinilla, *Agriculture and economic development* ... p. 346.

Table 9.9 Agricultural labour productivity, land productivity and land-labour ratio in Portugal and Spain (1950–1972)

Country	Year	Agricultural labour productivity (a)	Land productivity (b)	Land–labour ratio
Portugal	1950	1,211	536	2.26
Spain	1950	1,330	325	4.09
Portugal	1962	1,725	825	2.12
Spain	1962	2,017	447	4.51
Portugal	1972	2,215	760	2.92
Spain	1972	3,451	572	6.03

Note (a):1950–2005 (international 1999–2001 prices in dollars per worker) and annual growth rates from 1950 to 2005. (b) international 1999–2001 prices in dollars per hectare.

Source: Martín-Retortillo and Pinilla, 'On the causes of economic growth in Europe: why did agricultural labour productivity not converge between 1950 and 2005?', *Cliométrica*, 2014, DOI 10.1007/s11698-014-0119-5.

more delicate international situation than the Salazar regime. This led to Spain's greater adherence to US postwar hegemony. Franco's modernisation policies in agriculture were much more decisive in the 1950s than those of the *Estado Novo*. The best example of this can be found in the Franco regime's emphasis on agricultural structural policies and the extension of irrigation, which were directly related to the intensity of motorisation and the magnitude of structural change in the Spanish agricultural production of the 1960s. Meanwhile, the *Estado Novo* continually avoided any true change in national agricultural structures, as seen in the negligible results of the colonisation policy.[57] Clear differences exist in the political logic and internal social factors underlying these divergent behaviours.

Francoism demonstrated that it was possible to vastly increase the irrigated area while scrupulously upholding the rights of the large rural landowners who constituted one of its main social and political pillars. In fact, from the 1950s on, the colonisation policy served chiefly to capitalise their farms and give them access to maximum returns from new industrial agriculture. The Civil War and the benefits obtained from their large-scale participation in the 1940s black markets had erased any doubts among rural elites regarding the true intentions of Francoist agricultural policies.

In Portugal, the large agricultural lobbies with interests mainly tied to traditional dry crops in the south systematically opposed any modernisation projects that would alter crop systems or forms of landholding. Large landowners in Portugal formed part of the socio-political and ideological DNA of the *Estado Novo* and rejected almost all State attempts to reform the rural context. The structural transformation of the Portuguese countryside from the 1960s on was in a way almost natural, as it derived more from global changes affecting the national economy than from specific measures designed for agriculture.

Notes

1 Lourenzo Fernández-Prieto, Juan Pan-Montojo and Miguel Cabo, *Agriculture in the Age of Fascism*, Turnhout: Brepols, 2014, 22–23; 28–30. See also P. Brassley, Y. Segers and L. Van Molle (eds), *War, Agriculture, and Food: Rural Europe from the 1930s to the 1950s*, New York: Routledge, 2012.
2 Rafael Cavestany, *Una política agraria (discursos)*, Dirección General de Coordinación, Crédito y Capacitación del Ministerio de Agricultura, Madrid: Ministerio de Agricultura, 1958.
3 Ana Cabana and Alba Díaz, 'Exploring modernization: agrarian fascism in rural Spain', in Fernández–Prieto *et al.* (eds), *Agriculture in the Age of Fascism* ..., 2014, pp. 189–217.
4 International Bank for Reconstruction and Development (IBRD), *Informe del Banco Internacional de Reconstrucción y Fomento: el desarrollo económico de España*, Madrid: Oficina de Coordinación y Programación Económica, 1962; IBRD & Food and Agriculture Organization of the United Nations (FAO), *El desarrollo de la agricultura en España. Informe del Banco Internacional de Reconstrucción y Fomento y de la Organización de las Naciones Unidas para la Agricultura y la Alimentación*, Madrid: Ministerio de Hacienda, 1966.
5 Carlos Barciela, 'Historia del Ministerio de Agricultura (1936–1965)', in Ricardo Robledo (ed.), *Historia del Ministerio de Agricultura 1900–2008. Política agraria y pesquera de España*, Madrid: MARM, 2011, p. 213.
6 Eduardo Rico, *Política forestal e repoboacións en Galicia*, Santiago: USC, 1995.
7 Carlos Barciela and Inmaculada López, 'El fracaso de la política agraria del primer franquismo, 1939–1959. Veinte años perdidos para la agricultura española', in Carlos Barciela (ed.), *Autarquía y mercado negro: el fracaso económico del primer franquismo, 1939–1959*, Barcelona: Crítica, 2003, pp. 55–99.
8 Barciela and López, 'El fracaso de la política agraria ...', p. 82.
9 F. Javier Martínez and Andrés Sánchez, 'La ayuda americana en la modernización del regadío español: la enmienda McCarran y la financiación de la colonización pública', unpublished.
10 Cristóbal Gómez Benito, *Políticos, burócratas y expertos. Un estudio de la política agraria y la sociología rural en España (1936–1959)*, Madrid: Siglo XXI, 1996, pp. 183–191.
11 Barciela, 'Historia del Ministerio ...', p. 198.
12 Barciela and López, 'El fracaso de la política agraria ...', pp. 86–89.
13 Here we adhere to the conceptual distinction between mechanisation and motorisation offered by Auderset and Moser in their contribution to this volume, Chapter 8.
14 José Manuel Naredo, *La evolución de la agricultura en España*, Barcelona: Laia, 1974, p. 68; James Simpson, *La agricultura española (1765–1965): la larga siesta*, Madrid: Alianza, 1997, pp. 334–336; Barciela and López: 'El fracaso de la política agraria ...'. Apart from Spanish migration to Western Europe (which was already significant in the second half of the decade), internal inter-regional migrations toward the main industrial cities involved more than one million persons in the 1950s (3.5 per cent of the average population). See David Reher, 'Perfiles demográficos de España, 1940–1960', in Barciela (ed.): *Autarquía y mercado negro* ..., pp. 21–24.
15 Ernesto Clar, 'Contra la virtud de pedir ... Barreras administrativas a la difusión de tractores en España: 1950–1960', *Investigaciones de Historia Económica*, 13, 2009, p. 110.
16 José Ignacio Martínez, *Trilladoras y tractores: Energía, tecnología e industria en la mecanización de la agricultura española (1862–1967)*, Seville: University de Sevilla and University de Barcelona, 2000, pp. 164–170.
17 Thomas Christiansen, *The Reason Why: The Post Civil War Agrarian Crisis in Spain*, Zaragoza: Prensas Universitarias, 2012, pp. 87–90; Simpson, *La agricultura española* ..., pp. 324–326.

18 Clar, 'Contra la virtud …', pp. 114–124. Along with tractors, there was also a nationwide increase in petrol-powered threshers and irrigation motors.
19 Inmaculada López, 'Los efectos de la autarquía en la agricultura murciana', *Revista de Historia Económica*, XIV, 3, 1999, pp. 591–618.
20 Mikel Buesa: 'Una nota sobre la construcción de maquinaria y la producción de fertilizantes en la política industrial española'.
21 With the exception of rice cultivation. Lino Camprubí, 'One Grain, One Nation: Rice Genetics and the Corporate State in Early Francoist Spain (1939–1952)', *Historical Studies in the Natural Sciences*, vol. 40, no. 4, 2010, pp. 499–531.
22 Alberte Martínez, 'La ganadería gallega durante el primer franquismo: crónica de un tiempo perdido, 1936–1960', *Historia Agraria*, 20, 2000, pp. 197–223.
23 Rafael Domínguez, 'Las transformaciones del sector ganadero en España (1940–1985)', *Ager*, 2, 2004, pp. 54–55.
24 Ramón Garrabou and Xavier Cussó, 'La transición nutricional en la España contemporánea: las variaciones en el consumo de pan, patatas y legumbres (1850–2000)', *Investigaciones de Historia Económica*, 7, 2007, pp. 90–95.
25 Prior to this, the Ministry of Agriculture had three Directorates General: Agriculture, Livestock and Forests, Hunting and River Fishing, which were all internally reorganized in 1952.
26 Daniel Lanero, *Historia dun ermo asociativo: Labregos, sindicatos erticais e políticas agrarias en Galicia baixo o Franquismo*, Santa Comba: TresCtres, 2011.
27 Fernando Sanchez De Puerta, *Extension agraria y desarrollo rural*, Madrid: MAPA, 1996.
28 Lourenzo Fernández-Prieto, *El apagón tecnológico del Franquismo: estado e innovación en la agricultura española del siglo XX*, Valencia: Tirant Lo Blanch, 2007, pp. 205–357; Miguel Cabo and Antonio Bernárdez, 'Ciencia y dictadura: la investigación agronómica en Galicia durante el primer franquismo', *Noticiario de Historia Agraria*, 12, 1999, pp. 119–139.
29 Fernández-Prieto, *El apagón tecnológico …*, pp. 231–238.
30 Barciela, *Historia del Ministerio …*, p. 203; Fernández-Prieto, *El apagón tecnológico …*, pp. 233–234.
31 International Bank of Reconstruction and Development & FAO, *El desarrollo de la agricultura …*, pp. 122–124.
32 Juan Pan-Montojo, *Apostolado, profesión y tecnología. Una historia de los ingenieros agrónomos en España*, Madrid: Asociación Nacional de Ingenieros Agrónomos - Blake & Helsey, 2005, pp. 303–308; Juan Pan-Montojo, 'La depuración de los ingenieros del Ministerio de Agricultura, 1936–1942', in Josefina Cuesta (ed.), *La depuración de funcionarios bajo la dictadura franquista (1936–1975)*, Madrid: Fundación Largo Caballero, 2009, pp. 232–246.
33 Pan-Montojo, *Apostolado, profesión y tecnología…*, pp. 311 – 316; Carlos Barciela and Inmaculada López, 'La ingeniería agronómica española en la encrucijada. El Congreso nacional de 1950', *Historia Agraria*, 62, 2013, pp. 323 – 363.
34 *Falange Española Tradicionalista y de las Juntas de Ofensiva Nacional Sindicalista* (FET–JONS, 1937), was the Franco regime's single party.
35 Lanero, *Historia dun ermo …*, pp. 156–162; Juan Pan-Montojo, 'Sindicalistas e ingenieros en los conflictos político–agrarios del primer franquismo', in Daniel Lanero and Dulce Freire (eds), *Agriculturas e innovación tecnológica en la Península Ibérica (1946–1975)*, Madrid: MARM, 2011, pp. 243–268.
36 Fernando Rosas, *Portugal entre a Paz e a Guerra, 1939–1945*, Lisbon: Estampa, 2005.
37 Fernando Rosas, *Salazarismo e fomento económico*, Lisbon: Notícias, 2000, pp. 195–204.
38 Fernando Rosas (ed.), Vol. 7. *O Estado Novo*, in Jose Mattoso (dir.), *História de Portugal*, Lisbon: Estampa, 1994, 41–48.
39 Luciano Amaral, 'Reformismo Agrário', in Fernando Rosas and Jose M. Brandão (eds), *Dicionário de História do Estado Novo*, 2 vols, Lisbon: Bertrand, pp. 821–832.

40 Fernando Oliveira Baptista, *A política agrária do Estado Novo*, Porto: Afrontamento, 1993, pp. 78–80.
41 Luciano Amaral, 'Agricultura e política agrícola: o país que nós perdemos', in Rosas (ed.): Vol. 7. *O Estado Novo*, in Mattoso (ed.), *História de Portugal*, pp. 431–450.
42 Oliveira Baptista, *A Política Agrária* …, pp. 375–398. Dulce Freire, *Portugal e a Terra. Itinerarios da modernização da agricultura na segunda metade do século XX*, Lisbon, Universidade Nova, 2008, unpublished Ph.D. dissertation.
43 Pedro Lains, 'Agriculture and economic development in Portugal, 1870–1973', in Pedro Lains and Vicente Pinilla (eds), *Agriculture and Economic Development in Europe Since 1870*, Oxford and New York: Routledge, 2009, pp. 344–347.
44 Lains, 'Agriculture and economic …', p. 346.
45 V. X. Pintado, *Structure and Growth of the Portuguese Economy*, Lisbon: ICS, 2002, p. 95, p. 106. One of the strategic objectives of postwar industrial policy was to develop a national chemical fertiliser industry. Pedro Lains, *Os progressos do atraso: uma nova história económica de Portugal*, Lisbon: ICS, 2003, p. 171.
46 Oliveira Baptista, *A Política Agrária* …, pp. 326–328.
47 Manuel Belo Moreira, 'A revolução do leite no minifúndio de Entre–Douro–e–Mondego', in Jose Pais De Brito (ed.), *O voo do arado*, Lisbon: Museu Nacional de Etnologia, 1996, pp. 440–441.
48 Fernanda Rollo, 'Ambiciones frustradas: las vías de modernización y reorganización y el programa de asistencia técnica americana a la agricultura portuguesa en la posguerra (1948–1956)', in Lanero and Freire (eds): *Agriculturas e innovación* …, pp. 107–133.
49 Dulce Freire, 'Modernising ambitions: agronomists in action between dictatorship and democracy (Portugal, 1957–1986)', in Ana Delicado (ed.), *Associations and Other Groups in Science: An Historical and Contemporary Perspective*, Newcastle upon Tyne: Cambridge Scholars Publishing, 2013, pp. 92–107.
50 Freire, 'Modernising ambitions …', p. 96.
51 Daniel Lanero, 'The Portuguese *Estado Novo*: programmes and obstacles to the modernization of agriculture, 1933–1950', in Fernández–Prieto *et al.*, (eds): *Agriculture in the Age of Fascism* …, pp. 85–111; Cabana and Díaz, 'Exploring modernization: agrarian …', pp. 189–217.
52 Rosas, *Portugal entre a paz* …; Fernando Oliveira Baptista, 'Política Agrária', in Rosas and Brandão (eds), *Dicionário de Historia* …, 1996, 749–754.
53 Christiansen, *The Reason Why* …; Juan Pan-Montojo, 'Spanish Agriculture, 1931–1955: Crisis, Wars and New Policies in the Reshaping of Rural Society', in Brassley, Segers and Van Molle (eds), *War, Agriculture, and Food* …, pp. 75–95.
54 Pedro Lains, *Os progressos do atraso*…, pp. 230–234; Manuel Ennes Ferreira: `O império e as relações económicas com África´ in Pedro Lains and Álvaro Ferreira da Silva (eds.), *História Económica de Portugal (1700–2000)*, vol. III, Lisbon: ICS, 2005, pp. 343–371.
55 OECD, *Agricultural Development in Southern Europe: Report Adopted by the Committee of Agriculture and by the OECD Council*, Paris: OECD, 1969.
56 Dulce Freire and Daniel Lanero, 'The Iberian dictatorships and agricultural modernisation after the Second World War', in Peter Moser and Tony Varley (eds), *Integration through Subordination: The Politics of Agricultural Modernisation in Industrial Europe*, Turnhout: Brepols, 2013, pp. 183–201.
57 Ernesto Clar, 'Farm Policy under the Salazar and Franco Dictatorships in Portugal and Spain: Towards and Authoritarian Model of Intervention in Agriculture?', in Nadine Vivier (ed.), *The State and Rural Societies: Policy and Education in Europe 1750–2000*, Turnhout: Brepols, 2008, pp. 177–194; Pan-Montojo, 'Spanish Agriculture, 1931–1955: crisis, wars, and new policies…', pp.88–90.
58 Some 22,600 ha were colonised, all to the north of the Tagus River, between 1937 and 1951.

10 Tractorisation
France, 1946–1955

Laurent Herment

By the end of the Second World War French agriculture had declined in comparison with its position in 1939. The four years of German occupation saw much of its output carried off to supply Germany without agricultural resources being replaced. Urban areas consequently experienced great difficulties in obtaining food; the Liberation did not solve all of France's problems.

In November 1945, during a session of the "*Conseil Général*" (Departmental Council) of the *département* of Oise, lying to the north of Paris, a dispute occurred between the Prefect (*Préfet*), who embodied the central State, and the Président of the agricultural committee of the *département*. The latter said that French Administration was responsible for the lack of staple foods, and argued that farmers should have a free market for their products, especially potatoes.[1] Moreover he denounced the lack of petrol, of fertilisers, etc., and more generally the lack of resources that were supposed to be provided by the State. The Prefect wanted to protect the population of the *département* against the rapacity of farmers, even if he did not say that explicitly.[2] Between 1945 and 1955 the context changed very quickly. In a report published in January 1952, the Ministry of Agriculture pointed out that the aim for French agriculture was not to produce all staple products, but to redirect resources towards products capable of creating an export surplus.[3]

At the beginning of 1952, supplies of some agricultural products, taking account of imports, were already in excess of demand, despite the fact that the domestic output predicted by Monnet's first General Plan (*Plan Général Monnet*) had not been reached. The government faced a choice between three policies. The first was to restrict the supply of some products, but this hardly fitted with the desire for a rapid modernisation of French agriculture to satisfy the needs of the French population.[4] The second was to increase the supply of all products beyond the needs of French population. This would have been no better than the first, because at that time a large part of the working population was composed of farmers, and such a policy would have caused an agricultural crisis that could in turn have provoked an industrial crisis.[5] The third option was to adjust the production to need while taking account of the opportunity to export to other European countries. This policy was obviously the best, but it could be put into effect only if French agriculture was able to compete with foreign suppliers.[6] 'If we eliminate the authoritarian system, competition is the only stimulant to increased production.'[7] It appeared that this third way would allow French agriculture to produce more, to improve the quality of its products and to be modernised.

To modernise French agriculture and to increase production competitively, government wanted to increase first, agricultural labour productivity and second, crop yields. To achieve this it was necessary to transform radically the economic pattern of farms by the spread of artificial fertilisers, by increasing technical knowledge (especially about plants and cattle), and by motorisation. The third goal was the most popular for two reasons. First, tractors were the most visible element of the agricultural revolution. Second, tractors seemed to be the means by which the productivity of labour could be increased after the war. Although there may be little doubt about the first point, we might question the exact role of tractors in this agricultural revolution. It is also useful to ask why state-promoted tractorisation and why the spread of the tractor was so slow in France.

To respond to these questions, this chapter examines the issue of the tractorisation in the *département* of Oise. In the next section we examine the growth of global output of French agriculture during the crucial years of the so-called Agricultural Revolution. The following section examines the results of the agricultural surveys recorded in 1929, 1946 and the census of 1955, and a specific survey about tractorisation in Oise dated to 1950.[8] The *département* of Oise was divided between regions characterised by large and capitalist estates, already highly tractorised before the Second World War, and some other regions in which familial estates were predominant, and characterised by a very low level of tractorisation, but in which there were alternative methods of motorisation. The *département* is typical of the variety of French agriculture.[9] The sources examined demonstrate that the partition of the *département* continued long after the war and allow us to assess the limits of tractorisation in France. In the fourth section, I try to explain why tractorisation was so slow in France, with the aid of the literature about tractorisation in North America, which was a model for French agronomists after the war. These comparisons at different levels (local, regional, national and international) allow us to understand better the problems faced by French agriculture during the first decade of the Agricultural Revolution.

From food shortage to food surplus (1945–1955)

Like every other country in Europe, France suffered during the war. During the four years of German occupation, French agriculture had not only to feed the French population, but also to export food to Germany. In common with much of continental Europe, French agriculture suffered from a lack of materials, machinery, labour, fertiliser, etc. Consequently, rationing was very strict during the war. In contrast, the following decade from 1945 to 1955 was characterised by a huge growth in the total agricultural output. However, it is necessary to distinguish two sub-periods: 1946–1949 and 1950–1955.

Until 1949, rationing was very severe for the French population, especially in 1947. Despite the expectations of the French planners, harvest yields remained very low during the first five post-war years (see Table 10.1 below). The harvest of 1947 was very poor for wheat (0.96 tonnes per hectare on average for the whole country), against more than 1.5 tonnes per hectare before the war.[10] The harvests of other staples were also very poor. The aims of the French plan to produce more, to improve the quality of the output and to modernise agriculture could not be achieved. Consequently, in 1947, the French government needed help to feed France. In the short term, the Marshall Plan enabled France to avoid famine; in the long run, more depended on the French balance of payments.[11]

As Table 10.1 demonstrates, the production of the major crops increased considerably between 1950 and 1955. By the 1950–1954 period, the harvests exceeded the interwar output for wheat, barley, sugar beet, and even for rapeseed and maize, which were two minor crops in this period. Furthermore, land productivity improved too. The average yields for wheat reached 2.2 tonnes per hectare in 1955. For barley the yield was 2.0 tonnes per hectare, as against 1.5 tonnes during the interwar period. Figures for other crops are contradictory. The output of sugar beet did not increase, whereas that of potatoes increased by 30 per cent.

Thus, from 1950 onwards, French agriculture improved its performance in the output of products liable to create commercial surpluses: sugar beet, wheat, rapeseed and feed grains (barley and maize).[12]

For meat and milk, the growth of production was less impressive due to the time required to increase animal numbers and the lack of feed for them. However, if we except sheep, numbers of which had been decreasing since the middle of the nineteenth century, all herds increased, or at least reached the level of the interwar period. Thus, the supply of meat seemed to be sufficient if not overabundant (see Table 10.2). Like several other countries, France wanted to increase the production of milk, which was the best way to increase quickly the availability of protein in the short term. And although the cattle herd increased by less than 10 per cent, the yield per cow went up by more than 20 per cent.

Table 10.1 Output of the main food crops (except wine) between 1935 and 1955 (millions of tonnes). (Figures not available for the period 1940–1944.)

	Wheat	Oats	Barley	Maize	Potatoes	Rapeseed	Sugar Beet
1935–1939	7.76	4.75	1.14	0.56	15.43	0.01	9.04
1945–1949	5.99	3.16	1.1	0.246	10.45	0.076	7.2
1950–1954	8.56	3.55	1.95	0.667	13.12	0.139	11.82
1955	10.36	3.64	2.67	1.09	13.75	0.098	10.98

188 *Laurent Herment*

Table 10.2 Millions of cattle, sheep and pigs (millions of hectolitres of milk)[13]

	Cattle	Milk	Sheep	Pigs
1935–1939	15.6	133.2	9.87	7.13
1945–1949	15.4	132.0	7.48	6.76
1950–1954	17.3	180.0	8.01	7.57
1955	17.6	178.0	8.22	7.73

If the global efficiency of French agriculture remained quite low compared with some more advanced countries in the North Sea area, by the middle of the 1950s it had made substantial progress since the interwar period, and for some key products France was clearly self-sufficient.

Several elements could explain these improvements: institutional, political, scientific and technological. From the beginning of the interwar period onwards, the state *Institut des Recherches Agronomiques* (IRA, set up in 1921, but closed down in 1934) aimed to improve agricultural practices.[14] After the Second World War, state services improved and became more efficient. The Ministry of Agriculture and its decentralised services and, finally, INRA (*Institut National de la Recherche Agronomique*) set up in 1946, provided farmers with advice on how to adopt the best practices and choose the most suitable seeds, and with recommendations about the use of pesticides, fertilisers, etc.[15] Firms were also engaged to promote new seeds, fertilisers and pesticides. The land consolidation (*remembrement*) programme represented also a way of rationalising the rural landscape and the organisation of French farms. Finally, the French government wanted to improve the global standard of living of the rural population by electrification and the provision of water supplies.

From a technical point of view, there are several statistics that help to assess the progress of French agriculture (and see also Auderset and Moser's arguments in Chapter 8). During the interwar period, quantities of fertilisers used by French agriculture increased significantly. The rates of growth for nitrogen and potash are very impressive (more than 4 per cent per year), but slowed down during the crisis of the early 1930s. After the Second World War, the annual rate of growth remained very high, but, as Table 10.3 shows, nitrogen remained the weak factor. From this point of view, the postwar period continued the progress of the interwar period, but at a level never reached before, even for nitrogen.[16]

The figures for tractors and horses are the most striking in Table 10.3. The level of tractorisation was very low during the interwar period, but from 1954 onwards the number of tractors increased very quickly. It is often assumed that the ERP provided numerous tractors for French agriculture, but in fact, the spread of tractors occurred long after it had ended. As Figure 10.1 shows, the number of horses remained very high, even in 1955. Compared to other countries, it took a long time to replace horses by tractors. As Auderset and Moser show in Chapter 8, the number of tractors surpassed the number of

Table 10.3 Agricultural inputs (thousand tonnes of fertiliser elements; thousand units of tractors; millions of horses)[17]

	Nitrogen	Phosphate	Potassium	Horses	Tractors
1910-1914	73	352	42	2.31	
1915-1919					
1920-1924	96	451	94	2.86	
1925-1929	160	494	227	2.99	26.8
1930-1934	160	315	167	2.84	
1935-1939	225	323	278	2.69	33.1
1940-1944					
1945-1949	229	424	354	2.41	123
1950-1954	348	670	518	2.22	250
1955	353	701	542	2.16	306

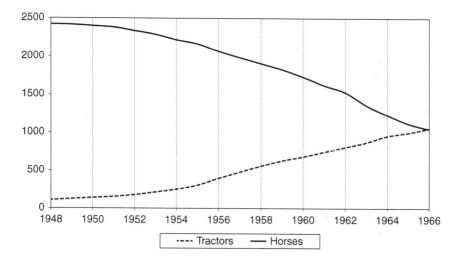

Figure 10.1 Evolution of tractors and horses (in thousands) 1948–1966[18]

horses between 1950 and 1960 in Great Britain, the USA and Sweden, whereas in France this phenomenon occurred later, in 1966. Despite the importance of tractors for modernisation, they took time to eliminate horses.

To assess the importance of the 300,000 tractors and more than 2 million horses in France in 1955, they should be compared with the number of farms and the age of farmers. At this date there were 2.25 million farmers, of whom 20 per cent were more than 65 years old. If we compare the data on farm acreage and the age of farmers, it appears that 30 per cent of farmers who had less than 5 hectares were more than 65 years old (see Figure 10.2). It is obvious that modernisation (and thus motorisation) could not be expected from the class of old and small farmers.

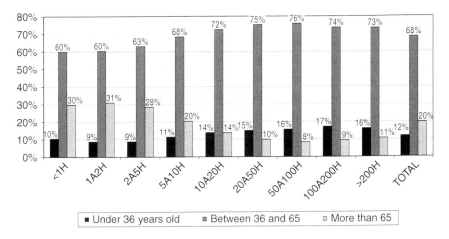

Figure 10.2 Age of farmers in 1955[19]

This brief overview of the progress of French agriculture after the Second World War suggests that to some degree the goals of the planners were reached by 1955. Consequently, it is possible to address two questions about tractorisation in French agriculture: why was it so slow, and why was it one of the main and most visible elements of the agricultural revolution?

Tractorisation in the *département* of Oise between 1929 and 1946

The department of Oise, located to the north of Paris, was one of the most motorised and advanced *départements* of France long before the Second World War (see Figures 10.3[20] and 10.4[21]). In 1929, as in 1955, this *département* was comparable to the more advanced regions in Europe. It was one of the most important providers of sugar beet and wheat, and also provided milk for Paris.[22] Beyond this crude description, the survey of 1929 allows us to understand the characteristics of this *département* which was divided between some regions dominated by capitalist farms that produced sugar beet and wheat, and other regions devoted to cattle breeding for milk, in which relatively small family farms were predominant. In these later regions, *bocage* (hedges) was the essential element of the landscape, while the former regions were characterised by large open fields.

I recorded the results of the survey of 1929 for 23 *cantons* from the South and the West of the *département*.[23] They were typical of the diversity of the *département* as a whole. It is thus possible to differentiate the two farming types statistically. In 1929, in the sugar beet and wheat regions, the number of tractors and the number of farms extending to more than 100 hectares were almost

Tractorisation: France, 1946–1955 191

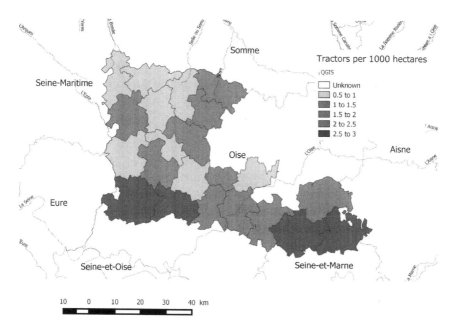

Figure 10.3 Oise, tractors per 1,000 hectares

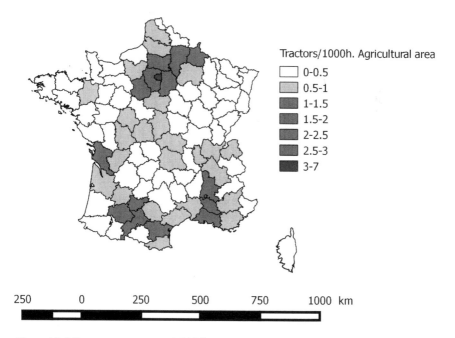

Figure 10.4 France, tractors per 1,000 hectares

the same, but despite the presence of tractors, these regions also used numerous horses. In addition, the density of wage-labourers was very high in the big farm regions, while it was very low in the milking regions. Second, in the sugar beet and wheat areas, the ratio of family labour to wage-earning labour was very low, while in the milking regions this ratio was very high. In other words, the areas with a lot of hired labour were also the areas where the tractorisation was more advanced. It therefore seems that in 1929, farms which used tractors could save neither labour nor horses. Tractors did not automatically reduce the need for hired labour or horses. How can we explain this paradox? If tractors increased the power of traction for ploughing, the necessity to weed still remained, and possibly increased, especially for sugar beet. It seems that the tractor could not replace horses for a lot of tasks.

Two further remarks are appropriate. The first is related to the very complex link between oats, horses and tractors. It is very important to note that the correlation between the wheat/oats ratio and the number of tractors is positive.[24] It means that when farmer used tractors, the acreage devoted to oats decreased. Thus, it seems that tractors partially eliminated horses and consequently oats. But as tractors did not produce a sharp decline in the number of horses at this time, the acreage devoted to oats remained very important, even in the most tractorised areas.[25] Big farms needed a lot of horses at this time, despite their use of tractors.[26] The second point relates to trucks and vans (*camions* and *camionettes*). Tractors were not the only means of motorisation. Trucks were very common, especially in the milking areas. Hence, during the interwar period, there were two ways of motorisation. The tractor was not necessarily the most popular, especially where family farms were predominant.

The 1946 survey of the working agricultural population, which in some ways is poor and for which I did not find any local data, provides very useful information at a departmental level for the very beginning of the postwar period. It proves that the predominant economic pattern in the *département* of Oise had not changed since 1929. It shows the agriculture of this *département* was highly capitalist. If we examine the number of wage labourers per thousand hectares, Oise is the fifth highest French *département*, after the Seine-et-Oise (where horticulture and early fruit and vegetables were very important to provisioning Paris) and the three big wine-making *départements* of the south of France (Aude, Hérault and Pyrénées-Orientales). Judged by the ratio between male wage labourers and the total male working population, Oise became the second *département*, just behind Seine-et-Marne.[27] But these global statistics conceal some very interesting peculiarities of this *département*. In fact, they hide the diversity that it is possible to detect at a micro-regional level, as the 1929 survey proved.

Tractorisation in the *département* of Oise between the end of the Second World War and 1955

The number of tractors increased after the war, but it is important to remember that there were more than 2 million farms in 1955 in France. I will examine below the reason why the spread of motorisation was so slow for the whole of France. For the moment, it is just necessary to assess the level and the features of motorisation in Oise.

As far as it is possible to disintegrate the data at a *départemental* level, tractorisation in the Oise followed, on the whole, the same pattern as in the rest of France. In 1945 the number of tractors in Oise was about 1,500 and a little less than 2,500 in 1950. In 1952 there were 5,300 tractors.[28] The modernisation of the *département* came late but happened quickly. More than any absolute figure, the relative figures (tractor by farm) permit useful comparisons with other *départements*. There were more than 11,000 farms in Oise at the end of the war. Thus, there was one tractor for seven estates in this department, compared to one tractor for 70 farms in the country as a whole. Compared to France, the degree of tractorisation in Oise remained very high.

Statistics produced in 1950 provide a guide to understanding the features of tractorisation in Oise and the limits of this phenomenon.[29] Using this survey, it is possible to know the number of individual farms, classified by area, which used tractors, horses and oxen. This statistic provides also the area of each class and the tractive power of every different means of traction by class. If we consider farms whose area was less than 50 hectares, about 6 per cent had a tractor. Between 50 and 100 hectares, about 75 per cent had a tractor and all farms of more than 100 hectares had one or two tractors.[30] The big farms which possessed one or two tractors were mainly located in the wheat and sugar beet area. Conversely, it is likely that the large number of small farms which were located in the milking areas had no tractors. The high degree of tractorisation of Oise was due to the very special structure of the agriculture of the department characterised by a large proportion of big farms.

Comparing the different means of power traction produces some surprising results. The bigger the farm, the higher the number of horses and/or oxen (see Figure 10.5). As this statistic concerns exclusively farms which had at least one tractor, it is not possible to explain the larger number of horses (or oxen) on big farms as a result of the lack of tractors.

Despite the progress of tractorisation, the basic economic pattern of big farms did not change between 1929 and 1950. They always used a lot of horses and in the bigger estates there were always a lot of oxen to plough.[31] However, although tractors provided a huge increase in the power available, the power per hectare on big farms was not all that great.[32]

For the very end of the period studied, I used data produced in 1955 and disintegrated at a municipal level. This census provides for each village the number of farms, the number of horses, the number of wage labourers, the number of tractors, etc. Owing to the very poor condition of the source, I could examine the survey for only 297 communes of the 700 covered.[33] It is possible to deduce from this data the average number of horses and the average number of tractors by farm for each village. We can also deduce the average

194 Laurent Herment

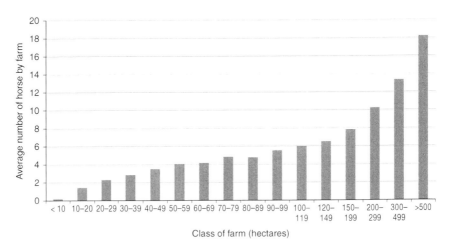

Figure 10.5 Horses on farms equipped with a tractor in 1950

number of wage labourers on each farm in each village. Figures 10.6 and 10.7 show that there are positive links between the average number of tractors and the average number of horses on each farm. The relationship is the same between tractors and wage labourers.

The increasing level of motorisation, and especially of tractorisation, between 1929 and 1955 did not cause a complete disruption in the ancient model immediately after the war. The number of wage labourers and horses

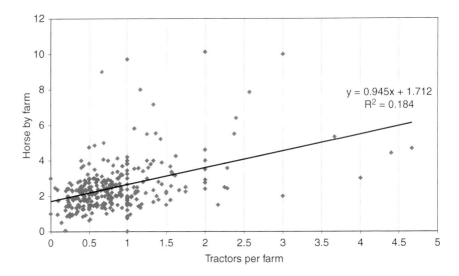

Figure 10.6 Horses and tractors per farm

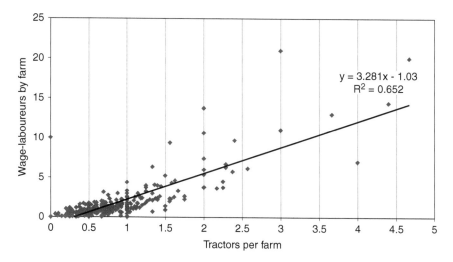

Figure 10.7 Wage labourers and tractors per farm

decreased on the biggest farms between these two dates, but the changes were far from complete.[34] It is also important to emphasise that tractorisation concerned more and more farms every year. Even in the dairy farming areas, the number of tractors increased substantially between 1950 and 1955. In this respect these two areas are representative of the diversity of French agriculture. Figure 10.8 shows this diversity at a *départemental* level for the whole of France.[35] By using principal components analysis (PCA), it is possible to detect several regional profiles.[36] The straight lines emerging from the central origin in the diagram show the variables. Among the numerous available variables, the number of tractors per 100 farms, the number of labourers per 100 farms, and the percentages of land in vineyards, grassland and cereals were chosen. The dots represent *départements*. The purpose of the PCA is purely descriptive, to see if it is possible to detect a structure or pattern in the dots (i.e. *départements*) in order to identify several regional profiles (in this case, Picardy, Lower Normandy and Brittany).[37]

It is not possible to summarise all the data, but we can focus on three areas. The first one, dark grey, is the area of big farms in Picardy (Oise (60)). The second one, in black, is the milking and cattle-breeding areas of Lower Normandy (the *départements* of Calvados (14), Manche (50), Orne). In this second area, where family farms were predominant, there were no tractors. The wealth of the farmers was based on milk, cheese and livestock farming. The performance of farming could be improved without tractors, by introducing artificial insemination, selection, improvements in forage production, pesticides, etc.[38] This area was similar to the west of the *département* of Oise. The third one, in light grey, is Brittany (Côtes-du-Nord (22), Finistère (29),

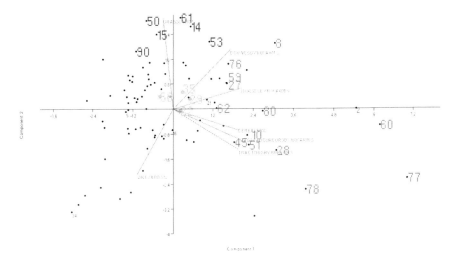

Figure 10.8 Diversity at a *départemental* level for the whole of France

Ille-et-Vilaire (35) and Morbihan (56)). In this last area, where small and medium-sized family farms prevailed, there were no tractors, no wage labourers, some cereal and some livestock farming. The economic pattern of farms was not well defined: it was a typical French mixed farming area. The position of Brittany epitomises the *retard français*. It is useful to remember all these points before trying to understand why tractorisation was so slow in France and why it was so necessary.

The obstacles to motorisation before 1955 and the necessity of tractorisation

It is possible to distinguish two main factors which hampered tractorisation: first, the fact that the French economy could not provide tractors for farmers, and second the behaviour of the peasantry. Although these two explanations are not mutually exclusive, it is worth emphasising that the first one was temporary, but the second was structural. If the structural explanation is the best, it is still worth examining the reasons why farmers did not use more tractors, and why they did not replace horses and oxen by tractors earlier.

The reluctance of French farmers?

When the *Plan Monnet* was enacted, agricultural mechanisation was considered very important for the modernisation of the French economy. The *Plan* anticipated a supply of 250,000 tractors in 1950.[39] In fact, there were only 124,000 tractors at this date.[40] To some extent the *Plan* failed because France was dependent on imports until the beginning of the 1950s. But after

1950–1951, production increased sharply.[41] One can explain the lack of tractorisation until 1950 by those facts, but the problem was more complex. As already indicated, there was no structural lack of tractors in the large farms in north-east France. Moreover, even if the aim of the *Plan* had been reached by 1950, there would still not have been a tractor for every single farmer in France. Tractors were first and foremost intended for big farms. In 1955, with only 270,000 tractors, it was impossible to provide a tractor for every single farm. Even after this date, the aim was to provide one to every single farmer who was *able to finance it*. Furthermore, the lack of tractors appeared to be one of the most important signs of the backwardness of French agriculture. To what extent can this be attributed to the reluctance of French farmers to buy them?

Two points should be distinguished in order to understand this structural explanation. The first is linked to the fact that tractors were not the sole improvement that needed to be implemented to increase productivity, and to improve the living standards of farmers and the rural population as a whole. The second is related to the fact that the introduction of tractors and the abandonment of horses and oxen for ploughing involved a complete change in the economic pattern of farms.

The effect of tractors on productivity was not very great. The author of the document entitled *Plan Monnet – son application à l'agriculture du département de l'Oise*, makes three points: first, that one driver replaced one carter, so the number of wage labourers did not diminish; second, that, with motorisation, the area per wage labourer had already increased by 40 per cent since 1929 (from 10 hectares to 14 hectares); and finally, owing to the introduction of tractors, the number of seasonal workers diminished from 25 per cent, so that overall motorisation saved about one third of the labour force.[42] In 1951, the French Society for Rural Economy published a vast work about tractorisation which gives some additional information on the extent to which tractors were responsible for the growth of productivity. The author examined the experience of the USA. He quoted an American work which calculated that motorisation accounted for 48 per cent of the economy of labour in American agriculture between the end of the First World War and 1944. Less than one third (14 per cent) was due to the use of tractors.[43] The authors also found that agricultural trucks and cars were responsible for 20 per cent of the economy, which is interesting because, as we have seen above, vans (*camionettes*) were very popular in the milking and dairy areas of the *département* of Oise. The report mentioned other means of increasing production and productivity, which were relatively cheap: in wheat and sugar beet regions the selection of seed, new seed such as monogerm varieties of sugar beet which diminished the need for labour; and for milking and cattle breeding areas artificial insemination, selection in breeding, irrigation, electric fences, etc. For all agricultural regions the transmission of technical knowledge and land consolidation (*remembrement*) were important. Finally, for wheat and rapeseed, combine harvesters had a bigger impact than tractors.

The tractor was hardly ever perceived as the essential feature of the agricultural revolution, even if it was its symbol. It was one factor among others and its status was not very well defined because of the lack of complementary implements. This shortfall was very important for the sugar beet, for example, because the volume of labour required did not decrease automatically on the introduction of tractors.[44] The tractor has two purposes: to cultivate and to transport. If the first purpose was suited to the economy of big farms specialising in wheat and sugar beet (especially for deep ploughing), for the second purpose it was in competition with horses and trucks. There were other investments that were more popular among the rural population, such as electrification and the establishment of mains water networks. The government was responsible for a large share of the investment in these services, which were in great demand. Creating them required considerable amounts of labour, and so was more related to the aim of the *Plan*.

Did farmers need tractors?

The previous explanations are attractive, but they do not help us to understand why tractorisation was so important for the modernisation of French agriculture. If we consider the economic pattern of farms, it may be possible to understand the behaviour of farmers and the wishes of French planners.

One of the long-term goals of the *Plan* was to turn France into an exporter of agricultural commodities, especially wheat, sugar, barley and maize. This objective was reached very quickly for the two first items, even if the global balance of French agriculture remained in deficit until the very end of the 1960s. Despite these first results, even in the big farms the acreage devoted to oats remained significant. For planners it was a leitmotiv; the acreage devoted to oats could and should decrease:

> A minimum of 2,200 tractors will be supplied to the Oise department, which, added to the 2,200 already there will bring the total to 4,400.
>
> Already 15,000 hectares of oats have disappeared from the rotation as a result of motorization and the disappearance of some outlets (Paris-la Chapelle, barge-towing horses).
>
> The acceleration of motorisation should bring about the disappearance of 9,000 horses out of a remainder of about 25,000 and the almost total disappearance of slow draught oxen. These reductions will have two results:
>
> a) A reduction of 11,000 hectares in the oat crop, since it is accepted that between 1 and 1.25 hectares are required to feed a horse for a year.
> b) Freeing up a quantity of pulp which would have been consumed by young oxen. To complete the fattening of these animals requires barley, so some of the land previously devoted to oats will have to be sown to this cereal.[45]

This quotation summarises all the challenges of modernisation. Indeed, this challenge was not specific to Oise. For the whole of France, it was possible to increase yields of oats, but the existence of 1.8 or 2 million horses occupied land and prevented the growth of more valuable crops.[46] Just before the war, 3.25 million hectares were devoted to oats. During the period 1944–1949 they remained very important (2.48 million hectares), and in 1955 there were still 2.08 million.[47] As oat yields increased, it was possible to feed more horses and thus, paradoxically, in some regions, cart horses could appear to be an economical way of modernisation until the middle of 1950s.[48]

If we take account of these considerations, we may reassess the role of tractorisation in the agricultural revolution and understand the reluctance of French farmers to mechanise. The whole pattern of French agriculture was supposed to be changed because farmers who bought tractors needed also to buy industrial inputs. Thus, tractors were important not just because the French tractor industry represented a key factor in the growth of the economy, but also because farmers would need to replace oats by oil and/or petrol, manure by chemical fertilisers and old tools with sophisticated new tools. To facilitate this modernisation, it would become necessary to multiply the contact points between farmers and the rest of the economy. If farmers became suppliers of food commodities they would also need to become buyers of industrial goods and services. From this point of view, tractors were a key factor.[49] The perceived importance of this goal is clear from the explanations that the service of agriculture of Oise used to justify help given to cooperatives to buy tractors and new implements in general: *augmentation de la rentabilité, diminution de l'autoconsommation de l'exploitation* (more profit, less home consumption) or *augmentation de la productivité, diminution de l'autoconsommation à la ferme* (higher productivity, less home consumption on the farm).[50]

Some international comparisons

French farmers were not alone in their reluctance to mechanise, as Ankli's work shows. He argues that in North America, the popularity of the tractor was not as great among American farmers as French agronomists assumed. He has demonstrated that various attempts to assess the cost per crop acre on farms operated with different types of power in Illinois during the 1930s produced very different and contradictory results. Sometimes, horses were cheaper than tractors on large farms, sometimes they were more expensive, etc.[51] In another article, Ankli *et al.* (1980) said: 'If the effects of the tractor upon prairie agriculture have been revolutionary ... the pace at which the tractor was adopted was not.' Later, they underline that 'the resistance of farmers ... to the overtures of tractor salesmen was based on much more than rural conservatism and that in the early 1920s there was good reasons to question if the new was more efficient than the old'.[52]

They presented numerous reasons for the slow progress of tractorisation: the lack of experience of the new technology; difficulties in finding repair facilities; the fact that 'most horse-drawn equipment ... was not adaptable to tractor operation' owing to the speed and power of the tractor; the cost of complementary equipment; and the fact that horses remained essential for many tasks because they were more adaptable.[53] In addition, the 1930s depression in agricultural prices restricted the adoption of tractors.[54]

In France, political authorities and scholars pointed out several types of obstacles to explain the limited spread of the tractor before 1951. As a report of the *service of agriculture* of Oise, dated from 1952, points out: '*L'effectif en chevaux (32.300 en 1951) n'a pas diminué dans la proportion prévue (35.000 à 24.000), les cultivateurs les ayant conservés étant donné l'instabilité économique et le prix des carburants*' (The number of horses (32,300 in 1951) has not decreased to the extent predicted (from 35,000 to 24,000), the farmers having clung on to them in view of the instability of the economy and the price of fuel).[55]

Among other explanations, the same report quoted the lack of expertise in tractor driving and the lack of repair shops. It is also noteworthy that the prices of many agricultural commodities decreased from the late 1940s or the very beginning of the 1950s. From all these points of view, the reluctance of French farmers is understandable because the cost of a tractor was not matched by the profit of the investment, and they also needed to buy further inputs whose prices increased.

French farmers faced the same problem as American farmers, so the behavior of North American farmers helps us to understand the reluctance of French farmers to adopt tractors. Like French farmers, they were obliged to modify radically the economic and technological pattern of the farm, and they had to take into account changes in output and input prices in order to assess the profitability of a tractor. Nevertheless, these factors alone do not explain the challenge to which French agriculture had to rise. To do so, it is necessary to return to the Oise department. As early as 1929, the economic structure of the large farms there seems similar to that of the large farms in North America, but in fact there was a significant difference between the two agronomic systems. Canadian prairie farmers had land available to increase the size of their farms.[56] Even in the great plains of North France, farmers could not increase the area sown to marketable crops without reducing the area devoted to oats and keeping fewer horses. In the milking and dairy districts, the problem of tractorisation was multiplied by the small size of many farms. From this point of view, these districts were more representative of French agriculture, because in them it is clear that the problem was almost insoluble. It was not possible for every single farmer to buy a tractor. The first remedy was co-operation, but it was inadequate. The only effective way to promote tractorisation was to encourage the retirement of old farmers so as to allow young and modern farmers, able to buy tractors, to increase the size of their farms.

Conclusion

In 1954, Rauscher and Carillon expressed the dilemma of French farmers facing motorisation: '*Encore faut-il que le moteur soit rentable. Cela signifie d'abord que les équipements de motoculture doivent, dans la mesure du possible, correspondre aux besoins des exploitations ou que les exploitations doivent s'adapter aux possibilités de ces matériels*' (Mechanisation must be profitable. That means first that mechanised implements should, as far as possible, conform to the needs of the farms, or that the farms have to adapt to the possibilities of this equipment.[57])

At first sight it appears that farmers had two choices, but the authors used a different formula to express the terms of the alternative. The adaptation of tractors to the farm is considered as something that might happen in future, whereas the adaptation of the farm to the tractor is considered as a necessity. And to clarify the problem the authors added: '*Autrement dit, la structure des exploitations doit évoluer vers la simplicité des spéculations, la compacité des parcelles et peut-être aussi vers des dimensions-types correspondant aux principales gammes d'équipements.*' (In other words, farm structure must evolve towards a more rational pattern of landholding and field sizes and perhaps also towards sizes corresponding to the scale of the implements.)[58]

From this point of view, it is evident that by 1954, and no doubt since 1951, the problem was not tractorisation per se, but the fact that the average size of French farms and of French fields was not suitable for the adoption of tractors and motorisation, except in some regions (north and east of Oise, for example). There were several ways of solving the problem: *remembrement*, destruction of *bocage* and *association* were the most popular. Another way was to eliminate the small mixed farms. However, from a social and political point of view, it was impossible to do any of these quickly. It was necessary to wait until old men went into retirement – and many young men decided to change their employment or to emigrate into town. Beyond this, two further points deserve emphasis: the lack of capital and the complexity of improvements. Tractorisation required much individual capital that farmers did not have or did not want to invest because it was unprofitable. In fact, tractorisation was one component of the modernisation of French agriculture, and not necessarily the most important one for French farmers. Their reluctance to mechanise was not due to a hypothetical suspicion of modernisation, but because such an investment was not necessarily the best and most useful from an economic point of view.

After 1955, however, in a sudden upsurge, tractorisation, and more generally mechanisation, became irresistible. This phenomenon was produced by a long period during which the French authorities set in place, very slowly, the conditions for change. In 1956 and 1957 these conditions were reached, and the French agricultural revolution could begin at an accelerated speed with the aim of integrating into the EEC, and providing, in the long term, substantial surpluses for the balance of trade.[59] Between 1954 and 1962, the people employed in agriculture decreased by 160,000 every year. In 1963 Roland Pressat emphasised that this figure '*dépasse tout ce que les calculs prévisionnels (notamment ceux effectués pour le 4e Plan), avaient laissé escompter*' (surpassed all the predictions (notably those in the 4th Plan) that had been made).[60] From another viewpoint, more important for the understanding of tractorisation, between 1948 and 1955 the number of horses decreased by 36,000 units per year, and by a further 90,000 between 1955 and 1962. The figures for tractors were an increase of 28,000 per year between 1948 and 1955, and an increase of 71,000 per year from 1955 to 1962. In 1970 only half a million horses remained, while the number of tractors had reached 1,230 million.[61]

Notes

1 From 1936 the French Government could control the price of wheat by the means of the *Office National du Blé*, later the *Office National des Céréales*. See A. Chatriot, E. Lynch, and E. Leblanc, *Organiser les marchés agricoles: Le temps des fondateurs*, Paris: Armand Colin, 2012.
2 *Rapport et délibérations du Conseil Général de l'Oise*, 2 November 1945, p. 25. Available in Gallica website of the Bibliothèque Nationale de France.
3 Ministère de l'Agriculture; Conseil Supérieur de l'Agriculture. *Les objectifs de productions agricoles*. January 1952. Rapport général, p. 3 Archives départementales de l'Oise (AD 60), 515W Mp10719.
4 AD 60, 515W Mp10719, p. 35.
5 AD 60, 515W Mp10719, p. 35.
6 French planners considered that the more important competitors were the USA, Argentina and Canada for cereals, and Denmark and Netherlands for dairy products and meat. *Résumé du rapport général des commissions de la production agricole et de l'équipement rural*, French Ministry of Agriculture, note 5, October 1953. AD60, 15W Mp10719.
7 '*Elimination étant faite du système autoritaire, il n'est qu'un stimulant capable d'accroître la production, c'est celui qui nous est offert par la concurrence*', AD 60, 515W Mp10719, p. 35, 1953. See also *Résumé du rapport général des commissions de la production agricole et de l'équipement rural*, 5 October 1953. AD60, 515W Mp10719.
8 Despite its flaws, this survey was the best source on agriculture before the Second World War. The structure of French agriculture did not change fundamentally between 1929 and 1939. There were about 26,000 tractors in 1929 and 35,000 in 1939. J. Bienfait, '*L'industrie du tracteur agricole en France*', *Revue de géographie de Lyon*, vol. 34, no. 3, 1959, pp. 193–216, p. 195.
9 For the level of tractorisation in France and in the different regions of Oise in 1929, see Figures 10.3 and 10.4.
10 Wheat is the main staple food for the French population, but potatoes became more important due to the very poor harvest during the war and immediate post-war years.
11 The focus of this chapter is not on the problem of supply. For a brief bibliography in French language about this issue, see J. F. Crombois: '*Le Fonds Monétaire International, le Plan Marshall et la reconstruction des économies européennes 1946–1951*', *Revue belge de philologie et d'histoire*, Tome 85, fascicule 4, 2004, pp. 995–1019; G. Bossuat, '*La contre-valeur de l'aide américaine à la France et ses territoires d'outre-mer: la mesure des rapports franco-américains*', in *Le Plan Marshall et le relèvement économique de l'Europe*, Comité pour l'histoire économique et financière de la France, Paris: Ministère des finances, 1993, pp. 177–199; G. Bossuat, *L'Europe Occidentale à l'heure américaine 1945–1952*, Paris: Editions complexes, 1992; A. Lacroix-Riz, '*Négociation et signature des accords Blum-Byrnes (octobre 1945–mai 1946) d'après les archives du ministère des affaires étrangères*', *Revue d'histoire moderne et contemporaine*, September 1984, pp. 417–447; M. Margairaz, '*Les finances, le plan Monnet et le plan Marshall. Entre contraintes, controverses et convergences*', in *Le Plan Marshall et le relèvement économique de l'Europe*, Comité pour l'histoire économique et financière de la France, Paris: Ministère des finances, 1993, pp. 145–175; Ph. Mioche, '*Le démarrage du plan Monnet: comment une entreprise

conjoncturelle est devenue une institution prestigieuse', *Revue d'histoire moderne et contemporaine*, September 1984, pp. 399–416. For the lack of staple food, see *Etudes et conjoncture-Union française/Economie française:* '*Le bilan alimentaire de la France avant la guerre et en 1947–1948*', 4o année, no 1, pp. 72–80.

12 Ministère de l'Agriculture, Conseil Supérieur de l'Agriculture. *Les objectifs de productions agricoles.* January 1952. *Rapport général*, p. 37. AD 60, 515W Mp10719. See also *Etudes et conjoncture-Union française/Economie française*: '*Le problème des investissements agricoles et le plan du Ministère de l'agriculture*', 4o année, no 1, pp. 81–95. It is quite important to remember that these new goals were linked with the European Recovery Program (henceforth ERP), often known as the Marshall Plan, and the Organisation for European Economic Co-operation (OEEC). The OEEC, established in April 1948, was linked with the setting up of the ERP.

13 Sources, *Annuaire statistique de la France. 2o partie. Résumé rétrospectif*, INSEE, 1956, p. 3.

14 Despite the suppression of the IRA, the research continued in various agronomic research stations. From several points of view, the war period did not constitute a break. In fact, the system organised after the war arose slowly during the interwar and war periods.

15 On INRA and its role in spreading new seeds, see Ch. Bonneuil and F. Thomas, '*L'INRA dans les régimes de production des savoirs en génétique végétale*', in *Sciences, chercheurs et agriculture: pour une histoire de la recherche agronomique*, Bonneuil, Ch., Denis, G. and J.-L. Mayaud, (eds), l'Harmattan, Paris, 2008, pp. 113–135; Ch. Bonneuil and F. Hochereau, '*Biopolitique et métrologie de la construction d'un standard variétal dans la France agricole d'après-guerre*', *Annales. Histoire, Sciences Sociales*, 2008–2006, pp. 1305–1340 ; Ch. Bonneuil and F. Thomas, *Gènes, pouvoirs et profits: Recherches publiques et régimes de production des savoirs de Mendel aux OGM*, Lausanne: Editions Quae, 2009.

16 About the importance of nitrogen fertiliser, see V. Smil, *Enriching the Earth: Fritz Haber, Carl Bosch, and the Transformation of World Food Production*, Cambridge, MA: MIT Press, 2001.

17 Sources, *Annuaire statistique de la France. 2o partie. Résumé rétrospectif*, INSEE, 1956, p. 3.

18 *Annuaire rétrospectif de la France. Séries longues, 1948–1988*, Paris : INSEE, 1990, pp. 323 and 325.

19 *Recensement général de l'agriculture. Caractéristiques générales des exploitations. I Premiers résultats pour la France entière et par département*, Paris: Ministère de l'agriculture-INSEE, 1958, p. 35.

20 Sources, AD60, Mp1415. I used all the figures available in the archives.

21 Source, *Statistique agricole de la France. Résultats généraux de l'enquête de 1929*, Ministère de l'agriculture, Imprimerie Nationale, 1936, pp. 493–495 and 670–673.

22 *Annuaire statistique de la France*, 1938, pp. 97 and 78–79.

23 A canton is an administrative district, a subdivision of a *département*, which usually includes several villages.

24 $r = 0.38261$.

25 The number of horses was correlated to the number of tractors: $r = 0.6365$.

26 The survey indicated that the number of oxen for ploughing was very important in the sugar beet areas.

27 P. Coutin, '*La population agricole en France*', *Bulletin de la Société française d'économie rurale*, vol. 1, no. 1, 1949, pp. 18–25, annexe, pp. 22–23.

28 AD 60, 515W Mp10719, *Comité départemental de production et d'équipement agricole*, April 1952.

29 AD 60, 515W Mp10751.

30 To make this calculation I used the number of farms provided by a document entitled *Plan Monnet – son application à l'agriculture du département de l'Oise*. In the same document there is further information that the number of farms was supposed to be

8,707. I could not use this last figure because it does not provide the distribution by classes. AD 60, 515 Mp10719.
31 There are some other tables in the same file. Table VII titled *Répartition de la puissance de tractions mécanique totale dans les exploitations agricoles classées suivant leur surface totale et dans les entreprises de travaux* provides us a very useful overview of the tractive power available.
32 These figures could be interpreted in terms of economy of scale.
33 I want to thank Mme M.-P. Duru from the Ministry of Agriculture. I would not have any information without her help.
34 In Oise, the number of wage labourers has decreased from around 24,000 in 1946 to around 13,000 in 1955.
35 Source: '*Statistiques récentes – L'agriculture française, caractéristiques moyenne des exploitations agricoles*', *Annales de Géographie*, vol. 66, no. 358, pp. 570–572.
36 In this model, the first axis opposes the *wheat/sugarbeet départements* to *other départements* (55 per cent of the variance), the second axis opposes the *wine-growing départements* to *cattle breeding and milking départements* (22 per cent of the variance). See annexe 1.
37 PCA attempts to reconstitute the position of elements (in this case *départements*) in relation to each other so as to obtain a less skewed picture after reducing the dimensions from n (in this case 7) to 2. The two first principal components were chosen because their eigenvalues were more than 1. The same exercise was carried out with several sets of variables but the differences between the three regions were always clear.
38 To assess changes in the use of fertilisers in France, see Table 10.3.
39 J. Bienfait, '*L'industrie du tracteur agricole en France*', p. 196 and M. Coquery, '*L'agriculture française et le plan de modernisation et d'équipement*', *Bulletin de la Société française d'économie rurale*, vol. 4, no. 3, 1952, pp. 76–81, p. 81. See also M. Catinat, '*La production industrielle sous la IVe République*', *Économie et statistiques*, no. 129, January 1981, pp. 17–36, p. 22.
40 From a certain point of view, it is necessary to wonder as Ph. Mioche did, if this aim was set to '*faire un geste en direction du monde paysan*' (to make a gesture to the rural world): Ph. Mioche, '*Le démarrage du plan Monnet: comment une entreprise conjoncturelle est devenue une institution prestigieuse*', *Revue d'histoire moderne et contemporaine*, September 1984, pp. 399–416, p. 410.
41 It is worth remembering that American firms produced in France some of the tractors used by French farmers.
42 AD60, 515W Mp10719. *Plan Monnet – son application à l'agriculture du département de l'Oise*.
43 Anon., '*L'utilisation des tracteurs agricoles dans quelques régions de la France (résultats d'une enquête dans 500 exploitations agricoles) Section II: Les conséquences de la motorisation*', *Bulletin de la société française d'économie rurale*, vol. 3, no. 1, pp. 30–43, p. 32.
44 '*L'utilisation des tracteurs*', p. 33.
45 AD60, 515 W Mp10719. *Plan Monnet – son application à l'agriculture du département de l'Oise*.
46 It is important to remember that, at this time, even the more optimistic planners did not predict the growth of yields which happened between 1955 and 1970.
47 Sources, *Annuaire statistique de la France. 2o partie. Résumé rétrospectif*, INSEE, 1956, p. 3.
48 In Finistère (Brittany), the prices of cart horses declined between 1945 and 1955 from 100,000 to 80,000 francs, while the prices of the *Farmall H 22/24 CV* tractor increased from 105,000 to 1,090,000 francs. '*L'utilisation des tracteurs*', p. 28.
49 See, for example, *Résumé du rapport général des commissions de la production agricole et de l'équipement rural*, AD60, 515W Mp 10719.

50 Cards established for the assessment of the progress of the *programme d'investissements agricoles [for] 1954*. AD60, 515W Mp10719. See also *Résumé du rapport général des commissions de la production agricole et de l'équipement rural*, pp. 15–16. French Ministry of Agriculture, 5 October 1953. AD60, 515W Mp10719; and the arguments of Auderset and Moser in Chapter 8.
51 R. E. Ankli, 'Horses vs Tractors on the Corn Belt', *Agricultural History*, vol. 54, no. 1, 1980, pp. 134–148, pp. 140–147.
52 R. E. Ankli, H. D. Hersberg and J. H. Thompson, 'The adoption of the Gasoline Tractor in Western Canada', in D. H. Akenson (ed.), *Canadian Papers in Rural History*, vol. II, Langdale Press, 1980, pp. 9–40, pp. 10 and 15.
53 R. E. Ankli, and alii., 'The adoption of the gasoline tractor', pp. 15–17.
54 R. E. Ankli, 'Horses vs tractors' pp. 146–147.
55 AD 60, 515W Mp10719, *Comité Départemental de Production et d'Equipement Agricoles*, p. 3. It seems that French farmers bought more auxiliary equipment than other European farmers. See *Résumé du rapport général des commissions de la production agricole et de l'équipement rural, op. cit.*, p. 6, AD60, 515W Mp10719.
56 R. E. Ankli *et al.*, 'The adoption of the gasoline tractor', p. 13.
57 M. Rauscher and R. Carillon, '*Moyens de tractions et machines*', *Economie rurale*, no. 19, 1954, pp. 49–52, p. 50.
58 M. Rauscher and R. Carillon, '*Moyens de tractions et machines*', p. 50.
59 All these goals were summarised in the *Résumé du rapport général des commissions de la production agricole et de l'équipement rural*, French Ministry of Agriculture, note 5 October 1953. AD60, 515W Mp10719.
60 R. Pressat '*La population active en France. Premiers résultats du recensement de 1962*', *Population*, 18o année, no. 3, pp. 473–488, p. 479.
61 *Annuaire rétrospectif de la France. Séries longues, 1948–1988*, Paris: INSEE, 1990, p. 313ff.

Part IV
Rural society and structural policy

Figure P4 A typical Swedish family farm of the 1950s (courtesy of Carin Martiin)

11 Structural policy and the State

Changing agricultural society in Belgium and the Netherlands, 1945–1960

Erwin H. Karel and Yves Segers[*]

Introduction

After the Second World War a period of recovery started for the agricultural sector in the Netherlands and Belgium (the Low Countries). In both countries the state was confronted with the task of repairing the damage and delays which were due to the years of occupation. This damage was considerable: destroyed farms, flooded areas, arrears of maintenance and insufficient investment in agricultural enterprises. Furthermore, both states were confronted by a number of pre-war problems which had been caused by the crisis in the 1930s and which also had their roots in structural bottlenecks in the agricultural system. The largest and most troublesome bottleneck probably was the high number of small farmers, which blocked the modernisation and rationalisation of the agricultural sector. In this group of farmers were many big families, with a large number of children for whom there would strictly speaking no longer be a future in agriculture. However, they were a significant electoral group.

In hindsight, the agricultural sector was at the beginning of a new phase in the industrialisation process which had characterised the sector since the end of the 19th century. The mechanisation and connections between farming enterprises, agro-industry and other links in the food chain which were then engendered were enriched after the Second World War by intensification, specialisation, rationalisation, and especially by an increase in the scale of agricultural enterprises. The emergence of agro-pharmacy and agro-chemistry created the conditions for a totally new approach to agriculture. In the Low Countries, the nexus to this new period can be situated in the 1950s. But developments which later proved to be of substantial value for the modernising processes had already manifested themselves before that time. During the years from 1944–1945 to about 1960, agriculture was balancing between repair of the old and emergence of the new.[1]

The agricultural policies developed by the state in Belgium and the Netherlands immediately after the occupation showed similarities, but also differed. Belgium's main concern was to become less dependent on other countries for its food supply. In 1951 it had to import around 75 per cent of its bread grain. It therefore instigated a moderately protectionist agricultural policy, also at the insistence of the agricultural organisations, flanked by a policy aimed at strengthening the facilities for farmers. In the medium term, the state nevertheless aimed at a free market in the agricultural sector. The Netherlands attempted this by regulating prices and exports in order to stimulate reconstruction, but after some time switched to a more structural policy in order to improve the international competitiveness of Dutch farmers. The Netherlands were not opposed to a free market, but the social-democratic influence on state policies resulted in a far more prescriptive approach than the Belgian one, which for that matter had already been the case in the 1930s. Both approaches led to political tensions between the two countries. The sting was removed from this conflict only after the start of the European Economic Community (1958), which featured a common agricultural policy.[2]

In this contribution we analyse the approach developed by both countries from 1944 to 1945 onwards in order to restore and renew the agricultural sector (and rural society). Comparing the two countries is appropriate, as on one hand they showed many similarities, but on the other they also displayed fundamental differences. For instance, both countries had a relatively small and open market, their agricultural systems were reasonably modern and of an intensive nature (with an emphasis on livestock and horticulture), and showed high yields. Also, in comparison with the neighbouring countries, their agricultural enterprises were on a very small scale. But there were also differences: the Dutch production costs were significantly lower, and the Belgian agrarian sector was much less export-oriented. Furthermore, the Dutch agricultural policies had, as early as the First World War, been characterised by a more dirigiste approach. As early as the 1940s, the Netherlands and Belgium had tried to achieve a greater similarity in their agricultural policies through the cooperative alliance of the Benelux. The question is therefore how far both states (and the farmers' organisations) approached the postwar challenges in a similar or different manner. Did they opt for a price- and market-oriented policy or for a more structural policy? And what were the results thereof?

This chapter is composed of three parts. The first part will give a brief overview of the pre-war developments, especially in order to provide an insight into the relationship between the state and the farmers. The next part will treat the problems and challenges immediately after the end of the war, and the manner in which production was restored. Finally, the new role of the state in both countries will be examined further and compared, whereby the main focus is on the so-called structural policy, and the social and cultural measures to improve and modernise the farmers' way of life.

Agricultural policies before 1945

During 1944–1945 farmers in the Low Countries had to contend with a difficult inheritance from the pre-war period. Economically speaking, the farmers in both countries had seriously suffered under the crisis of the 1930s.

They had only been able to survive the crisis thanks to far-reaching governmental measures. This had, however, led to a substantial number of them leaving the traditional political parties and becoming beguiled by extremists or national-socialists. After the Second World War, mainly in the Netherlands (although there were similarities with the situation in West Germany), this led to the notion that farmers had to be better integrated into national society.[3] However, the economic problems were rooted deeper than the political and cultural problems. In particular, the skewed ratio of people working in agriculture to the level of production represented by the industry caused many worries for the Belgian and Dutch governments. There were a significant number of small farmers and smallholders. Many family members continued to 'stick around' on the farm because they could not find work elsewhere. The standard of living of small farmers was depressed by this hidden unemployment.

Belgium had a very long tradition of smallholders in some regions, specifically in Flemish regions such as the Campine, the Hageland and inland Flanders. They were able to survive by putting their labour also at the disposal of crafts and industry. In 1910, about 67 per cent of the farms (or 195,913) were smallholdings between 1 and 5 hectares. After the agricultural crisis of the 1880s, the recovery of Dutch agriculture had led to an increase in small farms – i.e. farmers with less than 10 hectares of land. Between 1910 and 1921, the number of farms in the Netherlands with 1–5 and 5–10 hectares grew respectively from 55,366 to 60,610 (or 37 per cent and 25 per cent of the total numbers of farms) and from 37,331 to 44,468 (or 37 per cent and 27 per cent of the total number of farms). In some regions the move to farming had become attractive for labourers. The application of chemical fertilisers allowed for the cultivation of large areas of wasteland. Furthermore, the emergence of the agro-industry (among others in the dairy sector) enabled small farmers to sell their products more easily. Certainly, until the mid 1920s they could easily maintain themselves, but thereafter they faced hard times.[4]

In Belgium, the war damage after the end of the First World War proved to be extensive. During the years 1914–1918 farmers struggled with a shortage of chemical fertilisers, fodder and available manpower. The German occupier not only requisitioned a significant part of the harvests (both for the home front and for the army), but also confiscated cattle and horses. The agricultural and food markets fell under the control of the occupier and a few private organisations, which ensured the distribution of food and other products. Paradoxically, many farmers also benefited from the war situation, except for those who farmed in the area of the front in West Flanders, which was severely affected. Many farmers were able to amass a considerable fortune thanks to the very high prices for provisions (in part through the black market). After the war, they used this capital to acquire land, machines and cattle, and to modernise farm buildings.[5] In the neutral Netherlands, the compulsory state policies during the pre-war years had other consequences. In order to maintain the national food supply and to contain price rises, the

Dutch state intervened from 1916 onwards. The export of agricultural and horticultural products was limited, maximum prices were set and production was directed. For instance, the authorities forced farmers to convert grazing land into arable land. For horticultural products, there was even an obligation to auction (which resulted in the establishment of various auction houses). In other words, the authorities intervened extensively in the agricultural sector, which means that during the war years there was a planned agricultural economy (just as in occupied Belgium).[6] The policy was very much criticised. Farmers and horticulturalists wished to profit freely from the favourable prices. For this reason, farmers in both the Netherlands and in Belgium were pleased that some time after the war a more liberal agricultural policy could be developed further.

As early as the 1920s, Dutch and Belgian farmers suffered under the sometime wildly fluctuating prices on the global market, which became dramatic after the Wall Street Crash in 1929. Therefore, the Dutch state launched price support measures for agricultural and horticultural products from the start of the 1930s. Finally, in May 1933, the Agriculture-crisis Law followed, which combined existing and a series of new measures, and which gave the authorities extensive competencies concerning price setting, production limitation, distribution and international trade. In the same period the Belgian state also developed a protectionist policy, and tried to protect domestic agriculture by all sorts of import quotas, import taxes and quota restrictions. But a far-reaching support of the primary sector emerged late and would never be as far reaching as in the Netherlands. Belgium, as an industrial nation, opted mainly to keep food prices low, which inhibited wage rises, and which at the same time had a positive impact on the spending power of families. In a sense, in Belgium the interests of consumers outweighed the interests of the (small) farmers. From about 1935, the state chose a more dynamic agricultural policy which was aimed at a better quality of products and higher competitiveness. The agricultural sector only started to emerge from the crisis at the end of the 1930s, probably also because of the preparations for war at home and abroad, including in neighbouring Germany, which was an important market for both countries.[7]

During the occupation years (1940–1944/45), normal agricultural development was impossible. Because of the experiences during the First World War the authorities were better prepared. In both countries the state relatively quickly set up a reasonably efficiently functioning distribution system. The agricultural and food sectors had to deal with a strict prescriptive policy, which again imposed crop and cultivation plans, requisitioned harvests and determined prices. But the war years were not simply negative for the farmers. Just as during the previous world war, many of them benefited from the scarcity of food and the consequent high prices.[8] State intervention in the agricultural economy therefore showed various waves since 1900. Periods of relative free trade were exchanged for strict state intervention during crises. After the Second World War state interference intensified.

Postwar challenges

Immediately after the war, the authorities were faced with the problem of a necessary rebuilding of the economy and normalisation of social relations. Belgium, which had been liberated by the Allies during 1944, had suffered significantly less material damage than the Netherlands. For instance, the port of Antwerp was completely reopened and in full operation much earlier than the port of Rotterdam. Although the southern part of the Netherlands was indeed liberated in 1944, the Allied advance then faltered. As a result, famine broke out in the north of the Netherlands during the winter of 1944–1945. Because the rail connections were not working well enough, insufficient food could be shipped, especially to the western parts of the country. This led to food shortages and famine, mainly in the towns. So while reconstruction in Belgium had already started in 1944, Dutch reconstruction only fully started during the summer of 1945. Apart from the reinstatement of political relations, this reconstruction was in the first place aimed at repairing the war damage, fostering a general economical recovery and (especially in the Netherlands) relieving the overpopulation in the agricultural sector.[9]

War damage

A contemporary inventory showed that in 1945 approximately 9,000 farms had been destroyed in the Netherlands, most of them during battles at the end of the war. However, many farms had also been evacuated and destroyed at the start of the war in order to reinstate an old water defence line (Grebbe Line). In addition, farm buildings (40,000) had been damaged. So, in total about 25 per cent of the agricultural buildings had been damaged in some way. The damage to agricultural land was also substantial: about 375,000 hectares (or 16 per cent of the total agricultural area) had suffered damage, and of this about 215,000 (9 per cent) was unfit for use in 1945, mainly because it had been flooded by the Allies as well as by the German occupiers.[10] The livestock had also greatly suffered under the war conditions. Pigs and poultry had almost completely disappeared because they were mainly bred for export, which had come to a standstill. The cattle herd had diminished by 22 per cent.[11] Much grazing land had been turned into arable land on the orders of the occupier and therefore had to be reconstructed. Still, one must conclude, although exact calculations are not available, that agricultural production had decreased less than the production of other sectors of the economy.[12]

This conclusion is also valid for Belgium, where war damage to the production infrastructure was less dramatic than in surrounding countries. The damage was less than expected in comparison to the First World War. Agricultural land was less severely hit and the cattle herd had remained almost intact. However, the number of chickens and pigs had significantly decreased. According to recent research, about 31,000 arable and livestock holdings in Belgium were destroyed or damaged (or about 15 per cent of farms, which was clearly less than in the Netherlands). But notwithstanding the shortage of chemical fertilisers and fodder, which had to be imported on a grand scale, the postwar reconstruction went relatively smoothly (see Tables 11.1a and 11.1b).[13] Both in the Netherlands and in Belgium, agricultural production reached the pre-war levels in about 1950, and this growth rate was to increase during the next decade. Yields also rose rapidly between 1940 and 1960. This was on the basis of, among other factors, an increase in investment at an enterprise level, the stimulation of research and innovation, the expansion of knowledge networks and the introduction of new and efficient production techniques. Of course, increasing mechanisation also played a role. In both countries tractors increasingly replaced the traditional heavy horses on the farm during the 1950s. In the Netherlands, this mechanisation was significantly stimulated by the Marshall Plan, which allowed the purchase of agricultural machines from the United States.[14]

The recovery of the (agricultural) economy

In the postwar years, agricultural policy was fully focused on the reconstruction of the economy, both the industry and trade. Both countries had an

Table 11.1a Production of some agricultural products in the Netherlands, in tons (1935–1950)

	1935	1940	1945	1950
Butter	96,400	105,700	100,200	93,500
Cheese	117,500	107,800	37,000	129,400
Wheat and rye	920,890	837,993	424,005	711,554
Sugarbeet	1,526,262	1,893,884	449,249	2,913,000
Consumption potatoes	1,919,141	1,929,017	2,017,756	2,846,418

Source: Knibbe, *Agriculture in the Netherlands 1851–1950*, pp. 266–267 and 278–279.

Table 11.1b Production of some agricultural products in Belgium, in tons (1935–1950)

	1935	1940	1945	1950
Butter	47,444	c. 40,000	–	42,300
Cheese	–	–	–	1,143
Wheat and rye	815,551	726,842	459,560	786,617
Sugarbeet	1,539,050	c. 1,600,000	877,842	2,674,842
Consumption potatoes	2,981,082	c. 3,000,000	1,215,978	2,317,630

Source: Database Interfaculty Centre for Agrarian History, Leuven.

interest in low industrial wages, as this led to lower production costs and a greater competitiveness in the international market. Increasing industrial exports generated the necessary dollars. In order to keep the wages of factory workers low, and at the same time keep the purchasing power of households sufficiently elevated, the Dutch authorities subsidised Dutch farmers to sell their products on the domestic market, where the price level was lower in comparison with the international market. In Belgium such a support policy had already been ended in 1950 because the economy had sufficiently recovered. In fact, the Dutch policy was partially a continuation of the price and production policy used during the crisis years of the preceding turn of the century, which had proven reasonably successful. For that matter, this did not mean that export from the Netherlands was completely avoided. Agricultural products not required for the domestic food supply, or of which there was a production surplus (such as, for instance, dairy, vegetables and fruit), were indeed sold on the international market. Initially, exports were mainly agricultural and horticultural products, as the livestock herd first had to recover. At the start of the 1950s, however, exports were already higher than before 1935 across the board (see Table 11.2)[15] – and this is where Dutch and Belgian interests (again) emphatically collided.

In the decades preceding the Second World War, Belgian agricultural policy was relatively liberal. Due to this, foreign products could easily be sold in the Belgian market, but it also meant that the agricultural sector was certainly not self-sufficient for products such as grain and horticultural products. This became clear during the occupation through a serious shortage of food and a necessary prescriptive policy by the occupier and the competent authorities. For this reason, another course was chosen after the war: food security and self-sufficiency became the new aims. However, this meant that the borders had to be closed to foreign products, an option which was not entirely realistic. Because of this, Belgian economic policy had a somewhat ambiguous nature: on one hand, a desire for liberalisation (for the sake of the industry and consumers) and on the other a necessary protectionism (for the sake of the farmers). In the late 1940s and 1950s, food imports were still

Table 11.2 Agricultural exports in the Netherlands, 1935–1950 (1950– = 100)

	1935	1939	1946	1948	1950
Processed					
Arable products	34	38	8	43	100
Livestock products	67	72	2	30	100
Horticulture products	30	39	13	48	100
Unprocessed					
Arable products	73	84	78	107	100
Livestock products	64	101	4	39	100
Horticulture products	71	68	43	70	100

Source: Knibbe, *Agriculture in the Netherlands 1851–1950*, p. 212.

required in order to keep the Belgian food situation at an acceptable level. The rationing of basic food such as bread, butter and sugar was abrogated no earlier than late 1948, and until 1950 the price evolution of some foodstuffs remained under state control. The government of Gaston Eyskens, which was installed in August 1949, was the first after the war without a Ministry for Food Provisioning. The improvement of the food situation in Belgium was mainly due to increasing food imports. Because of a lack of sufficient investments and the increased production costs, Belgian farmers could not compete with foreign suppliers. Belgian farmers feared, among others, the Dutch dairy and horticultural products. Therefore, in 1949 the price of wheat was regulated again, and in late 1950 the Minister of Agriculture, Charles Héger, launched a five-year plan in order to stimulate production, especially of fodder and animal products. But the protectionist policy led to fairly lucrative smuggling in the border areas – for instance, the smuggling of butter from the Netherlands. As a result, relations between Belgium and the Netherlands became strained.[16]

Even before the war, Belgium had feared the 'agrarian expansionism' of its northern neighbours, and after the war this sentiment only became stronger. This was not entirely unjustified, because Dutch production costs of agricultural products were, immediately after the war, about 30 per cent lower, also thanks to lower land and tenancy prices and labour costs. It is therefore no wonder that the Belgian and Luxembourg farmers and horticulturalists tried to delay the agreement with the Netherlands, entered into during the war, to set up a joint customs union (Benelux). This finally led to a separate agricultural protocol (1947) whereby the domestic cost price applied as a minimum price for imports. This opened the door to a protectionist policy, which was later defended with tooth and claw by the Belgian farmers' organisations. Integration of the agricultural economies was deemed only to be possible after harmonisation of the agricultural policies of the three countries. Even when the EEC was established in 1958, a similar condition concerning the agricultural policy was included.[17] The shielding of the national market was, however, not an option in the long term and had to be replaced over time by a more international orientation of the agricultural policy. Increasing production also compelled Belgian farmers to look for foreign markets. Furthermore, autarky in the field of agriculture was only possible within a wider European context.[18]

The Dutch Minister of Agriculture and EEC Commissioner for Agriculture, Sicco Mansholt, described his agricultural policy in the postwar years as 'opportunistic'.[19] The long-term goals, production increases and a reasonable income for farmers, were in fact dictated by the changes in the market. As soon as prices dropped too much, the farm subsidy taps were opened. This meant that there was no free market development, and that countries such as Belgium felt disadvantaged in comparison with their Dutch colleagues. However, the Netherlands profited substantially from these market and pricing policies, because they were aimed at stimulating the reconstruction of industry and trade through a speedy increase of domestic, private consumption. Cheap food and low wages for labourers played a key role in this policy. Still, when the Benelux became reality in 1948, Mansholt had to promise that he would abolish the consumers' subsidies. In succeeding years, he pleaded for more market action, for some sort of 'liberal–socialist solution'.[20] However, it was political opportunism. In his own circles he presented himself as a proponent of economic planning and control, but where his policies were concerned, he often had to bow to the pressures from abroad. However, at the start of the 1950s a change occurred. The increasing prosperity led to rising wage levels, and this led to the obligation to let farming incomes rise as well, in line with post-war policy. Opposed to this there was a sharp drop in agricultural prices on the international markets. These were two opposing movements, which did not bode well for farmers in the Netherlands and Belgium.

In order to be able to continue his policy – namely, production increases in order to let the farmers' income rise – Mansholt looked for a way out in Europe, and in doing so discovered French support. Just like the Netherlands, France was an agricultural exporter. Politicians in both countries were striving for a European Agricultural Community (or a 'Green Pool') and proposed various plans. But at least three problems were identified in doing so: (1) should the community involve all agricultural products, (2) should a supra-national organisation (similar to the European Coal and Steel Community, ECSC) manage this, and (3) should as many countries as possible participate, or only the six ECSC members?[21] Belgium reverted to its 'old' position: it did not wish for extensive integration and liberalisation before a harmonisation of the competitiveness could be realised. Furthermore, Belgium objected to a supranational organisation. Actually, free enterprise was already rooted deeper in Belgium than in the Netherlands, where strongly prescriptive authorities had been in place since the 1930s (and even during the First World War). The Belgian Farmers' Union (Belgische Boerenbond) also feared that the European policy would have too much of an economically oriented approach and would have too little attention to the social dimensions of the farmers' concerns. In other words, the farmers' leaders were afraid that rationalisation and profit would prevail over people.[22]

Migration and population pressures in the agricultural sector

Apart from the reconstruction of the war damage and the recovery of the agricultural economy, there was a third problem which manifested itself in many European countries (such as Sweden, West Germany, etc.) immediately after the Second World War: overpopulation in the agricultural sector. Both in the Netherlands and in Belgium, especially in some Flemish regions, there was a shortage of agricultural land after the war and a surplus of successors to the farms. In the Netherlands, the authorities chose the stimulation of emigration by farmers and agricultural workers as a solution. This matter had already been studied during the occupation, and after the Second World War it was hoped that the Netherlands would be allowed to annex a part of Germany, but the Allies were not keen on this. Finally, more distant regions were considered. In 1949 a state commission estimated that 40,000 people employed in agriculture should emigrate. Between 1948 and 1956, exactly 22,887 farmers migrated. In the next six years no more than 3,257 farmers left the country. Through successful reconstruction more employment was created in industry and an income could be found close to home.[23]

However, in Belgium the situation was somewhat different. In the south of the country there was a shortage of manpower in industry and a rapidly declining interest in farming as a way of life. Many Flemish people, mainly originating from poor rural regions, commuted daily or weekly to Wallonia in order to work in heavy industries, especially in the coal mines, and to help with harvesting. Apart from that, Belgium attracted foreign migrants – for instance, from Italy – fairly quickly after the end of the war. There was also permanent internal migration: thousands of Flemish farming families moved to Wallonia during the years 1945–1960 in order to try their luck there. Especially in the provinces of West and East Flanders there was a shortage of farms and a surplus of successors due to the relatively large size of families and small size of farms. Emigration to France, which had attracted many farmers before the Second World War, became increasingly difficult, because after 1952 France needed the land to accommodate migrants from Algeria. Overseas, areas such as its own colony the Belgian Congo, and to a lesser extent Canada, could tempt Flemish and Walloon farmers after the Second World War, but the numbers remained all in all very limited (2,000–5,000 between 1945 and 1960).[24] And in contrast to the Netherlands, the Belgian authorities did not have an active and dynamic migration policy for farmers. The government rather aimed at slowing down rural depopulation through the development, from the 1950s, of a regional economic expansion policy (in deprived Flemish rural regions). Attracting industrial enterprises also ensured that it was easier for small farmers to leave the agricultural sector.[25]

A new structural policy in the making

As already described above, after the Second World War agricultural production in the Low Countries recovered relatively quickly. From the early 1950s, however, the position of the agricultural economy was in danger of deteriorating. The increasing domestic and foreign production and the strongly growing international competition caused a sharp drop of agricultural prices. A number of structural problems in the Dutch and Belgian agricultural economy and rural society, which had already put pressure on the sector in the 1930s, became painfully clear as a result. First, there was the low level of schooling of many farmers and their limited knowledge in the technical and economical fields. Second, one can refer to the socioeconomical deprivation of the rural areas in comparison with the towns. Very often farms were not connected to water and electricity supplies or the telephone network.[26] A third sticking point was the low income of most of the farmers. According to the Dutch policy makers, this socioeconomic deprivation had led to many farmers choosing the side of the National Socialists before the war. Therefore, they pleaded for a better integration of the farming population in society.[27] Fourth, agriculture in the Low Countries was characterised by a large number of smallholders and micro-agricultural enterprises. In the Netherlands these were mainly found on the sandy soil and low-lying watermeadows in the east and south of the country. In 1950 there were around 60,000 farms with 1–5 hectares of land and about 61,000 farms with 5–10 hectares, or respectively 30 per cent and 31 per cent of all farms. In Belgium, the small farms were mainly located in the sandy regions of Flanders. The income of these farming families was too low, and the income gap with industry and the service sector was too large. In Belgium, for instance, the official average farmers' income was no more than 55 per cent of the national average. Higher incomes were only possible if farms could increase their production.[28]

As early as 1945–1946, agricultural experts in the Low Countries discussed possible solutions.[29] During the 1950s, agriculture ministers in both countries chose to develop a so-called 'structural policy' at the same time as the pricing and market policies. In this way they wanted to give further support to the process of mechanisation and increases in scale which continued in the agricultural sector. Farming enterprises had to become larger, and especially had to be run in a more modern and efficient way.[30] What immediately stands out is that the Netherlands had already started this policy a number of years earlier and that this served as example for Belgium. The Dutch measures were also based on a more centralised and structured approach. The structural policy had a slower start in Belgium, was more ad hoc and also had a lesser impact. The Netherlands mainly pursued two important development programmes: land consolidation (1954) and rural area development (1956). The structural policy for agriculture was aimed in the first place at improving the farmers' work and production circumstances. The first measure was aimed at the techniques and economics of farm management, the second was mainly steered by sociological views. Below we examine which measures were included in these programmes and the impact they had. Furthermore, we compare the Dutch and the Belgian approach.

Land consolidation

Land consolidation was the undisputed core of the structural policy. The first Dutch land consolidation law had been passed in 1924, but a thoroughly revised law followed in 1954. A fundamental innovation was the role of the authorities. They could compel landowners to take part in planned land consolidation projects. The concept of agrarian land consolidation offered three important benefits for the farmer. First, this intervention ensured an extension of the arable areas. Hedges and hedge sides, partitions and unproductive strips of land disappeared. Second, the labour and land productivity rose, as the larger plots could be cultivated in a more efficient manner. Third, land consolidation ensured that farmers had to travel over shorter distances, which resulted in significant cost savings. Apart from that, there was also an effect on employment. The execution of rural engineering and land consolidation works such as the construction of new roads and bridges, the straightening and canalising of brooks and small rivers, ensured a (short-lived) increase of non-agricultural work in rural areas. According to the Dutch (and later also the Belgian) planners, land consolidation also offered social benefits. The farmers had more free time and could therefore improve their quality of life. The building of new farms also gave the farmers more modern comforts, such as telephone connections, main water and electricity. The number of land consolidation projects in the Netherlands was already rising during and shortly after the Second World War, but it was especially the law of 1954 which caused an increased activity. Almost 165,000 hectares were consolidated in the period 1955–1960. In the following decade, this was even extended to no less than 520,000 hectares across the whole country.[31]

In Belgium, things did not go at such a pace, although the arable areas were even more fragmented and spread out than in the Netherlands. The 1950 agricultural census showed that the average farm had a surface of 6.8 hectares. On average, it had more than six plots. Many plots had an uneven shape and were enclosed. The Belgian authorities decided first to enact a law concerning voluntary land consolidation (in 1949), but this law was unsuccessful. The approved requests covered only 215 hectares. Land consolidation only became mandatory when the law of 25 June 1956 was enacted. In contrast to earlier measures, from then on land consolidation went hand in hand with major land improvement work and with state funding. The explicit aim of the instrument was to improve the profitability of the small family farm and to combat rural unemployment. The Nationale Maatschappij voor de Kleine Landeigendom (NMKL) (National Society for Small Landownership) ensured the coordination and execution of the work. The large-scale land consolidation, land reclamation and draining projects in the Netherlands were deemed to be an example, especially at the technical level. The government was ambitious: it was estimated that land consolidation was required for one third of the Belgian arable areas, or some 500,000 hectares. But the land consolidation made a poor start. This was the result of a lack of financial means and personnel, and the strong opposition from the farmers themselves. In 1961 only five projects were realised, all of them in Wallonia (and covering only about 1,719 hectares). It took until 1962 before the first project in Flanders could be successfully finished (Gingelom, 735 hectares). In comparison with Wallonia, things went much slower in Flanders, especially because the land and waterways were even more fragmented and therefore had a more complex character from a technical point of view.[32]

In other words, the intervention of the state in both countries, through the postwar land consolidation, was intensive. First, this was because of the technical involvement of the ministries of agriculture and their related departments:

not only the land distribution of the country had to be adapted, but the public infrastructure also had to be intensively improved. Second, the states had an imperative economic interest in the restructuring of agriculture. After the war both the improvement of the export position and agrarian employment were deemed to be government tasks. The latter caused the Dutch authorities to take this even further than their southern neighbours.

Rural area development programme

In the Netherlands the land consolidation was accompanied by an extensive support programme in which the authorities and the farmers' organisations worked closely together. This happened in a framework, the 'Landbouwschap' (Agricultural board), established in 1954.[33] In Belgium the Ministry of Agriculture and the farmers' organisations also maintained good contacts. The Belgische Boerenbond especially was involved in framing the general agriculture policy. However, this did not happen through such a formal consultation. The 'Landbouwschap' actually was aimed at a harmonious cooperation between the authorities, employers and employees. Before the war, the power of the three large Dutch farmers' unions was already considerable. The cooperation between unions, employers' societies and political parties was especially close within Catholic and Protestant networks. At the start of the 1950s, there were still more than 400,000 farmers in the Netherlands (or around 12 per cent of the total active population). Together with the members of their families, they constituted a substantial part of the electorate. However, the interests of large and small farmers differed. Whereas small farmers often preferred protection from foreign countries (protectionism), large farmers wished for free trade. The extraordinary thing was that a number of organisations governed by private law (namely the unions) acquired the right to carry out government tasks. In contrast to Belgium, where the institutions, (co-)founded and funded by the state, had a rather facilitating function which fitted within a liberal mindset, the Dutch 'Landbouwschap' opened the way for a fairly prescriptive government policy.

This policy must be understood within the context of the 'feasibility conviction' which grew strongly in the 1950s, the belief that a fairer society could be achieved by state intervention, a society in which everyone had equal opportunities. In the Dutch agricultural sector feasibility was sought through the execution of a so-called *rural area development programme*, among other measures. After all, the civil servants of the Dutch Ministry of Agriculture were not convinced that land consolidation would be universally successful. They held the opinion that, especially in what they described as 'rural deprived areas' a flanking information policy was required. In this *social engineering* programme the social and cultural 'edification' of the rural population was central.

The basis of this programme was the modernising theory of the sociologist Evert Willem Hofstee. According to this theory, society was in transition from traditional agricultural crafts to modern industrial. Farmers had lagged behind in this process. Although they were physically part of modern society, mentally they had remained in the 19th century. They suffered a so-called *cultural lag*. It was the duty of the sociologists to guide the farmers and their families into the world of a modern cultural pattern.[34] But what did this modern farmer look like? According to Hofstee he managed his enterprise in a modern and rational manner, staking his success on mechanisation (e.g. the purchase of a tractor), an increase in scale, the use of an accounting system, etc. He read the newspaper and professional journals, went on holiday with his family and therefore knew the world outside his village. His equally modern wife ran the household on rational principles and with the newest kitchen appliances. The children received the best possible schooling. And if they did not want to take over the family farm, this was not a problem. It would simply be sold. In the eyes of the sociologists of Wageningen University during the 1950s and the early 1960s, the farmer was, after all, a 'market thinker'.[35] Furthermore, the discontinuation of small and medium-sized farms ensured that the others could grow, which was necessary to bring to a halt the increases in the income gap between farmers and other parts of the economy.[36]

The newly reclaimed Noordoostpolder in the former Zuiderzee was an ideal chance to apply the new concepts about farmers. This was the place where the modern farmer could settle and where the conditions for the modern farming enterprise, also in a technical and economical sense, could be created. The 1,600 new farms were between 12 and 48 hectares in size. Under other circumstances a similar policy was started during the 1950s in the so-called 'lagging areas'. These were the regions where the farmers retained their strong attachment to traditional forms and working methods. In these areas one could find many small mixed farms which had high production costs. They often formed isolated communities with little outside contact. In the families the patriarchal forms were prevalent and the eldest son was considered the designated successor.

Within the framework of rural area development, three types of programmes were developed. Information concerning enterprise economics and technology was mainly provided by the information and extension officials of the ministry. Housekeeping information and the agrarian-cultural information were provided by consultants of the farmers' unions. The latter was necessary because the confessional unions did not allow the state to interfere in family matters, and consultants working for Catholic unions were not allowed to advise Protestants and vice versa. These information programmes were partly inspired by developments in the United States.[37]

In 1953 a test project was started in two Dutch villages. Rottevalle was the model for farmers representing modern ideas and who were open to changes. The village of Kerkhoven was a rather closed society where traditionalism was standard. In 1956 it was finally decided to deal with the traditional farming societies first, as the more modern societies would change even without being urged by the state. In the next decade, a total of 132 regions followed, mainly in the east and south of the Netherlands. However, already by the end of the

1950s the collective approach of a village was increasingly exchanged for stimulation of the most 'promising' farmers. This was caused, in the first place, by the fact that from the early 1960s the confessional farmers' unions no longer resisted on principle a reorganisation of the small farming enterprises. Through the so-called Ontwikkelings- en Saneringsfonds (O & S, 1963; Development and Reorganisation Fund) the old farmers were bought out, and in this way the political parties could satisfy their electoral supporters in rural areas. Second, the Americanisation of European sociology played a role. The individual approach of the Americans found more and more followers on the 'Old Continent', and also found its way into the information methods in the agricultural sector.

In Belgium there was not immediately a planned approach. An equivalent of the Dutch rural area development programme, whereby the state and the agricultural organisations explicitly worked close together, was absent. The structural policy initially concentrated on land consolidation and it took until the 1960s for the authorities to start developing some new supporting instruments. By establishing the Landbouwinvesteringsfonds (LIF; Agriculture Investment Fund) in 1961 the state wished to stimulate the modernisation and mechanisation of the sector through private initiatives. Previous attempts to encourage the cooperative use of machines had after all had little effect. In 1965 the establishment of the Landbouwsaneringsfonds (Agricultural Reorganisation Fund) had to convince farmers to discontinue unprofitable small farms by offering financial support.[38]

Of course, after the Second World War both the Belgian state and the agricultural organisations paid more and more attention to the 'modern farmer' and to the farmer as an individual person. This was also expressed through a series of measures and especially through information programmes. Just as in the Netherlands, the main topics were the economics and technical aspects of farm management. For instance, the Landbouweconomisch Instituut (LEI; Agriculture Economic Institute) of the Ministry of Agriculture had been advising on the use of bookkeeping on farms since the end of the 1940s. A few years later (in 1953) the Belgian Farmers' Union started a similar advisory service. Furthermore, the number of extension officers and consultants of both the authorities and of the farmers' organisation significantly increased. They had to spread the new scientific and technical knowledge and insights, which were fitting for postwar modern agriculture, as efficiently as possible, among the agrarian population. In 1948 the Belgian state started a separate information and extension department, followed by, among others, the publication of brochures, a magazine aimed at the public and radio programmes.

The provision of sociocultural information in Belgium during the 1950s and 1960s was mainly in the hands of the agricultural organisations, as in the Netherlands. For the state, the sociocultural dimension only started to play a role at the end of the 1960s or beginning of the 1970s, at a time when the first sociologists were employed.[39] Within the agricultural sector it was especially the women's guilds and youth organisations of the Belgian Farmers' Union who were interested in a wider, general education. Striking in all this was that the sociocultural initiatives of the Farmers' Union were very much inspired by Hofstee's ideas. The thinking at the Farmers' Union was concentrated on the growing cultural conflict between the lifestyles and values of the farmers and traditional rural inhabitants on one hand and those of the city dwellers or temporary migrants to the towns from rural areas on the other hand. Farmers were described as conservative, and their 'traditional cultural patterns' were in marked contrast to the world around them, which modernised at an incredible speed. The Farmers' Union wished to better integrate the 'traditional farmers' in modern society, but that did not mean that they had to completely get rid of their old culture and be fully synchronised with the inhabitants of towns and cities. The aim was to further a 'modern rural culture'.

Already from the early twentieth century, the Boerinnenbond (Women Farmers Union) organised versatile family/social activities, next to economical and religious initiatives. These popular activities included amongst others lectures and short courses about cookery, crafts, child rearing, married life and sexuality, organisation of the household and embellishment of the farm. From the 1950s onwards, the Boerenjeugdbond (BJB) (Young Farmers Association) expanded into a wider youth organisation in which sports and games were the central themes. Theatre, singing, dancing and courses for young people about to be married were also part of the programme. In 1957, the Farmers' Union itself, which exclusively addressed the male farmers, hesitantly started a Culture Department. The department stimulated the local farmers' guilds to include in their programmes, from time to time, a cultural presentation, a visit to a film or theatre performance, a fun evening for families, etc. From 1957, the members' magazine *De Boer* (*The Farmer*) also contained an extra page focusing on social and cultural themes. However, the functioning of the Culture Department only really took off from the second half of the 1960s, when the first employees could be recruited, thanks to the granting of new subsidies. So, within the professional functions more attention was paid to the 'farmer as human being'. This was also expressed by the establishment of a Social department (in 1963), after an Economics department had already been established in 1961. Moreover, in the early 1960s the Farmers' Union also recruited various staff employees who had studied sociology.[40]

Conclusion

The question we asked is how far both states (and the agricultural organisations) in the Low Countries approached the postwar challenges in a similar or different manner and what results they obtained. First, one can conclude that in both Belgium and the Netherlands war damage was repaired relatively quickly. As early as 1948, agricultural production had surpassed the pre-war level (except for the livestock herd). Initially, the postwar agricultural policies in both countries were more or less a continuation of the policies of the 1930s.

The Netherlands developed its more prescriptive approach further. Here, the agricultural sector was an important support of the national economy, not least because of the very powerful export position. However, Belgium focused more on an industrial resurgence: the rapid modernisation of the agricultural sector did not attract as much attention and the state was more modest in its intervention, as there was an ambition to develop a more liberal agricultural policy in the medium term. The migration policies for farmers also differed. The Netherlands tried to alleviate population pressures in the agricultural sector by having an active emigration policy and continued to do so until the end of the 1950s. In Belgium this policy was much more limited. The internal migration of rural labour to the industrial sector was much more part of the solution.

Notwithstanding this, the agricultural policies in both countries were characterised by increasing state intervention. The problems were largely identical. Modernisation was especially hampered by the large number of small farmers. Joining the EEC forced both countries to internationalise further, including the inevitable modernisation (increase in scale, mechanisation, etc.). Apart from the old pricing and market policies, the development of a structural policy had become unavoidable. From 1954, the Dutch state chose a technical and economic modernisation in which land consolidation played a central role. Concurrently with this a social agrarian programme was developed from 1956 in the most deprived rural areas. The rural area development programme was 'a product of its time'. The belief that a socioeconomically fair world could be created through social engineering was clearly at the forefront of it. In an increasingly individualised world, the village collective approach was, however, already deemed to be outmoded in the 1960s. Although the economic effects of rural area development and improvement are hard to measure, it might be argued that they prevented an increased gap between prosperous and less prosperous agricultural enterprises.

Although in Belgium land consolidation started in 1956, it took until the early 1960s for it to reach some size and intensity (but it still remained much more limited than in the Netherlands). This is partly an explanation of why no separate state-led social and cultural programme was developed. The latter was, however, also determined by the different social structure: while in the Netherlands society became compartmentalised and therefore divided, rural Belgium (and in particular Flanders) had a much more homogeneous Catholic culture. In other words, in the Netherlands the relation between religious ideological organisations and the state was more complex than in Belgium, and clear guidelines for social programmes were essential in order to steer the various groups.

However, one cannot say that the Belgian state was far less interventionist in the agricultural sector than its Dutch colleagues. After the Second World War, it was probably difficult to imagine that the state would continue to be aloof to agricultural questions in most of the Western European nations. Modern food supplies did not allow for this and the building up of the welfare state had to incorporate the interests of the farming community as well. An analysis of the differences between policies, as made in this chapter between the Netherlands and Belgium for the years 1944–1960, still remains interesting. Comparative and transnational research concerning the 19th and 20th centuries is, in general, still too rarely undertaken. More in-depth research on various themes is desirable, such as postwar mechanisation, the increasing attention to and investments in research, education and extension, the growing impact of the agri-business complex and the position of the farmers therein. Some of the themes which are briefly discussed in this chapter could be researched in much greater depth, such as the approach to the land consolidation, the relationship between national authorities and agricultural organisations, and the attention to sociocultural developments in rural areas. This contribution nevertheless gives an insight into the reasons why, even after more than half a century of common agricultural policy in Europe, national and regional differences continue to co-determine the development of agriculture.

Notes

* We thank Leen Van Molle, Gesine Gerhard, the members of the Leuven 'Ruralia' Group and the editors for their valuable comments on previous drafts of this chapter.
1 J. Bieleman, *Boeren in Nederland: Geschiedenis van de landbouw 1500–2000*, Amsterdam: Boom, 2008, pp. 461–480; J. Blomme, *The Economic Development of Belgian Agriculture 1880–1980: A Quantitative and Qualitative Analysis*, Brussels: Koninklijke Academie voor Wetenschappen, Letteren en Schone Kunsten van België, 1992, pp. 292–297; Y. Segers and E. H. Karel, The Low Countries, 1750–2000, in E. Thoen and T. Soens (eds), *Struggling with the Environment: Land Use and Productivity: Rural Economy and Society in North-western Europe 500–2000*, Turnhout: Brepols, 2015; L. Van Molle, Le milieu agricole belge face à la concurrence européenne 1944–1958, in M. Dumoulin (ed.), *La Belgique et les débuts de la construction européenne de la guerre aux traités de Rome*, Louvain-la-Neuve: CIACO, 1987, pp. 119–143.
2 L. Van Molle, *Ieder voor Allen. De Belgische Boerenbond 1890–1990*, Leuven: Leuven University Press, 1990, pp. 326–329; W. H. Vermeulen, *Europees landbouwbeleid in de maak: Mansholts eerste plannen 1945–1953*, Groningen: NAHI, 1989, pp. 30–38.
3 E. H. Karel, *De maakbare boer: Streekverbetering als instrument van het Nederlandse landbouwbeleid 1953–1970*, Groningen/Wageningen: NAHI, 2005; Van Molle, *Ieder voor allen*, pp. 289–300.
4 E. H. Karel, De illusie van het maakbare platteland? Streekverbetering 1956–1970, in P. Kooij et al. (eds), *De actualiteit van de agrarische geschiedenis*, Groningen/Wageningen: NAHI, 2000, p. 73; Blomme, *The Economic Development of Belgian Agriculture*, p. 224.
5 B. Demasure, *Boter bij de vis: Landbouw en voeding tijdens de Eerste Wereldoorlog*, Leuven: Davidsfonds, 2014, pp. 40–44, 141–147; P. Scholliers, The policy of survival: Food, the state and social relations in Belgium, 1914–1921, in J. Burnett and D. Oddy (eds), *The Origins and Development of Food Policies in Europe*, London: Leicester University Press, 1994, pp. 39–53.
6 Bieleman, *Boeren in Nederland*, p. 267; N. Koning, *The failure of agrarian capitalism. Agrarian politics in the United Kingdom, Germany, the Netherlands*

Agriculture in Belgium and the Netherlands 227

and the United States 1846–1919, unpublished Ph.D. thesis, Wageningen, 1994, pp. 235–242, published under the same title, London: Routledge, 1994.
7 J. L. van Zanden, Modernisering en de toenemende betekenis van de overheid, in *Agrarische Geschiedenis van Nederland*, 's-Gravenhage: Staatsuitgeverij, 1986, p. 128; P. Brusse, A. Schuurman, L. Van Molle and E. Vanhaute, The Low Countries, 1750–2000, in B. van Bavel and R. Hoyle (eds), *Social Relations: Property and Power: Rural Economy and Society in North-western Europe 500–2000*, Turnhout: Brepols, 2010, pp. 199–224.
8 Bieleman, *Boeren in Nederland*, p. 294; Y. Segers and L. Van Molle, *Leven van het land: Boeren in België 1750–2000*, Leuven: Davidsfonds, 2004, pp. 107–108.
9 R. Ryckewaert, *Building the Economic Backbone of the Belgian Welfare State: Infrastructure, Planning and Architecture 1945–1973*, Rotterdam: 010 Publishers, 2011; G. Trienekens, *Voedsel en honger in oorlogstijd 1940–1945: Misleiding, mythe en werkelijkheid*, Utrecht: Kosmos, 1995.
10 S. M. Elpers, *Erfenis van het verlies. De strijd om de wederopbouw van boerderijen tijdens en na de Tweede Wereldoorlog*, unpublished Ph.D. thesis, University of Amsterdam, 2014; G. Andela, *Kneedbaar landschap, kneedbaar volk. De heroïsche jaren van de ruilverkaveling in Nederland*, Bussum: Uitgeverij TOTH, 2000, p. 31; M. Knibbe, *Agriculture in the Netherlands 1851–1950: Production and Institutional Change*, Amsterdam: NEHA, 1993, p. 210.
11 Andela, *Kneedbaar landschap*, p. 30.
12 Bieleman, *Boeren in Nederland*, p. 296.
13 P. A. Tallier (ed.), *Puin en wederopbouw: Oorlogsschadedossiers Tweede Wereldoorlog en verwante archieven: Bronnen voor een veelzijdige geschiedenis van de 20ste eeuw*, Brussels: Algemeen Rijksarchief, 2012; Segers and Van Molle, *Leven van het land*, pp. 107–108.
14 P.R. Priester, Boeren met machines: Paarden en trekkers, in J. Bielemand and A. van Otterloo (eds), *Techniek in Nederland in de twintigste eeuw: deel 3: Landbouw en voeding*, Zutphen: Walburg Pers, 2000, pp. 72–81; Bieleman, *Boeren in Nederland*, p. 463.
15 Knibbe, *Agriculture in the Netherlands 1851–1950*, pp. 212, 266–267, 278–279.
16 Van Molle, *Ieder voor Allen*, p. 327; Van Molle, Le milieu agricole belge, pp. 125–126.
17 L. Van Molle, 100 jaar ministerie van Landbouw 1884-1984, *Agricontact*, 1984, pp. 65–69, 81–85; Van Molle, Le milieu agricole belge, p. 121.
18 Th. E. Mommens, Agricultural integration in the Benelux, in R. T. Griffiths (ed.), *The Netherlands and the Integration of Europe 1945–1957*, Amsterdam: NEHA, 1990, pp. 49–68; Th. E. Mommens, Het landbouwprobleem in de vorming van de Benelux, in A. Postma, H. Balthazar and L. J. Brinkhorst (eds), *Benelux in de kijker*, Tielt: Lannoo, 1994, pp. 175–199; Segers and Van Molle, *Leven van het land*, pp. 112–114.
19 J. van Merriënboer, *Mansholt: Een biografie*, Amsterdam: Boom, 2006, p. 160.
20 Van Merriënboer, *Mansholt*, p. 165.
21 Van Molle, *Ieder voor Allen*, p. 334.
22 Van Molle, *Ieder voor Allen*, p. 335.
23 E. H. Karel, *Boeren tussen markt en maatschappij: Essays over effecten van de modernisering van het boerenbestaan in Nederland 1945–2012*, Groningen/Wageningen: NAHI, 2013, pp. 135–148.
24 M. Cheyns and Y. Segers, Fermiers flamands en Wallonie, in I. Goddeeris and R. Hermans (eds), *Migrants flamands en Wallonie 1850–2000*, Leuven: Lannoo Campus, 2012, pp. 70–97; C. Carbonez-Dejaeger, De Belgische aanwezigheid in Canada, *The Canadian Journal of Netherlandic Studies*, 2002, XIII, p. 45.
25 E. Buyst and W. Peeters, Regionaal expansiebeleid: een slag in het water? De lange weg naar economische convergentie 1950–1990, in J. De Maeyer and P. Heyrman (eds), *Geuren en kleuren: Een sociale en economische geschiedenis van Vlaams-Brabant, 19de en 20ste eeuw*, Leuven: Peeters, 2001, pp. 257–262; C. Mougenot and M. Mormont,

L'invention du rural: L'héritage des mouvements ruraux (de 1930 à nos jours), Brussels: Editions Vie Ouvrière, 1988.
26 Karel, De maakbare boer, p. 251.
27 Karel, De maakbare boer, pp. 84–85.
28 Segers and Van Molle, Leven van het land, p. 129.
29 About the National Congress for Agricultural renewal, organised in Brussels in September 1945, see L. Van Molle, Y. Segers and P. Brassley, Introduction, in P. Brassley, Y. Segers and L. Van Molle (eds), War, Agriculture and Food: Rural Europe from the 1930s to the 1950s, New York: Routledge, 2012, pp. 3–4.
30 Bieleman, Boeren in Nederland, pp. 467–468; Van Molle, 100 jaar Ministerie van landbouw, pp. 85–91.
31 In 1959 there was 2.31 million hectares agricultural land in the Netherlands. S. van den Bergh, Verdeeld land: De geschiedenis van de ruilverkaveling in Nederland vanuit een lokaal perspectief, 1890–1985, Wageningen/Groningen: NAHI, 2004, pp. 58–59, p. 207.
32 G. Dejongh and P. Van Windekens, Van Kleine Landeigendom tot Vlaamse Landmaatschappij. Vijfenzestig jaar werking op het Vlaamse platteland 1935–2001, Brussels, 2001, pp. 80–92; Van Molle, 100 jaar ministerie van landbouw, p. 89.
33 E.J. Krajenbrink, Het Landbouwschap. 'Zelfgedragen verantwoordelijkheid' in de land- en tuinbouw 1945–2001, Groningen/Den Haag: NAHI/LTO, 2005.
34 Karel, De maakbare boer, pp. 25–29.
35 Karel, De maakbare boer, p. 21.
36 A. Maris, C. D. Scheer and M. A. J. Visser, Het kleine-boerenvraagstuk op de zandgronden: een economisch-sociografisch onderzoek van het Landbouw-Economisch Instituut, 's-Gravenhage: LEI, 1951.
37 E. W. Hofstee, De plaats van de 'Land-Grant Colleges' in het landbouwonderwijs, de voorlichting en het onderzoek in de Verenigde Staten, Landbouwkundig Tijdschrift, 64, 1955, pp. 189–195; F. Inklaar, Van Amerika geleerd: Marshall-hulp en kennisimport in Nederland, Den Haag: Sdu Uitgevers, 1997, pp. 275, 309.
38 Segers and Van Molle, Leven van het land, pp. 125–129.
39 Van Molle, 100 jaar Ministerie van landbouw', p.91.
40 C. Bisschop, Meer dan boer alleen. Een geschiedenis van de Landelijke Gilden 1950–1990, Leuven: Leuven University Press, 2015, pp. 66–90; Mougenot and Mormont, L'invention du rural.

12 From food scarcity to overproduction

Saving the German peasant during the miracle years

Gesine Gerhard

After two decades of war, political upheavals and economic rollercoasters, the most dramatic changes for German agriculture and rural society were still to come. During the 1950s, West Germany underwent a rapid economic recovery that seemed miraculous compared to the hunger years of the war and immediate postwar period. Agricultural production increased dramatically, while the number of German farms decreased.[1] Tractors and machinery replaced horses, peasants became industrial workers, and lifestyles in the countryside were altered.[2] These developments were not unique to Germany; they happened in other Western European countries and could thus simply be understood as part of the long-term transition from a rural to an industrial society. The German case, however, is characterized by both dramatic changes and astonishing continuities over the course of the 20th century and deserves closer examination.[3] This chapter will analyze the agricultural transformation in Germany between 1945 and 1960. It will shed light on how new agricultural programs were worked out after the destruction of the war, what role agricultural organizations played in the process and how the new German state was able to direct the economic transformation without social conflict or political radicalization of the major players, the peasants.

At the eve of the destruction of the Second World War, few people would have predicted such a fast European recovery. Roads, bridges and train stations were destroyed, and cities and agricultural lands lay in ruins. In addition to the devastation, millions of people had been uprooted by the war. Refugees from the eastern territories, liberated camp inmates, prisoners of war and displaced persons as well as victims of bombed-out cities needed food and shelter. Many of them had no home to go back to or could not be repatriated. A large-scale hunger crisis was looming over central Europe and everybody was looking to the victorious Allies for help.[4]

While hunger and starvation had begun for many people in countries dominated by Germany years before, most Germans had had enough to eat until the last winter of the war. The Nazi government had implemented an efficient food rationing system at home, tightly controlled agricultural production, and carefully oversaw the distribution and consumption of food.[5] In their quest to stretch scarce resources as far as possible, Nazi propaganda had promoted

Spartan eating habits and made 'eating right' a patriotic duty. Housewives were asked to prepare satisfying dishes with local products and substitute foods, and the traditional Sunday roast gave way to 'one-pot meals' (*Eintopf*) prepared with leftovers and cheap cuts of meat.[6] Most of all, the ruthless exploitation of allied, occupied and defeated countries had ensured that German civilians and soldiers did not go hungry. In this way, the Nazi regime had been able to avoid the kind of collapse of the home front as had happened in the First World War.[7]

During the Third Reich, peasants as the producers of food were subject to tight regulations and production control. The Nazi regime, however, was able to overcome peasant resentment of the close oversight by elevating peasants' status in society. Spectacular mass events celebrated peasant contributions to the German 'Volk' and recognized peasants as the foundation of the 'Nordic race'. On the Bückeberg near Hanover in Northern Germany, hundreds of thousands of rural people came together every year to recognize peasant labor and to rally in support of agricultural producers.[8] Peasants were also indispensable for the Nazis' visions of the colonization and Germanization of Eastern Europe. The *Generalplan Ost* foresaw the removal and ethnic cleansing of millions of Slavs, who would be replaced with German settlers.[9] Finally, peasants' labor and agricultural production at home was a crucial part of the equation to achieve greater food autarky and to become less dependent on food imports.

Food shortages and hunger arrived in Germany only in the last year of the war, when the front closed in on Germany, the Red Army took Poland and millions of Germans found themselves fleeing from formerly Eastern German territory. Armies of soldiers could no longer be fed from the conquered territory, and the already tight resources at home had to be stretched further. By the winter of 1944/45, the food regime in Germany finally collapsed. The severity of the crisis would affect political decision-making in Germany and in Europe in the years following.[10]

The victorious American, Soviet, British and French Allies faced an enormous task in May 1945. After the foremost goal—the defeat of Nazi Germany—had been accomplished, the four powers knew that they had to tackle the hunger crisis next. While they disagreed profoundly on what economic system would be best to handle the crisis, all four of them saw themselves bound to continue some of the measures introduced by the Nazis. Few civil servants in the departments of agriculture were replaced in an attempt to use existing expertise, food rationing as set up by the Nazis was continued albeit without its racist components, and the control of production remained in place.[11] These first years after the war did not allow for a profound economic reorganization. At least in the western parts of the country, peasants were able to continue their way of farming and enjoyed a relatively sheltered existence. In the eastern parts, the Soviets did not wait long to pursue a radical restructuring of landownership. They expropriated large farmers and redistributed the land in small plots to the landless, a step that turned out to be far from successful in terms of economic and political outcomes.[12]

The year 1948 was a turning point for Germany's economy. Agricultural production started to grow, food rationing was lifted, and the administration of the occupation zones was left more and more in German hands. By the mid 1950s, the German economy was in the midst of an economic upward trend that promised to bring 'prosperity to all'. However, it also threatened the lives and work of the rural population. It was at this point that agricultural interest groups lobbied strongly for ways to 'save the peasants' and for a special treatment of their constituency. The Agriculture Act of 1955—the so-called Green Law—represented a great compromise that continued protectionist farm politics while at the same time promoting structural changes. Peasants' incomes and affordable prices for agricultural products were ensured, and the small family was endorsed as the preferred model that needed to be protected, while specialization and the enlargement of farms were encouraged. The Green Law provided incentives for farmers to modernize, and the number of small farms that couldn't afford to do so decreased. State subsidies effectively averted social conflicts or political opposition, and ultimately allowed for the peaceful integration of farmers in German society and into the European Economic Community.

Hunger and democracy after the war

In May 1945, few people would have predicted such an economic and political outcome. The food situation in Germany was dire. Food distribution systems had collapsed and fertilizers and machinery were in short supply. Access to food varied greatly across Germany, and hunger was prominent especially in the cities and industrial areas, where bombs had leveled houses, roads and factories. But the situation was hardly better in the villages. Here, the population had swelled with millions of refugees and expellees from the former German territories. The villagers had to make room for and share food with the newcomers, and the population in the villages doubled or even tripled. The newcomers were expected to help with harvesting and other chores, but the clash of cultures and lifestyles often put a strain on social relations. The situation became more difficult with an unusually cold winter in 1945/46, when even the most basic necessities for survival were in short supply.

In all four zones, the occupation powers continued the rationing system in an effort to secure food, but the average daily calorie supply dropped well below subsistence level. In mid-1946, people in the American zone had to survive on official rations of 1,330 calories per day, in the Soviet zone daily rations were at 1,083 and in the British zone at 1,050 calories. Inhabitants in the French zone fared worst with only 900 calories daily.[13] In the city of Stuttgart, officials estimated that people had to survive on 793 calories.[14] Another cold winter followed in 1946/47 and prolonged the crisis.[15] Two years after the war, food production was down 75 percent compared to the level of production in 1938/39.[16] In industrial areas like the Ruhr, strikes and unrest broke out among hungry workers, and desperate people embarked on foraging trips to the countryside or took the 'potato train' to more distant agricultural areas like Bavaria in search for something edible. Small garden plots and city parks were turned into vegetable gardens and potato fields to ensure survival. Balconies and cellars housed pigs, chicken and rabbits in desperate attempts to supplement meagre diets. Where this was not enough, people resorted to stealing and other illegal activities. The black market flourished, where everything could be bought or bartered for those who had anything to give. About one quarter of all manufactured food was funnelled through the black market.[17]

The widespread experience of hunger set the agenda for economic decision-making for the new superpowers. It became clear very quickly, however, that the political disagreements and the incompatibility of economic priorities between the United States and the Soviet Union would obstruct a consolidated effort to get things working again. At the first postwar conference in Potsdam in July 1945, Germany was split into four zones of occupation. Germany's eastern border was shifted westwards, and all territories east of the Oder–Neisse line were put under Polish jurisdiction. This was supposed to be a provisional solution until a peace treaty was drawn, but it became a de facto loss of Germany's most fertile agricultural lands, especially Prussia and large parts of Pomerania. Despite the division into zones, the Allies had intended to treat Germany as a single economic unit. This turned into an elusive goal when each power was allowed to take reparations from their own zone. The Soviets proceeded to remove as much as possible from their zone to compensate for the heavy losses sustained during the war. Industrial machinery and other movable items were taken and shipped east. Stalin was allowed to take another 10 percent of the industrial capacity from the western zones as war reparations. The chaotic disassembly of German industry affected Eastern Germany's recovery significantly.[18] The US—much less affected by war damage and loss of lives compared to its allies—tried to avoid any punitive measures that would disrupt the economic recovery in their zone, and consequently handled the question of reparation very differently. In the end, there was no agreement among the four Allies on how to increase German agricultural and industrial output, and each zone quickly went its own way.[19]

In the rapidly cooling climate of the Cold War, the division of Germany into four occupation zones would eventually lead to the emergence of two separate German states in 1949. The conflicting ideas crystallized over questions of agricultural and food policy. No agreement could be reached on whether it was more important to get the country back on its economic feet or if Germany should first be punished for its war crimes and the Nazi terror, or if the Allies should provide economic aid or insist on reparations and the disassembly of agricultural machinery and resources. While some believed that Germany had to be turned into a land of peasants and shepherds to ensure that Germany would never be able to build up military strength again (the so-called Morgenthau Plan), others argued that only a quick and forceful industrial revival would guarantee lasting peace.[20] Another contentious issue was the power of the former landed elites and the question of a redistribution of land—something that would be handled quite differently in the occupation zones. The ideological clash between the two new superpowers thus found its most direct expression in the agricultural decisions made over the next few years.

Both sides, however, realized the political risks associated with hunger, and took action to relieve the crisis. In the Soviet zone, people from the cities were organized to help the rural population with the harvest. Workers in critical industries were given special food rations. The main priority in Eastern Germany was the restructuring of farm sizes and the breaking of the power of the old landed elites.[21] A radical land reform was hastily introduced that would change the structure of landholding profoundly.[22] Large landowners with properties of more than 100 hectares, Nazi and war criminals were to be expropriated, and the land was redistributed among the landless in small parcels of 5–10 hectares. The land was free of prior debts or other obligations, but there was a price—an equivalent of one year's harvest was to be paid by the new owner in money or kind over the next 10–20 years. By the middle of 1946, the land commissions had completed their work. By January 1949, one third of all agricultural and forest land had been expropriated, a total of 3,225,364 hectares or 13,699 properties, 209,000 new peasant farms with an average size of 8 hectares had been created, and another 120,000 grants of land had been added to existing small farms. Most agricultural land was now held in units of 5–20 hectares. Farms larger than 100 hectares had declined from one third of all farms to 11 percent (by 1950).[23]

East German Communists celebrated the land reform as a great success. Within the short span of a few years, the old social structure had been demolished and the power of the great landowners had been destroyed. The land reform had created a new social order with a class of small peasants who were heavily indebted to the regime.[24] In socioeconomic terms, however, the land reform was far from successful. The hastily implemented land reform had disrupted autumn planning, and many of the more successful famers had been expropriated or fled to the west. There was great mismanagement of funds, seeds, and livestock. Widespread looting had further aggravated the situation. Many of the new farms were far too small to be profitable, and the overall agricultural output declined dramatically. Modernization or technological improvements were stalled, since the new peasants did not have the means or the state support to invest in machines. A great number of plots were left untilled and quickly abandoned by the new owners who could not make a living on such small areas of land. Over the years, many farmers returned their land to the state, left the country or abandoned farming all together.[25] For those who stayed, the living and working conditions in the countryside remained difficult. Many of the peasants withdrew their support for the new communist government, or the 'Workers' and Farmers' State', which was what the German Democratic Republic liked to call itself in the decades to come. In the 1950s, all peasants were forced into collectivization for a 'full socialization of agriculture', a move that was very unpopular with the peasants.[26]

In the western parts of Germany, existing social and rural structures were left intact. There had been talk about a redistribution of land, but no direct measures were taken. For the Western occupation powers, the main goal was the restoration of the economy; they quickly set up a democratic administration that would manage agricultural production and food distribution. Since Germany's agricultural production was considered crucial for a rapid recovery of Europe overall, the new authorities were careful not to disturb the fragile social order. Large landowners were allowed to keep their land and only a small amount of land changed hands. In addition to economic considerations, there was a political dimension to hunger. The US Military Governor in Germany, Lucius D. Clay, argued that only the prospect of a quick economic recovery would allow for a strong democratic foundation—and allow Western Europe to become a bulwark against the spread of communism. In Clay's words, there was 'no choice between becoming a Communist on 1,500 calories and a believer in democracy on 1,000 calories. It is my sincere belief that our proposed ration allowance in Germany will not only defeat our objectives in middle Europe but will pave the road to a Communist Germany.'[27] Since food was at the basis of the equation, the Americans avoided any disruption of agricultural production. The US government also argued that American taxpayers did not want to pay for German recovery in the long term, and economic necessities overruled the need to bring justice to all war criminals. These political considerations found their expression in the Marshall Plan, a massive European recovery program announced in 1947 that would give financial assistance to the rebuilding of European economies.[28] Over the next four years, a total of $14 billion dollars was pumped into Western Europe. The Soviet Union rejected the aid because of its economic regulation and American oversight, and pressured other Eastern European countries to decline the program. To the Americans, the Marshall Plan would create a stable and democratic Europe that provided the best protection against communism.

Food administration in the occupation zones

Following Clay's rationale that only a quick handling of the food crisis would allow for an overall economic recovery and stable political future, the American Office of Military Government for Germany, US (OMGUS) swiftly set up a central administration for food and delegated political authority to the Germans in their zone. The Central Office for Food and Agriculture led by Hermann Dietrich worked independently from the occupying forces with the goal to distribute food across the zone. The British also set up a German Central Office for Food and Agriculture in their zone and appointed Hans Schlange-Schöningen as the head.[29] Here, the Nazis' food administration, the Reich Food Estate (*Reichsnährstand*, or RNS) remained in place until 1948 and former personnel continued their jobs. In the industrial areas of the French zone the collaboration between the French and Germans proved especially difficult. The already scarce resources were stretched further to feed the occupying troops with local resources. The hunger in the cities and industrial areas caused protest and strikes among German workers. To overcome food delivery problems and collaborate more efficiently, the British and American zone combined their administrative offices for agriculture and food distribution and merged the two territories into the Bizonia in January 1947. The French united their zone with the other Western powers in March 1948.

Getting food production and distribution working again, however, was not without friction. Conflicts arose between German and Allied authorities and between peasants and consumer interests. Peasants allegedly exploited the situation for their own advantage and sold their produce at high prices on the black market. They resented the order to deliver food at low prices, and opposed the call to reduce their herds and focus on grain production. Peasants resorted to open sabotage when they proceeded to kill their animals rather than turning them over to the authorities.[30] The American authorities had little patience for this behavior. Clay voiced his frustration in a staff meeting on May 19, 1947:

> Maybe we had better let people starve if they don't run their affairs better than that. I am not going to get too worried about it. The point I am trying to make is I am not willing to bring food in to replace food that Germans didn't plant which they could have planted. Or to replace food that goes to animals they don't need that has 'come out of their ration. I think we might as well tell them so, but think we ought [to] ... bring home to the German people that the reason of their failure to get food is their own administrative failure to do the maximum with what they have got ...[31]

The tensions between the occupation powers and the German administration escalated over the issue of food. Schlange-Schöningen was often caught in the middle of the conflicting interests and had to manoeuver between what looked like egotistical peasants, ungrateful Germans or overly demanding occupation powers. The so-called food pantry law (*Speisekammergesetz*), that ordered peasants and food distributors such as restaurant owners and merchants to disclose every bit of food they stored, became the tipping point. Many openly resisted the 'emergency law against the peasants' and very few filled out the questionnaire.[32] In an inflammatory speech in early 1948, Johannes Semler, a German conservative politician and member of the Economic Council of Bizonia, expressed his anger with the American occupiers. He was dismissed shortly after he made his polemic comment.

> Americans sent us corn and chicken feed and we have to pay for it dearly. They don't give it to us for free. We have to pay for it in dollars from German work and German exports and we are even expected to be grateful. German politicians should stop saying thank you for these food deliveries.[33]

On both sides, more conciliatory voices prevailed. In March 1948, Ludwig Erhard was elected as the Director of Economics in Bizonia.[34] Over the next months, Erhard and the Economic Council prepared a currency reform that would replace the *Reichsmark* with a new currency, the *Deutsche Mark*. Announced only two days before the actual implementation on June 20, 1948, the currency reform eliminated all price controls and ended the food rationing system that had been in existence for almost a decade. The currency reform was a dramatic turning point. Overnight, the Reichsmark became useless. Everybody received a starting capital of 40 Deutsche Marks. Suddenly, stores were filled with food items that consumers had not seen in years. The hoarding of food came to an end, and shortages and bartering disappeared completely. Prices went up quickly as well, and the better prices seemed to have boosted agricultural production overnight. Peasants started to deliver and sell their products on the regular market, workers showed up for work and were paid in money that had value.[35] The foraging trips to the countryside in search of food were no longer necessary, since stores carried plenty of food for everybody who could afford it. This initial euphoria, however, quickly gave way to frustration, when consumers realized they could not afford many of the items at the new and higher prices.

The currency reform led to a different kind of food crisis in the city of Berlin. Angered by the unilateral economic step in the western zones, the Soviet occupation power decided to introduce a currency reform in their zone as well. To put pressure on the West and assure Berlin's status as a free city, the Soviets blocked all roads in and out of Berlin. Neither people nor goods could get into the city, and the Soviets threatened to starve Berlin if no political concessions were made. From April 1948 to May 1949, Berlin was cut off from its surroundings. The Western Allies responded to the pressure with an unprecedented rescue action. For twelve months, the United States and their allies delivered all daily necessities for people in Berlin by air. During the so-called airlift, aircraft affectionately dubbed 'raisin bombers' or 'candy poppers' delivered food and supplies to the city and its inhabitants. When winter set in and the city was still cut off from its surroundings, American and British aircraft delivered coal to heat the stoves. In total, the Western Allies brought over 2 million tons of food and supplies to Berlin on more than 200,000 flights. On average, an American or British aircraft landed every two minutes in Berlin for the entire duration of the blockade. Because of these supplies, Berlin's population did not starve. The Western Allies had not given in to the political pressure of the Soviets—and the Berlin Airlift constituted the first major victory in the Cold War.[36]

Changing farms, changing farm policies in the 1950s

After the currency reform, Germany's economic recovery proceeded quickly. The European Recovery Program (Marshall Plan) pumped US$2 billion in aid into West Germany over the next five years and contributed to the overall economic recovery.[37] Within a few years, food consumption reached pre-war levels, and food scarcity would soon become a distant memory. For peasants, however, the new economic realities brought new uncertainties. They had to produce more food at lower cost and had to pay high prices for new machinery. They faced pressures to rationalize production and modernize their farms. In the new economic climate, small farms were unprofitable and would have to be given up.

Agricultural politics had to find a way to make the transition amenable to the peasants. As more food was to be produced by fewer peasants, the change had to be actively embraced by those remaining in agriculture. Liberal market principles were promoted, but there was also the consensus that agriculture faced special circumstances and needed to be sheltered from market forces, just as it had been in the past. Politicians from all across the political spectrum saw the importance of secure domestic food production and of a stable peasantry. They all embraced the demands of agrarian interest groups for a continuous protection of the farming sector and for state subsidies. Between 1953 and 1959, the amount of financial aid spent by the federal government on agriculture increased from DM 317 million (or 1.1 percent of the federal budget) to DM 2.68 billion (or 5.3 percent of the federal budget), a clear indicator of the importance attributed to cushioning the transition for the farm sector.[38]

The greatest dilemma, however, was the inherent problem with prices for food. Prices had to be both high enough and 'fair' for the producers, and low and affordable for the consumer. The discussion over bread prices illustrates this dilemma. German domestic prices for grain were low compared to international prices in 1949–50. To raise peasants' incomes, the first Minister of Agriculture, Wilhelm Niklas, wanted to increase the national grain price. But since this would have led to higher bread prices—unacceptable in light of consumers' spending powers—another solution had to be found. In July 1950, the so-called *Konsumbrot* was introduced. The bread was made with less wheat and more rye, and it was sold at a fixed price. At first the *Konsumbrot* was brushed off as 'poor-people's bread', but soon it became quite popular and seemed to appease all sides. The government subsidy of the *Konsumbrot* was costly but worth its price.[39] Milk was another example of the attempt to make small dairy farming profitable, while also keeping the price for milk low for consumers. Special laws and subsidies were introduced in 1950/51 that secured prices for producers, and soon market regulations covered bread grains, cereals, fodder, meat, milk and sugar. In all, 75 percent of agricultural production was influenced by these regulations.[40]

When industrial growth took off in the 1950s, agriculture fell further behind. Agriculture's contribution to the GDP dropped from 10.2 percent in 1950 to 5.75 percent in 1960. The trend was the same for the number of people employed in agriculture—it fell from 25 percent of the working population to 13.7 percent. An average of 110,555 people left agriculture every year for jobs in industry.[41] At the same time, dramatic changes and rapid modernization took place in agriculture. By 1950/51, agricultural production had reached the pre-war level of 1935–39, despite the loss of agricultural lands in the East. In the course of the 1950s, meat and milk production increased by more than half. Across West German farms, mechanization, modernization and specialization took place at a rapid pace and ushered in the modern era in the agrarian sector.

In West Germany, farm sizes changed dramatically even without land reform. In 1949, almost two-thirds of the 2 million farms were small with a cultivable area of 0.5–7.5 ha. These farms were too small to be profitable. By 1960, the number of farms between 2 and 5 ha had declined by 30 percent and the number of farms larger than 10 ha had increased slightly.[42] Small farms were given up or lost their status as main income sources for a family and disappeared from the statistics. In many cases, the land was farmed part-time by a family member, but the main family income would come from jobs outside the farm sector.

The transformation included agricultural machinery. While more than one million draught horses were used on German farms after the war, they were almost entirely replaced by tractors over the next decade.[43] The number of tractors increased from 77,000 in 1949 to 900,000 by 1960, a more than tenfold increase.[44] While there had been fewer than three tractors per 100 hectares in 1949, the number had risen to 15 tractors per 100 hectares in 1960. Other changes in the social make-up of the rural world were the many newcomers—refugees and expellees. A law was introduced to provide land for settlement, and while about 50,000 refugees had settled by 1954, the success in terms of creating farmers was modest. Often the parcels were too small and could only serve for part-time farming.[45] Refugees were the first to leave agricultural jobs behind and find employment in industry or the cities. An increasing number of rural people commuted daily to jobs in industry, and farmed after regular working hours and on weekends. Life in the countryside itself started to look more like life in the city, and the distinction between rural and urban lifestyles became less noticeable. Work patterns and social customs changed. Many jobs on the farm became more specialized and professionalized, like the job of a milker.[46] Another characteristic of change was the decrease in the employment of non-family members. Farm work became entirely a family business, and was predominantly made up of female family laborers. The absolute number of family laborers dropped, too. In the end, it was only the wife that was left to do farm work, with extra hands hired only for the harvest. The workload for those remaining on the farm increased.

Agricultural productivity grew enormously, but for many peasants this came with a feeling of loss and anxiety. The miraculous economic boom left farmers more and more behind, and the gap between agricultural and industrial incomes grew. Remedial financial help was not enough to make the transition any easier and instead changes in agricultural policies were necessary. Agricultural interest groups demanded action to close the income gap and to tackle the problem of prices. They depicted the rural exodus as a socially explosive issue that had to be solved quickly. According to the agricultural interest groups, a parity law was needed that would secure peasants an equal share in the economic growth and ease the transition. In July 1955 just such a law was passed with the support of all political parties—the Federal Agriculture Act (*Bundeslandwirtschaftsgesetz*). The law envisioned closing the income gap between the farm sector and the industrial sector; it aimed at equal living standards, and promoted measures such as tax breaks for farmers, subsidies, price controls, investment assistance, and an agricultural social policy. The new law was also supposed to ensure sufficient food supplies, but this had become a secondary concern amid the general economic recovery. The main purpose of the law was to keep farmers content and satisfied with the social changes around them. The government was now required to give a comprehensive annual report on German agriculture with suggestions on how to help the farm sector. With the Agriculture Act, financial aid for the farm sector increased substantially, from 2.1 percent of the federal budget in 1955 to 5.8 percent just two years later.[47]

Agricultural organization and corporatist politics: the German Peasant League

The Agriculture Act of 1955 was a major accomplishment of the agrarian interest organizations. In the 1950s and 1960s, the newly founded agrarian interest group, the German Peasant League (*Deutscher Bauernverband e.V.*, or DBV), exercised considerable political influence, which is remarkable in light of the loss in significance of the agrarian sector for the overall economy. The interest group would influence all major agricultural laws, and the representation of the farm sector in the parliament (*Bundestag*) and on special committees was striking. The agrarian interest organization had a strong party affiliation with the conservative party, the CDU, and was in close contact with the Minister of Agriculture himself.[48]

The DBV had been founded in 1948 as a central organization representing all farmers, thus overcoming the splintering of agricultural interest groups characteristic of the past. In other regards, there was a lot of continuity. Many of its leading personalities were more than 60 years old and had worked in agrarian interest groups during the Weimar Republic. Like the earlier interest groups, the DBV favored protectionism, price supports, and government intervention, and its main focus was the perceived struggle to protect agriculture's position in society. It is remarkable how successful the DBV was in securing their constituency's interests considering the fast changing society around them.

One reason for the success of the DBV was its ability to represent itself as the voice of all farmers, large and small. It advocated that all farms had to be preserved and protected from the structural change. This advocacy was largely rhetorical, since in reality the economic measures supported by the DBV benefited the large and medium-sized farms.[49] However, the DBV successfully depicted its clientele as a group that had been pushed to the side and was becoming a small minority in the industrial society. Peasants' interests had to be defended and the DBV put itself at the forefront of the struggle. The agrarian sector was highly organized, with 90 percent of all full-time farmers belonging to the DBV.[50] The attendance at farmers' meetings was high and farmers were mobilized successfully during election campaigns. A weekly publication, the German Peasant Correspondence (*Deutsche Bauernkorrespondenz*, or DBK), reached a large readership. Local branches of the Peasant League provided services such as legal advice, technical information or other support. Members of the DBV also headed up local Chambers of Agriculture or Farmers' Mutual Loan Organizations that provided financing and other services for farmers.[51] The influence of the DBV on the farming population was thus considerable.

The DBV was closely associated with the Christian Democratic Union (CDU) or its Bavarian sister party, the Christian Social Union (CSU). Farmers provided a reliable source of support for the conservative parties in both regional and national elections.[52] In the 1950s, 60 percent of the farmers voted for the CDU; in the 1960s it was more than 70 percent. The Social Democrats (SPD) never gained more than 10 percent of the farm vote.[53] No other political party could count on such homogeneous support from one social group. The Minister of Agriculture in all states (*Bundesländer*) was affiliated with the CDU.[54] Some 70 percent of the agrarian representatives in the Bundestag were members of the CDU, and another 15 percent came from the Liberal Party, the FDP.[55]

The representation of agrarian interests in the Bundestag increased over the years despite its dwindling clientele. The majority of the representatives were also members of the DBV, including several presidents of local DBV branches. The influence of the DBV extended to the advisory committees to the Ministry of Agriculture (*Ausschuss für Ernährung, Landwirtschaft und Forsten*). A total of 16 out of the 27 members of this 'independent' committee were members of the DBV. The close relationship between the DBV and the Ministry of Agriculture was striking, too. The chancellor could appoint a Minister of Agriculture only after consulting with the DBV, and it was impossible to get a candidate through without approval from the interest group. Konrad Adenauer learned this lesson when he wanted to appoint Schlange-Schöningen as the first Minister of Agriculture. The DBV did not agree with his choice, and Wilhelm Niklas, a member of the Bavarian Peasant League, was chosen instead. Adenauer maintained a close relationship with the DBV during the fourteen years of his tenure. He institutionalized this relationship in the so-called Rhöndorfer meetings between the chancellor, the Minister of Agriculture and the president of the DBV. Here, the DBV could make proposals and demands directly to the head of government.[56]

The DBV was successful with its rhetoric of the beleaguered peasantry in industrial society. Agrarian interest groups had always described the forces of industrialization and modernization as threatening to the peasants and linked it to demands for protection. The depopulation of the countryside and the insistence on the special character of the peasantry and their cultural value for the state were familiar facets of the old peasant ideology. The DBV continued in this tradition. In the context of the Cold War, the peasant ideology could be used as a tool against communism and socialist agriculture. More importantly, the ideology was effective in stirring up strong feelings. Demands for higher prices, subsidies and tax cuts became more powerful if coupled with an outcry over the crisis for agriculture. The ideology also united small peasants and large-scale farmers. Peasants could be mobilized quickly and the prospect of peasant radicalization could be used as a threat to give demands more urgency.[57]

The DBV stirred up dissatisfaction and protest, but it was also able to control and direct it. Peasants who lost their livelihoods in the 1950s did not drift to the far-right or anti-republican political spectrum, as many had done during the crisis of the 1920s. In the end, the DBV's radical tone contributed to the stabilization of German democratic society and the integration of the peasants into industrial society.[58] The DBV's far-reaching demands cushioned the transition for farmers, made them feel heard, and allowed for peasants to keep their small plots while also pursuing more lucrative jobs in the booming industrial sector. Price support, transitional aid, and other protections were introduced to allow farmers to continue farming even if it was only a part-time or weekend occupation. The number of farmers diminished dramatically, but those who left seemed to have been given a choice. Many of them 'happily' took on new jobs in the booming industry, where incomes were higher and working hours more limited.[59] Those who left farming were not treated as the 'stepchildren' of the industrial society. They participated in its economic growth and in the end fared better than ever before.

Conclusion

The economic and political changes in agriculture during the 1950s described in this chapter went along with a dramatic sociocultural transformation of rural—and urban—life. Living standards in Western Europe rose quickly. In West Germany, the first Minister of Economics under Konrad Adenauer, Ludwig Erhard, was able to keep his optimistic promise to bring 'prosperity for all' (*Wohlstand für alle*). To observers at the time, the quick and profound recovery seemed in fact 'miraculous', and the term 'economic miracle' (*Wirtschaftswunder*) has since been used to refer to fast economic growth. Distinctions between rural and urban lifestyles diminished in the 1950s. New recipes and dishes appeared on the tables, and German diets changed.[60] People ate more poultry, meat and butter, and they consumed more alcohol, all indicators of the new prosperity. Soon the postwar hunger years made way for a wave of gluttony.[61] Large grocery stores replaced the small local stores, and food was offered at affordable prices for everyone. Consumerism replaced food rationing and thriftiness. New food-processing technologies allowed for a change in eating habits, and people could now consume corn, peas and spinach any time of the year from a can or from their newly acquired freezers. The changes in eating habits expressed themselves most symbolically in the decline of the potato that had once been the staple and everyday food for German families.

The other most significant trend in agriculture was the establishment of the European Economic Community (EEC) in 1957 and a Common Agricultural Policy (CAP) in the early 1960s. The coal and steel industry was the first to demonstrate that collaboration between European nations was beneficial for all its participants, and the European Coal and Steel Community (ECSC) became a model for creating a common European agricultural and food policy. Integrating the agricultural sector on a European level, however, was much harder than in other sectors. Agrarian systems and structures varied greatly across Europe, and different climates, customs and regulations made agreement on a common agricultural policy difficult. Nevertheless, negotiations were successful and the Treaty of Rome was signed in March 1957.[62] The European regulations ensured high prices for agricultural products and provided incentives for farmers to produce more even when the market was saturated. With its focus on agricultural producers' interests and protectionist price regulations, the CAP was largely a continuation of German agricultural policies of the 1950s albeit on a European level. The goal to secure food supplies was quickly accomplished and soon overproduction, rather than scarcity and shortages, became the biggest issue for the European Community. The hunger years of the immediate postwar period had become a distant memory.[63]

Notes

1 The number of farms fell by 19 percent between 1949 and 1962, small farms (less than 5 hectares) declined by 30 percent. See Gesine Gerhard, 'Change in the European Countryside: Peasants and Democracy in Germany, 1935–1955,' in Paul Brassley, Yves Segers and Leen Van Molle (eds), *War, Agriculture, and Food: Rural Europe from the 1930s to the 1950s*, New York: Routledge, 2012, pp. 195–211, 201. See also Friedrich-Wilhelm Henning, *Landwirtschaft und ländliche Gesellschaft in Deutschland*, 2 vols, Paderborn: Ferdinand Schöningh, 1978.
2 Daniela Münkel (ed.), *Der lange Abschied vom Agrarland: Agrarpolitik, Landwirtschaft und ländliche Gesellschaft zwischen Weimar und Bonn*, Göttingen: Wallstein Verlag, 2000.
3 Kiran Klaus Patel, 'The Paradox of Planning: German Agricultural Policy in a European Perspective, 1920s to 1970s,' *Past and Present*, vol. 212, 2012, pp. 239–269. On continuities in agricultural politics, see Ernst Langthaler and Josef Redl (eds), *Reguliertes Land: Agrarpolitik in Deutschland, Österreich und der Schweiz 1930–1960*, Innsbruck: Studienverlag, 2005.
4 See John E. Farquharson, *The Western Allies and the Politics of Food: Agrarian Management in Postwar Germany*, Leamington Spa, UK: Berg Publishers, 1985.
5 Gustavo Corni and Horst Gies, *Brot—Butter—Kanonen. Die Ernährungswirtschaft in Deutschland unter der Diktatur Hitlers*, Berlin: Akademie Verlag, 1997.
6 See Gesine Gerhard, *Nazi Hunger Politics: A History of Food in the Third Reich*, New York/London: Rowman & Littlefield, 2015.

7 See Adam Tooze, *The Wages of Destruction: The Making and Breaking of the Nazi Economy*, New York: Penguin Press, 2006 and Lizzie Collingham, *The Taste of War: World War II and the Battle for Food*, New York: Penguin Press, 2012.
8 Gerhard, *Nazi Hunger Politics*, Chapter 1.
9 Uwe Mai, 'Rasse und Raum.' *Agrarpolitik, Sozial- und Raumplanung im NS-Staat*, Paderborn: Schöningh 2002.
10 Farquharson, *The Western Allies*; Alan Milward, *The Reconstruction of Western Europe 1945–1951*, Berkeley, CA: University of California Press, 1984.
11 Patel, 'The Paradox of Planning', p. 246.
12 See Arnd Bauerkämper (ed.), *Junkerland in Bauernhand? Durchführung, Auswirkungen und Stellenwert der Bodenreform in der Sowjetischen Besatzungszone*, Stuttgart: Franz Steiner Verlag, 1996, and Elke Scherstjanoi, *SED-Agrarpolitik unter sowjetischer Kontrolle 1949–1953*, München, Oldenbourg Verlag, 2007.
13 On food distribution in the occupied zones, see Rainer Gries, *Die Rationen-Gesellschaft. Versorgungskampf und Vergleichsmentalität: Leipzig, München und Köln nach dem Kriege*, Münster: Verlag Westfälisches Dampfboot, 1991; Trittel, *Hunger und Politik: Die Ernährungskrise in der Bizone (1945–1949)*, Frankfurt: Campus Verlag, 1990.
14 Corni and Gies, *Brot—Butter—Kanonen*, pp. 581–2. These numbers are official estimates; they do not account for food people were able to acquire through other channels such as the black market.
15 On the economic situation in postwar Germany, see Alan Kramer, *The West German Economy, 1945–1955*, New York, Oxford: Berg Publisher, 1991; see also Günter Trittel, *Hunger und Politik*; Paul Erker, *Ernährungskrise und Nachkriegsgesellschaft: Bauern und Arbeiterschaft in Bayern 1943–1953*, Stuttgart: Klett Verlag, 1990; and Farquharson, *The Western Allies*.
16 Rainer Gries, *Die Rationengesellschaft*. pp. 26–27.
17 See Gries, *Die Rationengesellschaft*; Trittel, *Hunger und Politik*; and Michael Wildt, *Der Traum vom Sattwerden. Hunger und Protest, Schwarzmarkt und Selbsthilfe in Hamburg 1945–1948*, Hamburg: VSA-Verlag, 1988.
18 Historians estimate that the chaotic take from Germany by the Soviets accumulated to billions of dollars and led to the loss of about one third of East Germany's industry. See N.M. Nairmark, *The Russians in Germany: A History of the Soviet Zone of Occupation, 1945–1949*, Cambridge, MA and London: Belknap Press of Harvard University Press, 1995, pp. 168–9.
19 Hermann Graml, *Die Alliierten und die Teilung Deutschlands: Konflikte und Entscheidungen 1941–1948*, Frankfurt: Fischer Taschenbuch Verlag, 1985.
20 The Morgenthau Plan, first proposed by US Secretary of the Treasury Henry Morgenthau in 1944, proposed a defeated and occupied Germany that would be stripped of its armaments industry and other heavy industries. Thus, Germany would become a pastoral and agricultural country that would never again be in a position to start another war. See Michael Beschloss, *The Conquerors. Roosevelt, Truman and the Destruction of Hitler's Germany, 1941–1945*, New York: Simon & Schuster, 2002; Nairmark, *The Russians in Germany*.
21 Nairmark, *The Russians in Germany*.
22 See Elke Scherstjanoi, *SED-Agrarpolitik unter sowjetischer Kontrolle 1949–1953*, München, Oldenbourg Verlag, 2007; Gregory W. Sandford, *From Hitler to Ulbricht: The Communist Reconstruction of East Germany 1945–46*, Princeton, NJ: Princeton University Press, 1983; Martin McCauley, *The German Democratic Republic since 1945*, London: Macmillan Press, 1983; and J.P. Nettl, *The Eastern Zone and Soviet Policy in Germany, 1945–50*, London: Oxford University Press, 1951.
23 Nettl, *The Eastern Zone*, 176–177.
24 See also Antonia Maria Humm, *Auf dem Weg zum sozialistischen Dorf? Zum Wandel der dörflichen Lebenswelt in der DDR und der Bundesrepublik Deutschland 1952–1969*, Göttingen: Vandenhoeck & Ruprecht, 1999.

25 See Gesine Gerhard, 'Peasants into Farmers: Agriculture and Democracy in West Germany' (dissertation thesis, University of Iowa, 2000), pp. 78–79.
26 Humm, *Auf dem Weg*, 99.
27 Jean Edward Smith (ed.), *The Papers of General Lucius D. Clay*, vol. 1, Bloomington, IN: Indiana University Press, 1974; see also Gerhard, *Peasants into Farmers*, 70.
28 See Michael Hogan, *The Marshall Plan: America, Britain, and the Reconstruction of Western Europe, 1947–1952*, Cambridge: Cambridge University Press, 1987; Milward, *The Reconstruction of Western Europe*.
29 Hans Schlange-Schöningen was a conservative German politician and the most prominent German food administrator during the occupation period. Well known by his contemporaries—some called him a 'hunger dictator' while Schlange-Schöningen considered himself the foremost fighter in the 'battle against hunger' after the war—there is relatively little literature about him. See Günter Trittel, 'Ein vergessener Politiker der "ersten Stunde"', in *Vierteljahreshefte für Zeitgeschichte*, 35, no. 1, 1987, pp. 25–64.
30 Gerhard, *Peasants into Farmers*, 98–99.
31 Here quoted from Trittel, *Hunger und Politik*, p. 116; see also Gerhard, *Peasants into Farmers*, p. 85.
32 Here quoted from Trittel, *Hunger and Politik*, p. 166; see also Gerhard, *Peasants into Farmers*, p. 109.
33 Quoted from Benz, *Von der Besatzungsherrschaft*; see also Gerhard, *Peasants into Farmers*, p. 102.
34 Ludwig Erhard became the first Minister of Economics under Konrad Adenauer in 1949 and was Chancellor of the Federal Republic of Germany from 1963 to 1966.
35 Erker, *Ernährungskrise*, p. 246.
36 See Andrei Cherny, *The Candy Bombers: The Untold Story of the Berlin Airlift and America's Finest Hour*, New York: Penguin Books, 2008, and Helena P. Schrader, *The Blockade Breakers. The Berlin Airlift*, Stroud: The History Press, 2008.
37 Charles S. Maier and Günter Bischof (eds), *The Marshall Plan and Germany: West German Development within the Framework of the European Recovery Program*, New York and Oxford: Berg, 1992. To what extent the Marshall aid contributed to Germany and Europe's economic recovery remains contested in historiography.
38 Andreas Eichmüller, *Landwirtschaft und bäuerliche Bevölkerung in Bayern. Ökonomischer und sozialer Wandel 1945–1970. Eine vergleichende Untersuchung der Landkreise Erding, Kötzing und Obernburg*, München: Hanns Seidel Stiftung, 1997, p. 77 and Karl-Heinrich Hansmeyer, *Finanzielle Staatshilfen für die Landwirtschaft. Zur Theorie einer sektoralen Finanzpolitik*, Tübingen: Hanns Seidel Stiftung, 1963, p. 215.
39 Gerhard, *Peasants into Farmers*, pp. 129–130.
40 Ulrich Kluge, *Vierzig Jahre Agrarpolitik in der Bundesrepublik Deutschland*, vol. 1, Hamburg and Berlin: Verlag Paul Parey, 1989, pp. 116ff.
41 Gerhard, 'Change in the European Countryside', p. 201.
42 Arnd Bauernkämper, 'Agrarwirtschaft und ländliche Gesellschaft in der Bundesrepublik Deutschland und der DDR. Eine Bilanz der Jahre 1945–1965', in *Aus Politik und Zeitgeschichte. Beilage zur Wochenzeitung „Das Parlament,"* B 38/97, 12 September 1997', pp. 25–37; Gerhard, *Peasants into Farmers*, p. 135.
43 Gerhard, *Peasants into Farmers*, p. 136.
44 Friedrich-Wilhelm Henning, *Landwirtschaft und ländliche Gesellschaft in Deutschland*, vol. 2, Paderborn: Schöningh, 1988, p. 267.
45 Gerhard, *Peasants into Farmers*, p. 147.
46 Gerhard, *Peasants into Farmers*, p. 151.
47 Eichmüller, *Landwirtschaft*, p. 77.
48 On the German Peasant League, see Paul Ackermann, *Der deutsche Bauernverband im politischen Kräftespiel der Bundesrepublik: Die Einflussnahme des DBV auf die Entscheidung über den europäischen Getreidepreis*, Tübingen, 1970; Rolf Heinze, *Verbandspolitik*

zwischen Partikularinteressen und Gemeinwohl: der Deutsche Bauernverband, Gütersloh, Bertelsmann-Stiftung, 1992; Kiran Klaus Patel, 'Der Deutsche Bauernverband, 1945 bis 1990: vom Gestus des Undedingten zur Rettung durch Europa' in *Vierteljahreshefte für Zeitgeschichte*, vol. 2, 2010, pp. 161–179.

49 See Patel, *Der Deutsche Bauernverband*.
50 Ackermann, *Der DBV*, p. 29.
51 Ackermann, *Der DBV*, pp. 34–35.
52 Pavel Uttitz, 'Partizipation und Wahlabsicht der Landwirte in der Bundesrepublik Deutschland – neigen die Landwirte zur Wahlenthaltung?', in *Zeitschrift für Parlamentsfragen*, vol. 18, 1987, pp. 243 ff., p. 245.
53 Hans-Joachim Krekeler, Das 'Wahlverhalten der landwirtschaftlichen Bevölkerung in der Bundesrepublik: Analyse und Diskussion von Ergebnissen der empirischen Wahlforschung–Ein Beitrag zur ländlichen Soziologie', (dissertation thesis, Bonn, 1976).
54 With the exception of Bremen and Berlin, two city states with a mostly urban electorate.
55 Sönke Boysen, 'Struktur und Einflußmöglichkeiten der landwirtschaftlichen Abgeordneten in den Parlamenten der Bundesrepublik Deutschland von 1949 bis 1969', (dissertation thesis, Kiel, 1971).
56 Gerhard, *Peasants into Farmers*, p. 177.
57 Gerhard, *Peasants into Farmers*, p. 181.
58 See Patel, *Der Deutsche Bauernverband*, and Gesine Gerhard, 'Politische Bauernbewegungen zwischen Systemkonformität und –opposition: Der Deutsche Bauernverband (DBV) und die politische Eingliederung der Bauern in die Bundesrepublik Deutschland', in *Österreichische Zeitschrift für Geschichtswissenschaft*, vol. 13, no. 2, 2002, pp. 129–138.
59 Patel, 'The Paradox of Farming', p. 260.
60 Ursula Heinzelmann, *Food Culture in Germany*, Westport, CT: Greenwood Press, 2008, p. 29.
61 Wolfgang Protzner (ed.), *Vom Hungerwinter zum kulinarischen Schlaraffenland: Aspekte einer Kulturgeschichte des Essens in der Bundesrepublik Deutschland*, Wiesbaden: Franz Steiner Verlag, 1987.
62 See Alan Milward, *The European Rescue of the Nation-State*, London: Routledge, 1992; Kiran Klaus Patel, *Europäisierung wider Willen. Die Bundesrepublik Deutschland in der Agrarintegration der EWG, 1955–1973*, Munich: Oldenbourg Wissenschaftsverlag, 2009; and Ann-Christina L. Knudsen, *Farmers on Welfare: The Making of Europe's Common Agricultural Policy*, Ithaca: Cornell University Press, 2009.
63 Kiran Klaus Patel (ed.), *Fertile Ground for Europe? The History of European Integration and the Common Agricultural Policy since 1945*, Baden-Baden: Nomos, 2009.

13 Farm labour in the urban–industrial Swedish welfare state

Carin Martiin

One of the characteristics of the post-war history of Western European countries is to find fewer people in farming, and increased numbers and shares of labour in other sectors. This was also the case in Sweden, which exemplifies the general Western European process in this book, albeit with some deviations. Increasing governmental intervention is one of the similarities, whereas a striking difference is that Sweden escaped the Second World War and was immediately able to carry on with its social and economic development. The plans for postwar Sweden were greatly influenced by Social Democratic visions of a welfare state based on intensified industrialization and urbanization with agriculture in a more subordinated position. There had been similar visions in the late 1930s which were not completely forgotten during the war, when, although factories and suburbs continued to expand, the popularity of farming experienced a short revival, in contrast to both the critical debate of the late 1930s and the agricultural programme of 1947, in which the phasing out of smallholder farming was one of the major points.[1]

A decline in farm labour, including farmers and farm family labour, had begun decades earlier, from roughly one third of the total workforce in 1930, to slightly less by 1940, one fifth in 1950, and only one tenth in 1965.[2] Especially in the eyes of the Social Democrats, farm labour issues were a structural problem that was characterized by too many people in too many and too small farm holdings, which meant low living standards for farmers and risks of rural proletarization, quite contrary to the political aims for equalized socio-economic progress and improved material welfare.

In the late 1940s, the idea of reducing the number of people who tried to make a living in farming was carried out more or less without knowing much about alternative jobs for those who left.[3] Soon, however, the decline in farm labour came to coincide with a rapidly increasing demand for labour in other sectors, due to an unforeseeably rapid expansion of the Swedish economy. By this time – the first half of the 1950s – Swedish economic experts were deeply concerned about what was by then an overheated economy with high demand, labour shortages, limited capital for investments, and high inflation. Lack of labour was thus considered a big issue and the reallocation of farm labour to urban sectors was expected to be of importance, although the more detailed forecasts for the 1950s and early 1960s did not present this as the big solution. Generalized statements about the importance of reallocating farm labour to other sectors were formulated now and then but were not claimed in forecasts by contemporary economists.[4] Repeatedly, the forecasts for the early and mid-1950s stated, in retrospect, that large-scale decline in farm labour certainly had taken place, but that this would probably not go on at the same rate.[5] Repeatedly, the forecast proved to be wrong; the amount of farm labour decreased drastically in the early 1950s, at a comparably more modest pace during the second half of the 1950s, but then again more rapidly in the 1960s. Not until the early 1960s would the forecasts actually suggest that the down-turn in farm labour might continue even more rapidly.[6]

The Swedish rural narrative about the 1950s and 1960s sometimes tells of people who were pushed out from farming through a politically driven pressure on farm product prices at the same time as the expanding industrial sector called for labour, offering better pay and a more comfortable life. Another version tells about a massive resistance to give up farming. Neither of these versions is untrue but they suggest a more consciously organized and imperative process than was, in fact, pronounced in the 1947 agricultural programme (discussed later) and the overarching Swedish long-term plans. The reasons that made people leave farming were often a complex mix of push and pull factors with different impacts on individual decisions and over time, but the determining factor was generally the situation at the labour market.[7]

Smallholdings and family labour

Swedish farming of the mid-twentieth century was characterized by smallholdings, family labour, mixed farming with grains, forage and dairy production. Many farms had also forest land and forestry could be an important complement to cultivation and animal husbandry, especially in well-forested areas. Agricultural production was comparably labour intensive, due to small farm sizes and animal husbandry. Dairy production was generally highlighted as the backbone of Swedish farming and had experienced a peak in the 1930s and 1940s, just before entering a dramatic journey downwards, sometimes talked about as 'the last dairy herd', which came to symbolize a decline in farm holdings, dairy cattle and the farm population. From a high and stable level of 307,000 registered units in the 1920s and 1930s, the number of farm holdings had begun to decline in the mid-1940s. In 1961, about 79 per cent remained, and five years later 63 per cent.[8] The changes are shown in more detail in Table 13.1.

Table 13.1 demonstrates the dominance of smallholdings and that the decline was almost solely a matter of farms with less than 10 hectares. The table reveals a dramatic reduction in the number of the smallest holdings in the late 1940s that later, in the 1950s and 1960s, was accompanied by a decline in the number of somewhat bigger farms, up to the 'model farm' size of 20–30 hectares. Of the 109, 000 holdings that disappeared from the records between

Table 13.1 Number of farms in different farm size categories

No. of farm units	2.1–5.0	5.1–10.0	10.1–20.0	20.1–30.0	30.1–50.0	50.1–100.0	100.1–	Total
1944	107,776	94,144	58,477	17,030	10,710	5,065	2,325	295,527
1951	95,945	89,755	59,790	17,719	11,234	5,419	2,325	282,187
1956	87,554	83,246	59,561	18,479	11,667	5,373	2,221	268,101
1961	66,635	75,017	53,446	18,266	11,960	5,410	2,186	232,920
1966	47,301	55,025	43,754	18,433	13,231	6,280	2,243	186,267

Source: *Statistical Yearbook of Agriculture*, 1970, Table 2, pp. 46–47.

1944 and 1966, more than half had at most 5 hectares of arable land and as many as 91 per cent had at most 10 hectares of arable. Meanwhile, almost nothing changed in the number of bigger farms. The figures do not reflect all kinds of leasehold or other arrangements, but the trend is crystal clear.[9] It should also be noted that the rate of decline increased over time, from around 27,000 farms between the mid-1940s and mid-1950s to around 82,000 between the mid-1950s and mid-1960s. As shown later, these changes followed a somewhat different pattern compared with the decline of farm labour that was less dramatic in numbers during the second half of the 1950s. Moreover, the number of dairy herds was also reduced, from being found at 90 per cent of all farms in 1947 and 80 per cent in 1961 to only 70 per cent in 1966. At the same time the total number of dairy cows was halved whereas the dairies received almost unchanged quantities of milk.

It is important to distinguish between the rural population, its share of the farm population, and the number of people working in farming. It should also be remembered that the figures are approximate and that statistical figures are not always from the same year.[10] Of the total Swedish population, about 50 per cent, or 3.25 million of the total of 6.5 million Swedes, lived in rural areas in the mid-1940s, 44 per cent or 3 million of the then total of 7 million people in 1950, 40 per cent or 3 million of a total of 7.5 million people in 1960, and 38 per cent, or 2.9 of the 7.7 million people in 1965. In the words of the agricultural economist Folke Dovring, the Swedish countryside was obviously experiencing an 'absolute exodus' from the midst of the 1940s, no longer just a relative but also an absolute decline in comparison with the urban population.[11] The farm population represented substantial parts of the rural population and was roughly estimated as 1.9 million people of all ages in 1940, 1.7 million in 1950 and 1.1 million in 1960, excluding forestry and fishery. Alternatively formulated, the farm population declined from 29 to 15 per cent of the total Swedish population from 1940 to 1960. It is interesting to note that almost two-thirds of the rural population made a living from farming by 1950 but only one third one decade later.[12] The number of people working in farming and how this changed in the 1950s and early 1960s is shown in Table 13.2.

Table 13.2 Total labour in Swedish farming, 1951–1966

Year	Farmer and family labour		Employees, permanent		Employees, casual		Total		Total
	Men	Women	Men	Women	Men	Women	Men	Women	
1951	369,520	304,390	66,470	23,260	69,430	36,370	50,420	364,020	869,440
1956	293,200	222,420	44,860	9,390	28,060	14,690	366,120	246,500	612,620
1961	262,900	192,810	31,990	8,380	23,120	13,480	318,010	214,670	532,680
1966	179,090	123,620	22,370	4,430	10,410	5,250	211,870	133,300	345,170

Source: Based on a farm sample survey, *Statistical Yearbook of Agriculture 1970*, Table 16, p. 65.

According to Table 13.2, the total number of people working in farming went down about 40 per cent in the 1950s and 60 per cent between 1951 and 1966. This and other observations from this table will be further examined in the section of this chapter that deals specifically with changes in farm labour.

Many farm families identified themselves strongly with their farm, which had often been inherited over many generations, and made far-reaching efforts to continue farming by supplementing their incomes or accepting a lower standard of living. Among these farm households the increased prioritization of urban–industrial development and the relative downgrading of farming contrasted sharply with the war crisis years, when agriculture had been widely appreciated among politicians and ordinary people. At that time, there were relatively high prices for farm products, and publicly financed campaigns to encourage farmers to do their best and to persuade other people to help the farmers. This produced a positive atmosphere, from an agricultural perspective, during the crisis years of the war, and increased farmers' confidence in the future for a short while. However, it was soon turned into an even greater disappointment about the harsher political approach that followed after the war.

Other farmers, farm family members and employees welcomed increased opportunities to leave farming for more regulated work and leisure, and for the lights of the city. Even though many people left, the countryside was still comparatively well populated by the mid-century. Active farming from the south to the very north was taken for granted during the period studied here and was also an explicit political goal that combined Sweden's regional and defence policies. In brief, the major changes dealt with a modest scaling up of farm sizes, to about 20–30 hectares, changes in methods of production, and with the reduction of farm labour.[13]

The reduced official interest in Swedish agriculture stands in notable contrast to the contemporary international efforts to enlarge the output of food.[14] The simple reason behind the lukewarm Swedish political interest was that the production of food was already in line with domestic demand, as it was in Denmark (see Chapter 7). Moreover, the difficulties of the 1930s on the world market were still fresh in the authorities' minds and, unlike the Danes, the Swedish authorities were far from tempted by surplus production for the international food market. The economist Gunnar Myrdal had already in 1938 drawn attention to the risks of the approaching Swedish overproduction. Myrdal saw it as a major threat to Swedish farmers who, he argued, risked a vicious circle of declining prices for their produce and accompanying backwardness in the countryside.[15] Myrdal's warning from 1938 was again brought up in the agricultural programme of 1947 (discussed below). In between, during the war crisis years, the Swedish population had enjoyed an average calorie intake around 3,000 calories per head per day, of which more than 40 per cent came from animal foods, a similar level as in the late 1930s, although of slightly different kinds of food.[16] Some years later the figures for 1951/53 reported 120 per cent self-sufficiency in bread grains, 116 per cent in butter, 108 per cent in eggs, 102 per cent in pork and 100 per cent in feed grains, potatoes and poultry meat, whereas figures slightly below self-sufficiency were reported for veal, 96 per cent, cattle meat 92 per cent, margarine 84 per cent, and sugar and syrup 83 per cent. Feed concentrates were said to cover about 50 per cent of the country's needs. Remembering the surplus production of butter, it can, be argued, however, that the 'needs' could have been modified.[17]

The fact that Sweden was not very hungry and not interested in food production for export was central to the 1947 agricultural programme that paid most attention to price regulation and structural problems in farming. Yet, the agricultural sector was not left to its fate. Rather the contrary, the postwar agricultural programme has been described as making agriculture a planned sector in the Swedish economy. The programme had its roots in the early and late 1930s, was produced between 1942 and 1946, and was passed by the Swedish *Riksdag* in 1947.[18] Some modifications followed later on but the major principles were actually maintained until just a few years before Sweden's membership of the European Union in 1995. A key message in the 1947 programme was that Swedish farming had too many people, and too many and too small farm units to make possible the narrowing of the current gap in material welfare between town and country, in line with social democratic ideals on socioeconomic equity, and to some extent also to prevent rural proletarization. The formal aims of the programme were summarized as improving farmers' incomes, making farm production more efficient, and maintaining the farm output in line with domestic needs, which can alternatively be formulated as aiming at fewer farms with more modern and labour-saving methods of production, or, more frankly, phasing out of smallholder farming. In practice, it was envisaged that the reduction in smallholdings and people in farming would be managed successively during the following decades and through a combination of economic pressure, obstacles to sell smallholdings as separate units, and active favouring of family farms with about 20–30 hectares arable land, identified as the model farm. Remembering the huge number of smallholdings but modest number of 20–30 hectare farms in Table 13.1, the 1947 programme was a challenge that required far-reaching structural changes and that certainly meant that more chilly winds would blow across the Swedish countryside. All changes were intended to be voluntary, but the means combined the stick and the carrot, such as pressure on farm product prices on one hand and favourable tax rules for machinery investments and offers on state-guaranteed loans on the other.

The investigation behind the 1947 programme was accompanied by some separate sub-investigations, one of which was a special study on the possibility of creating more non-farm jobs in the Swedish countryside. The study discusses the importance of making it more attractive for young women to stay and to prevent depopulation of the vast Swedish countryside for military and civil emergency purposes. Among the suggested improvements were: better public communications, more non-farm jobs for women, and arrangements so that seasonal peaks in farming could periodically be combined with non-farm work. The mere existence of this report implies that the late 1940s ideas of reducing the farm population were not primarily a response to urban–industrial demands for labour but rather to the problem of surplus labour in farming. Similarly, the investigation behind the 1947 programme said that an over-rapid reduction in farm labour could pose risks for unemployment in other sectors.[19]

The relations between the farmers' organizations and the government had been comparatively good in the 1930s, and both good and favourable during the war years, but became more problematic in the late 1940s when the 1947 agricultural programme was set in train.[20] Still, the two farmers' organizations, the SL (*Sveriges lantbruksförbund*) and the RLF (*Riksförbundet landsbygdens folk*), appear to have been eager to stay at the negotiation table and to care for their relations with other organizations and the government. The former organization, SL, was founded in 1917, with roots among estate owners, but by the mid-century was primarily serving as an umbrella organization for the then well-established national producer cooperatives in branches such as milk, meat and grains. The RLF, which was established in 1929, was closely related to the farmers' party (*Bondeförbundet*) and more of a union that aimed at representing farmers and smallholders, and the countryside in general. The internal relations between the SL and the RLF were not always without friction, especially during the early days of RLF.[21] The impression is that farmers' frustration was more ventilated around farm kitchen tables and at local farmers' meetings of the RLF than in Stockholm. Still, the contacts in Stockholm were quite important, for agriculture and the entire Swedish society of the mid-twentieth century, when the interplay between big organizations like the labour unions were very influential on the shaping of post-war Sweden.

Planning for the further development of the Swedish society and its labour force

Having escaped the Second World War without either physical or mental damage, Sweden enjoyed an extremely favourable starting point by the mid-1940s. The surrounding war had brought about enlistment for military service and had also created a far-reaching rationing system that, it is suggested, was more motivated by the desire to make the population feel safe and protected by the authorities than by any shortage of food. Generally speaking, ordinary life and the Swedish economy had been functioning well, and the ruling Social Democrats were eager to get ahead with the urban–industrial welfare project.

This post-war period was indeed a time of social democratic hegemony, an era when the idea of the Swedish so-called 'folk's home', coined by the legendary Social Democratic leader Per-Albin Hansson in the late 1920s, was successively replaced by aims for a welfare state with enlarged public expenditures and higher ambitions for improved material standards of living. The Social Democratic Party held the premiership from 1932 to 1976, albeit shortly interrupted during the summer of 1936, and periodically in coalition, first during the war when the Social Democrats ruled in coalition with the farmers' party (*Bondeförbundet*), the conservatives (*Högerpartiet*) and the liberals (*Folkpartiet*) and second, in coalition with the farmers' party between 1951 and 1957.[22] The farmers' party worked for farming and the countryside, and argued against the downgrading of farming and the countryside, and was thus considered a natural alternative for the rural population in general, including smallholders and most farmers, although some farmers with the biggest farms preferred the conservatives. The farmers' party was part of the government in the 1950s when many of their voters were angry and worried about the agricultural policies. The party appears, however, to have been clearly subordinated to the Social Democratic leadership who were not entirely happy about the alliance with 'the farmers', although we do not know what things would have looked like without the coalition.[23]

Not having to worry about how to feed the nation, political ambitions were concentrated on full employment, education, pensions, health insurance and other social security issues, house building, improved socioeconomic equality and material standards of living. To realize these aims high priority was given to the expansion of export industries and export markets, including efforts to direct labour and other limited resources to these sectors.[24] Among useful contacts were the OEEC (the Organization for European Economic Cooperation) in Paris that administered the Marshall programme in which Sweden took part, despite not having been at war. According to the memoirs of prime minister Tage Erlander, Sweden did not need the money; it appreciated the dollars as such, but even more that other countries were supplied with dollars to pay for Swedish deliveries.[25] Like other members of the OEEC, Sweden was in 1948 urged to produce a plan for economic development. In the Swedish case, this plan came to be the embryo for a long subsequent series of greatly influential long-term plans, especially about the economic development of Swedish society and generally aiming at five-year periods. In brief, the Swedish report to the OEEC in 1948 paid much attention to the prevailing imbalance in foreign trade and expressed concern about the overheated Swedish economy, in which a shortage of labour was considered a key issue.

Farm labour in the urban–industrial Swedish state 253

The link to the Marshall programme was still present in the following plan for 1950–1955 that combined a report to the OEEC and a comprehensive internal plan for Sweden. The authors were happy to announce that Sweden's foreign trade was already in balance, so that the focus could now be turned on to the so-called inner balance, such as domestic investments and how to prioritize between investments in the export industry, infrastructure and urban expansion. Similar questions were highlighted in the long-term plans of 1956 and 1961 that paid much attention to priorities between various needs and desires, and to public versus private consumption.[26]

Considerable attention was paid to labour issues in the long-term plans, primarily in terms of labour shortages due to low birth rates in the 1930s, which resulted in fewer young people in the labour market in the 1950s, just at the time of the postwar expansion of the Swedish economy.[27] According to Table 13.3, the total number of working people increased steadily over time, but included a temporary dip in the number of young people in the 1950s. The first row shows the number of men and women between 16 and 24 years of age, considered as young people of working age, and the second row presents the total number of men and women of working age up to retirement. The third row shows how many of these people were part of the labour market, while the difference between the second and third row indicates housewives and other people outside the labour market.

Lack of labour was considered a bottleneck that put obstacles in the way of the development of the Swedish economy, but the consequences of the low fertility rates in the 1930s could not be changed overnight. In the long-term plans, the discussions and suggested solutions varied over time, from a somewhat passive approach in the late 1940s to more intensive efforts to increase the number of people at work in the early 1950s, after which more attention was paid to less quantitative means, such as various ways to increase industrial production through labour-saving investments and other means to improve labour productivity.[28]

The 1948 Swedish report to the OEEC predicted a slower decline in farm labour in the years to come, compared with the 1930s and earlier 1940s.[29]

Table 13.3 Number of people in working age and at work in Sweden, 1945–1965 (estimates for 1965)

	1945	*1950*	*1955*	*1960*	*1965*
16–24 years of age, men and women	880,000	794,000	790,000	928,000	1,107,000
All people in working age	4,485,000	4,593,000	4,664,000	4,817,000	5,027,000
Approximate no. of working people	–	3,335,000	3,419,000	3,540,000	3,715,000

Source: SOU:1962, 10, p. 92.

Similarly, the 1951 report made a cautious assessment forecast of some decline in farm labour, although even lower than before because of fewer remaining employees to reallocate from agriculture to other jobs.[30] Instead of calling for the reallocation of farm labour, the 1951 report saw married women as the most important labour source potential, and suggested increased numbers of part-time jobs to make this possible.[31] The forecasts for the second half of the 1950s appear to have been less concerned. Little attention was paid to the potential reallocation of farm labour, although 'transfer benefits' from the reallocation of labour were discussed, exemplified by comparing farming in less fertile regions with employment in a 'highly profitable export industry'.[32] The percentage decline of farm labour was expected to be maintained, which meant fewer numbers over time, but at the same time the frequency with which women entered the labour market had increased, and bigger cohorts of young people born in the 1940s would soon also enter it.[33] Moreover, a former focus on number of people at work was increasingly accompanied by attention to efforts to raise the efficiency per worker, such as labour-saving investments and improved management.

The long-term plan for the early 1960s included two changes. For the first time it predicted that the decline in farm labour would increase, rather than continuing at a similar or lower pace, as assumed in the earlier reports.[34] Second, migrant labour from abroad was taken into account. Before then, representatives for the industrial sector had advised the authors not to include migrant labour in their calculations of the total Swedish labour force, despite the fact that the total net migration to Sweden amounted to almost 110,000 people between 1950 and 1960, and nearly 200,000 up to 1965, primarily from Finland but in the 1960s also from Italy, Yugoslavia and Greece.[35] The figures do not record working age, but a large proportion were young men who were rapidly employed in car factories and other sectors of the export industries. Notwithstanding the modest explicit calls for the reallocation of farm labour in the forecasts, the real changes were huge, in absolute numbers and in comparisons between farming and other sectors, shown in Table 13.4.

The number of people in farming made up about one third of the working population in 1930, slightly lower in 1940, one fifth in 1950, and only about

Table 13.4 Proportions (%) of the labour force in agriculture and other sectors

Sectors	1930	1940	1950	1960	1965
Farming, forestry and fishery	32	28	20	14	10
Industrial and construction sectors	34	36	41	42	44
Other sectors	34	36	39	44	46
Total	100	100	100	100	100

Sources: 1930 and 1940: SOU 1956:53, p. 107; 1950–1965: SOU 1966:1, p. 76.

one tenth in 1965, although the absolute decline was somewhat lower due the contemporary increase of the total Swedish labour force (Table 13.3). At the same time, the industrial and construction sectors increased throughout the period and the category 'Other sectors', essentially the service sector – meaning work in shops, offices, schools, hospitals and with transport – increased slightly more, which mirrors various parts of the emerging Swedish welfare state. Only two sectors decreased substantially – agriculture and domestic service – both in line with the social democratic aims and ambitions. The following section analyses the changes in farm labour in more detail with regard to farmers and employees, male and female labour, and the way in which the changes were distributed between farm holdings of different sizes.

Changes in farm labour

Substantial numbers of people, primarily young family members and employees, had already left farming and the countryside in the 1920s and 1930s, whereas the number of farms and farm households had been stable. The census of population registered 876,000 people working in farming in 1930, 832,000 in 1940 and 632,000 in 1950, while the number of farms remained at around 300,000.[36] The number of households was thus little changed, although there were fewer plates on the kitchen tables. This early migration to town was lamented and discussed in terms of 'the flight from the countryside' and, as already mentioned, not even the economic experts writing the long-term reports could imagine that the number of people in farming would go down much more. This would, however, prove to be wrong.

The fact that many employees had already left and that many farms were small (Tables 13.1 and 13.2) meant that the share of employed farm labour was low at the beginning of the 1950s. As Table 13.5 (which repeats the information in Table 13.2 in percentage terms) reveals, family labour provided for 77 per cent of the labour in 1951, 85 per cent in 1961 and as much as 88 per cent in 1966.

Table 13.5 Types of labour (%) in Swedish farming, 1951–1966

Year	Farmer and family labour			Employees, permanent			Employees, casual			All male and female farm labour		Total
	Men	Women	Total	Men	Women	Tot	Men	Women	Total	Men	Women	
1951	42	35	77	8	3	11	8	4	12	58	42	100
1956	48	36	84	7	2	9	5	2	7	60	40	100
1961	49	36	85	6	2	8	4	3	7	59	41	100
1966	52	36	88	6	1	7	3	2	5	61	39	100

Source: Based on the farm sample survey in *Statistical Yearbook of Agriculture 1970*, Table 16, p. 65.

Swedish farming was obviously not equipped with masses of hired labour to be reallocated to other sectors. What was left was primarily the farm family, with or without children of working age, and eventually elderly relatives and others. We do not know exactly how much each person worked over the year, but the average employee (permanent or casual) worked for more than 1,600 hours per year, according to an investigation of hired labour.[37] From 1951 to 1961 the number of permanently employed men was halved while only a third of the women remained, and in 1966 the numbers had diminished to one third and one fifth, respectively. The scaling down was even more dramatic with regard to casually hired labour, which was about equal for males and females. The changes over time are shown in Table 13.6.

The lower decline in total change during the second half of the 1950s is interesting in itself and is also important to remember when studying the following tables that have had to be based on the time between 1956 and 1966, due to lack of figures from the early 1950s.

Due to the small-scale character of Swedish farming, it can be assumed that the decline in hired labour took place primarily at bigger farms whereas smaller farms generally speaking were operated without hired labour. Tables 13.7 and 13.8 show the average numbers of males and females on farms of different size, including the male and female farmer, and how the average numbers per farm was changed. The two tables demonstrate the fact that most Swedish farms were operated by only the male and female farmer who, generally speaking, can be assumed to have done all the practical work at farms with figures 1.0 or less in

Table 13.6 Percentage changes in various types of farm labour, 1951–1966, 1000 people

	Farmer and family labour		Employees, permanent		Employees, casual		Total change	
	Men	Women	Men	Women	Men	Women	Men	Women
1951–56	–76	–82	–22	–14	–41	–22	–139	–118
1956–61	–30	–30	–13	–1	–5	–1	–48	–32
1961–66	–84	–69	–10	–4	–13	–8	–106	–81

Source: Based on a farm sample survey, *Statistical Yearbook of Agriculture*, 1970, Table 16, p. 65.

Table 13.7 Average male labour on Swedish farms of different sizes, 1956–1966

	2.1–5.0	5.1–10.0	10.1–20.0	20.1–30.0	30.1–50.0	50.1–100.0	100.1–
1956, men /farm	0.97	1.24	1.40	1.69	2.16	3.42	8.62
1961, men /farm	1.01	1.20	1.44	1.61	1.93	2.88	7.14
1966, men /farm	0.68	0.96	1.20	1.37	1.62	2.34	5.65

Sources: Based on a farm sample survey in *Statistical Yearbook of Agriculture 1970*, Table 17, p. 66 and Table 1, p. 45.

the two following tables. Figures over 1.0 indicate that some work was done by other members of the farm family and/or by permanent or casual labour.

According to Table 13.7, the smallest holdings had on average 1.0 men working, most probably the farmer, in both 1956 and 1961. The lower figure for 1966 indicates that smallholder farming had become more of a part-time occupation where the farmer had to manage both the farm and another job. On farms with 5–30 hectares of arable land, the average number of men per farm was between one and two – the farmer and in some cases also some permanent or hired labour. More than two working men (usually the farmer and one employee) were found only on the biggest farms. In 1956, this was the case for farms with more than 30 hectares, but by 1961 it only applied to farms with more than 50 hectares. Only in the biggest size category was the number of men enough to provide a significant possibility of reducing the number of employees, most likely through labour-saving technologies. The number of farms of this size was, however, small (Table 13.1), which meant a modest total reduction in labour from big farms and estates. This implies also that labour-saving technologies had a limited direct impact on the total number of people in farming. Only at the biggest farms was it possible to replace one man through labour-saving means, while investment in, for example, a tractor, on a smaller farm certainly could save days of work but did not make it possible for the farmer to leave.

Similarly, Table 13.8 includes the female farmer, often married to the male farmer. About one woman on average was working on each farm, irrespective of farm size and with little average change from 1956 to 1961. On small and middle-sized farms, this woman can be assumed to have been the farmer's wife but, it is suggested, some bigger farms had a woman employed in the cowshed whereas the wife was more of a housewife, and was thus not recorded as working in farming in the farm sample survey. Between 1961 and 1966, the average number of women dropped to less than one, also irrespective of farm size. Among the reasons for the decline in the 1960s, it is suggested that increasing numbers of women worked outside the farm too, at least part-time, in order to manage the price-pressure on farm products.

Tables 13.7 and 13.8 demonstrate that the potential to release labour for other full-time work – for example, in the export industries – was limited to

Table 13.8 Average female labour on Swedish farms of different sizes, 1956–1966

	2.1–5.0	5.1–10.0	10.1–20.0	20.1–30.0	30.1–50.0	50.1–100.0	100.1–
1956, women/farm	0.78	0.94	0.99	1.02	1.05	0.98	1.41
1961, women/farm	0.79	0.93	1.02	1.01	0.99	0.94	1.17
1966, women/farm	0.51	0.70	0.84	0.90	0.83	0.76	0.59

Sources: Based on the farm sample survey, in *Statistical Yearbook of Agriculture 1970*, Table 17, p. 66 and Table 1, p. 45.

situations when the farm had two or more people, which may have been the case on some farms with less than 30 hectares, but was usually possible only on farms with more arable land than that. According to Table 13.7, the average male labour force (including the male farmer) in the three biggest farm size categories was reduced by, on average, 0.5, 1 and 3 men respectively, between 1956 and 1966. The explanation is most probably that these farms had been able to benefit from labour-saving technologies to an extent that made it possible to terminate the employment of one or more men and still continue farming. On smaller and middle-sized farms, one male fewer meant that the male farmer would leave, which in practice could be to give up the holding. Investment in a tractor could save time in comparison with a pair of horses, but the amount of saved time was probably not enough to make it possible to reduce the labour force on any but the very big farms. In addition, the biggest farms would probably have been able to reduce their labour force even more if it had not been for the usually intensive animal production that still required a lot of manual labour, in spite of milking machines and other technologies. Hay-making, for example, was still very labour intensive and a motive to hire casual labour. In spite of the low or non-existing potentials to reduce the number of people in smallholder farming, the greatest share of those who left came from holdings with at most 10 hectares of arable land. Table 13.9 demonstrates that about one fifth of those leaving came from the 10–20 hectare category, which had actually been the model farm size in the early 1950s, while only about one tenth came from farms with more than 20 hectares, and slightly more from the biggest size category. This was in line with the previous observation claim that the potential to replace labour by new technology was primarily found on big farms that still had a number of employees, some of whom could leave while the farming was continued.

Accordingly, the reduction of farm labour followed two main pathways. On one hand, large numbers of people were released when smallholder farming was given up (Table 13.1), primarily farmers and farm household members. In that process entire farm households left agriculture and family members of all ages and both sexes had to find other ways of making a living. Of course not everyone entered the factory gates or found other non-farming jobs, but retired, or became housewives, etc. Holdings that were given up may alternatively have been planted with pine trees, sold to and merged with another farm unit, or sold and used for other purposes, such as urban expansion or new

Table 13.9 Decline in male and female farm labour on holdings of different farm sizes, per cent of the total decline

Years	2.1–5.0	5.1–10.0	10.1–20.0	20.1–30.0	30.1–50.0	50.1–100.0	100.1–	Total
1956–66	36	34	19	3	2	2	4	100

Source: Based on the farm sample survey in *Statistical Yearbook of Agriculture 1970*, Table 17, p. 66.

roads. The decision to give up was often difficult for the individual and was in many cases made gradually, in order to get used to the new order and to keep a door open in case of later unemployment.[38]

On the other hand, farm labour was reduced on the biggest farms, as a consequence of labour-saving technologies such as tractors and chemical fertilizers. Despite the fact that the time period under discussion here coincides with the 'tractorization era' in Sweden, tractors and the use of other labour-saving equipment explains only a little of the direct decline in farm labour between 1956 and 1966.[39] The effects of labour-saving technologies may, however, have had substantial indirect effects by making it possible to operate enlarged farm units without having to engage additional labour, which was in line with the 1947 agricultural programme, and provided a market for tractors, fertilizers and other farm chemicals.

Concluding discussion

The changes in farm labour discussed here took place in a Swedish context that had similarities and differences in comparison with other Western European countries. We have to deal with general trends, such as an increasing share of industrial labour at the expense of the rural share, but also with variations due to different political, economic, social, cultural and natural conditions. Detailed comparisons have to be left to readers with special knowledge of each country, while the following discussion is limited to some general Western European trends and the Swedish case.

It is important to consider the unique Swedish situation by the mid-1940s when Sweden was unhurt by the Second World War, was a democratic country and was able to feed its population. These extremely favourable conditions made possible immediate industrial and urban expansion, and further improvements of the welfare state, eagerly undertaken by the ruling Social Democrats. A study of agrarian Sweden and its labour force requires awareness of the dominance of smallholdings and family labour, and that the sector was not supplied with masses of hired farm labour that could easily be reallocated to other jobs. This chapter deals with all categories of people working in farming – farmers and other farm family members, and permanent and casual employees – and the use of general terms such as farm labour, working in farming, etc. includes all these categories.

The already sufficient domestic production of food paved the way for the 1947 agricultural programme that focused on structural changes, rather than production, and was a gradual, voluntary reform that aimed at phasing out smallholder farming in favour of family-operated farms of modest size with little or no hired labour. This meant that the authorities considered about two-thirds of all registered farm units to be too small to survive in the long run. This was indeed provocative, and many farmers were taken aback by such a turnabout soon after the war, when the seaways had been blocked and all kinds of farming had been appreciated.

The agricultural programme was passed by the Swedish *Riksdag* in 1947, when it was not yet clear to what extent other sectors would be able to absorb the many former smallholders, which suggests that early parts of the process was a matter of smallholders being pushed out from agriculture, rather than pulled into other sectors. The agricultural programme happened to coincide with severe concerns for the lack of labour in the early 1950s, when low birth rates in the 1930s meant that few young people entered the labour market, at the same time as the Swedish economy was overheated by successful exports and high domestic demand. By then, shortage of labour was seen as a bottleneck for continued expansion, and in this situation former farm labour certainly played an important role. Already in the late 1950s the situation was considered less problematic thanks to high fertility rates in the 1940s, migration from abroad, increased number of women at the labour market, more efficient management and better access to capital for investments in laboursaving technologies, especially in the industrial sector. In spite of the worries for shortages of labour in the early 1950s, the authors of the long-term plan did not argue explicitly for the reallocation of farm labour, which contrasts with common views in Swedish rural narratives. Instead, the authors of the long-term plans underestimated the decline in the number of farms and people in farming. They said repeatedly, in one plan after another, that a big reduction in farm labour had already taken place and that the process was expected to slow down. Not until the 1960s was it realized in the long-term plans that the decline in the number of farms and people in farming would, in fact, continue or even increase.

The decline in farm labour was comparably concentrated in time in Sweden, where more than 50 per cent of the working population was engaged in farming until 1900 but only 10 per cent by the mid-1960s. According to David Grigg, Italy experienced a similar time period of change, whereas the downturn from 50 per cent to 10 per cent was more drawn out in Britain, the Netherlands, Ireland, Belgium, France, Switzerland, Germany (West), Denmark and Norway, which in many but not all cases can be explained by a slower process of change in countries where industrialization began earlier, with the UK as the most striking example.[40] Of the thirteen Western European countries in Grigg's comparison, only Italy, Portugal and Spain reached the 50 per cent level later than Sweden. In a more short-term comparison, Michael Tracy shows how labour in agriculture changed in eleven Western European countries between 1955 and 1960, and that the percentage decline in Sweden was at about the same level as in Belgium, Ireland and the Netherlands, significantly lower in Britain and higher than in Austria, Denmark, France, Italy, Norway and West Germany.[41] The decline in the number of people in Swedish farming was obviously exceeded by many other Western European countries, but the short time period of transition, within a lifetime, made the changes in Sweden dramatic.

The Swedish case is an illustrative example of what Grigg discusses in terms of the selective decline of the Western European agricultural population.

Typically, young people and employees were the first to leave whereas the number of farmers did not decline markedly until after the Second World War, before which 'very few "core" farmers were lured away by the attraction of industry or urban life', to quote Giovanni Federico.[42] The early postwar period can thus be seen as the point in time when farming in at least some Western European countries began to be given up by the farmer him/herself, which was a more complicated process than when other family members or employees left while the farm remained. The former situation required almost irreversible and also emotionally difficult decisions that included not only the giving up of farming for oneself and younger generations, but in many cases also that the family had to leave the countryside and start quite another kind of life. The Swedish rural narrative is greatly influenced by stories about why people left, often in terms of factories in desperate need of labour and offers of better pay, but also about losses of the rural idyll. The circumstances varied from person to person, but generally speaking the first and most decisive factor that made people leave appears to have been the occurrence of alternative employment opportunities in Sweden as well as in other Western European countries.[43]

In the Swedish case, the largest decline in the number of people in farming was due to the giving up of smallholdings as separately cultivated units, which released large numbers of smallholders and their family members for other jobs. At the same time, large farms replaced parts of their working staff by labour-saving technologies, but the total direct impact of technologies was much smaller than of the decline in the number of smallholdings, due to the small number of big farms and the fact that many employees had already left in the 1920s and 1930s. The indirect impact of labour-saving technologies was, however, considerable, even on smaller farms where a tractor could carry the aims of the 1947 programme into effect, to merge smallholdings into somewhat bigger units that were still able to manage the business on the basis of family labour.

Notes

1 Among the critics were G. Myrdal *Jordbrukspolitiken under omläggning*, Stockholm: Kooperativa förbundets bokförlag, 1938.
2 SOU 1956:53, p. 107; SOU 1966:1, p. 76. SOU stands for *Statens Offentliga Utredningar*, The Swedish Government's Official Reports, which is an extensive series for various kinds of governmental reports. Note that the term 'farm labour' and similar formulations in this chapter are used not only for hired labour but also for male and female farmers and farm family labour.
3 The committee behind the 1947 agricultural programme (see below) had a complementary investigation made about opportunities for the farming population to find non-farm jobs (SOU 1946:78).
4 SOU 1956:53, p. 109.
5 SOU 1948:45, p. 15; SOU 1951:30, pp. 22 and 35; SOU 1956:53, pp. 109–110.
6 1962:10, p. 27; 1966:1, p. 121.
7 C-E. Odhner, *Jordbruket vid full sysselsättning*, Stockholm: KF:s bokförlag, 1953, p. 104.

8 *Statistical Yearbook of Agriculture 1970*, Table 2, pp. 46–47.
9 Difficulties due to such aspects are repeatedly discussed in O. Gulbrandsen, *Strukturomvandlingen i jordbruket*, Uppsala: Almqvist & Wiksell, 1957.
10 The official statistics on farm labour are of two kinds. The census of population counted farm labour on the basis of the profession declared by the informant him/herself, which may have overestimated the number of male farmers because of the status of being a farmer (Gulbrandsen, *Strukturomvandlingen i jordbruket*, pp. 54–55). The number of female farm labourers may have been underestimated for similar reasons. The second official source was a farm sample survey that counted the number of people who worked on selected farms on 1–3 particular days, spread over the year. The figures are therefore approximate rather than exact and are not always comparable.
11 *Historical Statistics of Sweden, Part 1, Population, 1720–1967*, Stockholm: National Central Bureau of Statistics, 1969, Table 4, pp. 47–48 and Table 14, p. 66; F. Dovring, *Progress for Food or Food for Progress? The Political Economy of Agricultural Growth and Development*. New York: Praeger, 1988, p. 39.
12 SOU 1966:30, p. 73. SOU 1946:78, p. 5 estimates the share for forestry and fishery at 11.6 per cent in 1940, which has been used to calculate agriculture excluding forestry and fishery in 1950 and 1960, *ceteris paribus*.
13 For changes in methods of production, see C. Martiin, 'Modernized Farming but Stagnated Production: Swedish farming in the 1950s emerging welfare state', in *Agricultural History*, vol. 89 (4), Winter 2015 pp. 559–583.
14 Neither was Sweden very keen on becoming a member of the FAO. Sweden did not join the UN organization until 1950, after all Western European countries except for Germany (1950) and Spain (1951); (www.fao.org).
15 G. Myrdal, *Jordbrukspolitiken under* omläggning, Stockholm: Kooperativa förbundets förlag, 1938, pp. 30–32.
16 SOU 1946:42, p. 73; SOU 1952:49, p. 135. Extensive food rationing was applied in Sweden between 1940 and 1948, despite the comparably rich supply of food (SOU 1952:49, p. 406.
17 SOU 1977:17, pp. 131, 133. Until the late 1950s the import of oil cakes was maintained at the same level as during the Second World War (Historical statistics III, Table 3.5, p. 219 and Table 3.7, p. 230).
18 The 1947 programme is here referred to in the form of the preceding comprehensive investigation (SOU 1946:42, 1946:46 and SOU 1946:61) that was little changed in comparison with the final governmental bill.
19 SOU 1946:78, p. 7 and SOU 1946:42, p. 149.
20 C. Martiin 'Farming, Favoured in Times of Fear: Swedish agricultural politics 1935–1955', in P. Brassley, L. Van Molle and Y. Segers (eds), *War, Agriculture and Food*, New York and London: Routledge, 2012, pp. 156–171; S. Osterman, *Satt och osatt: Fyra decennier I och runt Jordbrukarnas Föreningsblad*, Stockholm: Land/LTs förlag, 1973.
21 M. Morell, *Jordbruket i industrisamhället*, Stockholm: Natur och kultur/LTs förlag, 2001, pp. 164–171.
22 The first Social Democratic Prime Minister Per-Albin Hansson was succeeded by the also legendary Tage Erlander in 1946, who was in turn succeeded by the internationally more well known Olof Palme in 1969. The farmers' party, the *Bondeförbundet*, was from 1958 named the *Centerpartiet*; *Högerpartiet* is now named *Moderaterna* whereas *Folkpartiet* has recently been changed to *Liberalerna*.
23 T. Erlander. *1949–1954*. Stockholm: Tidens förlag, 1974, pp. 336–337 and 339.
24 SOU 1948:45, pp. 14–15.
25 T. Erlander. *1940–1949*. Stockholm: Tidens förlag, 1973, p. 369.
26 SOU 1948:45; SOU 1951:30; SOU 1956:53 and SOU 1962:10. Over time, the Swedish long-term plans become ambitious investigations, taking a long time, in which highly qualified experts were engaged together with political representatives,

representatives of private and official business, and other concerned actors. Among the experts, Professor Ingvar Svennilson, a professor of economics with special competence in the planned economy, was a leading figure in several plans, from 1948 to 1966.

27 The demographic situation in the 1930s was investigated and debated, not least by Alva and Gunnar Myrdal in their book *Kris i befolkningsfrågan* (1934). They were also engaged in official investigations and other political work on these issues. Swedish birth rates were low in a European context, and extremely low in the 1930s (H. Gille, 'An International Survey of Recent Fertility Trends' in *Demographic and Economic Change in Developed Countries*. New York: Columbia University Press, 1960: pp. 19–22).
28 SOU 1948:45; SOU 1951:30 ; SOU 1956:53; SOU 1962 :10.
29 SOU 1948:45, p. 15.
30 SOU 1951:30, pp. 22 and 35.
31 SOU 1951:30, p. 24.
32 SOU 1956:53, p. 29. It is again worth remembering that the discussion includes farmers, farm family labour and employees.
33 SOU 1956:53, pp. 110–111.
34 SOU 1962:10, p. 27.
35 SOU 1966:1, p. 26.
36 SOU 1956:53, p. 107; *Statistical Yearbook of Agriculture 1970*, pp. 46–47.
37 *Statistical Yearbook of Agriculture 1970*, p. 66.
38 SOU 1966:30, pp. 77–78. Half of the farms that were abandoned in 1956–61 were given up gradually. Similar observations are discussed in J. Mellor, *The Economics of Agricultural Development*, New York: Cornell University Press, 1966, p. 32.
39 The number of tractors rose from 20,000 in 1944 to 69,000 in 1951, 148,000 in 1961 and 163,000 in 1966, after which the increase came to a halt until the 1970s (*Statistical Yearbook of Agriculture 1970*, Table 34, p. 96 and *Statistical Yearbook of Agriculture 1980*, Table 41, p. 100). Investments in tractors in different farm size categories are shown in C. Martiin, 'Modernized Farming but Stagnated Production: Swedish farming in the 1950s emerging welfare state', in *Agricultural History*, Winter 2015, pp. 575–576.
40 D. Grigg, *The Transformation of Agriculture in the West*, Oxford: Blackwell, 1992, pp. 22–24.
41 M. Tracy, *Agriculture in Western Europe: Challenge and Response 1880–1980*, London: Granada Publishing, 1982, p. 236.
42 Grigg, *Transformation of Agriculture*, p. 29; G. Federico, *Feeding the World: An Economic History of Agriculture, 1800–2000*, Princeton, NJ: Princeton University Press, 2005, pp. 56 and 58; C-E. Odhner, *Jordbruket vid full sysselsättning*, Stockholm: KF:s bokförlag, 1953, pp. 107–108.
43 Grigg, *Transformation of Agriculture*, pp. 27–28; Odhner, 1953, p. 104.

Conclusion

14 Similar means to secure postwar food supplies across Western Europe
A conclusion

Paul Brassley, Carin Martiin and Juan Pan-Montojo

Agriculture plays a minor role in most of the historical accounts of the post-Second World War period in Europe. Books on European contemporary history dedicate a few paragraphs to rural societies and even less to agriculture as if after 1945, once feeding and sheltering refugees and the local population in devastated areas or in occupied Germany stopped being an urgent task, nothing important had happened in this field. Mentioning the decline of agriculture as a productive activity and the fall in the numbers of farmers serves very often to underline the short-term irrelevance of a long process, more often than not read as inevitable.[1] The only exceptions are some works on the origins of the European Economic Community (EEC), discussed in the Introduction. The well-known central position of agriculture in budgetary and legislative terms in the early Common Market deserves an explanation and therefore many authors have attempted to construct one that brings agrarian lobbies and rural electorates into the picture.[2]

This book was born in order to overcome the teleological bias of such dominant analyses on agriculture in the early post-Second World War period. The fact that, in 2016, agriculture appears as a marginal economic sector in most Western countries should not lead us to ignore it when we talk about European history seventy years ago. The fact that in 1957 the Treaty of Rome gave birth to an ambitious project that, in 1962, turned agriculture into its first integral economic policy should make us think twice about the role of the primary sector in the Europe of the 1950s. It should not induce us, however, to see everything before 1962 as a one-way street to the Common Agricultural Policy. Food on one hand, and rural society on the other, and through both agriculture, were immediate and even urgent concerns for Western political forces in 1945 and remained so when food surpluses replaced food deficits in the early 1950s. The way the earlier and later concerns were faced had its roots in pre-war visions, discourses and projects, although new economic, political and institutional realities, with the state in the centre, determined their results. Moreover, the comprehensive political answers given to the problems of Western European agriculture in the 1940s and 1950s were much more homogeneous from every point of view than those that had been put into effect after 1918. As we will sum up in these pages, common Western

European trends can be identified in 1945–1960, whereas the same cannot be said so clearly of the 1920s and 1930s.

The first part of the book, on international politics, clearly shows this combination of continuity and discontinuity after 1945. Pan-Montojo traces the origins of political discourses on agriculture and international projects for agrarian policies that prevailed in the 1950s to the interwar period, and even before. His chapter explains that many of the international institutions created after the Second World War were rooted in the ones that had appeared after the First World War and had become very active in the 1930s, after the Great Depression. They all shared exceptionalism, the consideration of agriculture as an economic sector that deserved a special treatment, given its strategic role for national societies. They also utilised in various ways the discourse of international coordination – that is to say, the alleged need to stabilise prices and achieve a balanced nutrition all over the world through some kind of supranational or intergovernmental authority. However, their leaders clung to the principle of autarky, stressing the decisive role of a high degree of national self-sufficiency if a new war broke out. And their documents often took for granted the necessity of the organisation of agriculture: the thorough regulation of agricultural trade and production, with the participation of producers. These approaches supplied the bases for ambitious projects of old, renovated and new organisations that dealt only with agriculture and food, like the Food and Agriculture Organization (FAO), or had broad agricultural and food competences, like the Organisation for European Economic Co-operation (OEEC), the International Labor Organization (ILO) and the United Nations Relief and Rehabilitation Administration (UNRRA).

However, there were as well important changes beyond the foundation of new international agencies. The Cold War and the hegemonic position of the USA in the West favoured the export of the American interventionist agricultural administration, the technical solutions it was supporting, and the models of farms and farmers it was protecting in the United States. If world trade agreements like the General Agreement on Tariffs and Trade (GATT) did not reach agriculture, product standardisation and amplified information first, and regional agreements subsequently, promoted growing flows of agricultural products among the most developed countries. And beyond trade, even if there was not a direct copy but a partial and heterogeneous adaptation of American models, domestic price policies, technological solutions and structural programmes for the farming sector were homogenised, with a significant role for the transnational polity of technicians and agricultural economists that was created between 1943 and the 1960s.

The Cold War had a direct impact in European agriculture at two different levels. Food and agricultural inputs were prominent items in the American aid to 'free' Europe. Once European deficits were overcome, feeding local populations kept on being a central weapon of the USA diplomacy for the whole world, especially after decolonisation opened new challenges to the Western bloc. Moreover, food remained a priority in military plans for a possible direct conflict that only in the late 1950s seemed for a while less plausible. However, in spite of the pre-eminence given to food itself as a geostrategic resource, Western politicians had a wider approach to agriculture. They thought that it needed to be modernised in order to avoid possible political unrest and stabilise societies. That is why, as Bernardi shows, the 1950s were a time of far-reaching programmes of reform that included redistributionist measures, like the land reform in Italy, and other social policies for rural society, at the same time as large investments were made in technical change. Although industrial development received far more funding than the European primary sector, the communist threat strongly contributed to the design of a new Western agriculture.

González Esteban, Pinilla and Serrano complete the assessment of the period 1945–1960 with a general approach to international trade in agricultural commodities. As a result of production and export subsidies in rich countries, designed to sustain agricultural incomes and ensure a certain degree of self-sufficiency, too much food was grown in the developed world a few years after the end of the Second World War. At the same time, other agro-exporters, especially the Latin American and African ones, lost a part of their share in world markets and their agricultural output did not expand as much as it could have done otherwise. Notwithstanding the various barriers to international exchanges and the increase of protection to agriculture after 1950, agricultural trade grew between 1945 and 1960, but mainly because of intra-European flows of agricultural products. The internal liberalisation of agricultural trade within the EEC and the Europeanisation of protection gave birth to an upsurge of trade in Europe in the 1960s, but its basic guidelines and its negative consequences for extra-European producers were already there in the 1950s when world agriculture started to be 'in disarray'.[3]

Looking back, it is apparent that price policies in the OEEC countries were to blame for world agricultural problems that were already visible in the 1950s. Our book examines three very different cases: Greece, Denmark and the United Kingdom. They obviously do not exhaust all variants of Western agricultural policies after the war, but they provide examples of the type of problems faced by post-war governments.

In Greece, Petmezas argues that wheat policies after 1945 were simply the final materialisation of measures initiated between the wars. Economising on foreign currency was the main objective of a policy that aimed at attaining self-sufficiency in wheat in the 1920s and 1930s. This policy, very similar to the contemporary Italian and Portuguese ones, was initially run by private and corporate institutions and then, after the crisis of 1929, by public institutions, and implied a total control of wheat transactions. Post-war Greece kept guaranteed prices for wheat, gradually extended to other products, and long-term contracts with the flour industry. However, the post-war monarchy added an intense technical programme to increase land yields with a relevant foreign support. By the late 1950s, the country achieved 'nutritional self-sufficiency' through this integral regulation system of agriculture oriented to the domestic market, which coexisted with a diminished export agriculture.

Denmark, a country with a large and successful export agriculture, did not try to find a new model in the interwar period. The successive Danish governments, faced with the reduction of international agricultural trade in the 1930s, resorted to economic support to farmers in the form of minimum prices and subsidies negotiated for certain products, the so-called commodity arrangements. It did the same after the war, when Danish exports fetched lower prices or were hampered by quotas in foreign markets: the government reintroduced commodity arrangements as a defensive measure. There was, however, no systematic control of agricultural production or trade, although in the 1940s the government imposed rationing of certain products to improve the foreign balance. As soon as exports fared better in the 1950s, subsidies were cut down or suppressed and a more liberal regime was restored. But from 1958 onwards, a new crisis of Danish international trade forced the government to introduce minimum farm prices and fiscal benefits among other transfers to farmers.

In the late 1940s, the world food situation, coupled with British financial difficulties, brought about constant food shortages in Britain, a country that depended on agricultural imports to feed its population. In fact, after 1945 rationing had to be more wide-ranging and strict than during the war. For this reason, the Labour government passed the 1947 Agriculture Act and embarked on a state-directed plan to increase agricultural production. Shortly after the Conservatives returned to power in 1951, food surpluses began to emerge and improving the economic efficiency of agriculture while, at the same time, limiting the rising cost of public support to farmers became central items in the political agenda. The 1947 Agriculture Act remained the basis of the state's approach to supporting agriculture and subsequent legislation such as the 1957 Agriculture Act merely helped to modify the state's relationship with the agricultural sector. The differences in approach between the Labour and Conservative governments could be explained, according to John Martin, in terms of the degree to which the country was able to achieve food security.

Net food importers and net food exporters alike resorted in the 1940s to measures that fostered domestic agricultural production and tried to ensure price stability and stop the decrease in farmers' incomes. Since the size and the structure of agricultural sectors and their connection to world markets were very different in Western European countries, the actual policies varied from country to country. They all reflected, though, the fact that no government was prepared to leave the fate of their producers and the security of food consumers in the hands of the existing international markets. The techniques for market regulation that had been developed in the interwar period were thus improved to deal with deficits in the 1940s and to confront surpluses in the 1950s. These techniques included the participation of agricultural organisations in the negotiation of quotas, tariffs and prices. Perhaps for this reason, agrarian interventionism has often been read as a consequence of the power of agricultural lobbies.[4] Why such lobbies appeared to be so effective everywhere when the agricultural population was declining and hence losing its electoral relevance is a question that most probably cannot be answered, unless we consider the experiences and expectations of politicians and society on food, and its social and strategic meaning in the postwar context. Avoiding the radicalisation of rural society and preventing a 'red' or a 'nationalist' contagion in the countryside could be other important motives in certain countries like West Germany, but even where such fears had no rational bases, we find that agrarian organisations were promoted to the rank of co-actors in the design of agrarian policies.

Expanding production and raising productivity were the common aims of most national agrarian policies in the postwar period and the core element in the programmes of international organisations. Technological transformation of farms, and especially motorisation, were presented as key instruments. As Auderset and Moser remind us:

> the old attempts to develop a tractor shaped along the multifunctional lines of the draught animal while simultaneously transcending its constraints, limitations and peculiarities made its breakthrough in the 1940/50s, and, therefore, created the conditions which enabled a broad and rapid diffusion of the now versatile motorised technology.

This was a change, they maintain, that integrated agriculture in the industrial economy, through its liberation from its previous dependence upon organic resources, since the growth of machines did not entail increasing numbers of draught animals as the mechanisation process had done. At the same time, in the 1950s wide cultural changes among farmers enabled the rapid diffusion of tractors. Local studies, like the one by Herment on the French department of Oise, show that tractorisation implied not only investments that for many farmers were beyond their saving capacity, and auxiliary services that needed a critical mass of tractors to be profitable, but changes in production systems, in the organisation of the fields, and in the size of farms. Credit, land consolidation, or specialisation were not short-term processes, although in France active state support managed to get them through in less than a decade, and tractorisation was very advanced by the late 1950s.

Less effective were technological policies in Spain and Portugal in the 1950s, although in those years there were institutional innovations that would have major consequences in the following decade, more clearly in Spain where, after twenty years of reaction to war and technological breakdown, indicators of agricultural change were becoming much more positive. Lanero and Fernández-Prieto argue that the very different reach of structural policies in Spain and Portugal was the main cause of the divergent levels of modernisation, understood as labour and land productivity growth, in both Iberian states. They argue that whereas in Spain large irrigation schemes and land consolidation plans had started to be put into practice by in the 1950s and gained speed after the adjustment plan of 1959, in Portugal, land reforms of any type were much slower because of the successful resistance of agricultural lobbies.

In any case, productivity growth could not be equated to motorisation and motorisation was not limited to tractors. As Herment explains, lorries and vans multiplied their number in the French countryside after 1945, an evolution that could be found in other European societies and that, no doubt, had a direct impact in productivity. So, too, did the fact that the scarcity of chemical fertilisers, which had affected production during the war and in the early post-war period, was gradually overcome after 1950, and gave birth to a constant increase in their utilisation. Certain biological innovations, especially high-yielding cereal (wheat, maize, rice, etc.) and grass varieties, were developed, tested and diffused in Europe in massive terms thanks to the international institutions, to national research institutes like the *Institut National de la Recherche Agronomique* (INRA) in France, and to their collaboration with extension services set up in the 1950s. In fact, in the fifteen years after the war, the construction of national integrated systems of research, development and diffusion transformed the nature of the relations between scientific agronomy and agriculture. Farmers became increasingly dependent upon innovation paths that were configured in public and industrial institutions. Perhaps we should call this the European 'green evolution' in order to underline that it was very similar in content to the green revolution, but was not presented as a radical break with the past as elsewhere in the world.

Technical modernisation, as it was understood in the 1950s, demanded structural policies. Small farms, whatever the political rhetoric about family farming, were ill suited to many of the innovations promoted by agricultural plans, and increasing agricultural incomes seemed difficult below certain farm sizes. Producing more food with fewer farmers was either the explicit aim or the perhaps regrettable but, according to contemporary analysts, inevitable, side effect of agricultural development. Channelling, smoothing out or compensating the process of decline of the agricultural workforce were the basic questions that Western governments sought to address via their agrarian structural policies. In the Netherlands, an active policy of land consolidation to achieve viable farms, put in place in 1954, was supplemented in 1956 with a rural area development policy that encouraged economic, social and cultural transformations. Land reclamation was also utilised to promote new model farms. The intense Dutch intervention, in a country where export agriculture had a strong weight, and religious and ideological divisions in rural society were profound, served as an example to the policies put into practice in Belgium mainly in the 1960s, as Karel and Segers demonstrate. In Germany, the 1955 Agriculture Act aimed at parity between non-agricultural and agricultural incomes. Although it did not imply a land reform, Gerhard suggests that it simplified the reduction of the number of small farms and the specialisation of agricultural ventures, a process that went very quickly in Germany in the 1950s. Social democrats in Sweden did not act very differently from the Christian Democrats, who held power alone or in coalition in the Federal

Republic of Germany. They promoted middle-sized family farms through various incentives and paved the way for a smooth exit of labour from the countryside, which affected mainly the families who ran smaller farms and had their members hired as labourers in bigger farms, as Martiin shows. If there were differences between socialists and Christian Democrats, they appear to have been more relevant at the rhetoric than at the policy level.

In sum, our book shows that after a quick and successful reconstruction of the agricultural sector in most countries during the 1940s, very similar measures were adopted all over Western Europe in the 1950s. All governments aimed at keeping or achieving high production levels and disposing of the resulting surpluses via subsidised exports (or, in the case of the UK, substituting for imports). Market and foreign trade regulation, via price guarantees, import quotas and public subsidies were the tools to ensure that production did not fall. Politicians, electorates and military leaders shared the desire for a secure and diversified food supply. Political leaders and technicians wanted to increase production with higher labour productivities or at least higher yields. This policy nearly everywhere implied technical changes (motorisation, high-yielding varieties, better and more fertilisers and pesticides), led by a techno-scientific public apparatus with dense and continuous contacts, and a fluid relationship with the ancillary input and processing industries, with a strong American position, and an increasingly redundant agrarian workforce. Welfare ideology and political stability in the context of the Cold War prevented a passive policy in the face of rural unemployment or poverty: agricultural associations became political partners of governments of different political orientations. Notwithstanding the political defence of family farming, there were no land reforms except in Italy. Consolidation legislation was passed in very many countries, while financial, tax and technical support subsidised 'adequate' farm sizes, and extension programmes fostered cultural changes among the younger farmers, who were supposed to remain on the land. Despite the evident continuities at every level with previous trends, between the end of the Second World War and 1960, the main features of a new Western European agricultural model were established.

Notes

1 For example, Mazower only discusses agriculture in Eastern Europe, while Judt's otherwise excellent *Postwar* includes just short discussions of agriculture that usually emphasise the negative: agriculture is seen as either conservative and static, or problematic when output increases led to decreasing prices, or simply in decline. Hobsbawm, however, puts European agriculture in a world context and has a neat summary of its technical changes. See M. Mazower, *Dark Continent: Europe's Twentieth Century*, London: Penguin, 1999, pp. 273–274; T. Judt, *Postwar: A History of Europe Since 1945*, London: Pimlico, 2007, pp. 87, 227, 236, 305, 328; E. Hobsbawm, *Age of Extremes: The Short Twentieth Century*, London: Abacus, 1995, pp. 261, 289–292.

2 See, for example A-Ch. L. Knudsen, *Farmers on Welfare: The Making of Europe's Common Agricultural Policy*, Ithaca: Cornell University Press, 2009; A.D. Sheingate,

The Rise of the Agricultural Welfare State: Institutions and Interest Group Power in The United States, France and Japan, Princeton, NJ: Princeton University Press, 2001.
3 D.G. Johnson, *World Agriculture in Disarray*, London: Macmillan, 1987.
4 In political science and economic theory of institutions there are wide theoretical and comparative approaches to lobbying and policy-making in agriculture. See, for example, W.P. Grant and J.T.S. Keeler (eds), *Agricultural Policy, Volume I: Agricultural Policy in Western Europe*, Cheltenham: Edward Elgar, 2000; A-Ch. L. Knudsen, *Farmers on Welfare: The Making of Europe's Common Agricultural Policy*, Ithaca, Cornell University Press, 2009; K. Lynggaard, *The Common Agricultural Policy and Organic Farming: An Institutional Perspective on Continuity and Change*, Wallingford: CABI Publishing, 2006; Adam D. Sheingate, *The Rise of the Agricultural Welfare State*, Princeton, NJ: Princeton University Press, 2000; J. Swinnen, J. (ed.), *Policy and Institutional Reform in Central European Agriculture*, Avebury. There are, however, far fewer historical studies on the subject.

Index

Acerbo, G. 26
Acheson, D. 53, 56
Adenauer, K. 54, 240–1
Africa 67
agrarian-industrial knowledge society 147, 152, 159
agrarian question 54, 150, 173
agribusiness 28, 34
agricultural: exceptionalism 24, 268; interests 70, 231, 237–40, 242; liberalization 75; pressure groups 175
Agricultural Adjustment Act 68, 74
Agricultural Marketing Act 1949 (UK) 116
Agriculture Act (Green Law) 231, 239
Agriculture Act 1947 (UK) 107–12, 121; Agriculture Act 1957 (UK) 107, 121
Agriculture-crisis Law (NL) 212
airlift 236
Alderson, M.A. 149
Alentejo 173–4
Alentejo Irrigation Plan 175
Alivizatos, B. 96
Alsop, J. 51
American aid 31, 34, 97, 167, 268
American Foreign Operations Administration 31; Office of Military Government for Germany (OMGUS) 234
Anderson, K.L. 77
animal production *see* livestock
Ankli, R. E. 199
anti-agricultural bias 71
antibiotics 12
Argentina 6, 10, 120
artificial insemination 157, 177, 197
Asia 28, 55, 66
Association of Flour Industries 94

Attlee, C. 53, 108, 110, 114, 116
Auderset J. 17, 271
Australia 6, 8, 73, 120
Austria 3–5, 7–9, 11, 15, 45, 48, 260
autarky 8, 26, 32, 37–8, 69, 91, 171, 178, 218, 230 268; economic autarky policy 169
automated milking 177
Aykroyd, W. 26
Azevedo Gomes, M. 177

Bairoch P. 158
balance of payments 45–6, 69–70, 75, 108, 187
balance of trade 201
Balfour, E. 112
Bandoeng (Java) 27
barley 3, 9, 89, 99, 118, 170, 180, 187, 198
Barros, H. 177
Bavaria 16, 232
Beglinger, H. 154
Beiras 174
Belgium 3–4, 7, 9, 11, 13, 15, 18, 33, 45, 76, 209–26, 272
Berlin 236
Bernardi, E. 17, 269
biosphere 145, 151
biotic resources 146–8, 157–9
birth rates 253
Bizonia 235–6
black market 2, 70, 181, 232, 235, 243
Bording, K. 138
Brassley, P. 64, 70
British zone 231
Brittany 195–6
Bückeberg 230
bulk products 66

276 *Index*

Cairncross, A. 110
Calabria 52–4
California 24
calories 5, 109, 127, 231, 234, 250
Calouste Gulbenkian Foundation 177
Canada 5, 120, 218
Cánovas, C. 173
CAP *see* Common Agricultural Policy
Cardon, P. 30
Carillon, R. 200
Cassa per il Mezzogiorno 54
Castro Caldas, E. 175
Catholic Church 48
Cavestany, R. 166, 167, 173
Central Committee for the Protection of Domestic Wheat (KEPES) 94–6, 99
Central Service for the Administration of Domestic Production (KYDEP) 97–8; Central Service of Domestic Wheat (KYDES) 96–7
Centro de Estudios de Economia Agrária (CEEA) 177–8
Centro Superior de Investigaciones Científicas (CSIC) 172
cereal production 3–4, 97, 99
China 49–50, 53
Christiansen, T. 17, 70
Christliche Deutsche Union (CDU) 33, 239, 240
Christliche Soziale Union (CSU) 240
Churchill, W.S. 28, 70, 112
Civil War 5, 57, 97, 165, 169–70, 172, 181
Clay, L. D. 234–5
Cold War 24, 27–8, 31, 38, 44, 47–50, 58, 68, 166, 232, 236, 241, 268, 273
collectivization 45, 56, 234
colonisation 165, 167–8, 174, 176, 181
Combined Food Board (CFB) 28–9
combine harvester 197
combustion engine 147, 152
Cominform 45, 49
Commission Internationale d'Agriculture (CIA) *see Confédération Internationale de l'Agriculture* (CIA) 23, 25
Committee for Timber 31; Agricultural Problems 31; Experts on Indigenous Labour (CEIL) 28; Work on Plantations 28
commodification 89, 158
Common Agricultural Policy (CAP) 1–2, 13, 17, 35–6, 38, 59, 79, 210, 226, 242, 267

Common Market (EEC) *see* European Economic Community
communism 28, 44–5, 47–8, 55–6, 82, 234, 241; communist revolution in China 49
Confédération Européenne de l'Agriculture (CEA) 33
Confédération Internationale de l'Agriculture (CIA) 23, 25–6, 33
Confederazione Coltivatori Diretti 51
Conference for European Economic Cooperation 31
Conference of European Rural Life 27
Conference on World Tenure Problems 56
Conford, P. 112
Consortium of Unions of Agricultural Cooperatives for the Administration of Domestic Wheat (KESDES) 96
consumption 4–5, 32, 46, 90, 108, 170, 217, 229, 237, 253
convertibility crisis 109
cooperatives 28, 87, 94, 96, 177, 199, 251
corn 70, 170, 235, 241; hybrid corn 46
cotton 46, 70, 75
credit 29, 46, 54, 89, 96, 135, 157, 169, 171, 272
Cripps, S. 114
cultural lag 222
currency reform 236

dairy production 136, 211, 215–16, 247; milk 5, 15, 115, 127–8, 171, 177, 187, 237, 251
Dalton, H. 108, 113
David, E. 146, 150
deficiency payments 72, 76
De Gasperi, A. 53–4
de Gaulle, Ch. 5, 8
Denmark 4, 6–7, 9–11, 14, 17, 45, 117, 125–41, 269–70
Deutsche Bauernkorrespondenz (German Peasant Correspondence) 240
Deutscher Bauernverband (German Peasant League), (DBV) 239
developing countries 34, 71, 73, 78–9
diet 5, 15, 26, 109, 168, 171, 232, 241
Dietrich, H. 234
Directorate General for Agricultural Services 177
Directorates General of Coordination, Credit and Agricultural Training 171
Dodd, N.E. 30

Donnelly, D. 112
Dovring, F. 17, 248
draught animals 7, 133, 145–60, 271; selective breeding 152; *see also* horses
draught power 6–7, 145–60
Duque, R. 174

Eastern Bloc 31
Economic and Financial Organisation of the League of Nations (ECO) 26, 31
Economic Commission for Europe 7
economic modernisation 173–4, 225; economic modernisation model 179
ECSC *see* European Coal and Steel Community
EEC *see* European Economic Community
elasticity of demand 67–9
electricity 152, 218; electric fences 197; electrification 152, 188, 198
elites: academic 167; industrialist technocratic 173; political 36, 88, technical agronomy 175, 177
emigration 54, 100–3, 217–18, 225
Emilia region 49, 52
energy 125, 147–9, 151–4, 156–60
entropy 153
equalized socioeconomic progress 246
ERC *see* European Recovery Program
Erhard, L. 236, 241
Erlander, T. 252
Estado Novo 165, 173–4, 176–9, 181
Ethiopia 26
European Coal and Steel Community (ECSC) 13, 217, 242
European Committee for Agriculture (ECA) 30, 38
European Economic Community (EEC) 15, 35, 134, 138–9, 201, 216, 225, 242, 267, 269
European Free Trade Association (EFTA) 134
European integration 1, 23, 35–6, 66, 75–6
European Productivity Agency (EPA) 15, 31, 35
European Recovery Program (Marshall Plan) (ERC) 17, 31, 33, 38, 41, 67, 70, 114, 166, 177, 187–8, 234, 236, 244, 252
Evans, S. 115
Expanded Programme of Technical Assistance (EPTA) 30
export 71–2, 76, 79, 81, 84, 125, 127, 129–32, 136, 210, 212–13, 215, 252

extension 17, 35, 38, 46, 52, 70, 87, 93–4, 100, 167, 272; extensionism 177–8
externalisation 36–7

Falange Española Tradicionalista y de las Juntas de Ofensiva Nacional Sindicalista (FET – JONS) 173
family farming 14, 33, 101, 135, 176, 190, 220, 231, 238, 249, 259, 273; *see also* labour
FAO *see* Food and Agriculture Organisation of the United Nations
farm adjustment problem 64, 68
Farmers' Rights Association 111
farmers' unions 33, 71, 110, 217, 223–4, 251
farm income 67–8, 71–2, 75, 77
farm labour *see* labour
farm management 37, 219, 223
farm population 247–8
farms: fragmentation 15, 101; number and size 11, 14, 16, 18, 133, 209, 211–12, 218, 221, 225; 233, 238–9; smallholder farming 211, 246, 257–8; small landed property 46
fascism 48, 50, 165, 167 173; agrarian fascism 165, 167, 173, 178
fats 5, 32, 114
Federação de Grémios da Lavoura da Beira Litoral (Beira Federation of Farmers' Guilds) 177
Federico, G. 156, 161
Fellenberg-Ziegler, A. 150, 152
female farm labour *see* labour
Fernández-Prieto, L. 18, 271
Ferreira Dias, J. 173
fertilisers 5, 12, 35, 52, 101, 136, 157, 169, 188, 211, 214, 272
Finland 117, 254
First Development Plan 173
First National Conference of Agronomic Engineering 172
First World War *see* World War I
Fish, H. 5
folk's home 252
food: aid 28, 30, 34, 76, 79, 81; energy food 26; food order 29, 38; markets 168, 211; policy 232, 242; power 81; protective food 26; security 28, 75, 267; shortages 67, 69–70, 75, 79, 230, 236, 242; substitute food 230; supplies 2, 5–6, 8; surpluses 68–71, 74–6, 79–81, 137, 158

Food and Agriculture Committee of the OEEC 31–2, 35
Food and Agriculture Directorate 32
Food and Agriculture Organisation of the United Nations (FAO) 3, 5, 8, 13–14, 27–31, 33–6, 38, 40, 51, 57, 166, 183, 268
Food and Agriculture Technical Information Services (FATIS) 31
Food for Peace Program 58, 76
food pantry law (*Speisekammergesetz*) 235
Forest Services 177
fossil resources 159
Fossum, Ch. 171
France 3, 7, 9–11, 13–16, 18, 33, 70, 75–6, 83, 145, 150, 185–205, 271
Franco regime 48, 50, 57, 165–7, 177–9, 181
Francoism 166, 172, 181
Freie Demokratische Partei (FDP) 240
French zone 231
Friedmann, H. 79

General Agreement on Tariffs and Trade (GATT) 34, 73–5, 268
Generalplan Ost 230
Geneva 26
Georgescu-Roegen, N. 158
Gerhard, G. 18, 230
German occupation 97, 125–7, 185–6
Germany 2–4, 6–13, 15–16, 18, 50, 70, 75–6, 83, 229–45; East 58; West 33, 229, 272–3
Giedion, S. 154
globalisation 65, 145
González Esteban, A.L. 17, 266
Great Depression 23, 37, 64, 88, 90, 94, 268
Greece 2, 7, 9, 11, 15, 44, 56, 87–103, 254, 269
green revolution 36, 38, 272

Hansson, P-A. 252
Harberler Report 78
Hartman Report 27
Havana 73
Heady, E. 68
Health Committee of the League of Nations 27
herbicides 12, 96, 100
Herment, L. 18, 271
Hermes, A. 25
high-yield varieties 35, 272
Hobson, A. 25

Hoover, H. 68
Hops Marketing Board 119
horses 7, 9, 145–7, 151, 169, 189, 192–4, 199, 211, 214, 238, 258; *see also* draught animals
horticulture 192, 210, 215
Hot Springs 29
hunger 34, 38, 57, 68, 76, 229–35, 241–2; Freedom from Hunger Campaign 30
hydraulic agriculture 174; Hydraulic Agriculture Plan 174; infrastructures 167; Law on on Hydraulic Agriculture 174; policy 168
hygiene 27

Iberian dictatorships 165, 178
Iberian Peninsula 165, 179
Identification with farming 249
Illinois 199
II Plano de Fomento (Second Stimulus Plan) 175
import 9–10, 13, 57, 74, 90–2, 108, 125–6, 132, 209, 212, 273; import quotas 74, 212, 273; import substitution 67
India 6
Industrial: agriculture 181; cattle farming 170; countries 64, 68–9, 75, 78; development 173–4, 179
industrialisation 66, 71, 145, 147, 150, 158, 246; industrialism 174–5; regional 168
Industrirådet (Industrial Council), Denmark 134
Ineichen, F. 153
inflation 91–2, 116, 169, 246
infrastructure policies 168
Institut des Recherches Agronomiques (IRA) 188
Institut National de la Recherche Agronomique (INRA) 188, 272
Institute for Crop Improvement (IKF) 94, 100
Instituto de Investigaciones Agrarias (Agrarian Research Institute) (IIA) 172
Instituto Nacional de Investigaciones Agrarias (National Agrarian Research Institute) (INIA) 171–2
Instituto Superior de Agronomía (Higher Institute of Agronomy) 175
insurance policies, agriculture 171
Intergovernmental Conference of Far-Eastern Countries on Rural Hygiene 27

International Bank for Reconstruction and Development (IBRD) 182
International Commodity Clearing House 30
international coordination 26, 29, 37, 268
International Emergency Food Council (IEFC) 28–9
International Federation of Agricultural Producers (IFAP) 33
International Institute of Agriculture (IIA) 23–7, 30, 36
internationalism 24, 28–9; new internationalism 26
International Labour Organisation (ILO) 26–8, 33, 268
International Monetary Fund (IMF) 166
intervention, economic 165, 168, 173; economic interventionist policies 166
investment; private agricultural 168; public 168, 176; in tractors 258
Ireland 2, 4, 7, 9, 53
irrigation 46, 52–3, 167–8, 176, 179, 197, 268
Italy 3, 6–7, 9, 10–11, 15–16, 26, 33, 36, 39, 44–59, 75, 76, 83, 254, 269, 273

Jacob, F. 153
Japan 50, 57, 78
Johnson, D.G. 69
Judt, T. 5
Junta de Colonização Interna (Internal Colonisation Board), (JCI) 174
Junta Nacional das Frutas (National Fruit Board) 177; do Azeite (National Oil Board) 177; do Vinho (National Wine Board) 176–7

Kanslergade-agreement 129
Karel, E.H. 18, 272
Kautsky, K. 150
Kennan, G. 5
Keynes, J. M. 108, 110
knowledge: agricultural 35, 166; networks 214
Konservative Folkeparti (Conservative Party), Denmark 134
Konsumbrot 237
Korean War 17, 55, 58, 117, 166

labour 10–11, 14–16, 152–3, 157–8, 246, 263; casual 249, 255–6; family labour 246; female 251, 254, 257–8; labour productivity 10, 101, 181, 187, 197, 199, 219, 253, 272; labour-saving technologies 258–9; male 256–8; migrant labour 254; part-time farming 257; permanent 249, 255–6; reallocation 246
Labour government 53–4, 76, 107–9, 121, 267; Labour Party 107, 110–12
land 2, 10; consolidation 15–16, 36, 46, 50, 55, 167–8, 171, 188, 201, 271–3, 223, 225–6, 271–3; ownership restructuring project 175; ownership structure 174–5; reclamation 15, 36, 52, 101, 229, 272; reform 36, 42, 49–58, 233, 238, 243, 269, 272–3
Landbrugets Rationaliseringsfond (Agrarian Rationalisation Fund) 136
Landbrugsrådet (Agrarian Council) 129, 134
Lanero, D. 18, 271
Laur, E. 25
Law on Agricultural Improvement 176
League of Nations (LoN) 25–7, 31
Ligutti, L. 51
lithosphere 145, 147, 153, 156, 158–9
livestock 81, 210, 213, 215, 224; animal production 4; intensive animal production 258
Lloyd, G. 116
loan 108, 168m 176, 240, 251
lobbying 25, 32, 34, 69, 157, 174, 181, 267, 270, 272
long-term plans 247, 253, 260
Lower Normandy 195–6
Lubin, D. 24
Lucas Commission 116
Luxemburg 15

machinery 12, 35, 46, 101, 135, 149, 169, 179, 186, 231–2, 251; Centre for Testing Agricultural Machinery (SDGM) 94
Madrid 166
Madrid School of Agronomic Engineering 172–3
male farm labour *see* labour
Mallett, V. 53
malnutrition 26, 34, 109, 114
Malthus, T.R. 68
Mansholt, S. 13, 36, 216–17
Mao Zedong 53
Marshall Plan *see* European Recovery Program (ERP)
Martiin, C. 18, 273
Martin, J. 17, 270
McCormick, A. O'Hare 51

McCormick, C. J. 57
McDougall, F. L. 26
mechanisation 11, 31, 133, 135, 145–6, 148, 152, 157, 176, 209, 214, 219, 222–3, 226–7, 238, 271
Mejeribrugets Rationaliseringsfond (Dairy Rationalisation Fund) 136
Méline, J. 25
Metaxas, I. 95–6
military cooperation 166–7
Milward, A.S. 24, 35
mineral resources 145, 147–8, 156–7
Minister of Agriculture: Economy, Portugal 174; Portugal 174; Spain 173; UK 116
Ministry of Agriculture: Denmark 129, 134; France 186, 188; Greece 87, 94–6, 99; Spain 171–3, 183
Ministry of Food, UK 107, 109, 115
Ministry of Purveyance and Autarky 91
modernisation 18, 37, 175, 177–8, 181, 233, 237–8, 240; modern cultural pattern 222; modernising agrarian reformism 175; paradigm 165, 167, 172, 177; programme 167
Molotov, V.M. 45
Montini, G.B. 48
Morgenthau plan 50, 232
Moser, P. 17, 271
most favoured nation treatment 73
motorisation 35, 37, 145, 148–9, 154, 156–7, 159, 168–9, 175–6, 181, 269, 272–3; organic motor 145–8
multilateral agreements by product 33
Myxomatosis Advisory Committee 117

National Bank of Greece 91
National Catholic Rural Life Conference 51
National Confederation of Unions of Agricultural Cooperatives (ESSE) 96, 102
NATO *see* North Atlantic Treaty Organisation
nazi 5, 50, 229–30, 232–4, 242–3
Netherlands 2, 4, 6–7, 9, 10–11, 13, 15–16, 18, 33, 209–28, 272
New Deal 38, 50, 69
New Zealand 8
Niklas, W. 237, 240
Nominal Protection Coefficient (NPC) 77
Nominal Rate of Assistance (NRA) 77
non-tariff barriers 72, 77
Normandy 16, 145, 195

North America 35, 109, 154, 186, 199
North Atlantic Treaty Organisation (NATO) 31–3, 38, 57, 166
North Sea Area 188
Norway 11, 14, 45, 70, 260
nutrition approach 26, 29

occupation powers 231, 234–6
occupation zones 231–2, 234
Oceania 67
Oder-Neisse line 232
OECD *see* Organisation for Economic Cooperation and Development
OEEC *see* Organisation for European Economic Cooperation
oil crisis 178
Oise 185–203
one-pot meals (*Eintopf*) 230
organic economy 149, 158
Organisation for Economic Cooperation and Development (OECD) 41, 184
Organisation for European Economic Cooperation (OEEC) 8, 12, 28, 31–5, 38, 45, 134, 166, 252, 268–9
Organismos de Coordenação Económica (Economic Coordination Organisations) 176
Organização Corporativa da Lavoura (Corporative Farm Organisation) 176
Organización Sindical Agraria (Agrarian Trade Union) 171
Orr, J. 26, 29
output, animal 127–8, 130, 133, 136; vegetal 127–8, 130, 133, 136
overheated economy 246, 252
overpopulation 15, 101, 217
overproduction of food 250

Pakistan 6
Pan-Montojo, J. 17, 268
Papadakis, J. 100
Paris 25, 44, 185, 190, 198
Partisans for peace 49
peasant ideology 241
Permanent Agricultural Committee, ILO 27
pesticides 12, 188, 195, 273
Petmezas, S. 17, 269
Pflimlin, P. 13
Picardy 16, 195
Pinilla, V. 17, 269
Plan Monnet 50, 70, 185, 196–7
plantation products 66
Point IV 47–8

Index 281

Poland 10, 45, 230
political stabilization 44, 48, 50, 56
Pomerania 232
Pope Pius XII 48, 51
Portugal 2, 6, 7, 9, 15, 18, 50, 83, 165–81, 271
potatoes 4, 9, 114, 170, 180, 187, 214, 250
Potsdam 232
Potter, V. 5
price 65, 70, 72, 74–80, 83–4, 231, 233, 235–8, 241–2; control 129–32, 136; fixed 70–2, 76, 176; guarantees 71–2, 168; minimum 71–2, 76, 168; policy 168, 215–16, 219, 225; pressure on farm products 247, 257; supports 69–72, 74–6; target prices 71–2
Privileged Anonymous Society of General Warehouses (PAEGA) 91, 94, 102
productivity 10, 31–2, 44–5, 50–1, 70, 93, 112, 134–5, 145, 153, 158, 167–8, 177, 197, 238, 271–2
protectionism 24, 26, 33, 35, 38, 64, 67, 71, 73, 75, 77–8, 179, 215, 221, 239, 269
protection policies 35, 38, 73, 77, 92–4, 109, 178, 221, 237, 269
provincial Guild Federation 177
Prussia 232
Public Law 480 34, 76

quality standards 31, 35
quantitative restrictions 72, 74

rabbit 117
Rabinbach, A. 152
radicalisation 229, 241, 271
Radikale Venstre (Social Liberal Party), Denmark 134
rapeseed 136, 187, 197
rationing 2, 27, 32, 44, 70, 97, 107, 114, 132, 186, 216, 229–31, 252, 270
Rauch, E. 154
Rauscher, M. 200
rearmament 50, 54–6, 58
recovery 4, 9, 34, 44, 64, 67, 126, 170, 214, 229, 234
reforestation 52, 167, 176
reform: agrarian 28, 50–2, 61, 175; structural 49, 54, 167, 173
refrigeration 177
refugees 29, 229, 231, 238, 267
regional policy 249
regulations 13, 23, 26–8, 64, 89, 95, 137–8, 178, 230–1, 237, 242, 268–70

Reichsnährstand (Reich Food Estate), (RNS) 234
Rein Segura, C. 173
research 35, 87, 99–100, 166, 171–2, 179, 214, 219
Rhöndorfer meetings 240
Ribatejo 174
rice 6, 76, 179–80, 272
Robertson, A. 113
Rome 24, 27, 29, 52–4, 56
Roosevelt, F.D. 28, 68
Ruhr 231
rural: development program 219, 221–3, 225; exodus 135, 169, 172, 174, 176, 179; hygiene 27; population 248; proletarization 246, 250; reform 69, 71; risks for backwardness 250

Salazar regime 173, 181
San Francisco 166
Sardinia 15–16, 54
Schlange-Schöningen, D. 234–5, 240
Schweizerische Baurnverband (SBV) 25
Second World War *see* World War II
Secretary of State for Industry 173, 177
Segers, Y. 18, 272
selection of seed 100, 197
self-sufficiency 17–18, 26, 32, 66–7, 75–6, 89–90, 114, 215, 250, 268–9
Semler, J. 235
Sen, B.R. 30
Serrano, R. 18, 269
Servicio de Extensión Agraria (Agricultural Extension Service), (SEA) 167, 171
Servicio Nacional de Concentración Parcelaria (National Land Consolidation Service) 168
Servicio Nacional de Crédito Agrícola (National Agricultural Credit Service) 169
Sicily 52–4
Social Democrats, Sweden 246, 250, 252; hegemony 252; *Socialdemokratiet* Denmark 131–2, 138–9
Sozialdemokratische Partei (SPD) 240
social engineering 221, 225
Société des Agriculteurs de France (SAF) 25
socioeconomic deprivation 219
South America 67
Soviet Union *see* Union of Soviet Socialist Republics (USSR)
Spain 2, 6, 7–9, 15, 18, 50, 70–1, 83, 165–81, 271

Spanish Civil War 165, 169, 170, 172, 181
Stalin, J. 31, 45, 48, 232
standard of living 26, 158, 197, 211, 239, 246, 249, 252
starvation 2, 34, 109–10, 128, 229
state intervention 18, 50, 70, 77, 88, 135, 167, 172, 212
steam engine 145–6, 149, 151
stockpiling 32
Strindberg, A. 145
structural policy 169, 181, 209–10, 218–19, 223, 225
Stuttgart 231
subsectors to agriculture 178
subsidies 217, 224, 231, 237, 239, 241; consumer subsidies 130–2; export subsidies 71–4, 76, 78, 83; input subsidies 76; producer subsidies, Denmark 130–1, 136; production subsidies 74, 77; state subsidies to agriculture 136
sugar 5, 32, 76, 118, 170, 179, 190, 197–8, 216, 237, 250
supply management policy 69, 76, 81
surplus production 13, 17, 117, 125, 132, 138, 249
Sweden 3–4, 7, 9, 11, 18, 33, 70, 117, 189, 246–63, 272
Switzerland 2, 11, 76, 150, 154

Tagus River 175
Tarchiani, A. 53
tariffs 64, 67, 72, 77
taxes 136, 176, 251
technical assistance 30, 55, 167, 169; Technical Assistance and Productivity Program 177; Technical Assistance Program 47
technological innovations 147–8, 154–5, 177; technological package 172
technology 18, 148–60, 199, 222, 258, 271; technology transfer 172, 177; labour saving *see* labour
thermodynamics 152–3
thermo-industrial revolution 146, 149
threshing machine 151
tractors, tractorisation 7, 12, 18, 48, 101, 151, 154–7, 169, 186, 202, 214, 238, 258–9, 271
Tracy, M. 1, 10, 17, 107, 121
trade 6–7, 9–10, 17, 64–5, 67–8, 71–4, 76–8, 129, 133–4, 137, 185–6, 198; free-trade 26, 32, 38; international policies 64, 68, 72–3, 75, 77–8

traditional agriculture 176
Treaty of Rome 2, 167, 242, 267
Trentman, F. 26
Truman doctrine 45
Truman, H. 47–9
Turkey 44
Tyres, R. 77

United Kingdom (UK) 2, 4–7, 9, 11, 13, 17, 32, 70, 75–6, 83, 107–24, 150, 189, 269–70, 273
United Nations (UN) 5, 27, 29, 36, 166; Conference on Food and Agriculture, 29; Economic and Social Council 31; Economic Commission for Europe (UNECE) 31, 33, 35–6, 38; Relief and Rehabilitation Administration (UNRRA) 7, 29–30, 36, 38, 268
Union of Soviet Socialist Republics (USSR) 3, 7, 28, 166, 232; Soviet zone 8, 231, 233
United States (US) 5, 6, 17, 24–5, 27, 34, 37, 39, 64, 67–76, 78–81, 83, 166, 169, 171, 177, 181, 189, 197, 232, 236, 268; Agricultural assistance program 179; Cooperative Extension Service 167; Department of Agriculture 37; Economic Mission in Spain 171; modernisation model 178; technical assistance 167; US government 166, 167; US States Congress 34
urbanisation 66, 170, 176, 179, 246; urban-industrial welfare project 252

variable import levy 74
Vatican 48–9, 51, 54
Venstre (Liberal Party), Denmark 129, 132, 138
Virginia 29
Vittorio Emmanuele III 24
Vogüé, L. de 25
Voluntary export restraints (VER) 74
Voluntary restraint agreements (VRA) 74

wages 12, 91, 102, 215
Wall Street Crash 212
Washington 28–9, 48, 54
water 188, 198
weather conditions 92, 157
Weimar Republic 25, 239
welfare state 108–9, 246, 252; material welfare 246
western Communist parties 44, 49

wheat 3, 7, 9, 15, 34, 75–6; *Campanha do Trigo* 179; Canberra wheat seed 100; centres for the Improvement of Wheat Cultivation 100; hybrid wheat seed 100; International Wheat Agreement 33; Mentana wheat seed 100
Whetham, E. 115
WHO *see* World Health Organisation
Williams, T. 113
Wirtschaftswunder (economic miracle) 241
Wiskemann, E. 9
working age 253

World Bank 166–7, 172
World Health Organisation (WHO) 28
World War I 108–9, 114, 154, 210–13, 217, 268
World War II 25, 27, 64, 67, 69, 71, 73, 108–9, 112, 125, 157, 165–6, 173–4, 178, 209, 211–12, 215, 217–18, 220, 223, 267–9

Yates, P.L. 14, 17, 30, 68
Yugoslavia 3, 10, 254

Zweiniger-Bargielowska, I. 109, 112

Taylor & Francis eBooks

Helping you to choose the right eBooks for your Library

Add Routledge titles to your library's digital collection today. Taylor and Francis ebooks contains over 50,000 titles in the Humanities, Social Sciences, Behavioural Sciences, Built Environment and Law.

Choose from a range of subject packages or create your own!

Benefits for you
- Free MARC records
- COUNTER-compliant usage statistics
- Flexible purchase and pricing options
- All titles DRM-free.

Benefits for your user
- Off-site, anytime access via Athens or referring URL
- Print or copy pages or chapters
- Full content search
- Bookmark, highlight and annotate text
- Access to thousands of pages of quality research at the click of a button.

Free Trials Available
We offer free trials to qualifying academic, corporate and government customers.

eCollections – Choose from over 30 subject eCollections, including:

Archaeology	Language Learning
Architecture	Law
Asian Studies	Literature
Business & Management	Media & Communication
Classical Studies	Middle East Studies
Construction	Music
Creative & Media Arts	Philosophy
Criminology & Criminal Justice	Planning
Economics	Politics
Education	Psychology & Mental Health
Energy	Religion
Engineering	Security
English Language & Linguistics	Social Work
Environment & Sustainability	Sociology
Geography	Sport
Health Studies	Theatre & Performance
History	Tourism, Hospitality & Events

For more information, pricing enquiries or to order a free trial, please contact your local sales team:
www.tandfebooks.com/page/sales

 The home of Routledge books

www.tandfebooks.com